Second Printing with
updated information to
January 1995

Docks and Destinations

Coastal Marinas and Moorage

A west coast cruising dock-to-dock destinations guide
San Juan Islands to Port Hardy
Docks • Facilities • Services • Launch Ramps

Peter Vassilopoulos

By The Same Author
Antiques Afloat
From the Golden Age of Boating in British Columbia

Photographs, text, drawings and diagrams copyright 1994 Peter Vassilopoulos.
Seagraphic Publications Ltd. Vancouver. Box 1312, Delta, BC. V4M 3Y8.
In the USA:Box 984, Point Roberts, WA. 98281-0984
Prepress graphics and typesetting Seagraphic Publications Ltd.
Photo scanning and production assistance–Stephanie Bold.
Prepress services, Bridgeport Graphics, Richmond, BC.
Printed in Canada by Consolidated Graphics, Saskatchewan.
Photographs by author unless otherwise indicated.

Second Printing–March 1995.

Library of Congress (Number pending)

Canadian Cataloguing in Publication Data

Vassilopoulos, Peter, 1940–
Docks and Destinations

ISBN 0-919317-20-0

1. Pacific Coast (B.C.)–Guidebooks. 2. San Juan Islands (Wash.)–Guidebooks. 3. Marinas–British Columbia–Pacific Coast–Guidebooks. 4. Marinas–Washington (State)–San Juan Islands–Guidebooks. I. Title.
FC3845. P2V37 1994 917.11'1044 C94-910629-1
F1089.P2V37 1994
Copies available from marine stores, marinas and book stores. Distribution and acquisition enquiries to Seagraphic Publications (604) 273-4333. Fax (604) 273-0813

Peter Vassilopoulos

Docks and Destinations

Destinations and marinas of the British Columbia inside waterways, the San Juan Islands and the Gulf Islands.

East Vancouver Island,
Lower Mainland, Sunshine Coast, San Juans,
Gulf Islands,
Desolation Sound To Port Hardy

Seagraphic Publications • Vancouver

PREFACE

Words alone are not adequate to describe the beauty of the coastal cruising waters of British Columbia and Washington State. I don't believe Shakespeare with his copious collection of adjectives and flamboyant superlatives could have found adequa description for some of our landscapes, waterfalls, mountain peaks and deep waterways. Photographs and other illustrations may help but the best descriptions of the islands and inside passages of the area known as the Pacific Northwest have probably been coined in the names of some coastal places such as God's Pocket, Village Island Minstrel Island, Telegraph Cove, Kingcome and many others.

Like the tide tables, this guide is a listing of primary ports (marinas) with referenc to secondary ports (public docks). It covers docks with and without services and, by casual reference, some anchorages in the vicinity. Also, like the tide tables, this guide should be referred to whenever approaching any of its ports in order to know what do layout and services are to be found there.

Some incidental notes may serve also as a reminder to the boat operator of how they should run their boats and manage their crew during passage into moorage facilities. All boat owners using this guide are kindly asked to observe proper etiquett on the water and at the various facilities referred to. At some places there are severe water shortages and mariners are requested to use available water with discretion. Garbage cannot be disposed of easily at most island locations and mariners are asked not leave their garbage at the docks. Expectations by mariners of the marina operators can sometimes be unreasonable. Please consider the difficulties under which people o the coast have to function. Their season is extremely short—about two and a half months to possibly three months of the summer holidays. They have to make a living and cover their annual costs in those short months. They have to bring in supplies fro varying but often long distances. This means not only the produce and groceries whic they offer for sale but also their materials to build and maintain their properties. And remember they have established themselves in an area of wet wintery conditions whe the slightest neglect results in a quick return of their property back to nature. There ar many experienced people working at marinas but staff who assist for summer are not always experienced and it is difficult for them to know the specific preferences of individual arriving boat operators. The facilities found along the coast are the mom and pop type of businesses and mariners arriving on their doorsteps in need of replenishment are more than welcome, giving the operators an opportunity to meet people a communicate on a friendly, personal level.

You are on holiday. Give them a friendly greeting and you will be gratified with their welcoming response. Operators who welcome you with a grunt rather than a warm, friendly smile, are rare on the coast. If you do come across any such operators, try to be understanding, or just respond by using an alternative facility in future.

In assembling the material for this book, many options were considered. It had to be presented in such manner as to provide the mariner with a quick reference to the various facilities and destinations. It had to be uncluttered with personal whimsical

Typical islands scene reflecting the ambience of a choice cruising destination.
View across Preedy Harbour, Thetis Island looking towards Chemainus.

observations just for the sake of padding it into a voluminous book. Rather it had to be functional, allowing the user an easy access to information needed and advice and guidance on available facilities and conditions to watch for so as not to have unexpected unpleasant surprises. It is therefore presented in its existing format showing principal marinas throughout the coast along with reference and charted location of public docks and marine parks which have docks and mooring buoys. It is designed to provide guidance but not to remove the joy of exploring for yourself, rather it is intended to encourage you to moor your boat at a marina or anchor it at a protected anchorage and go exploring ashore or gunkholing in your shore boat.

Boating friends and acquaintances have offered advice on what to include in this guide. I wanted to listen to all of their advice and produce the kind of guide they suggested. I thank them for their advice and input and have used many suggestions, but had I done everything suggested this would have been a kaleidoscope of different styles and probably would never have reached print. The final format is mine alone but input from boating friends has definitely influenced it. I must thank the following for their input and information, some of which has come to form part of the guide:

My wife Carla, Walter and Rita Lee, Henry and Jeanne Karcz, Chris and Sue Fraser, Warran Buck and Helen Vieser and those fellow boat owners who have told me or reminded me about places I may otherwise have missed. Thanks also to John Shinnick of *Pacific Yachting Magazine.* Thanks to the friendly neighbours at marinas we have used as home base and destinations. Their input and encouragement helped push the book to conclusion.

Marinas–Guest Moorage

San Juan Islands 19

Roche Harbor 22
Friday Harbor, Port of 24
Snug Harbor Marina 26
Rosario Resort Marina 30
Deer Harbor Resort & Marina 32
West Sound Marina 34
Blakely Marina 36
Islands Marine Center 38
Islander Lopez Marina Resort 41
Point Roberts Marina 42

Vancouver Island (south) ... 43

Victoria 45
Oak Bay Marina 46
Port Sidney Marina 48
Van Isle Marina 50
Canoe Cove Marina 52
Brentwood Inn Resort 54
Angler's Anchorage Marina 56
Goldstream Boathouse 57
Bird's Eye Cove 67
Mill Bay Marina 58
Cowichan Bay 63
Genoa Bay Marina 64
Maple Bay Resort 66
Manana Lodge & Marina 72
Inn of the Sea Resort 73

Gulf Islands 77

Salt Spring Island 79
Fulford Marina 80
Ganges Marina 85
Salt Spring Marina 86
The Pender Islands 91
Bedwell Harbour Marina 94
Port Browning Marina Resort 96
Otter Bay Marina 98
Mayne & Saturna Islands 100
Thetis Island 104
Telegraph Harbour Marina 106
Thetis Island Marina & Pub 109
Galiano Island 110
Montague Harbour 112
Gabriola Island 114
Silva Bay Boatel 115
Page's Marina 116
Silva Bay Marina 117

Nanaimo 119

Nanaimo Boat Basin 121
Dinghy Dock Pub 122
Nanaimo Harbour City Marina ... 123
Nanaimo Shipyard 124
Stone's Marina and RV Park 125

Vancouver area marinas .. 126

Fraser River, Crescent Beach 127
Richmond 128
Vancouver 130
North & West Vancouver 131
Indian Arm and Port Moody 133

Howe Sound 136

Sewell's Marina 139
Union Steamship Co. Marina 140
Lions Bay Marina 142
Sunset Marina 142
Gibsons Marina 146
Squamish 149

Sunshine Coast 151

Secret Cove Marina 152
Buccaneer Marina 154
Pender Harbour marinas 158
Coho Marina 160
Garden Bay Hotel & Marina 161
Fisherman's Resort & Marina 162
Irvine's Landing 165
Madeira Marina 166
Duncan Cove Marina 166
Headwater Marine 167
Lowe's Resort 167
Bathgate Marina 169
Royal Reach Marina & Motel 171
Beach Gardens Resort 172
Powell River/Westview 174

San Juan Islands to Port Hardy

Lasqueti Island Hotel & Resort .. 175
Lund 176
Ragged Islands Marine 178

Vancouver Island (central) 179

Schooner Cove Resort 180
Beachcomber Marina 183
Blackfin Pub & Marina 184
Des Reid Marina 186
Pacific Playgrounds Resort 188
Salmon Point Resort 191
April Point Lodge & Marina 192
Sportfish Marina/Discovery 194
Discovery Harbour Marina 197
Brown's Bay Marina 198

Desolation Sound 200

Gorge Harbour Marina & Resort 202
Manson's Landing 203
Whaletown 203
Heriot Bay Inn 204
Cortes Island 211
Refuge Cove 212
Big Bay Marine Resort 216
Shoal Bay Lodge 218
Cordero Lodge 219
Blind Channel Resort 220

North of Desolation Sound . 222

Minstrel Island Resort 226
Lagoon Cove Marina 228
Telegraph Cove Marina 230
Alert Bay Boat Harbour 235
Port McNeill Boat Harbour 236
Echo Bay Resort 238
Windsong Sea Village 241
Greenway Sound Marine Resort . 242
Shawl Bay (Brown's Marina) 244
Sullivan Bay Resort 246
Port Hardy public docks 248
God's Pocket. 249

Index 251

Parks and Public docks, buoys & floats

San Juan Islands marine parks: 28, 29.
Vancouver Island South public docks: 46, 51, 53, 55, 58, 63, 66, 68, 71.
Gulf Islands marine parks: 74.
Gulf Islands public docks: 81, 88, 97, 99, 100, 101, 102, 111, 115.
Nanaimo marine park and public docks: 121, 122
Vancouver area marine parks: 133.
Vancouver area public docks: 127, 133.
Howe Sound marine parks and public docks: 139, 142, 143, 144.
Sunshine Coast marine parks and public docks: 152, 153, 157, 166, 169, 171, 174, 175, 176, 177.
Vancouver Island central public docks: 182, 185, 187, 195, 197.
Desolation Sound and north marine parks and public docks: 201, 204, 211, 218, 225, 226, 234, 235, 248, 249.

At Anchor

Preface 4
Home Marinas 8
Balladeer Notes 13
Docks and Destinations 17
Coastal Marine Parks 27
Cruising up the Coast 44
Doing it Right 60
Fuel in Gulf Islands 65
Fulford–A Summer Place 77
Crossing the Strait 135
Pender Harbour 154
Sandy Beaches....................... 155
Heriot Bay 205
Gateway North 213/222
Native Indian Villlages 231
Alert Bay 236

Home Marinas

- Victoria
- Oak Bay
- Sidney
- Brentwood Bay
- Maple Bay
- Ladysmith
- Nanaimo
- Vancouver/Port Moody
- Richmond
- Delta/Surrey
- Comox
- Campbell River
- Washington mainland

Compromises are sometimes necessary when boating and frequently these begin right at your home marina. Consider all the options when planning to leave the dock, monitor the weather and don't be reluctant to postpone a departure for the sake of safety. Home ports or marinas are basically storage areas for boats, some of which seldom are used for long voyages. Most marinas in this guide cater to those who cruise away from home, particularly in summer. Sometimes conditions are not favourable for leaving one's home port and it may be surprising to find there are nearby alternatives, some of which will show up in the following pages.

The above departure points for cruising the many and varied destinations in the Strait o Georgia and beyond are places where most privately owned pleasure boats are stored an maintained throughout the year. As the dawn breaks each year on a new spring and the chil of winter is diminished owners and yacht club members in particular take to scrubbing an polishing their boats in preparation for a colourful sailpast followed by as many weekend and prolonged periods away as possible on the water. Cruising to general destinations suc as the the San Juans, the Gulf Islands or Desolation Sound is the trend. Frequently there ar no specific plans for overnight moorage other than a vague intention to stop if there is suitabl anchorage or moorage at one of several possible overnight shelters. Increasingly, and wit more boats converging on popular destinations, it is becoming essential that reservations fo moorage be made in advance. This guide is intended to help mariners decide where to sto in safe, sheltered moorage overnight and where services, needed by the boat owners or thei crews, can be readily acquired. To this end it provides phone numbers, details of marin facilities and other pertinent information.

Most mariners travelling to popular cruising destinations begin their journey from one o another high density population area of the coastal lower mainland British Columbia o Washington. If you keep a boat in any marina in the areas listed above you are probably face with several possible variations of compromise in your place of moorage as well as you access to holiday moorage and anchorages on the coast. These compromises range fron limitations to easily access and enjoy your boat at its permanent mooring to your ability t leave or return to the general environs of your marina. In some cases your marina's geographical location is the compromise, or the effects of current and tide where you ar moored, or sometimes it's simply the weather combined with an inability to determin adequately what sea conditions prevail until you are well on your way and committed to you passage.

Victoria and vicinity mariners require a passage around an often rough and tide-rippe Trial Islands and up through a sometimes testy Haro Strait before they reach the placid water ff Sidney. Fortunately most Victoria residents can take one look out to sea and determine he ease of passage. Checking with the tide and current tables is always sound logic as well o ensure a comfortable beginning of a cruise.

Sidney and Saanich Inlet mariners are in much the same position, but they have the dvantage of being where they are going without even leaving the dock (that is—in the heart of the Gulf Islands). And the same applies to Maple Bay, Ladysmith and Nanaimo. Mariners n these areas have enviably easy access for extended seasonal periods to the anchorages and narinas of the Gulf Islands but often look farther afield for their major trips and their favoured lestinations include Desolation Sound and beyond. For them access out of their marinas is subject to little more than a decision to go. Swift currents and windy conditions through some passages could delay the more cautious and slower travelling mariner leaving from any of hese latter destinations, but usually little compromises their departure and returning plans. At Nanaimo mariners, locals and visitors alike, may await the slack at Dodd Narrows before venturing south into the islands, or may stay at the docks while seas off Entrance Island settle after a storm before crossing the Strait en route north.

Vessels at marinas on the Sunshine Coast or at places north of Nanaimo are already part way to cruising in Desolation Sound or north. For some of them the Gulf Islands are quick and easy to access. But many in places such as Pender Harbour have their boats at that location because of the good fishing and, especially smaller boats, seldom leave the area. Be sure to check your marine charts for area WG and ensure it is safe and that no military exercises are in progress before crossing this part of the Strait.

Mariners on the Vancouver side of the Strait of Georgia are probably the most compromised in their endeavours to leave their moorings and return home. Cautious boat operators will spend days monitoring weather forecasts prior to a major trip, and certainly will listen to the reports on VHF prior to any other departure. Wind and wave height is of utmost interest, tidal changes and currents can be critical and even openings of fishing to the commercial industry can affect one's plans to set off on a voyage. Vessels leaving Vancouver and Port Moody are subject to the currents under Lions Gate bridge and Second Narrows. An easy alternative for weekends out of Port Moody or Vancouver Harbour is Indian Arm, even though sheltered anchorage is limited to Bedwell Bay and little else, and dockside moorage is practically nonexistent, especially for overnight.

Leaving False Creek is quite straight forward and bumpy conditions off Stanley Park are the quick indicator that worse stuff lies ahead, usually at Point Atkinson. Boats departing Richmond and running down the North Arm of the Fraser may reach open water before determining that it was not such a good idea to leave the dock. One can usually tell from the wind force at the marina whether there is likely to be rough conditions out of the river, but how rough? Listen to the reports on VHF before leaving. And one can always wait in Coward's Cove for conditions to ease.

Most vessels from these Vancouver and Richmond areas have Howe Sound as their playground. The facilities in Howe Sound are among the best on the coast and increasing numbers of yachtsmen are finding enough satisfaction in spending time at places on Bowen Island or Gibsons that they decline to cross the Strait to the Gulf Islands other than for extended trips. Out of Surrey or Delta, on the other hand, the Gulf Islands are closer than Howe Sound. And mariners mooring their boats at Ladner, Crescent Beach or Point Roberts can be in the midst of the Gulf Islands in less than an hour (a little longer in a sail boat). But leaving the Fraser River is one of the biggest challenges on the west coast. (Returning may be another). The currents at the Sand Heads lightship are vicious at times. A receding tide near low water, especially against a moderate breeze (don't even think about a strong wind or or worse) can be dangerous in the extreme. Refer to the government publication on Weathe and Thompson's Oceanology for interesting information about current, wind and wav patterns at the river mouth. Bear in mind that while the weather report covers Sand Heads i does not provide wave height at the river mouth, a sadly lacking service, especiall considering the dangerous nature of the seas at that point. You can always turn back and wai at Steveston for improved conditions or return to your marina, but coming back from acros the Strait you reach a point where you are committed.

Leaving Crescent Beach is straight forward enough except that it is a long run across a open bay before entering the Strait. This may be easy and safe when departing, but it i difficult to assess conditions for returning. Point Roberts is well located for quick, visua assessment of condition in the Strait and close enough to the Gulf Islands that a crossing o the Strait is quick enough even for slower travelling vessels. But it is very exposed to ba weather conditions for a return trip and mariners should carefully determine what they ca expect off Point Roberts before leaving the safety of a comfortable mooring on the other side One of the compromises for Canadians who keep their boats moored at Point Roberts is th need to clear customs both by road and when cruising. Most who keep their boats at Poin Roberts feel the compromise is a minor one especially considering benefits of being there such as an excellent marina with superior facilities and the close proximity to some of the bes destinations on the coast, plus the immediate access out of the marina onto the Strait and, fo sports fishermen, fishing right off the point.

Boats cruising to Canada out of the States have the easy compromise of extra distance t travel through US waters to reach their Canadian destinations. The San Juan Islands ar popular for cruising destinations, with excellent marinas and facilities. Vessels passin through en route to Canada have to be mindful of wind and tidal conditions at severa passages, but with careful VHF weather monitoring and the ability to wait out unfavourabl seas at safe and interesting places, the passage can be most pleasant.

Canadian boats travelling to the San Juans are equally subject to monitoring conditions Know where you are headed and check the route before you leave. Watch for obvious curren swept waterways and check the tide and current tables. When cruising any unknown water watch what other boats are doing. If there are no other boats about be doubly cautious an double check your current predictions and weather reports.

Vessels travelling into Canada or the USA must stop at a customs dock for clearance an should carry their clearance reporting number for checking back into their home country.

Once you have managed to clear your marina and the possible obstacles of weather currents and tide you are on your way to the fabulous Gulf Islands, Desolation Sound o beyond. Enjoy your cruising and make use of the information in this guide.

The format of this book takes the reader in a south to north progression from one dock t the next. The intention is to provide a logical sequence of references to fuel stops or overnigh moorage en route to a final destination. The information accompanying the graphics is up t date but constant changes are being made at various marinas. To keep your references in this guide updated simply pencil in any new information for your own personal future reference. This book will be updated periodically depending on the frequency and extent to which coastal facilities are altered and improved.

Wherever possible space has been included for your own notes. Keep this guide up to date and feel free to pass along to the author any cruising tips and observations for future editions.

A peaceful early morning in Ganges prior to the busy summer rush in contrast with boats and people at the docks of Telegraph Harbour Marina on Thetis Island in mid season.

Top: Near Echo Bay, quiet passages and remote wilderness.
Above: The drying canal between Thetis and Kuper Islands allows passage at high tide between Clam Bay and Telegraph Harbour.

Balladeer Notes.

Rising early to set off on yet another day's quest in search of that elusive tranquil anchorage I find myself at odds with my own desire to simply remain where we have spent the past day and night rather than raise the anchor and go. Then it strikes me. This is where I want to be. This or any other anchorage on the coast of British Columbia where the feeling of well-being is so deep you don't realise what it is. It is the ambience of the morning as you lie at anchor in a quiet mooring with the light mists rising off the water and swirling up among the overhanging branches of tall firs and cedars and gnarled arbutus trees tangling their way among them.

I am where I want to be. This anchorage and not the one I hope to find later today or perhaps tomorrow. This is the place that I have been searching for these many years.

Years of travelling around the British Columbia coast by boat has led to the inevitable conclusion that there are many moorings in numerous coves and bays that can be shared among the region's thousands of pleasure boat owners and operators. Some of these are yet to be explored by a surprisingly large number of us.

My random text that ties together some of the destinations is intended to take the reader on mini voyages of discovery to some of the delightful places on this coast: anchorages where you can just sit and watch the sun set or take your dinghy and explore the rocky shores, poke into tiny beaches or slowly troll around the vicinity and bring back a salmon for supper. Or spend a day scuba diving to view some of the magnificent marine life that exists in these chilly but magnificent waters.

There are places on this coast where international history was made, where battles were fought among the aboriginal native peoples and where art has taken its form. There are places where nature refuses to allow man's intrusion to destroy, where she fights back and says "no, you cannot have this land" and simply reclaims what man has tried to steal from her. There are places where time has stood still.

Balladeer, our boat for 16 years served me and my wife, Carla, as a worthy vessel in which we discovered the British Columbia and adjacent Washington State coasts. *Balladeer* (and now *Balladeer II*) took us comfortably where the seas, inlets and passages would allow. We found our way through rough seas and calm, rain, shine and fog. On some of our voyages we had the company of other pleasure boats, friends with whom cruising is a shared delight and adventure, and who, being taught some of the ways of boating by our example, also taught us many lessons of operating a boat in local conditions as well as the importance of functioning as a team—a cruising "buddy" system that plays a major role in providing safety and peace of mind that comes only from knowing that you are not alone out there. In the same way a cruising companion provides company I have experienced a deep satisfaction at the presence of coast guard cutters and fellow yachtsmen met along the way and of the isolated but manned lighthouses scattered along the coast.

Villages, towns and cities have been visited and enjoyed. These make up the structure of hubs from which all adventures begin, just as it did in the gold rush days when prospectors gathered in places like Victoria and took off from there for the Klondike. In this cruising guide I invite you to vicariously revisit those places on the BC coast which are accessible by boat and in many cases only by boat or seaplane, and which have something special to offer, be it ideal walks ashore, fine cuisine from a waterfront restaurant or just a simple, quiet anchorage with no signs of civilisation about for miles. Share the sites of tall mountains, massive forests, Indian villages, small communities, city waterfronts, river mouths, inlets and current swept passages. Cruise through the fog to a safe haven, run the rapids of the swiftest passages and sit back on the deck of your own boat, reminiscing as you watch the sun go down. Notes in italics in the text are from my log.

I have included in this guide information about boat operation and handling which many boat owners may find of value. Photographs from my collection are intended to illustrate as well as inform. Use this guide as a reference and picture book, and most of all go out and enjoy your boat in safety and to the fullest extent.

The coast and islands of British Columbia and the San Juans

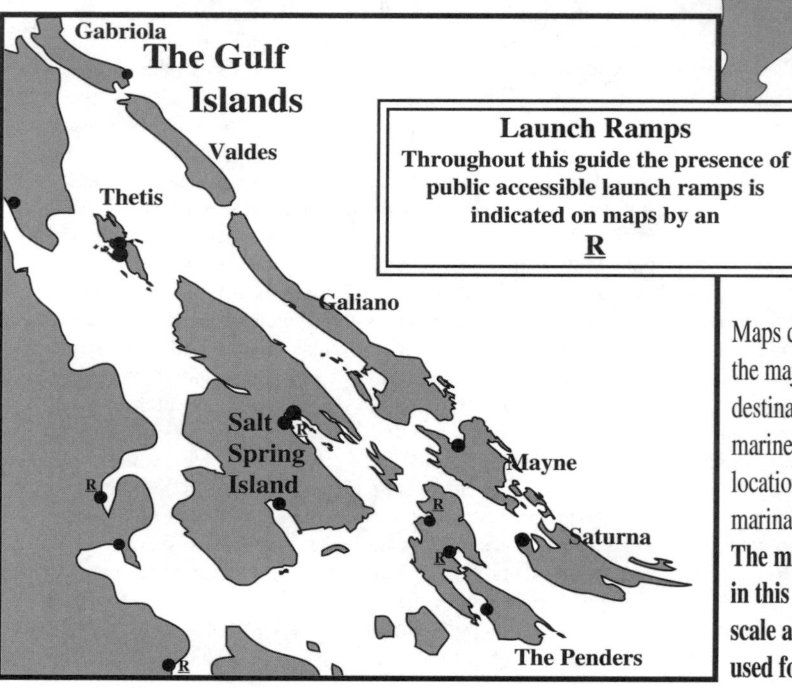

Maps depicting some of the major cruising destinations favoured by mariners. Dots show location of marina or marinas in the area. **The maps and diagrams in this guide are not to scale and are not to be used for navigation.**

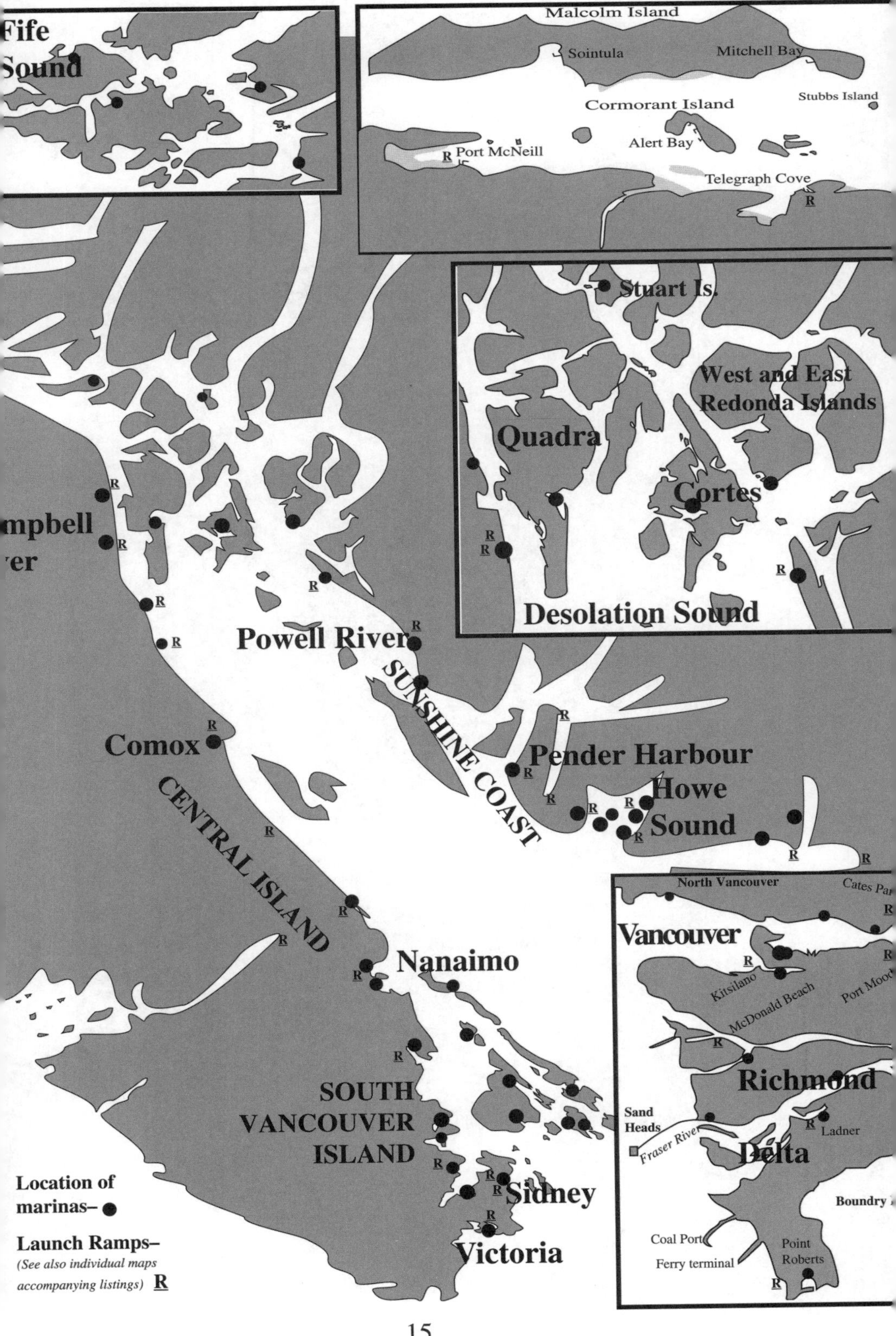
Fife
Sound
Malcolm Island
Sointula
Mitchell Bay
Stubbs Island
Cormorant Island
Alert Bay
Port McNeill
Telegraph Cove
Stuart Is.
West and East
Redonda Islands
Quadra
Cortes
Desolation Sound
mpbell
er
Powell River
SUNSHINE COAST
Comox
Pender Harbour
Howe
Sound
CENTRAL ISLAND
Nanaimo
North Vancouver
Cates Par
Vancouver
Kitsilano
McDonald Beach
Port Mood
Richmond
Sand
Heads
Fraser River
Ladner
Delta
Boundry
Coal Port
Ferry terminal
Point
Roberts
SOUTH
VANCOUVER
ISLAND
Sidney
Victoria
Location of
marinas–
Launch Ramps–
(See also individual maps
accompanying listings) R

One of the most appealing destinations on the coast–Princess Louisa Inlet.

Docks and Destinations

As you travel up the coast out of your home marina you may ponder your course to your final route. Or you wisely will have planned it well in advance. As you plan your route this guide will help you finalize and consumate that plan by enabling you to call ahead and make reservations one dock ahead for your progress along the way. Your timing for arrivals and departures at your chosen marinas will be subject to the weather and sea conditions and any astute boat operator will make allowances for this as do the marina operators. Although they are sometimes fully booked in advance, no-shows can mean a space for a late arriving boat that has either made no reservations or has been accepted on a stand-by basis. It is wise if you are arriving at a marina on stand-by and the docks are possibly going to be full that you choose in advance a marina where there is an alternative dock or anchorage nearby, preferably one that offers total protection in all weather conditions.

THIS BOOK IS AIMED AT PROVIDING MARINERS WITH GUIDANCE TO PROTECTED OVERNIGHT MOORAGE INCLUDING MARINAS, GOVERNMENT DOCKS AND MARINE PARKS, DOCKS, MOORING BUOYS AND ANCHORING.

The geography of the book follows the coast from mainland Washington State and BC's lower mainland. It begins with destinations in the San Juan Islands, continues to Victoria, B.C., and on up the east coast of Vancouver Island, taking in Sidney, Saanich Inlet, Cowichan, Maple Bay and on up through Crofton to Ladysmith. Then it returns to the Gulf Islands and follows them geographically, more or less up to Nanaimo. It goes across to Greater Vancouver with its Fraser River, False Creek, Burrard Inlet and Indian Arm facilities. Then continues into Howe Sound, up the Sunshine Coast with its inlets and harbours, until it reaches the entrance to Desolation Sound. It moves across to Comox and Campbell River then on to Desolation Sound and vicinity before continuing up through Big Bay to the world beyond Desolation Sound. Through the rapids and passages it goes up Johnstone Strait, acknowledging Kelsey Bay and branching off to Minstrel Island before continuing to Alert Bay. At this juncture it heads through the Broughton Archipelago to Fife Sound via Echo Bay to Sullivan and across to Port Hardy and finally God's Pocket in the Bull Harbour area.

All of the marinas listed have protected moorage and facilities in varying degrees to offer the mariner. Some offer limited casual moorage but no marina on the coast, including those operated for permanent mooring clients only, is likely to turn away an overnight guest if there is room. And it is only in the months of July and August as well as some weekends and long weekends in other boating months that space at marinas is at a premium. Many mariners who operate their boats year round enjoy the quiet and solitude of marinas during the off season. Their monitoring of weather conditions allows them access from their base to the destination of their choice which is usually one that assures them complete protection against changing weather conditions.

Historic buildings and places of interest can be found adjacent to many waterfront landings such as the Orcas Hotel, top, and the West Sound Store, above.

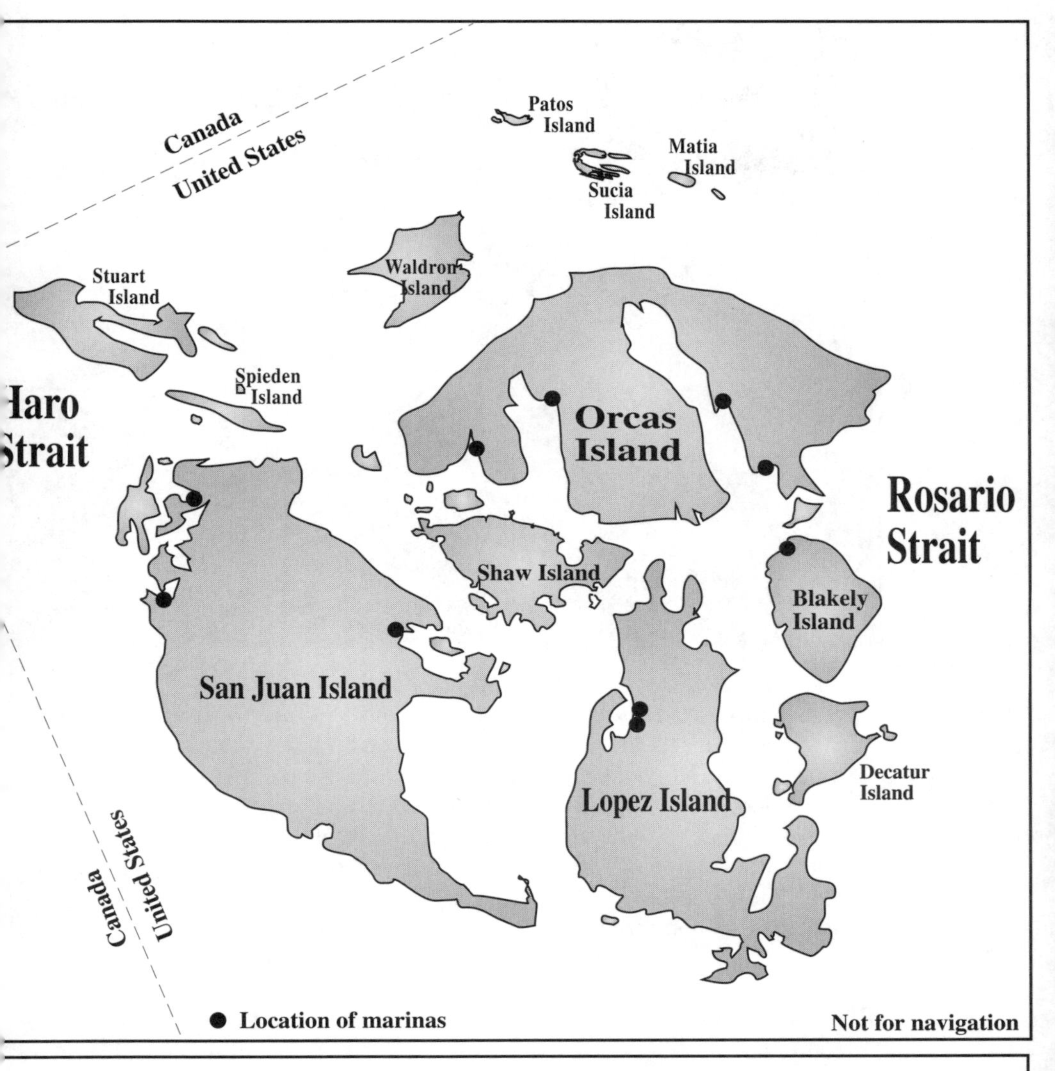

San Juan Islands

Journeying into the San Juans mariners have the pick of some excellent marinas, fine restaurants, well-stocked marine, grocery and hardware stores as well as arts and crafts centres. There are fast food places, ice cream vendors, pubs, hotels, good accommodations and rustic bed and breakfast places. There are walking and hiking trails and roads as well as car, bicycle and motor scooter rentals. Some of these include dining at places such as Hemingway's in Deer Harbor or the quaint West Sound Store and Deli for a good bowl of soup, a sandwich, salad or dessert. At Friday Harbour there is such a wide choice of

restaurants as well as other stores it would take an entire vacation to enjoy the place to its fullest. The annual Jazz Festival on the last weekend in July is a busy time so get in early or keep away if you want to avoid crowds. A more tranquil place may be Fisherman Bay with its good anchorage and marinas, nearby Lopez Village and pleasant dining facilities. Roche Harbor is a busy customs port and attracts some of the larger cruising yachts to its busy marina. It's a place to visit if you like to look longingly at some of those mega vessels that frequent and even monopolize it. The Hotel De Haro usually has fine dining and it's entertaining to watch the evening color ceremony at sundown. Fascinating history of the islands include the early explorations of the Spanish, the presence of the English and the famous Pig War which nearly led to an international confrontation between the British and Americans. One of the more charming remnants of recent history of the islands is Rosario Resort on Orcas Island. A stop at this facility will provide sheltered moorage as well as a chance to acquaint yourself with its splendid history.

A short or long stay in the San Juans can provide a complete vacation, and many Canadians make the trip once in a while just as their American counterparts are steaming through the San Juans en route to the Canadian Gulf Islands and points beyond.

Above: The massive marina at Roche Harbor. Big expansions are planned. Left: an outlook from Rosario Resort on Orcas Island. Below: on Lopez Island–Fisherman Bay has protected moorage.

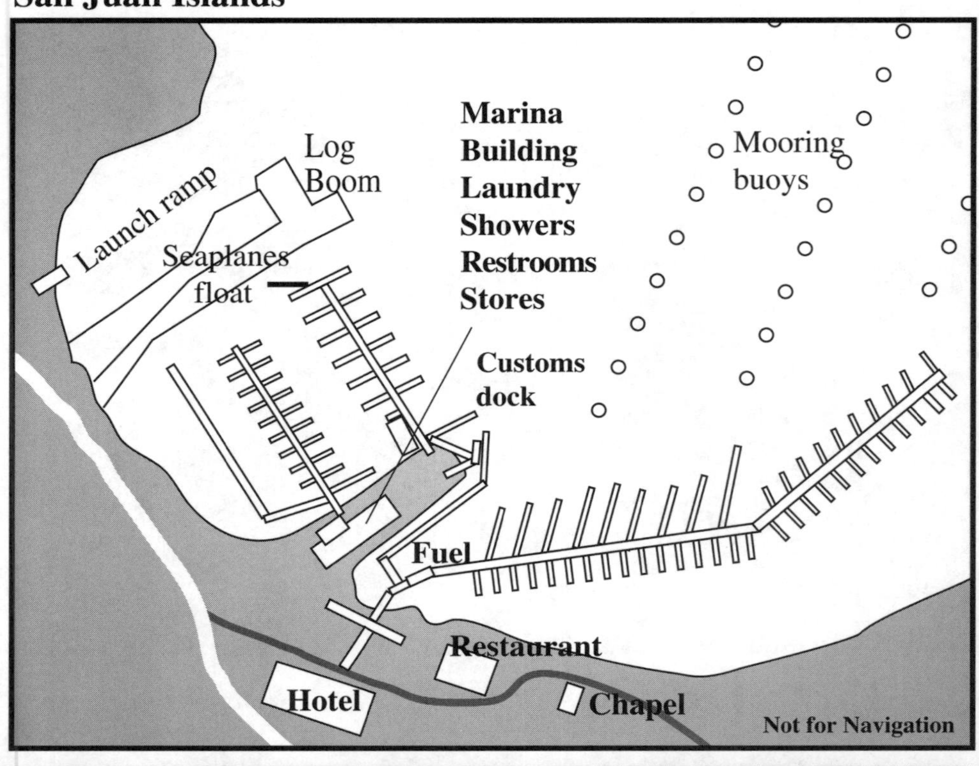

Roche Harbor

Roche Harbor

Bart Mathews
Box 4001, Roche Harbor,
Washington. 98250
Phone: (360) 378-2155 Fax 378-6809
Chart 18421/33 VHF call 78

Marina services:

Moorage. Transient all sizes to about 130'
Power at docks: 20 30 50/ 220 amps.
Water.
Fuel : Gas, diesel. Propane. Oil

Customer services:

Showers, laundry, washrooms
Public phones ashore. Phone hook up avail.
Walking: Road access walking, cycling.
Adjacent facilities: Store–groceries, a wide range of provisions. Hotel, fine dining, accommodations. Arts and crafts. Clothing, apparel, gifts, groceries. Ice, fishing tackle, licences, marine supplies. Moped rentals. Horse riding. Hiking trails. Boat rentals, kayaks. Good fishing nearby. New seafood deli, pool and tennis courts with burger bar at pool side. Jazz festival late July–call for information. Fourth of July celebrations and fireworks. Color ceremony each sunset.
Taxi or bus service to island centres and ferry to Anacortes. All facilities open March through November. Moorage and basic facilities open year round. Mooring buoys managed by marina.
Note: New docks planned for 1995.
Major Customs Port of Entry.

Facilities at Roche Harbour include the well stocked store whose name commemorates the historic Lime Stone company for which Roche Harbour was founded. Approaching the marina and fuel dock.

Roche Harbor

Hotel de Haro is the historic landmark at this famous harbor. It is a magnificent building exemplifying the type of construction and opulence of its day. There is a lot to see and do at Roche Harbor. The resort is a museum in its own right, its buildings dating back to the turn of the century. It was founded in conjunction with the adjacent lime kiln and barrel manufacturing. Massive changes and additions were planned for the marina to be ready in time for the next season.

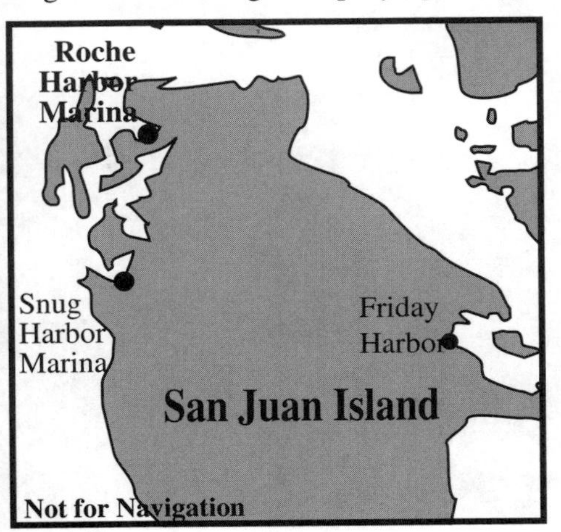

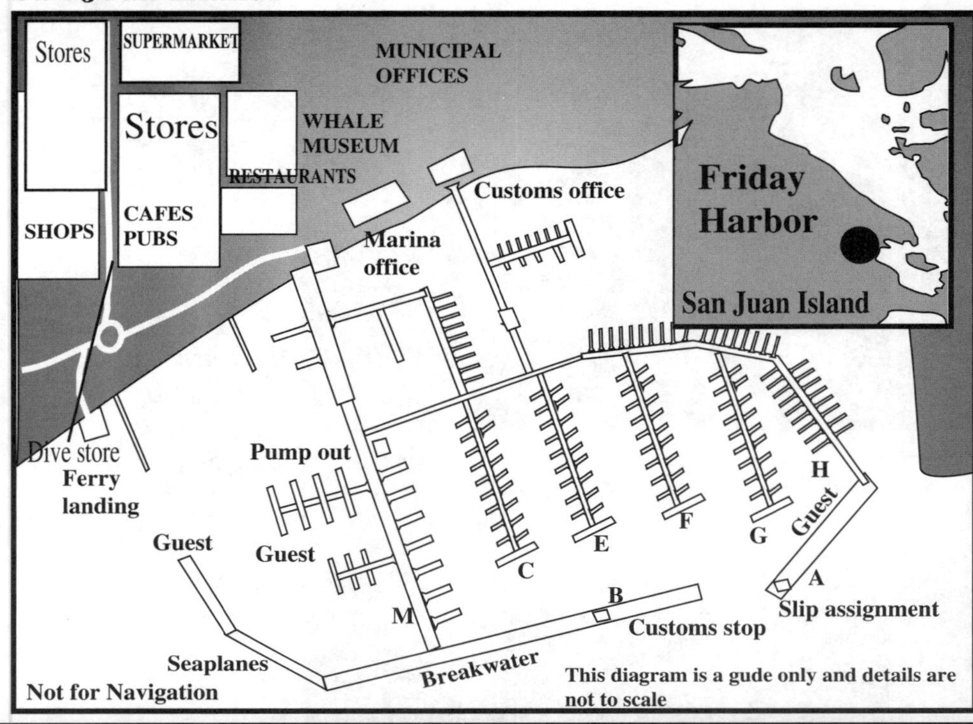

Friday Harbor

Port of Friday Harbor

Box 889, Friday Harbour,
Washington. 98250
Phone: (360) 378-2688
Chart 18434. 18421. Waterproof #43

VHF 66A (US mode)

Marina services:

Moorage. Guest and permanent.
Power at docks: 30 amp.
Water.
Fuel dock adjacent: Gas, diesel, propane.

Customer services:

Pump-out station.

Friday Harbor

Its large marina is one of the busiest in the Pacific Northwest. This is a major customs stop entering United States waters for Canadian boat operators and one of the major centres for returning American mariners. Located on the east side of San Juan Island it competes with Roche Harbor as a customs stop but the two towns are vastly different. Friday Harbour has a large town comprising everything from city hall to cinema, supermarkets to specialty shops, hardware store, marine chandleries and a wide variety of restaurants, pubs and bistros. As a major ferry landing, Friday Harbor sees the comings and goings of a vast number of people: islanders, cyclists coming to visit, campers, boaters and fly-in sightseers. During summer crowds of boaters flock to the town for the major event of the year, the Summer Jazz Festival. A Pig War barbecue is held in June.

For the boat owner there is fuel, moorage, water, showers, laundry, 30 amp electrical service and all the amenities one could imagine necessary for a major stopover. There are two anchorages in the immediate proximity of the huge marina, one adjacent to the north west marina entrance and the other out in the middle of the harbour.

Laundry, showers, ice, bait.
Public phones ashore.
Nearby church/es: multi-denominational.
Pharmacies and other necessities.
Scuba diving arrangements and charters–ask at nearby dive store or marina for details.
Walking: Road access walking, cycling, car and scooter rentals.

Entertainment:

Regular annual music festival late July, Pig War Barbecue in June. Many other events.

Adjacent facilities: Marine stores–charts, marine hardware, supplies, books, fishing licences, tackle, etc. Post office, liquor, restaurants, banks, accommodations, pubs and specialty stores. Golf, cinema, nearby airport. Ferry to Anacortes

Note:

When arriving at Friday Harbor first check in at the customs dock on the breakwater. The flag up means the office on the dock is open. Down means you can check in at the office ashore or by telephone if that office is closed. Then proceed to dock A for slip assignment.

Major Customs Port of Entry Phone (360) 378-2080. Or 1 800-562-5943

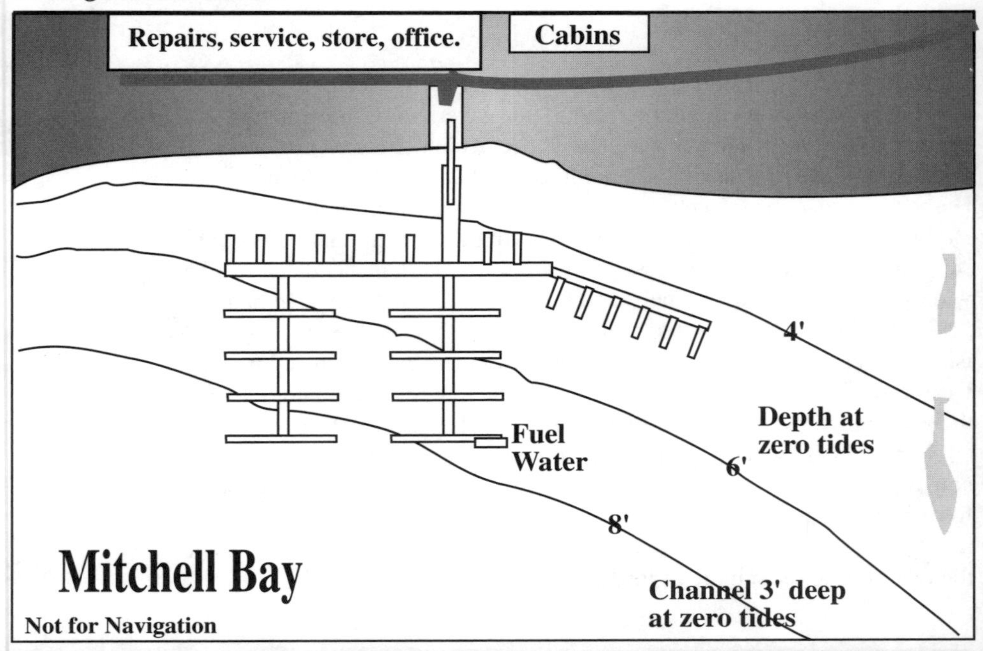

Snug Harbor Marina

Snug Harbor Marina Resort

Dick Barnes, Barbara Begley
2371 Mitchell Bay Rd., Friday Harbor, Washington. 98250
Phone: (360) 378-4762
Chart: Waterproof #43. 18421

Marina services:

Moorage. 71 slips. Guests welcome.
Power. 15 amp.
Water.
Fuel : Gas. Repairs. Supplies.

Customer services:

Garbage bins.
Shower, laundry. By arrangement.
General store, groceries, provisions. Charts, books, clothing, gifts. Hardware. Marine. Fishing equipment. Public phones ashore.
Walking: Road access walking.
Adjacent Facilities: Accommodations. Ten self contained, fully equipped bungalows. RV park. Launch ramp. Scuba charters.

Note: Rocks in entrance. Channel to left. Depth 3' at zero tides. Use large scale chart Waterproof #43 for navigating inside Henry Island.
Clear customs at Roche Harbor.

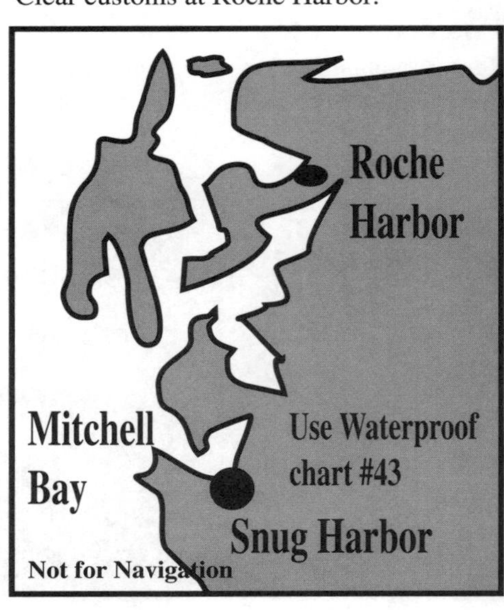

Snug Harbor Marina in Mitchell Bay is protected from the open waters of Haro Strait by a shallow entrance and drying reef. The channel at zero tides drops to three feet.

Coastal Marine Parks

Marine Parks in the San Juan Islands as well as British Columbia offer tranquil and delightful moorage. The parks have been established for use by the general public and attract hikers, backpackers, cyclists, RV campers and all sizes of boats . Many parks have picnic and overnight camp sites with walking or adjacent hiking trails or beaches. Some have docks adequate to moor dinghies only, some to moor a number of small to medium sized craft and others none at all. Most have mooring buoys and boats of all sizes make use of these for safe overnight mooring. Fees are charged for tying up at the docks at a fixed rate per foot or per meter (USA and Canada respectively), and flat fees are levied for use of mooring buoys. These fees change from time to time but at present they are about $5 per mooring buoy per night and the charges usually apply after a certain hour of the afternoon, 3 pm to 8 am in the San Juans and after 6 pm in Canada.

Marine Parks in BC are representative of the best of our waterways and their adjacent landfalls. They have been preserved for recreation, conservation and posterity. The authorities ask that they be respected and that they be kept clean. Garbage should not be disposed of unless there is a specific disposal station. Sewage should not be discharged in marine park anchorages and noise should be limited to daylight hours. Radios and other sources of noise are not to be operated from 11 pm to 7 am.

There are marine park hosts at some Marine Parks and in BC their presence will be indicated by the flying of a BC Parks Marine Park Host burgee. The host is usually a member of a power squadron, a yacht club, a sailing association or is an individual who has volunteered to assist visitors to the parks.

In the San Juans it is possible to purchase an annual moorage permit which allows use of mooring buoys and docks at the various locations throughout the year without further fee. Fees are in effect year round at some facilities while at others only between May and September. In the San Juan Islands these include Sucia Island, Stuart Island, Jones Island, James Island and Matia Island.

For more information on marine parks in US waters contact Washington State Parks Headquarters, PO Box 42664, Olympia, WA. 98504–2664 (360) 753-5771. In Canada, RR #6, 2930 Trans Canada Hwy, Victoria BC. V9B 5T9. (604) 387-4363.

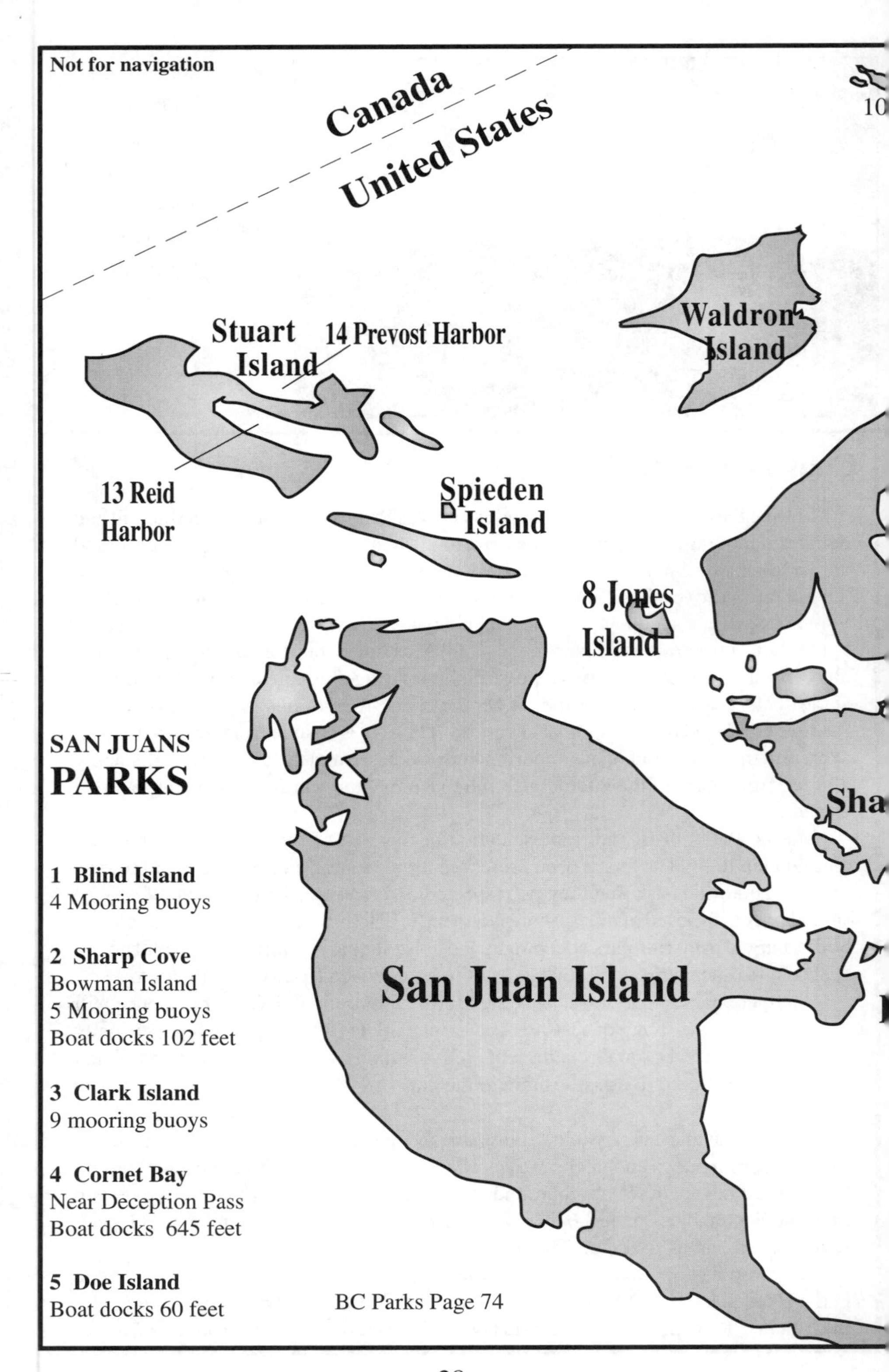
Not for navigation
Canada
United States
Stuart Island
14 Prevost Harbor
13 Reid Harbor
Spieden Island
Waldron Island
8 Jones Island
San Juan Island
SAN JUANS
PARKS
1 Blind Island
4 Mooring buoys
2 Sharp Cove
Bowman Island
5 Mooring buoys
Boat docks 102 feet
3 Clark Island
9 mooring buoys
4 Cornet Bay
Near Deception Pass
Boat docks 645 feet
5 Doe Island
Boat docks 60 feet
BC Parks Page 74

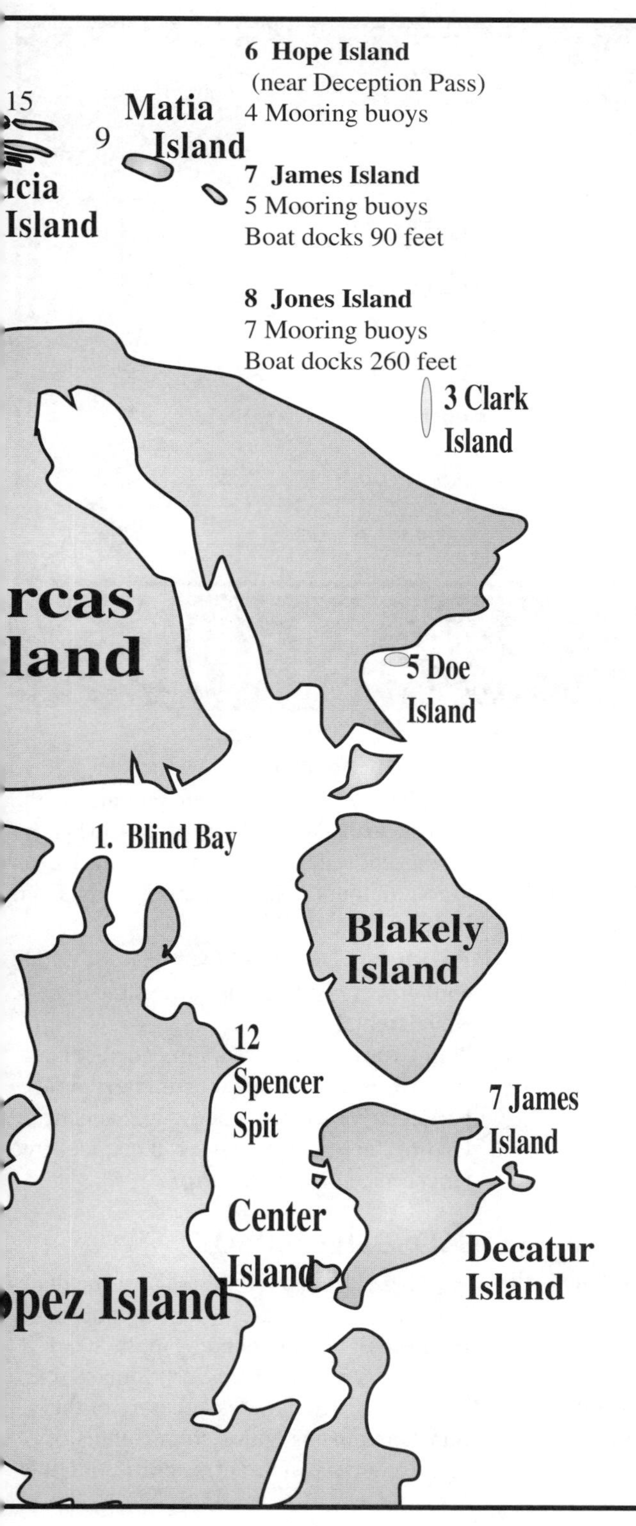

6 Hope Island
(near Deception Pass)
4 Mooring buoys

7 James Island
5 Mooring buoys
Boat docks 90 feet

8 Jones Island
7 Mooring buoys
Boat docks 260 feet

9 Matia Island
2 Mooring buoys
Boat docks 128 feet

10 Patos Island
2 Mooring buoys

11 Skagit Island
Near Deception Pass
2 Mooring buoys

12 Spencer Spit
16 Mooring buoys
Porta potti dump station

13 Reid Harbour
Stuart Island
15 Mooring buoys
Boat dock 219 feet

14 Prevost Harbor
Stuart Island
7 Mooring buoys
Boat docks 539 feet

15 Sucia Island
Echo Bay
14 Mooring buoys

Fox Cove
4 Mooring buoys

Shallow Bay
8 Mooring buoys

Ewing Cove
4 Mooring buoys

Snoring Bay
2 Mooring buoys

Fossil Bay
16 Mooring buoys
Boat dock 778 feet

16 Turn Island
3 Mooring buoys

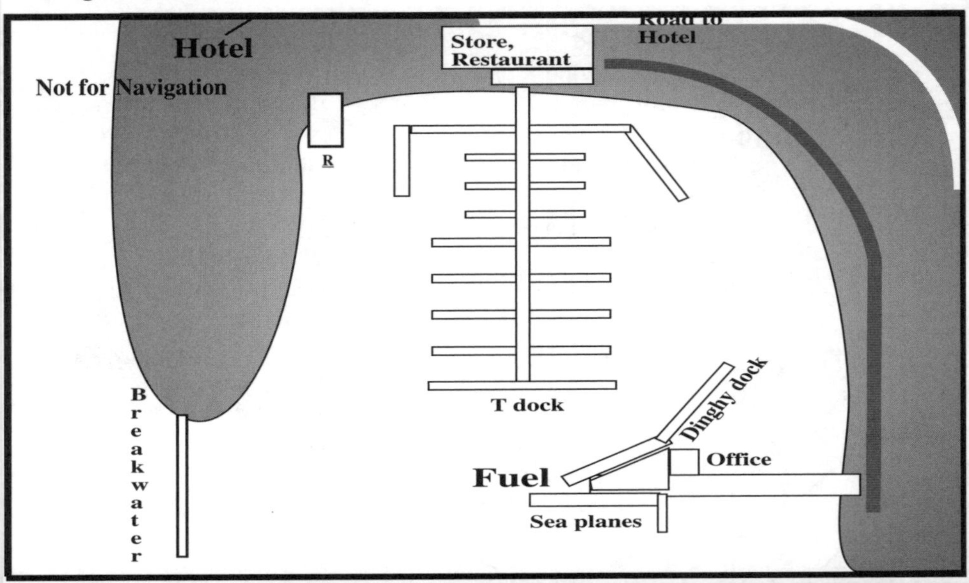

Rosario Resort Marina

Rosario Resort Marina

Richard Hansen
Orcas Island
East Sound, Washington. 98245
Phone: (360) 376-2222 Fax 376-3680
Chart 18421, 18430/34. WP #43

Marina services:

Moorage. Guest and permanent.
Power at docks: 30, 20 amp.
Water.

Customer services:

Laundry, showers, ice, bait.
Public phones ashore. Garbage bins.
Hotel, pub, spa, pool (indoor and outdoor), retaurants–fine dining or casual. Beauty salon. Gift shop. Accommodations and all hotel services.
Nearby church.
Scuba diving arrangements and charters–ask at dive store or marina for details.
Walking: Road access walking, cycling, car rentals. Scooter rentals arranged.

Entertainment:

Regular live music, organ recitals in the historic mansion. Slides and Rosario history narration. Golf nearby. Tennis courts. Kayak tours. Air tours. Whale watching tours. Fishing charters.

Adjacent facilities: Cascade Bay Cafe and grocery store, supplies. Rental cars. Kayak rentals.

Note: Reservations recommended for marina or resort, in peak summer months particularly. Mooring buoys and anchoring landing fee includes passes to spa and free taxi service. **Launch ramp.**

Rosario Resort

There is sheltered moorage at the docks behind the breakwater. Mooring buoys are not necessarily sheltered from the wind and waves that blow up East Sound some afternoons. The hotel is a feature of the San Juan Islands with a colourful history and excellent restaurant. Facilities include

The docks are protected behind a breakwater with a fuel dock at the entrance. The mansion, below, looks over the sweep of East Sound.

water, showers, store and a swimming pool with hot tubs.

Robert Moran, who built Rosario Resort after retiring in 1904, was a former shipbuilder in Seattle. He used shipbuilding methods and materials in the construction of the mansion. The building's walls are made of 12 inch concrete and the roof is sheathed in copper. Windows are 7/8 inch plate glass and many sections of the interior are panelled in mahogany. One of the resort's major features is the Kimball pipe organ, said to be the largest installed in a private residence in the United States. The mansion was listed in the National Register of Historic Places in 1979. The estate was sold in 1938 and the current ownership created the resort in 1960.

Rosario is the closest sheltered moorings for accessing East Sound, a quaint but bustling village that attracts many visitors each summer, mostly by ferry. East Sound has restaurants, stores, banks, post office, medical clinic, movie theater, pharmacy, churches, galleries and many other services and facilities. It has an airport and air tours are popular among visitors wanting a lofty look at the San Juans. Nearby is the town of Olga with its quaint village and community docks. Stop for lunch at the village Arts co-op. Moorage is an incredible 25 cents per foot. A sign on the dock reads: "Dock maintained with community labor and moorage fees collected after 6 pm."

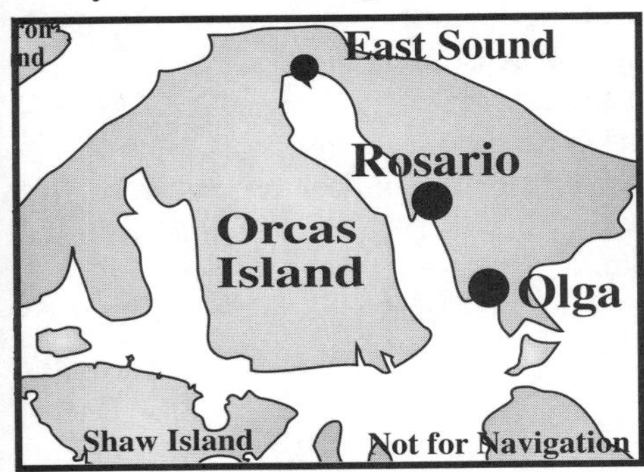

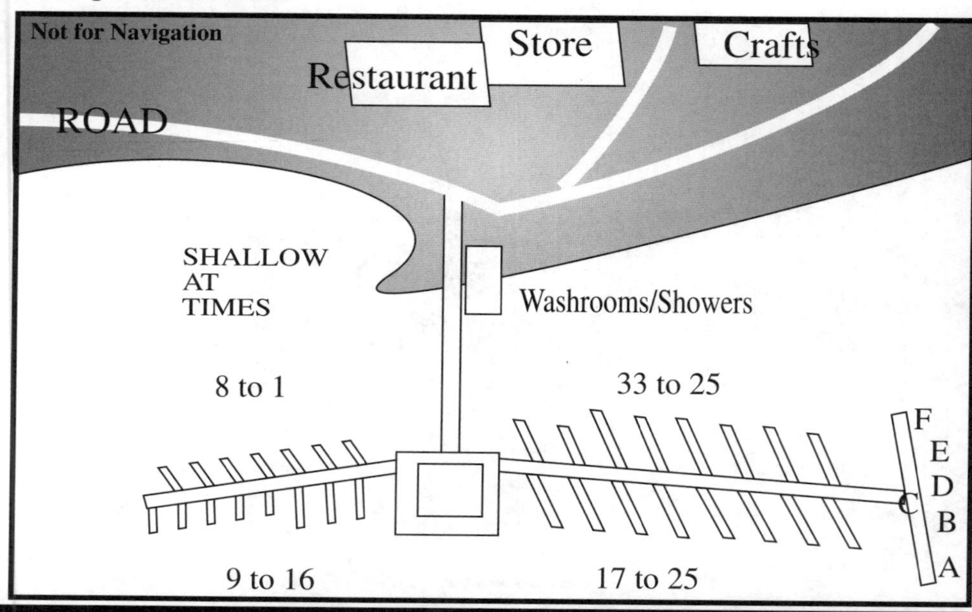

Deer Harbor

Deer Harbor Resort & Marina

Linda and Peter Casale
Box 200, Deer Harbor, Orcas Island
Washington. 98243
Phone: (360) 376-4420 Ext. 33
Chart 18421/34 VHF call 66 (US mode)

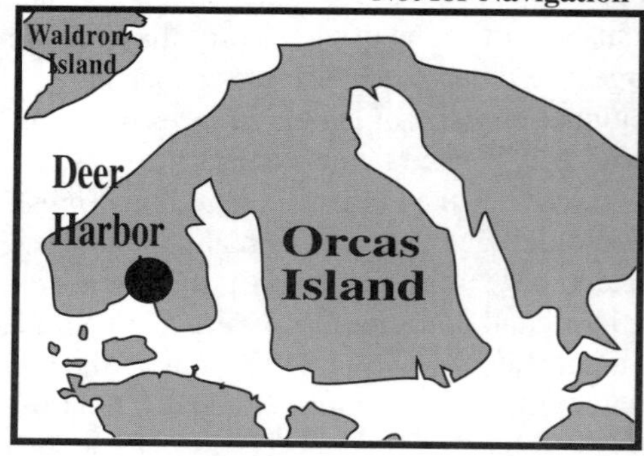

Marina services:
Moorage. Transient and permanent.
Power at docks: 15 amp.
Water.
Fuel: Gas, diesel.

Customer services:
Barbecue area. Accommodations.
Showers, washrooms. Ice.
Public phones ashore.
Walking: Road access walking, cycling.

Entertainment:
Small boat rentals, whale watching tours, kayaking, sunset cruises and fishing charters. Heated swiming pool and spas.

Adjacent facilities: Store–groceries, deli and provisions. Store–gifts, postcards, clothing and arts and crafts. Hemingway's by the Sea restaurant–fine dining.
Taxi service to island centres and ferry to Anacortes. Seaplane service to Seatac.
Note:
Clear customs for USA destinations at Roche Harbor or Friday Harbor.

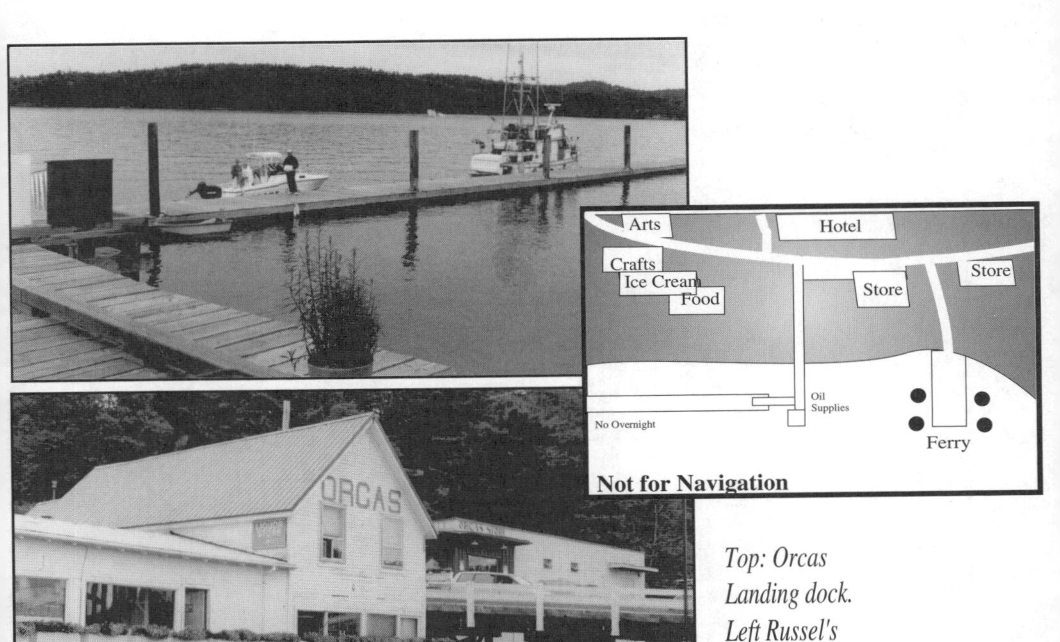

Top: Orcas Landing dock. Left Russel's and other buildings at the landing.

Orcas Landing

Russel's Store (Independent operator)
Box 200, Deer Harbor, Orcas Island
Washington. 98280
Phone: (360) 376-4389 (Russel's Inc.)
Chart 18430/4, VHF call 66 (US mode)

Marina services:

Moorage. Stopping briefly only.
Water.
Fuel: Gas, diesel. Oils

Customer services:

Stores and facilities ashore. Ice.
Public phones ashore.
Walking: Road access walking, cycling.

Entertainment:

Sightseeing by cycle popular.
Adjacent Facilities: Store–groceries. Stores–gifts, clothing, arts and crafts. Orcas Hotel nearby. Taxi service to island centres and ferry to Anacortes.

Deer Harbor

This cosy corner of Orcas Island is a pleasant stopover at docks that face a semi-protected open bay. Most wind conditions do not bother boats at the marina but a southerly or south westerly wind may cause a bit of movement, especially off season. In season many boats visit the docks to stay overnight and enjoy excellent cuisine at Hemingway's Restaurant. The marina offers fuel, water, showers, ice and the opportunity to relax in the comfort of a well maintained swimming pool with a couple of hot tubs.

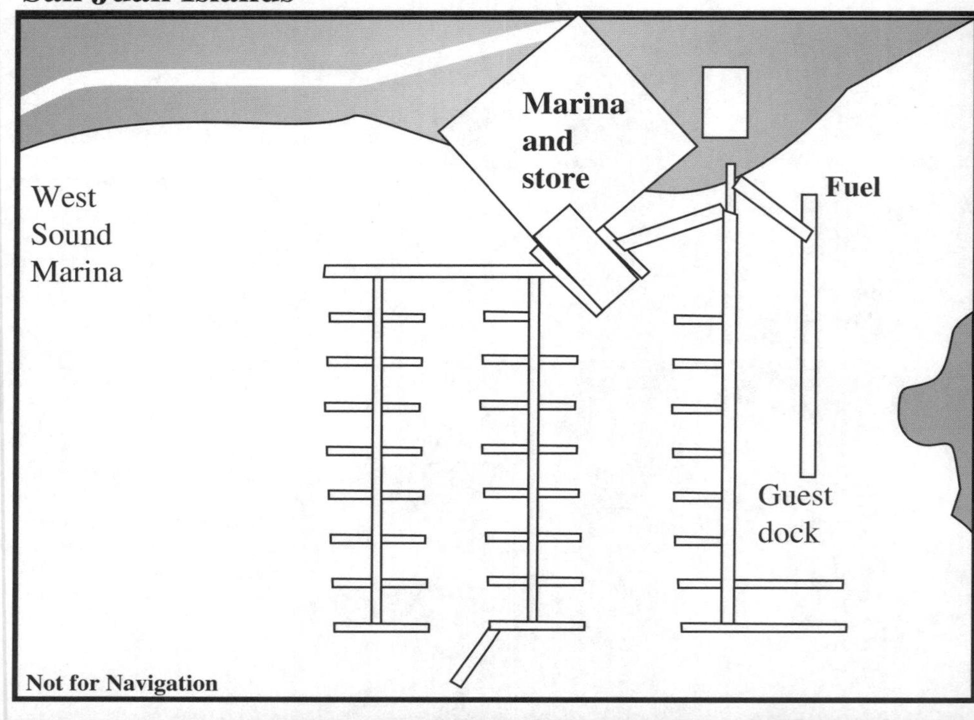

West Sound

West Sound Marina

Mike & Peggy, Ian, Betsy Wareham.
Box 19, Orcas Island
Washington. 98280
Phone: (360) 376-2314
Chart 18421/34 VHF call 16
Hazard: Island reef near guest dock.

Marina services:

Moorage. Transient (primarily permanent.)
Power at docks: 15 amp.
Water.
Fuel: Gas, diesel, oils.

Customer services:

Marine ways and repairs. Major shipyard. Complete marine chandlery.
Showers, washrooms. Ice. Public phones ashore.
Walking: Road access walking, cycling.
Nearby facilities: Store–groceries, deli and provisions. Meals.

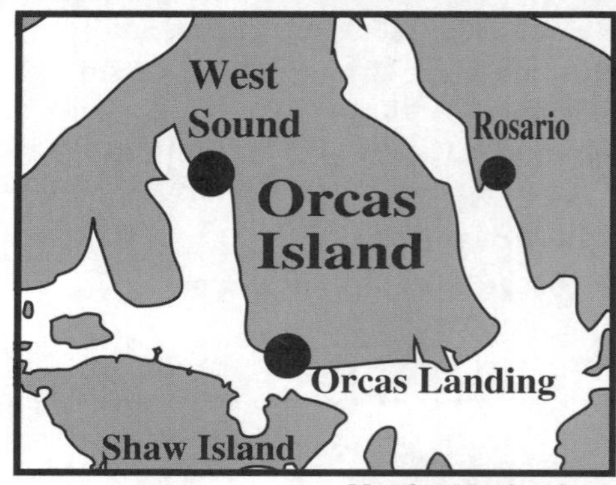

Not for Navigation

Taxi service to island centres and ferry to Anacortes.

Note:
Clear customs for USA destinations at Roche Harbor or Friday Harbor.

West Sound

This protected moorage is largely for long term resident boats. However, it has an excellent marine service facility with 30 ton travel lift and comprehensive repair services. It has a well stocked marine store and the buildings ashore include a large, modern, heated bay where refinishing and mechanical work can be done in any weather conditions. The facility caters to all of the San Juan Islands with a 24 hour emergency service. Transient moorage accommodates a number of boats on a 250 foot long finger that is an extension of the fuel dock. Gas and diesel are available and are generally priced competitively with fuel at places such as Friday Harbor. It has a pump out station.

A short walk up the road is a deli which serves hot light meals at lunchtime. An island taxi service out of East Sound is available for transportation to other parts of Orcas Island such as Orcas ferry landing or the town of East Sound. The facility is owned and operated by Mike and Peggy Wareham, son Ian and daughter Betsy. The chandlery offers Johnson outboard products, fishing gear, marine supplies of a wide variety, propane and ice.

Orcas Landing

A quaint village at the ferry landing serves the community on Orcas Island. It has an historic hotel as a focal point. The Orcas Island Hotel has rooms and pub and restaurant, the latter of which is open only at week-ends but is reputed to serve excellent meals. Through the week food is served at the pub, a tiny indoor, smoky room, or at the pub's outdoor terrace area. The dock at Orcas is for transient mariners only. It is long and accessible both sides although the shoreward side has a narrow entrance and if a boat is tied up at the end entry for anything but a small boat would be tight. Fuel is available at the dock as well as other marine products and services. On shore there is a gift and craft store, Russels, which has a wide selection of wares. The settlement is popular among transient mariners and land based visitors alike. Summer sees thousands of cyclists, campers and motorists arriving on the island in a constant stream off the ferries. At Orcas it is a common sight for crowds of vacationers to be lining up for their trip home mingling with those just arriving as they flood into hotel, craft stores, grocery store, fast food restaurant, ice cream store or other facilities.

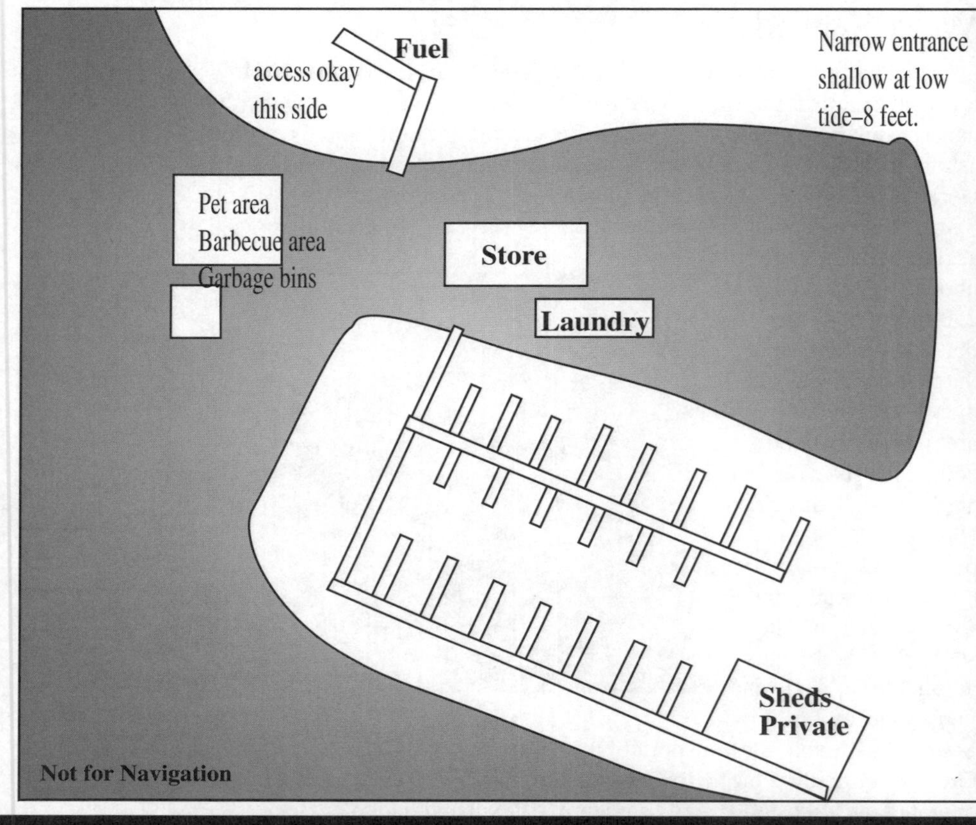

Blakely Marina

Blakely Island General Store and Marina

Lloyd and DeNeane Thurman
Blakely Island
Washington. 98222
Phone: (360) 375-6121 Fax 375-6141
Chart 18421 18430

Marina services:

Moorage. Guest moorage.
Fuel: Gas, diesel.
Power at docks: 30 amp.
Water.

Customer services:

Showers, laundry, washrooms.
Store. Provisions. Fresh produce. Food. Clothing, gifts. Marine hardware.
Tackle, bait. Fishing reports taken. Licences. Ice. Hot dogs, snacks. Patio. Banquet and meeting space.
Public phones ashore. Garbage disposal for customers.

Adjacent facilities: Covered barbecue pits in cabana on the waterfront. Firepit. Pet area. Play area. Cleaning facilities–sink and power. Club bookings, facility day use.

Note:
Entrance depth to 8' at zero tides. Fuel dock accessible either side.
Covered docks at entrance are private.
Clear customs for USA destinations at Roche Harbor or Friday Harbor.

The store at Blakely Marina with the patio out front. It faces the open passage and overlooks the fuel dock. The fuel dock is accessible from either side.

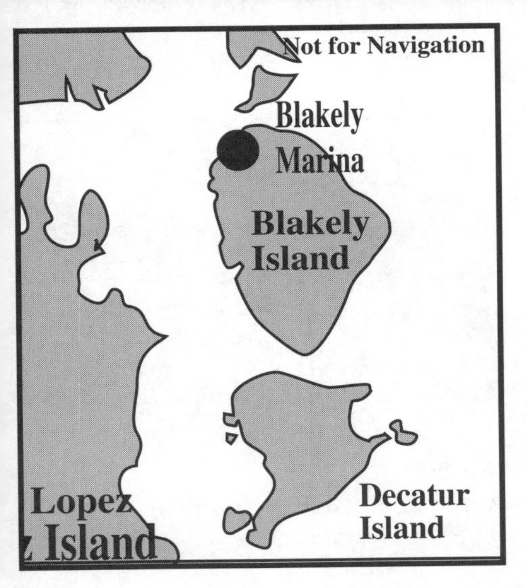

Blakely Marina

Private property with no access to the island. The marina has facilities for guest boats and a sheltered bay where a number of boats can moor. Access is limited to higher tides for deep draft vessels. The depth through the channel is 8' at zero tides. A current runs past the entrance. This is a beautifully landscaped island and although it is private the scenery is enjoyable from the marina or the patio ashore.

San Juan Islands

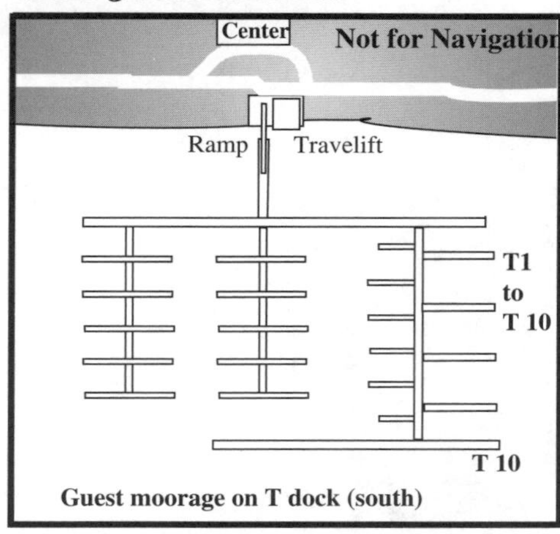

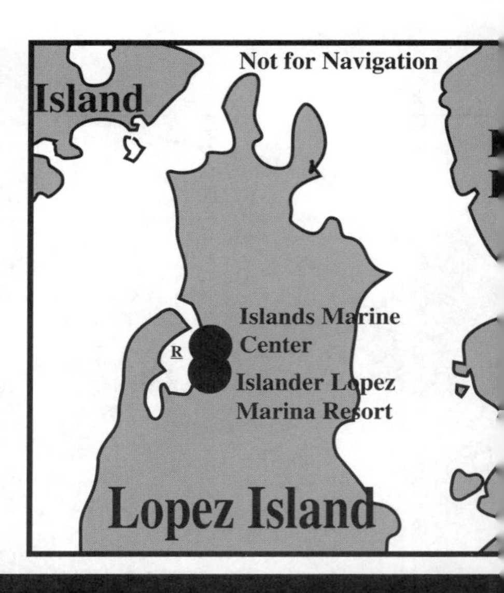

Islands Marine Centre
VHF call 16, 69. CB 9

Islands Marine Center

Islands Marine Centre

Ron & Jennifer Meng
Box 88, Lopez Island,
Washington. 98261
Phone: (360) 468-3377 Fax 468-2283
Chart 18421/30/34 VHF call channel 69

Marina services:

Moorage. Permanent and guest. (South side of marina).
Power: 30 amp.
Water.
Fuel: Next door at Islander Lopez Marina.
Boatyard. Reairs and service. Haulouts.
15 ton travel lift. Launch ramp.

Customer services:

Showers, laundry, washrooms
Yacht sales and service. Various makes of outboard motors and boating equipment. Marine chandlery, hardware, charts, clothing, gifts, electronics, fishing tackle and information. Licences. NAPA store. Ice. Public phones ashore.

Walking: Road access walking, cycling.

Entertainment: Golf nearby. Picnic and barbecue area. Bicycle rentals. Wine tasting at nearby vineyards.
Adjacent facilities: Lopez Village less than one mile. Stores–groceries, provisions, inn, meals, accommodations. Islander Lopez Marina Resort next door.
Courtesy van service to ferry, airport, golf, by arangement.

Note:
Customs Port of Entry at Friday Harbor or Roche Harbor.

The entrance, above, to Fisherman Bay is narrow and shallow, but deep enough for a safe passage for most craft at low tides. A sign on marker number five reminds mariners to round marker number eight inside the bay leaving it to starboard. It is located not far from the outer floats of Islands Marine Center docks shown in the distance and to the right in the accompanying photograph. The chandlery and service facility at Islands Marine Center appear in the photo on the opposite page.

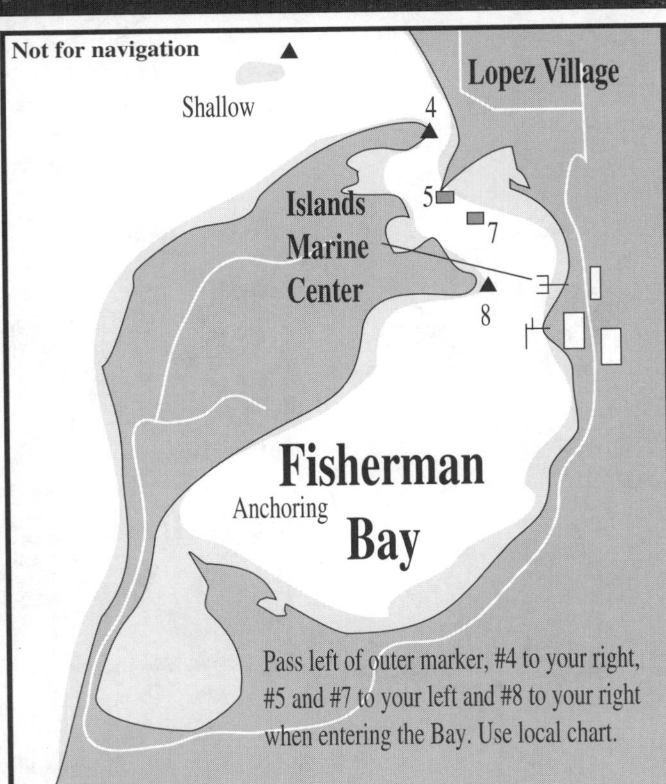

Lopez Island Vineyards are open to the public and wine tasting is available June to September 7, Wednesdays to Sundays from 12 noon to 5pm. Other months on Fridays and Saturdays. The vineyards are a short distance beyond the Lopez Island village and a reasonable walk or a quick drive away. Lopez wines are made from local Madeleine Angevine, Siegerrebe and from Yakima Valley Chardonnay and Cabernet Sauvignon/Merlot. Lopez Island is one of the easiest islands in the Strait of Georgia for cycling. Bicycle rentals are available adjacent to Islander Lopez Marina and Islands Marine Center. An extensive road system allows wide exploration of the many interesting things to see and do on the island.

Pictured: Islander Lopez Marina and village scenes.

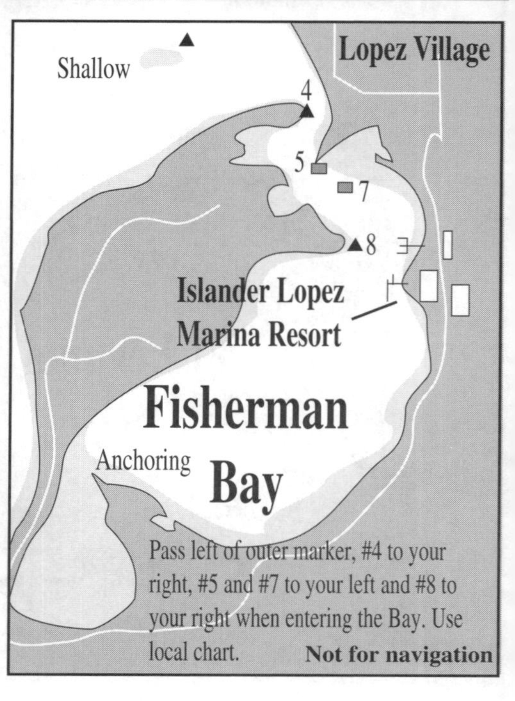

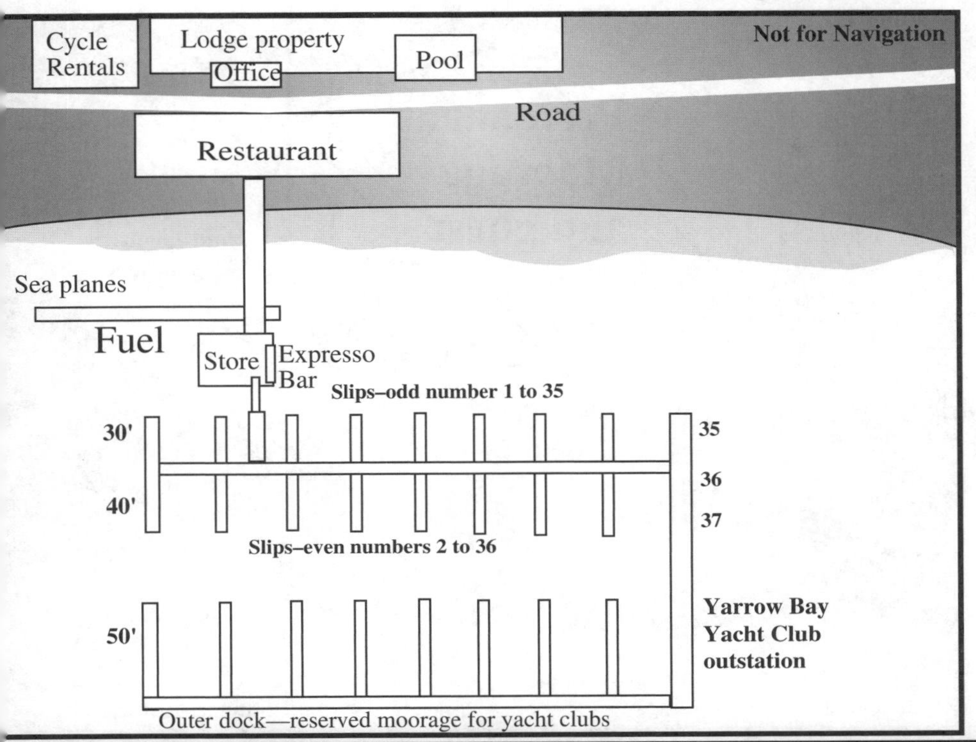

Islander Lopez Marina

Islander Lopez Marina Resort

Box 459, Lopez Island,
Washington. 98261
Phone: (360) 468-2233 Fax 468-3382
Charts 18421/30/34
Dock 468-3383 VHF 78

Marina services:

Moorage. Guest mooring.
Power: 30, 50 amp.
Water.
Fuel: Gas, diesel
Sea plane float

Customer services:

Showers, laundry, washrooms.
Store on dock, groceries, provisions, charts, clothing, gifts, books, bread, fishing tackle. Ice. Public phones ashore.
Courtesy phone on dock.
Hotel accommodation–28 rooms. Swimming pool. Hot tub. Conference and banquet facilities. Salmon fishing and scuba diving charters. Wildlife & whale watching.
Additional docks boats to 50' in 1995.
Restaurant (360) 468-2234. Patio service. Expresso bar on dock. Dockside welcome package June to September.
Walking: Road access walking, cycling.
Entertainment: Golf nearby.
Bicycle and small boat rentals.
Kayak rentals and guides.
Adjacent facilities: Lopez Village less than one mile. Stores, arts and crafts, churches, accommodations. Near ferry service. Float plane calls at marina.

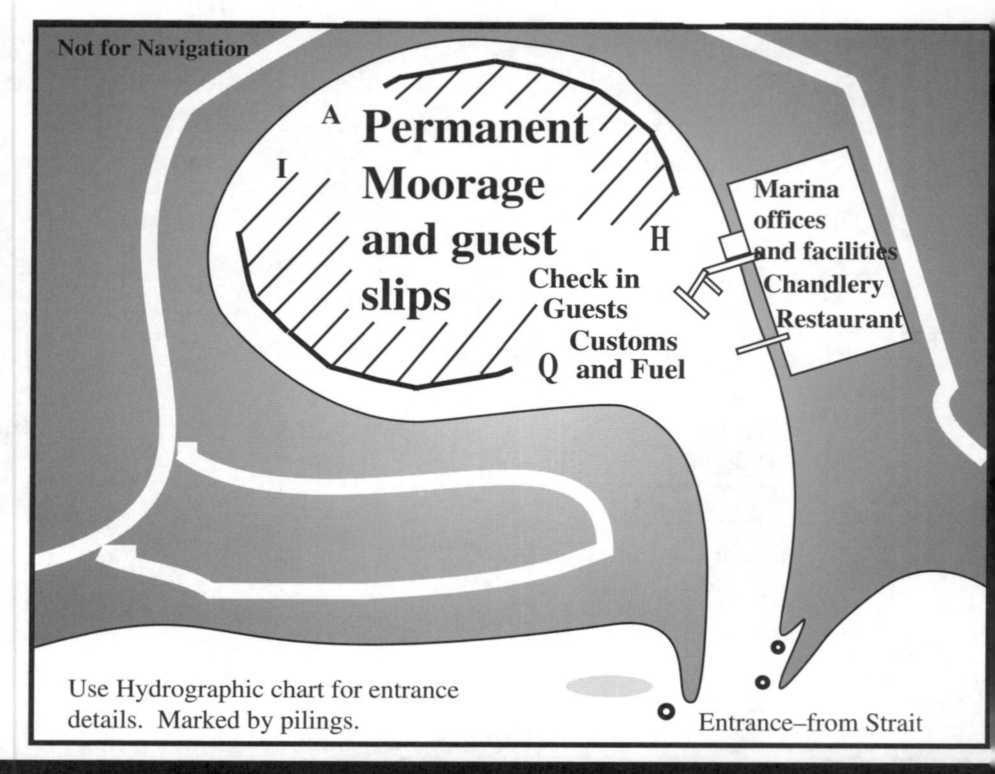

Point Roberts Marina

Point Roberts Marina

Bruce Gustafson
713 Simundson,
Point Roberts, WA. 98281
Phone: (360) 945-2255
Charts: Cdn: 3450. US: 18400

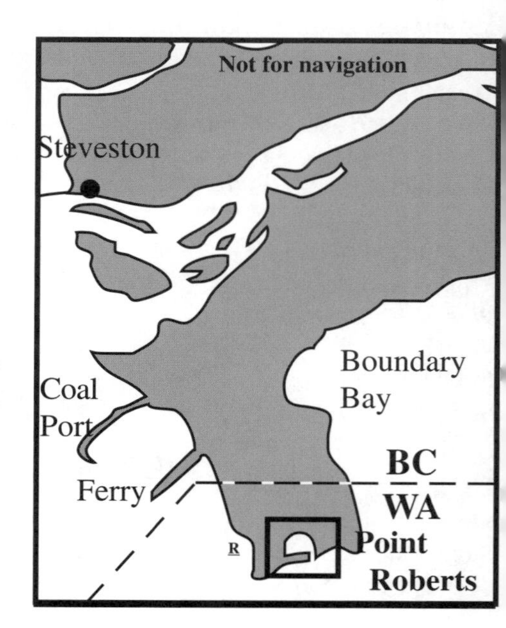

Customer Services:

Moorage 24' to 125'.
Fuel: gas, diesel, propane.
Water, Power 30, 50 amp, **Showers, laundry, washrooms.** Public phones. Chandlery, bait, tackle, fishing licences, repairs, service, pump out facility. Workyard. Cafe. Restaurants. Haulouts–35 ton travelift, monorail sling hoist–boats to 22 feet.
US Port of Entry. Customs.

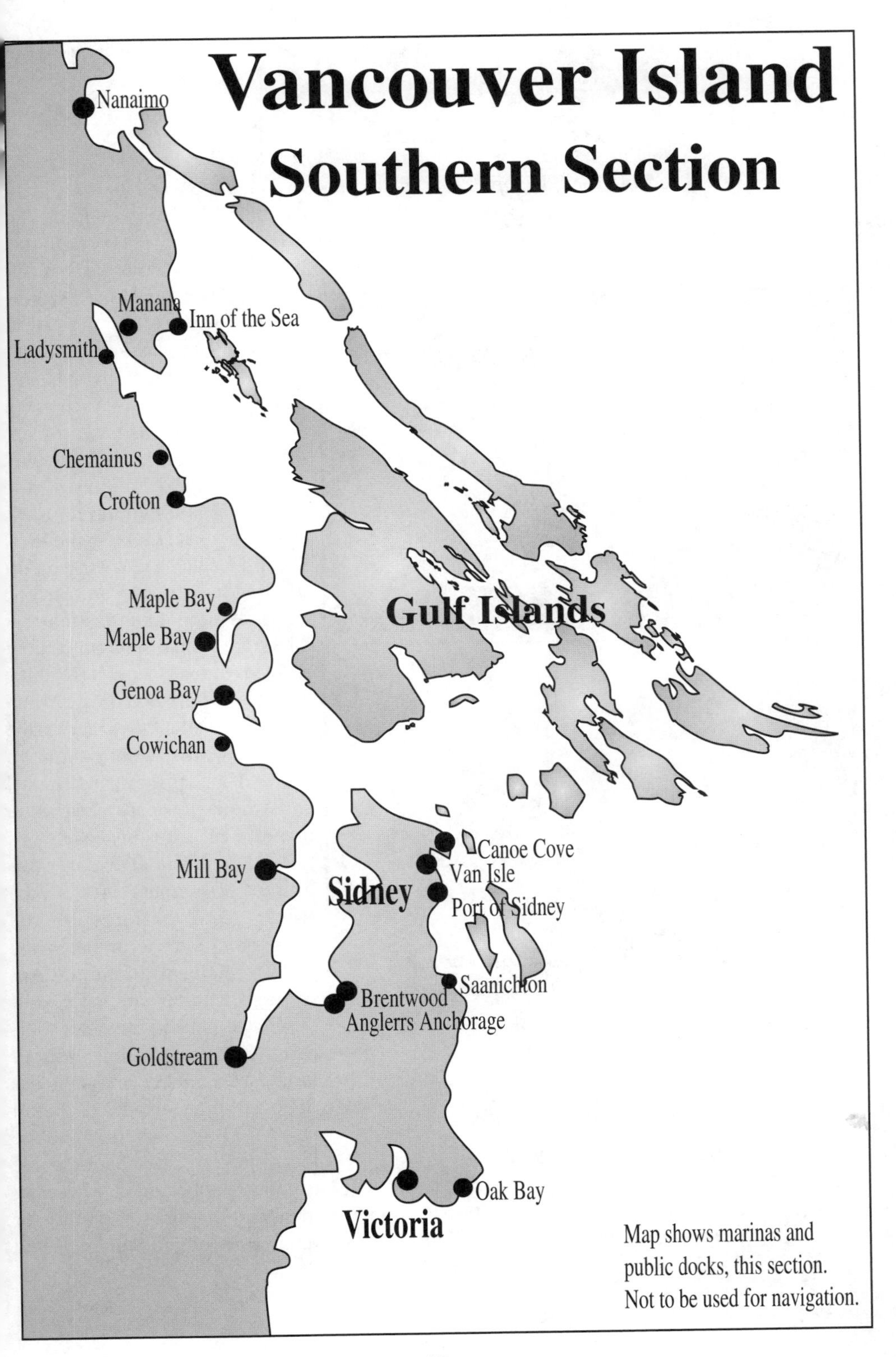
Vancouver Island
Southern Section
Nanaimo
Manana
Inn of the Sea
Ladysmith
Chemainus
Crofton
Maple Bay
Maple Bay
Genoa Bay
Cowichan
Gulf Islands
Canoe Cove
Van Isle
Mill Bay
Sidney
Port of Sidney
Saanichton
Brentwood
Anglerrs Anchorage
Goldstream
Oak Bay
Victoria
Map shows marinas and
public docks, this section.
Not to be used for navigation.

Cruising up the coast

The fabled Gulf Islands are steeped in history and folklore and there are many books on many subjects dealing with these fascinating islands as well as the San Juans. But this guide is not intended to keep you reading reams of historic notes, rather it encourages you to pick up the more complete works of other authors who have spent far more time researching those subjects for publication. As you make passage along the east shore of Vancouver Island, stopping possibly in Victoria or Sidney to clear customs, you unfold places and people that will surprise you with interest and character. You may prefer to tie up at a dock and take in the local facilities. Such a place is the Port of Sidney, a busy summertime customs stop and destination. There are good restaurants ashore and a favourite is the Hotel Sidney where you can sit on the patio and have an excellent view across the water towards Sidney Spit on Sidney Island in the near distance, and where you can take in the magnificent crimson sunsets.

The public docks at the entrance to Victoria Harbour are busy year round with fishermen, commercial and transient pleasure craft. In the inner harbour area options include the Wharf Street civic marina and the floats in front of the Empress Hotel. Those shown above are private, located to starboard at Laurel Point.

In Saanich Inlet discover waterfront restaurants such as the Rusty Duck alongside the Brentwood ferry terminal, or the Brentwood Inn itself. Stop at Anchorage Marina and take your dinghy around to Butchart Gardens for a day of strolling in one of the most magnificent masterpieces of landscaping anywhere. Or pull into Mill Bay and walk up to the local shopping centre for some excellent cappuccino or shopping at the well-stocked Thrifty Store. Continue up the coast through Genoa Bay for a safe overnight stop and fine dining, or visit Maple Bay for good moorage and a sumptuous meal at the marina restaurant.

Victoria

There are many reasons to put into Victoria. It is a major customs port with a customs dock alongside the large public marina on Wharf Street. After clearing customs it is usually easy to find a slip at the public dock. Another public dock with limited space on either side of a single slip is located just before the Johnson Street bridge and additional moorage under the same control as the Wharf Street dock is located right in front of the Empress Hotel. Private docks in front of local residences are located beyond the Johnson Street bridge in The Gorge, and if you are ever in Victoria for a while a slow cruise up The Gorge is a worthwhile undertaking, just for the scenery. West Bay has a number of floats and is the location of West Bay Marina with its narrow entrance and rock lined passage. A variety of services can be had at this marina but only occasional overnight moorage can be arranged for smaller vessels.

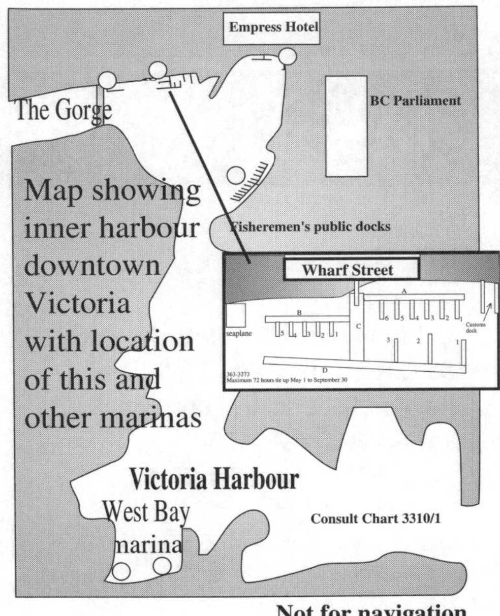

Not for navigation

As far as Victoria is concerned there are not only a wide variety of stores but also the charm of an array of British styled shops, pubs and restaurants. British imports are the specialty and if the atmosphere of old England does not strike you immediately go and reserve afternoon tea at the Empress Hotel. Tourists flock to Victoria each summer and the attractions, apart from the above, include Parliament, wax museum, undersea gardens, scenic London-bus tours and much more. There are festivities, shows and numerous public events in the city throughout summer.

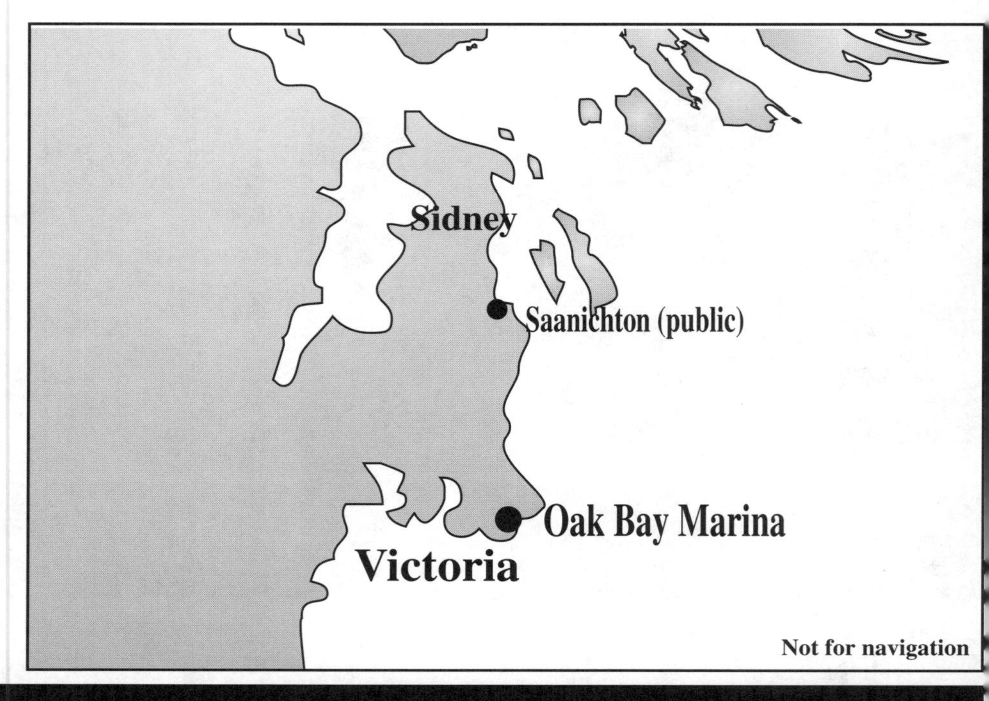

Oak Bay Marina

Oak Bay Marina

Steve Huxter
1327 Beach Drive, Victoria, BC,
V8S 2N4 (604) 598-3369
Chevron fuel dock, Oak Bay,
Phone: (604) 598-3366
Chart 3310, 3462 VHF 68

Hazard: Rocky entrance. Shoals and shallows–marked with buoys. Consult charts.

Marina services:

Fuel: Available at fuel dock.
Mechanic and services available from local and nearby marine operators and facilities.
Moorage: Permanent moorage and overnight slips. Reserve in summer.
Water at dock.
Power: 15 amp – upgrading to 30 amp.
Laundry, showers, washrooms.
Security gate.

Saanichton, Sidney Public.
Transport Canada dock
Chart 3310, 3441, 3462
Manager • Float length 10 m
Lights •
Adjacent city restaurants, shops, churches.
All services and facilities in Sidney.
Ferries nearby to mainland and US ports.

Customer services:
Customs/phone.
Nearby village. Oak Bay Avenue. 6–8 blocks.
Chandlery. Tackle shop. Gift shop and others within walking distance.
Deli at marina. Restaurant–dining.
Walking road and beachfront.
Entertainment.
Nearby Victoria. Shuttle service available.
Adjacent services:
Boat haulouts. Service. Launch ramp nearby.

The Crofton wharfinger's assistant. It's a town with charm and character and a good place to stop in summer. Information on page 69.

In the Gulf Islands you will probably linger longer than intended when you discover such treasures as Ganges and its Saturday morning fair, its fine restaurants, arts and crafts, clothing stores, food stores and the famous Mouat's Trading Store, or Port Browning with its weekly farmer's market. Or simply the serenity of tying to a mooring buoy at Montague Harbour or the dock at Wallace Island as you watch the sun go down. You may never want to leave Telegraph Harbour when you walk up to the Pot of Gold coffee suppliers and find a variety of coffees and freshly roasted coffee beans, or watch the spinning of wools and other fibres at the nearby Alpaca farm and arts and craft facility.

Entering a sheltered moorage area take care. Check your wake well before you arrive at the moorage and slow down a good distance off. Check again and if it is still creating a large wash ease off further on the throttle. Your wash should not be big enough to be felt in the marina. It will follow you in, possibly overtake you and it can damage boats at the floats. The person who creates a wash is liable for any damage it causes.

The charming hospitality or the outstanding milkshakes at the marina may do it for you, or the stop at nearby Chemainus with its great artistic murals, or an evening dining at the Manana Lodge restaurant on the waterfront in Ladysmith Harbour.

Pub atmosphere is sought by some and if you missed the one at Thetis stop at the Vesuvius pub or Nanaimo's Dinghy Dock Pub where you will linger a lot longer than you originally intended. Cross the Nanaimo harbour to the Boat Basin with its Lighthouse Pub and Bistro, or spend the night farther up at Stone's Marina with its Muddy Waters Pub and restaurant.

There's a good deal to see and do at Nanaimo and if you arrive at the time of the Bathtub Race in July you will want to be on hand to see the spectacular send-off and other activities that take place in the town. You may just want to enjoy a long walk on Newcastle Island, one of the coast's prime marine parks.

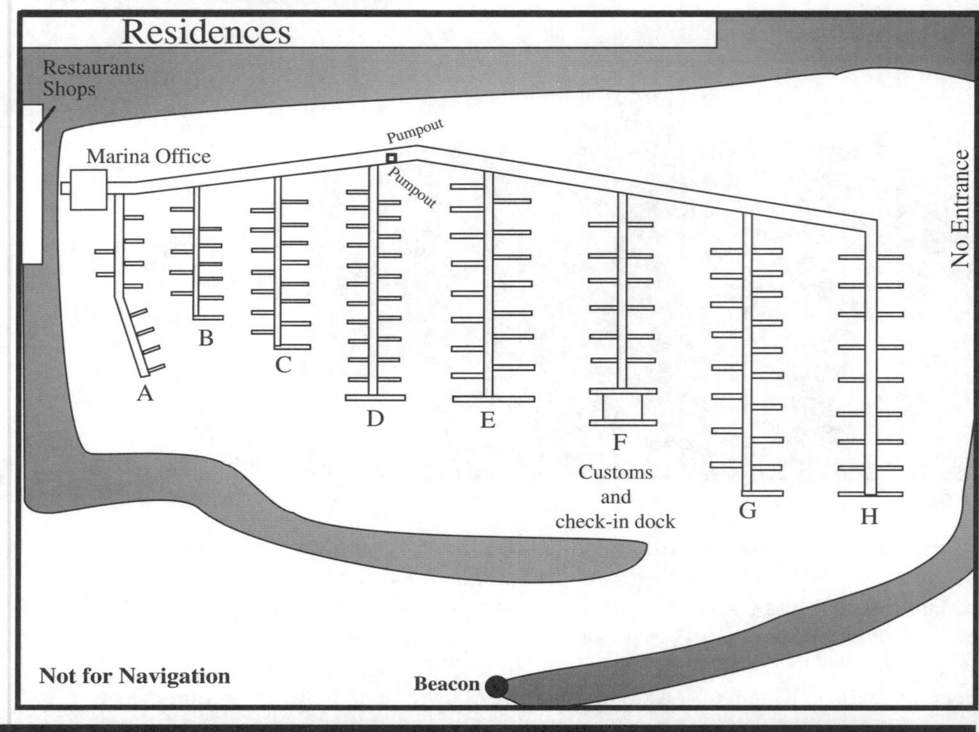

Port Sidney Marina

Port Sidney Marina

9835 Seasport Place,
Sidney, BC. V8L 4X3
or P.O. Box 2130,
Sidney, BC.
V8L 2P6
Phone: (604) 655-3711
Fax: (604) 655-3771
Chart 3310, 3476, 3441 VHF 68

Marina services:

Fuel: not available. Fuel docks at Tsehum Harbour and Canoe Cove (nearby, north) Mechanic and services available from local and nearby marine operators and facilities. ***Note: Breakwater extended.***
Moorage: 300–400 slips. Permanent moorage and plenty of overnight slips. Reserve in summer. Excellent moorage.
Also dockominium ownership available.
Water at dock. Taps at all fingers.
Power at docks: 50 , 30 , 20 , 15 amp.
Laundry, showers, washrooms.
Activities dock–reserve for group private functions.

Customer services:

Nearby church/es, post office, general stores, books, charts, fishing licences, tackle, bait, fresh produce, groceries, bakery, butchery, hardware, dry cleaning, liquor, pharmacy, clothing, gift stores all within walking distance.
Restaurants open 7 days a week. Many to 11 or 12 pm. Neighbourhood pub at top of dock.
Walking trails or road access. Some beachfront walks.
Town streets and waterfront roads allow

The Port Sidney Marina attracts many boaters from BC and Washington. It is a busy customs port and allows access to the many shops and services in the town.

views while walking.
Kayak and other small craft rentals available. Scuba diving arrangements and charters–ask marina for details.

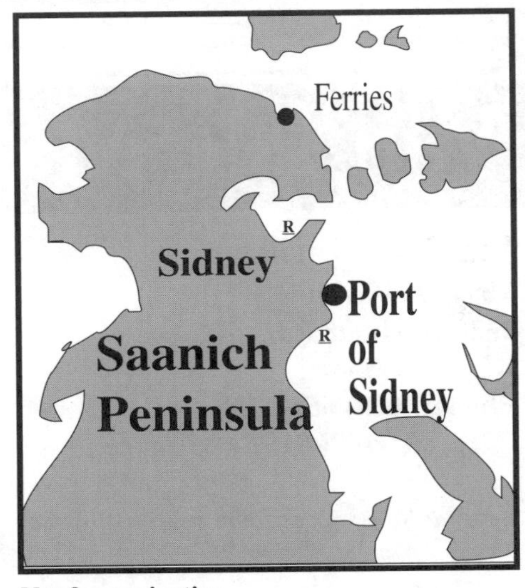

Not for navigation

Entertainment.

Live music at marina in summer holiday months.
July 1 to 4: Fireworks display, dinner on the docks and live entertainment.
August: Model ship regatta.
Sponsored events all summer.
Nearby historic Butchart Gardens. Shuttle service in summer. Also to downtown Victoria, Airport, Ferries.
Sidney Museum summer hours–7 days per week. Features whales with murals and other historic exhibits.
Golf, tennis and other recreation nearby.

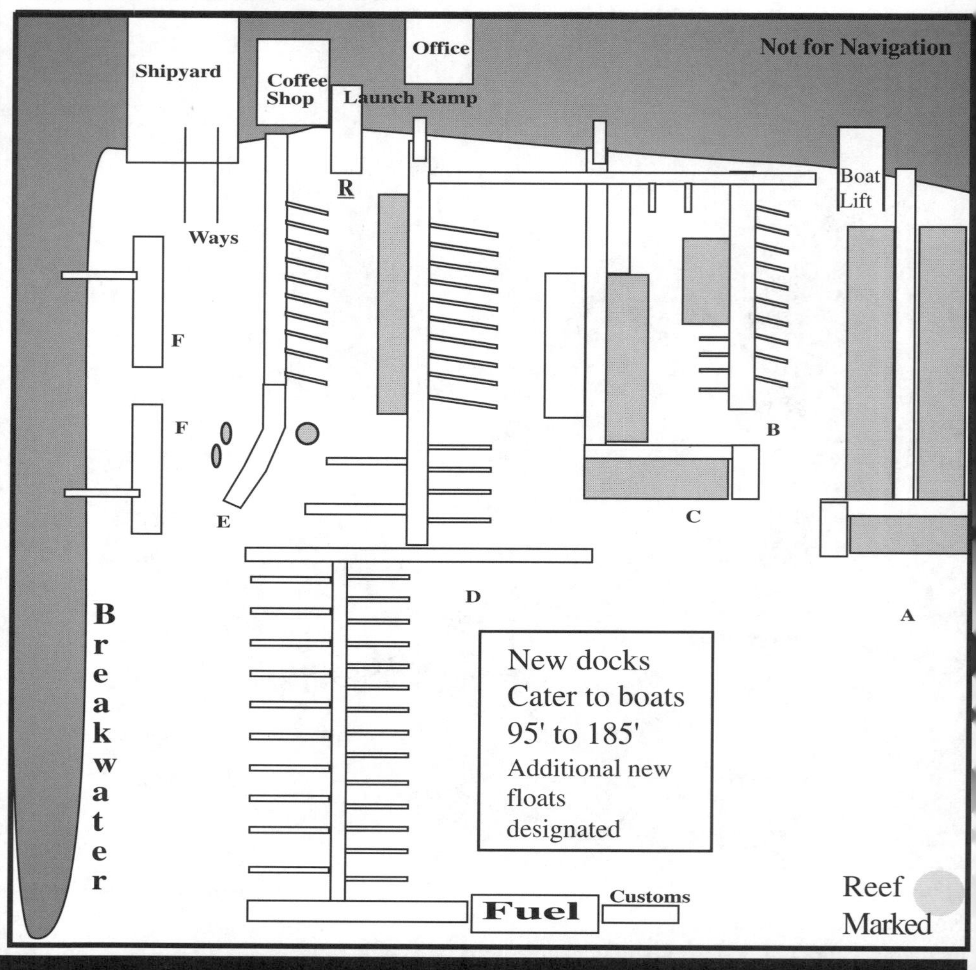

Van Isle Marina

Van Isle Marina

Mark Dickinson
2320 Harbour Rd., Sidney, BC. V8L 3S6.
Phone: (604) 656-1138
Fax: (604) 656-0182

Hazard–Rocks in channel marked by beacons.

Customs services.

Designated marina for courtesy customs clearance. Customs dock. Phone on dock.

Chart 3310, 3476, 3441 VHF 68

Marina entrance.

From around breakwater at entrance to Tsehum Harbour. Most visitor moorage is at east end of fuel and adjacent floats.

Marina services:

Guest Moorage

Fuel: Gas. Diesel. Stove oil: PetroCanada fuel dock. Outboard mix.

Water at dock. Multiple outlets.

Power: 50, 30 , 15 amp. 120, 208 amp available. Public phone–ashore and on docks.

Marine store on fuel dock. 656-1138.
Waste oil disposal, holding tanks pumpout, Ice. Charts, fishing tackle, licences, bait, life jackets etc.
Mechanic and services available from local and nearby marine operators and facilities.
Haulouts. Philbrooks Shipyard within marina complex–vessels to 110 feet. Coffee shop ashore. Yacht sales and service in marina complex. Boatlift within marina to 30 tons. New docks to accommodate craft to 185 feet. Large permanent marina with many overnight mooring slips. Reserve in summer. Excellent moorage. Facilities ashore.

Customer services:

Laundry, showers, washrooms.
Nearby church/es, licenced restaurant/s.
Nearby fine restaurants open 7 days a week.
Walking trails or road access. Some beachfront walks. Town streets and waterfront roads allow views while walking.
Scuba diving arrangements and charters–ask marina for details.

Entertainment.

Cablevision available. TV and telephone hook-ups.
Nearby historic Butchart Gardens. Bus, taxi and rentals plus water shuttle to downtown Sidney, easy access to Victoria, airport, ferries.
Golf, tennis and other recreation nearby.
Walk Roberts Bay Bird Sanctuary nearby.

Adjacent facilities:

Philbrooks Shipyard, All Bay Marine, The Boat Yard, Jensen Marine, Sidney Marine Supply.
Tsehum Harbour Government dock nearby.

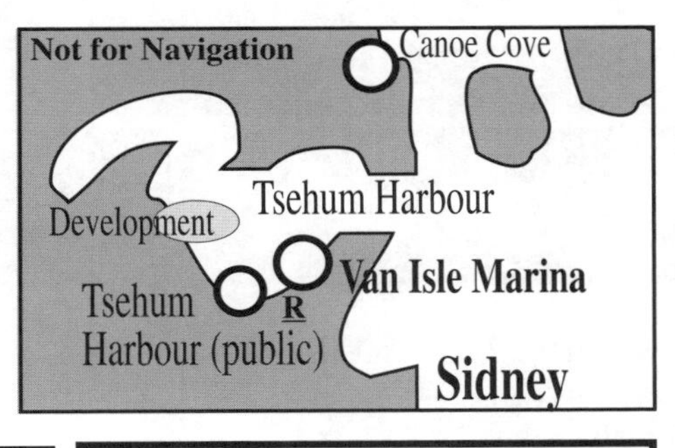

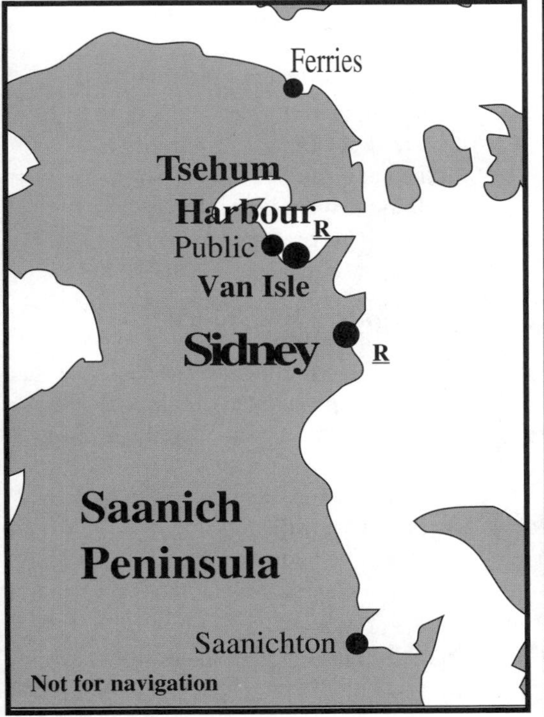

Tsehum Harbour
(Shoal Harbour Public)
Sidney, Vancouver Island.
Fish & Oceans
Chart 3310, 3476, 3441.
Managed •
Float length: 318 m
Ramp •
Breakwater •
Garbage •
Waste oil disposal •
Parking •
Water •
Lights •
Power •
Telephone •
Washrooms •
Adjacent marinas, restaurants, chandlery, haul outs,
marine repairs and full shipyard services.

Canoe Cove Marina

Canoe Cove Marina

Mike Townsend
2300 Canoe Cove Rd. Sidney, BC. V8L 3S6
Phone: (604) 656-5566
Fax: (604) 655-7197
Chart 3310, 3476, 3441 VHF 68

Customs services.

Designated marina for courtesy customs clearance. Phone on dock.

Marina:

Some visitor moorage. Phone ahead to reserve.

Hazard: Rocks in north entrance marked by poles. Narrow waterway to fuel dock. Go Slow. Use right-of-way.

Marina services:

Fuel: Gas. Diesel. Stove oil. Propane. Ice.
Marine chandlery: Charts, fishing tackle, licences, bait, life jackets etc.
Mechanic and services available from local and nearby marine operators and facilities.
Haulouts. 35 ton travel lift. 50 ton ways.

Moorage: Large permanent marina with limited overnight moorage slips. Reserve.
Water at dock. Multiple outlets.
Power at docks: 50, 30, 20, 15 amp.
Laundry, showers, washrooms.

Customer services:

Customs dock/phone. Churches in Sidney and nearby. Coffee shop.
Walking neighbourhood roadways.
Scuba diving arrangements and charters–ask marina for details.
Public pay phones ashore.

Entertainment.

Nearby historic Butchart Gardens. Bus, taxi and rentals plus water shuttle to downtown Sidney, easy access to Victoria, airport, ferries.
Golf, tennis and other recreation nearby.

Adjacent facilities:

Marine pub and restaurant (The Stonehouse–phone 656-3498) open 7 days a week. BC Ferries Swartz Bay to Vancouver and Gulf Islands.

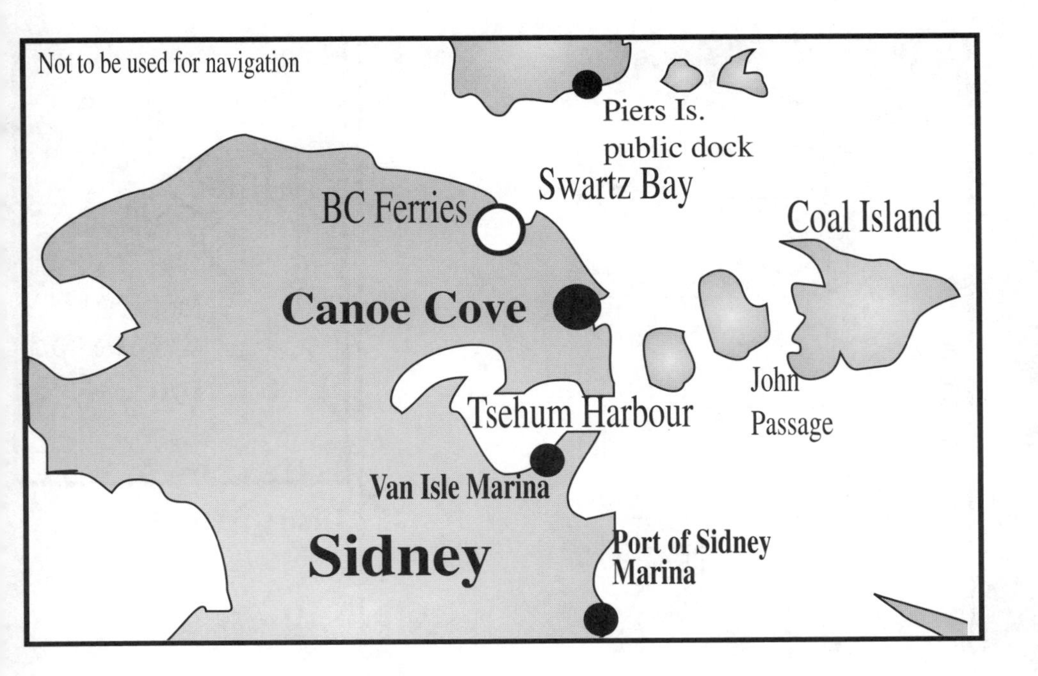

Canoe Cove

This cosy marina is a classic, with many permanent resident boats and little room for guests. Mariners stop in for fuel at the dock tucked away between dock C and D or to clear customs. There is a homey cafe for breakfast or lunch and early light dinner in the summer. For finer fare the Stonehouse Pub a short way behind the marina has an atmosphere that matches its good dining. Special events are celebrated at the restaurant with appropriate meals for the occasion.

The large boat yard adjacent to the marina has haulout and dry storage space and is operated by the service centre at the head of dock B. The ways will allow haulouts of larger vessels and the travel lift caters to more average sized boats. A chandlery situated near the cafe carries a wide range of items for repairs, service and annual maintenance.

The property is quite extensive with a resident artist and a couple of well-known yacht brokerage companies. It is the former home of the Canoe Cove shipyard.

Many boat owners at the marina commute by ferry from the mainland and other parts taking advantage of the marina's close proximity to some of the most favoured cruising destinations on the coast.

Piers Island, Sidney (public)
Transport Canada dock
Chart 3310, 3476, 3462, 3441
Manager • Float length 63 m
Used primarily for local residents' access.
Opposite BC Ferries Swartz Bay terminal (Sidney).

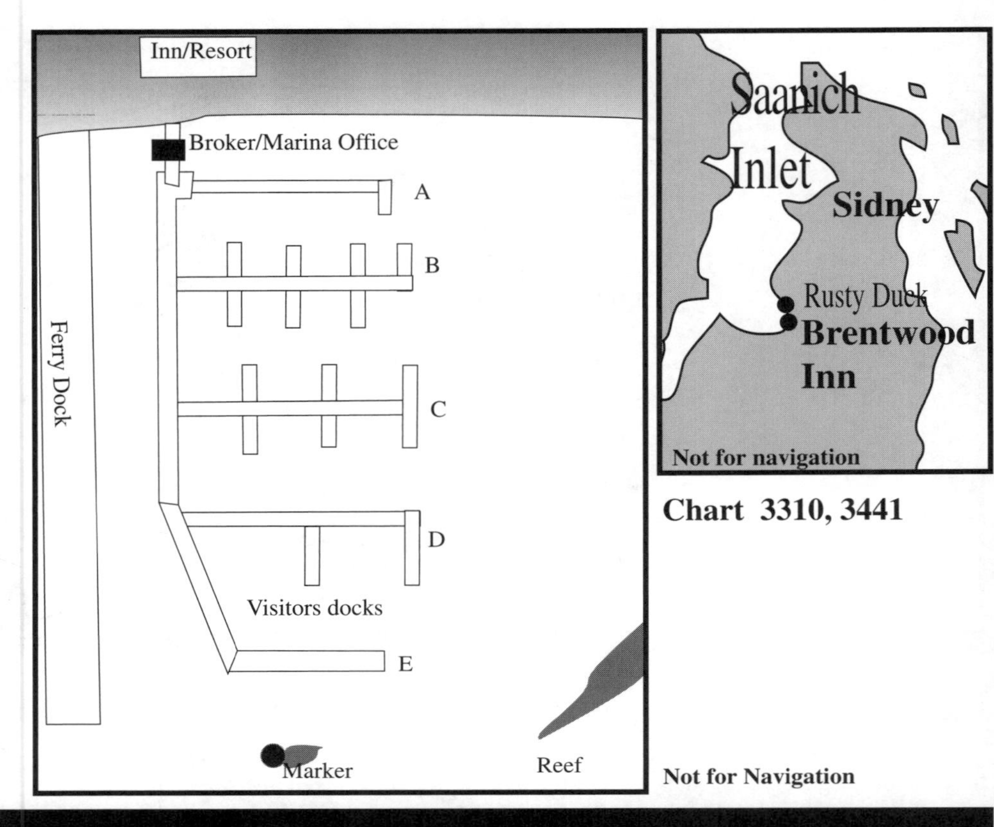

Chart 3310, 3441

Not for Navigation

Brentwood

Brentwood Inn Resort

Mike Keepence
7172 Brentwood Drive., Brentwood Bay, BC. V0S 1A0
Phone: (604) 652-2413
Fax: (604) 652-2402

Customs services.

At adjacent Anglers Anchorage Marina. Phone on dock.

Marina Entrance.

Hazard–Reef off outer dock. Best route keep marker to starboard. Approach dock from ferry terminal. Check your chart.

Marina services:

Convenience store: Ice, fishing tackle, licences, bait, some provisions.
Mechanic and services available from local and nearby marine operators and facilities can be arranged.
Moorage: 65 slip permanent marina with limited overnight moorage. Reserve.
Water at dock. Multiple outlets.
Power at docks: 30, 15 amp.
Laundry, showers, washrooms.

Customer services:

Nearby church/es, Dockside restaurant and pub with view. Deck open in good weather and restaurant open 7 days a week.
Restaurant. Specialty–seafood.
Walking trails or road access. Some beachfront and parkland trails.
Professional fishing guides available.

The dock at the Rusty Duck is tucked in north of the ferry landing. Small to medium boats only and it is shallow at low tide. Below, docks at Brentwood Inn.

Rental runabouts - 16 footers.
Scuba diving arrangements and charters–ask marina for details.
Public pay phones ashore.

Entertainment.

Nearby historic Butchart Gardens.
(Dinghy in to Butchart Gardens)
Bus, taxi and rentals to downtown Sidney, easy access to Victoria, airport, ferries.
Golf, tennis and other recreation nearby.

Adjacent facilities:

Rusty Duck Restaurant–dock for restaurant customers.
Fuel at Mill Bay, Goldstream or Sidney.

Public dock

Brentwood Bay

Saanich Inlet
Transport Canada dock
Chart 3310
Manager • Float length 22 m
Adjacent: Private marina and Angler's Anchorage Marina
Walk in adjacent park.
Used mostly by commercial traffic for loading.

Angler's Anchorage

Angler's Anchorage Marina

Mark Tigchelaar
933 Marchant Rd. RR #1,
Brentwood Bay, BC. V8M 1B5
Phone: (604) 652-3531
Fax (604) 652-9923

Canada Customs

Designated marina for courtesy customs clearance.
Phone on dock.

Marina Entrance.

Near Brentwood Inn Marina
Refer to your chart.

Marina services:

Mechanic and services available from local and nearby marine operators and facilities can be arranged.

Moorage: Large permanent marina with limited overnight moorage slips. Reserve.
Water at dock. Multiple outlets.
Power at docks: 30, 15 amp.

Chart 3310, 3441
VHF 68

Customer services:

Laundry, showers, washrooms.
Nearby church/es, Dockside restaurant. Marine restaurant open 7 days a week.
Public pay phones ashore.

Entertainment.

Nearby historic Butchart Gardens.
Bus, taxi and rentals to downtown Sidney, easy access to Victoria, airport, ferries. Walking trails or road access. Some beachfront walks.
Golf, tennis and other recreation nearby.

Adjacent facilities:

Brentwood Inn Resort/Marina. Government dock. Clinker's Galley & Restaurant.
Note: Major changes planned for marina.
Shopping in nearby Brentwood Bay.
Note: Major changes are planned for early 1995.

Pictured above, the dinghy dock at Butchart Gardens. Shallow at low tides, most mariners boat in by dinghy from anchorage or nearby marinas. Opposite: Angler's Anchorage Marina.

Goldstream Boathouse

Mark Aitken and Doug Spence
2892 Trans Canada Highway, RR 6,
Victoria, BC. V9B 5T9
Phone: (604) 478-4407
Chart 3310, 3441 VHF 68

Marina services:

Fuel: Gas. Oil filters, etc.
Marine supplies. Marine repairs. Haulouts.
Moorage. Transient available.
Water at dock.
Power at docks: 30, 15 amp. (For transient moorage customers–15 amp.) **Washrooms.**

Customer services:

Nearby church/es
Road access walking. Parkland trails at Goldstream Park nearby.
Rental boats. Bait, ice, tackle, fishing licences. Groceries, snacks.
Scuba diving arrangements and fishing charters–ask marina for details.
Public pay phones ashore.

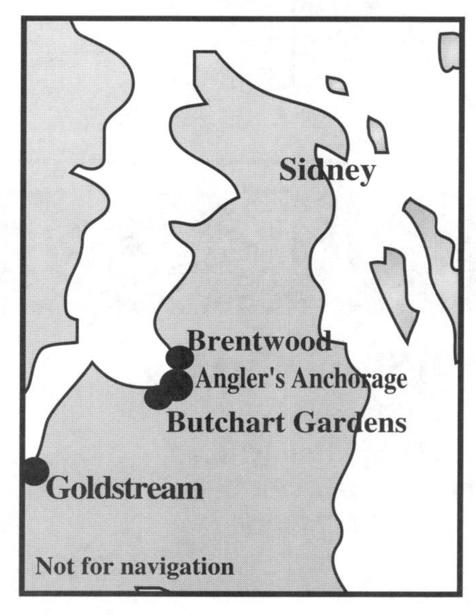

Entertainment.

Historic landmark boathouse.
Up inlet to Butchart Gardens.
Bus, taxi and rentals to downtown Victoria. Golf nearby.

Adjacent facilities:

Campsites. Launch ramp.

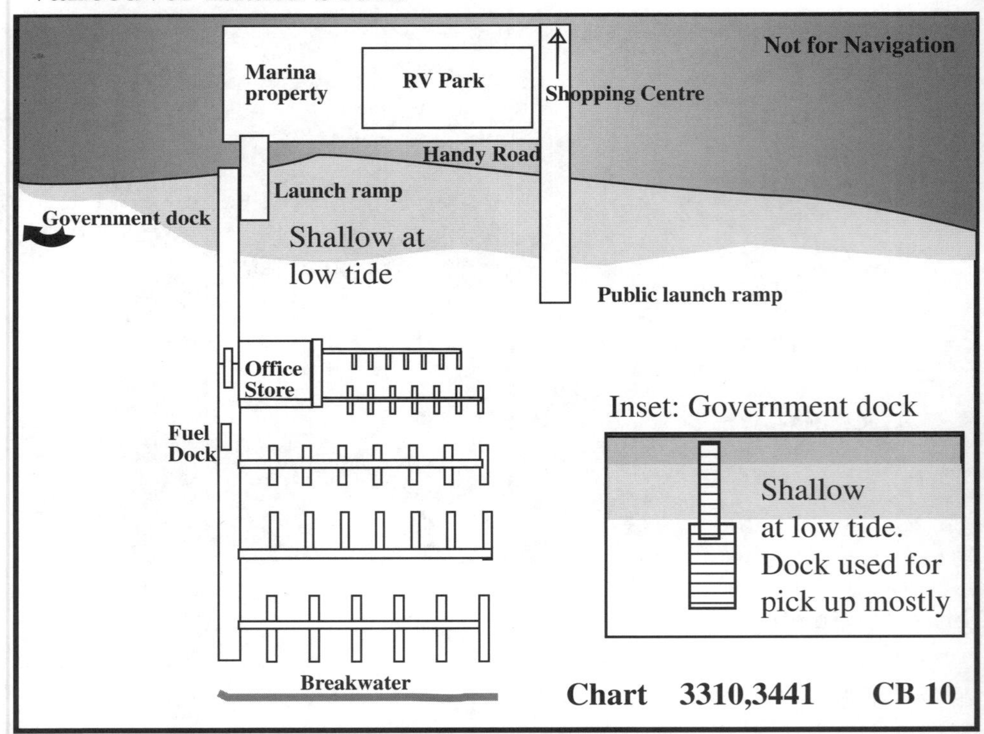

Mill Bay Marina

Mill Bay Marina

Fred and Marilyn Laba
Box 231 740 Handy Road,
Mill Bay, BC. V0R 2P0
Phone: (604) 743-4112

Marina services:
Fuel: Gas. Diesel. Launch ramp.
Water at dock. Multiple outlets.
Power at docks: 15 amp. Multiple outlets.
Laundry, showers, washrooms.
Boats for rent. Charters. Bed & breakfast.
Marine supplies. Ice, fishing tackle, licences, bait.
Mechanic and services can be arranged.
Moorage: 158 plus slips–permanent marina with 540' overnight moorage. Reserve.

Customer services:
Nearby church/es. Road access walking. Some nearby river and beach trails.
Rental boats. **Launch ramp**
Shopping centre and grocery store nearby (Thrifty) will deliver purchases to your boat.
Public pay phones ashore.
Entertainment.
Across inlet to Butchart Gardens.
Bus, taxi and rentals to downtown Victoria.
Golf nearby.

Mill Bay, Vancouver Island
Fisheries & Oceans public dock
Phone 743-9764
Chart 3310, 3441, 3462
Manager • Float length 15 m

The shopping centre at Mill Bay has good grocery shopping as well as a variety of interesting stores, arts and crafts, restaurants, expresso and coffee shops among others.
The marina is a short walk from the centre. The main float to the south includes a fuel dock and overnight moorage for larger vessels. Small craft will be assigned slips inside.

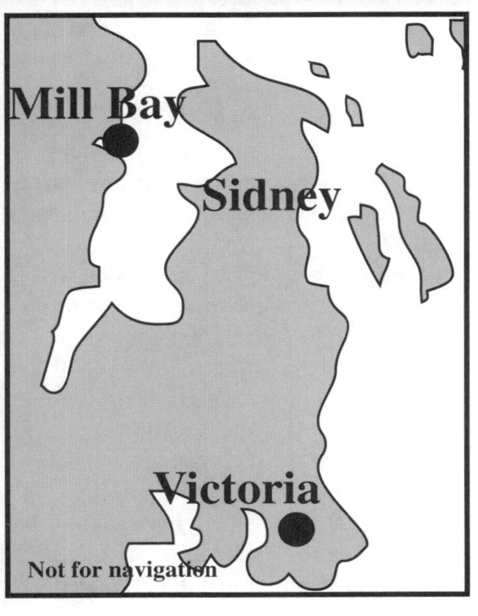

Notes:

Doing it right.

Marinas are a home away from home. And when you tie up to a dock at a private marina you are in effect stopping in to visit with other boat owners and with the owners and operators of the marina. What you do and how you operate your vessel says a lot about you and a lot about your experience as a mariner. Your reception from marina managers and fellow boat owners will be determined by the impression you create from the moment you nudge your boat up to the dock.

Some boat owners, and often this applies to novi ces, don't really care how they are perceived by others. Some want to conform to a certain standard yet will not avail themselves of any form of training or take any advice. Those same people also tend to not learn from their errors. But for mariners who wish to fit in, be they newcomers or old hands here are some basic tips:

To begin with it is usually advisable during the peak of summer to phone ahead and make reservations when you intend to stay over at a marina. Usually early that same day would suffice. In some cases marinas are fully booked well in advance for some dates, particularly at weekends or long weekends. So plan your overnight stops to coincide with marinas that will have space or if not then at least have an alternative nearby, such as a safe, all-weather anchorage. To that end I have listed some good, sheltered anchorages and government docks close to marinas in the same general location in which the marinas are listed in this book.

Quite often you will see a boat operator slow down at the last moment on approaching a marina. He will then swing around in his seat in consternation to see who is making a wash as he approaches the dock, not realising it is his own wake.

Before you arrive at a marina ensure you are not passing other marinas or installations at speed. Slow down well before you reach the dock. Sitting at a dock in West Sound in the San Juans once I saw a large boat came by at full speed leaving a wash in excess of two feet that caused some damage at the dock. He was heading for a club dock at the head of the bay and had totally ignored the existence of the marina tucked in behind the island to his starboard. As it turns out he also created so much wash at the marina he was entering that he must have been very unpopular among his peers. That same week I saw a similar sized vessel do the same thing entering the marina at Bedwell Bay. A boat operator is liable for any damage his boat's wash causes, so take it easy and know the area you are entering. Marine charts show marinas and facilities along the shoreline and these should not be ignored.

As you arrive at the marina assess exactly where the slip is that you will be occupying. In some marinas there is an arrivals dock where you are assigned a slip, but most will do so over the VHF on the channel they monitor to assign slips. The dock diagrams in this book should help you easily locate the slip or general area of the slip to which you have been assigned. As you approach your slip note effects on the water and your boat of current and wind and plan your docking manouvres accordingly. It's always easiest to angle in towards the dock against the flow of water or direction of the wind. If you are backing your boat into a tight slip, which is more difficult, it is even more essential that you are aware of these conditions. Have your crew at the ready and prepared for landing. I find it best to have only one person assist with landing. A second person on the side of the boat opposite to the docking side can be helpful in the event there is a need to help fend off on that side. But the primary assistant should be experienced or well instructed in what you plan to do and how they should assist.

Play it the way the pros do. They attach a line to a cleat in the centre of the boat and hold the end coiled in one hand as they step ashore. Snubbing the line to a cleat on the dock when the boat is as close to that cleat as it is going to get will keep it there and prevent the bow or stern from breaking away and swinging out, as often occurs when only a line at the bow or the stern is used. Have fenders down at a height compatible with the height of the docks and positioned at least one ahead of the centre cleat and one aft or at the approximate locations they will be while docked. Once the boat is stopped the skipper can casually step ashore, secure the bow and stern lines and adjust fenders at leisure.

Other people may come up to you as you approach the dock and offer assistance. Usually they expect to be handed a line and all too often when they take it they totally destroy your docking plan. This is usually done by their yarding on the bow line, bringing the bow in too close towards the dock and thus disabling you from handling the stern. Politely thank docksiders for standing by to lend a hand as they reach out for your lines, but don't give them over unless absolutely necessary or until the skipper has the boat in such position that all they can do with the lines is hold them until the crew or skipper of your boat takes over. No harm saying to a person "here is the line, please just hold it" or have two docksiders haul you in by yarding on bow and stern lines simultaneously. This is especially helpful if you are docking against a wind that will push the boat off before a reasonable chance can be gained to step ashore and secure it. Don't try to look as though you are proficient if you cannot pull it off. You are better off to say to anyone watching as you are approaching your slip that you are new at this and would appreciate some experienced help in docking. You'll be surprised how readily people will come to your aid and how pleasant they will be when you are up front about your docking abilities.

Docking is just the beginning. You will not enamour yourself or your crew to anyone at the dock if you yell, either at them or at your crew.

At many marinas there are full time personnel employed to assist boaters docking. They are not always the most experienced but as long as you follow some of the above advice their assistance will enable you to perform a good landing.

If you are tying up parallel to a long open dock, tie up your boat in such a way that you allow maximum room for the next boat coming in. If you have a dinghy in the water tuck it in under the bow of your boat while you are not using it in order that you leave room for the next boat.

Anchoring off and going ashore to visit a marina and its facilities, perhaps to have a meal, a snack or browse for some souvenir is a common practise during summer. Also common is the individual who does this and brings with them a huge bag of garbage. This may be fine at a mainland destination where garbage disposal is a matter of course, but on small and especially remote islands, this is a major problem and your attempts to dispose of garbage can really cause animosity, particularly if you are not a paying tenant at the marina. And if you are a mooring guest you may do well to assess how convenient it will be to leave piles of garbage behind, even though some places have disposal bins. If you know you are going on to a large mainland or Vancouver Island facility soon, save the bulk of the garbage for that stop rather than drop it at a tiny island with limited facilities. The same applies to water. If you are travelling to an island with limited water resources fill up before going there and use water sparingly until you reach a destination that has plenty of water. Certainly do not use water to wash your boat when there is barely enough to replenish domestic supplies.

Boats tied up alongside the dock at Wallace Island Marine Park in the Gulf Islands. Limited space suggests mooring close to other boats, rafting or anchoring out and using a dinghy to go ashore. Balladeer *anchored at Prevost.*

Some boat owners have been known to tie up at a marina for long periods during the day, fill up with water, perhaps use the facilities such as shower and laundry and then take off and anchor across the bay for the night. That may be fine some of the time but there are times when such moorage has denied a prospective overnight moorage customer space to tie up. Marinas have a very limited season in which to prosper and boats that cause marina operators lost overnight moorage will not be appreciated.

Most marina operators will be happy to have you stop for a short period if you don't plan to spend the night. Some have a charge per hour. Others, like government docks, allow two hours free and then an overnight charge is levied.

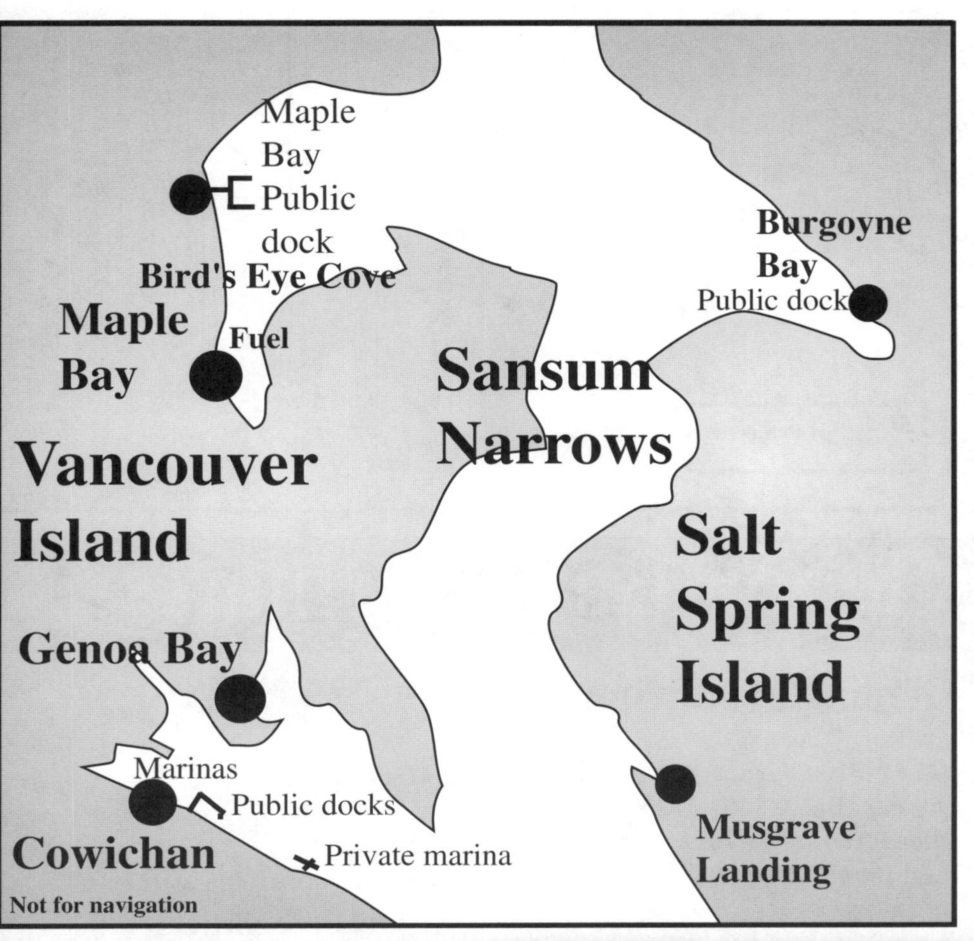

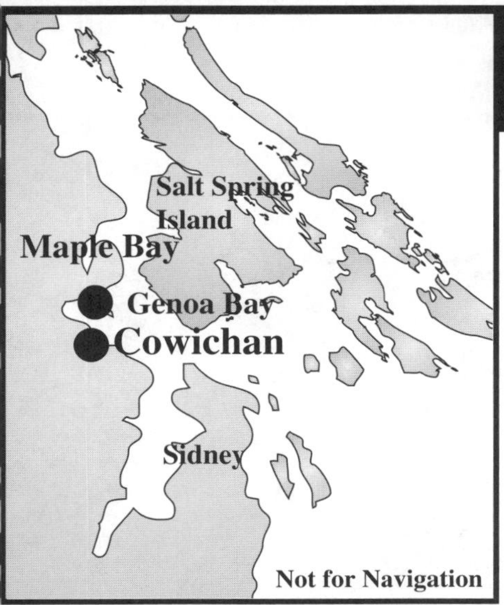

Cowichan

Cowichan Bay

Fisheries & Oceans dock
Phone 746-5911
Chart 3310, 3478
Manager • Float length 287 m
Breakwater • Garbage • Waste oil service • Water • Lights • Power • Public phone • Washrooms •
Other marinas in the area are private. There are stores and marina services but changes are underway. Check with public dock manager for details. Best nearby overnight moorage is at Genoa Bay.

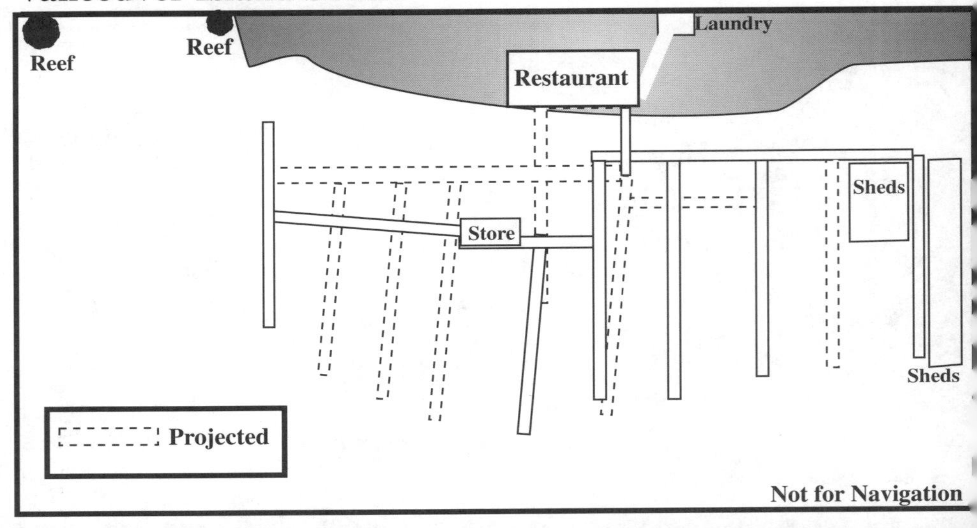

Genoa Bay Marina

Genoa Bay Marina Ltd

Kay Kirkby and Jim Kiedaisch
RR #1 5100, Genoa Bay Road,
Duncan, BC., V9L 1M3
Phone: (604) 746-7621
Fax: (604) 746-7316

Hazard: Entering bay keep to port of day beacon. Avoid shore-side reef–marked.

Marina services:

Moorage. Large marina with permanent and transient moorage.
Water at dock.
Power at docks: 15 amp. 30 amp
Laundry, showers, washrooms.
Ice. Propane. Service available.

Customer services:

Restaurant. Bistro.
Breakfast, lunch, dinner. Licenced.
Also patio service. Tenting.
Barbecue area.
General store: Groceries. Fishing gear, licences, fresh baked goods. Gifts.
Art and crafts gallery.

Chart 3310, 3441, 3442 VHF 68

Entertainment:

Road access walking or cycling. Nearby hiking trails.

Public pay phones ashore.

Adjacent facilities:

Anchorage. Southeasterly winds may cause some discomfort.

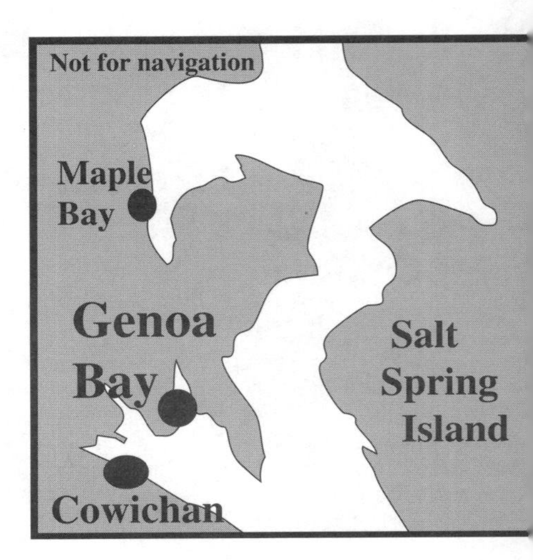

Genoa Bay Marina. Big changes to the docks are in the works. The restaurant is licenced. There are excellent roads and trails for walking.

Fuel in the Gulf Islands

Many wonder about the availability of fuel in the Gulf Islands. It is true that it became more difficult to obtain fuel in the Gulf Islands in recent years. But Ganges Marina on Salt Spring Island installed new storage tanks and is pumping Shell seven days a week. Montague Harbour has fuel again in 1995.

Apart from Ganges fuel is available among the Islands at Fulford to the south or Saturna Island's Lyall Harbour, Active Pass to the north-east or Telegraph Harbour in a northerly direction. Fuel is also available at Maple Bay or in Ladysmith. There is fuel also at Bedwell Harbour (reported January 1995).

On the perimeter of the Gulf Islands fuel can be purchased at Silva Bay, Van Isle Marina in Sidney's Tsehum Harbour, Canoe Cove Marina, Goldstream Boathouse, Angler's Anchorage and Mill Bay in Saanich Inlet. Some places sell gas but not diesel so if your reserves are low check the references in this guide or call ahead to double check.

Silva Bay is another favoured fuel stop. There is fuel at Page's Marina. The bay has always been a major centre for overnight moorage, a place to refuel and to have repairs and service done to your boat..

Changes at Silva Bay Marina are in the works but Page's and Silva Bay Boatel are open.

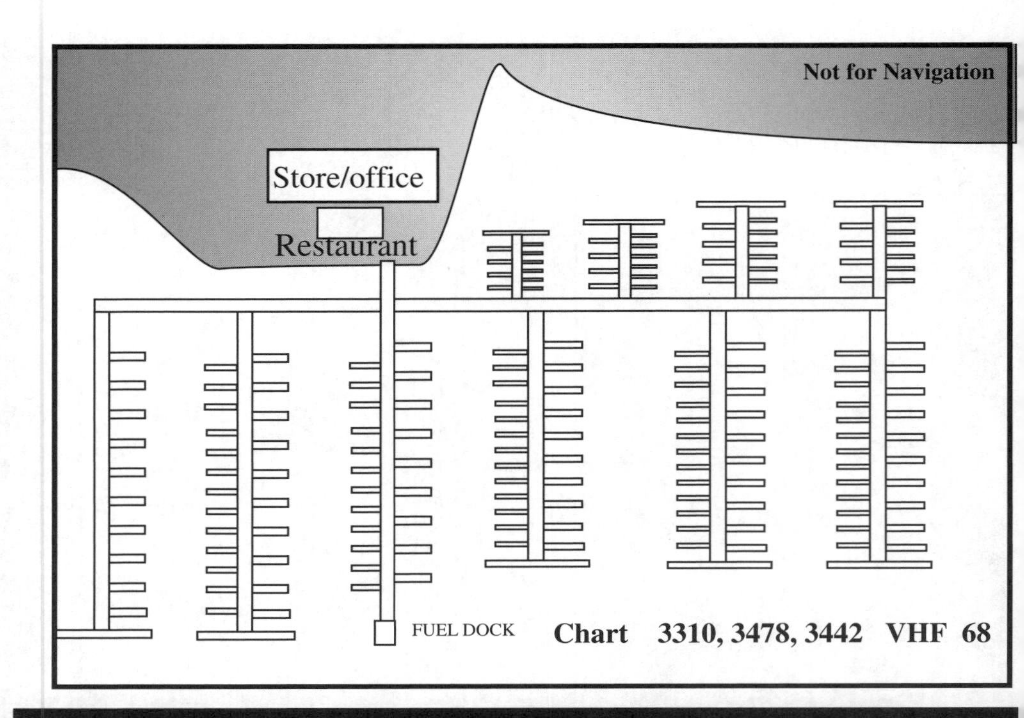

Maple Bay Resorts

Maple Bay Resorts

Ted McLeod
6145 Genoa Bay Road,
Duncan, BC., V9L 1M3
Phone: (604) 746-8482
Fax: (604) 7468490

Marina services:

Fuel: Gas, diesel. Service available.
CNG. Propane.
Marine supplies. Fishing gear, licences, charts, bait.
Guest and permanent moorage.
Water at dock.
Power at docks: 15, 20 amp.
Laundry, showers, washrooms.

Customer services:

Restaurant. Licenced.
Also patio service.
Gift Shop. General Store.
Road access walking or cycling.
Scuba diving arrangements and charters–ask marina for details. Scenic boat tours.
Public pay phones.
Daily float plane service.

Entertainment.

Nearby restaurants with special atmosphere.

Adjacent facilities:

Excellent bed & breakfast accommodations at nearby lodge.

Public dock

Maple Bay,

Fisheries & Oceans dock
Phone 746-7101
Chart 3310, 3441, 3462
Manager • Float length 46m
Water • Lights • Public phone •
.

The public float at Maple Bay is in the bay before entering Bird's Eye Cove. It is suitable for a brief stop to access the store. Birds Eye Cove Marina is a major fuel stop and service and repair centre while Maple Bay Marina is farther down and a major moorage marina.

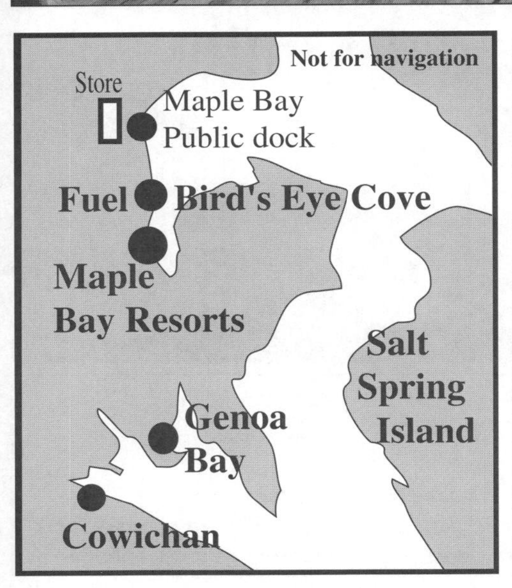

Bird's Eye Cove (Fuel)

Cove Yachts
6261 Genoa Bay Road
RR #1 Duncan BC
V9L 1M3
(604) 748-8183
Fax 748-7916
Fuel dock–all fuels and oils. Service and repairs Transient moorage for service and repairs customers.

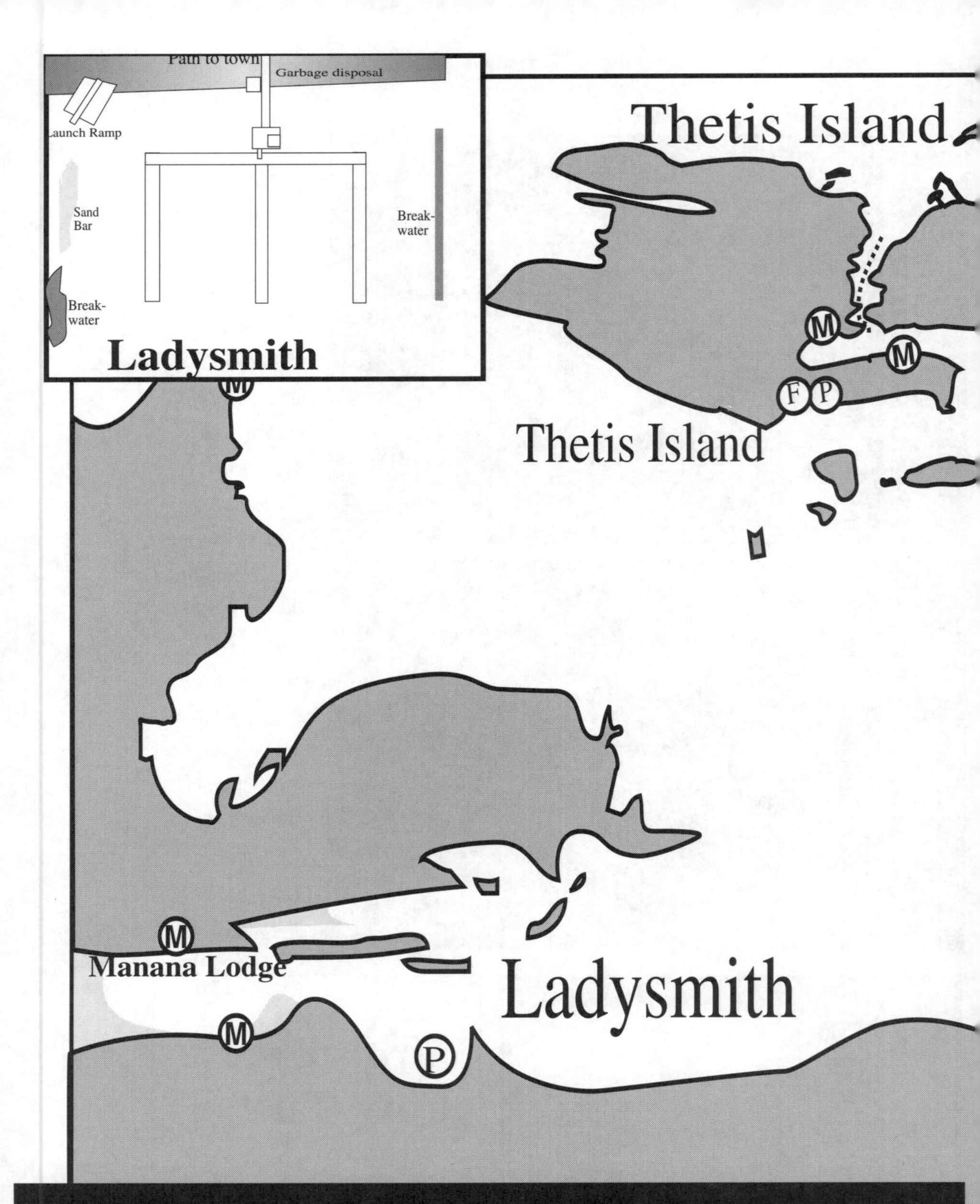

Ladysmith, Chemainus & Crofton

Chemainus
Transport Canada dock
Manager • Float length 175 m

Chart 3310, 3463

Crofton, Vancouver Island
Fisheries & Oceans dock
Phone 246-4512
Manager • Float length 158 m
Launch ramp • Breakwater • Garbage •
Water • Lights • Power • Public phone •

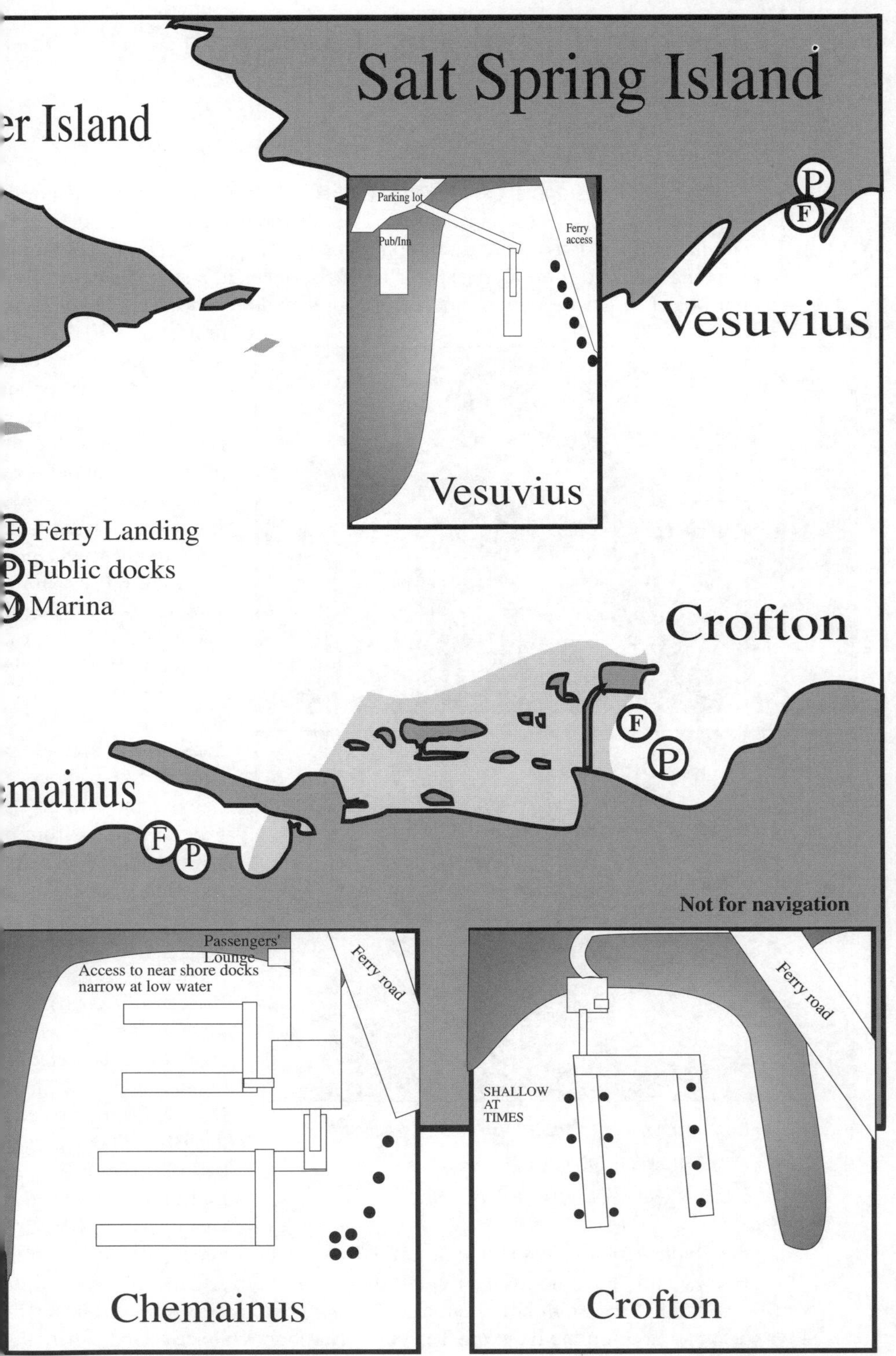
Salt Spring Island
er Island
Parking lot
Pub/Inn
Ferry access
Vesuvius
Vesuvius
F Ferry Landing
P Public docks
M Marina
Crofton
mainus
Not for navigation
Passengers' Lounge
Access to near shore docks narrow at low water
Ferry road
Chemainus
Ferry road
SHALLOW AT TIMES
Crofton

Crofton, Chemainus, Ladysmith

An overnight stop at the sheltered harbour of Crofton can be a most memorabl experience. The government dock has lots of room for transient boats in th summer. Off season if there is no room to tie up it is possible, preferably for nc too long a stay, to come alongside a docked fishing boat. Fishermen generally d not object to having a boat moored temporarily alongside them, but you ma prefer to be tied directl to the dock for easier ac cess to and from your boa

Crofton docks are emptier of fish boats in summer than winter, providing lots of guest moorage.
Chemainus looks busy but there is often space to tie up.

The docks at Manan Lodge are most hospita ble to recreational boats During summer a stead stream of craft call at th lodge for overnight moor age, fuel and very limite supplies. Also a regula clientele check in for th sumptuous meals serve at the lodge. Moorage i safe at all times and th docks are available spe cially for guest boats. A Ladysmith, within eas walking access from th government docks, on can find every conven ience and requirement supplies and services an a touch of coastal history It is an old coal minin town named for the tow in South Africa which wa under siege during th Boer War and relieved b the British coincidenta to the founding o Ladysmith in BC. So i was named in honour o the South African town which in turn was named for the charitable wife of Si Harry Smith, governor of the Cape Province of South Africa.

Out of Ladysmith boats can easily and quickly access several outstandin destinations. Among them are Telegraph Harbour, Wallace Island, Chemainu

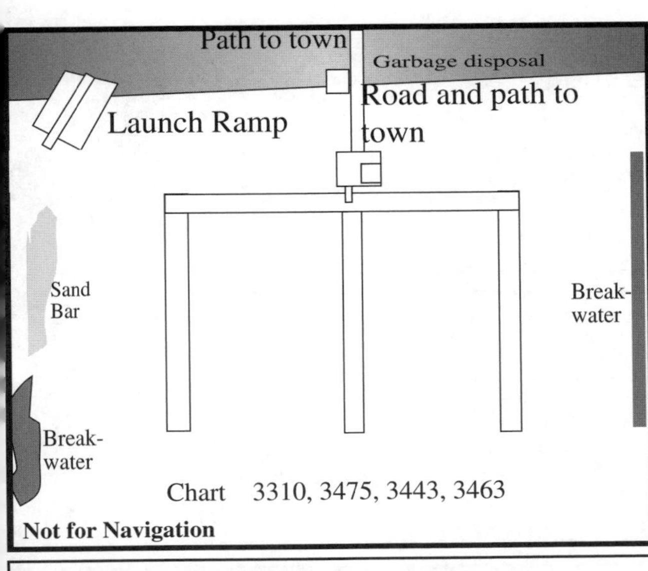

Left: The docks layout at Ladysmith public marina. Note location of launch ramp. Below: The docks at Ladysmith are generous with lots of room to manouvre between fingers.

Ladysmith, Public dock
Vancouver Island
Fisheries & Oceans dock
Phone 245-7511
Manager • Float length 213 m
Launch ramp • Breakwater •
Grid • Garbage •
Waste oil disposal •
Water • Lights • Power
• Public phone •
Near uptown restaurants, shops.

and Pirate's Cove. Some excellent stops in this general area include North Galiano, Vesuvius, Crofton and Retreat Cove.

Visit Wallace Island Marine Park nearby for its excellent paths and scenery, for its history and protected overnight moorage. It's a cross-roads for people on the move, enjoying the outdoors by boating, canoeing and tenting. The park attracts many boats every season and many campers take advantage of the recreational facilities provided by the Parks Branch and maintained by Power and Sail Squadron members.

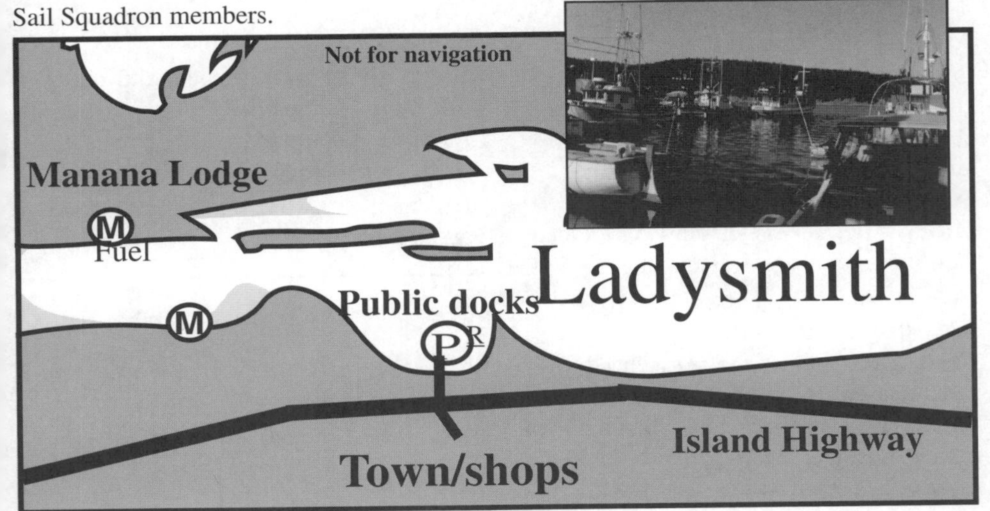

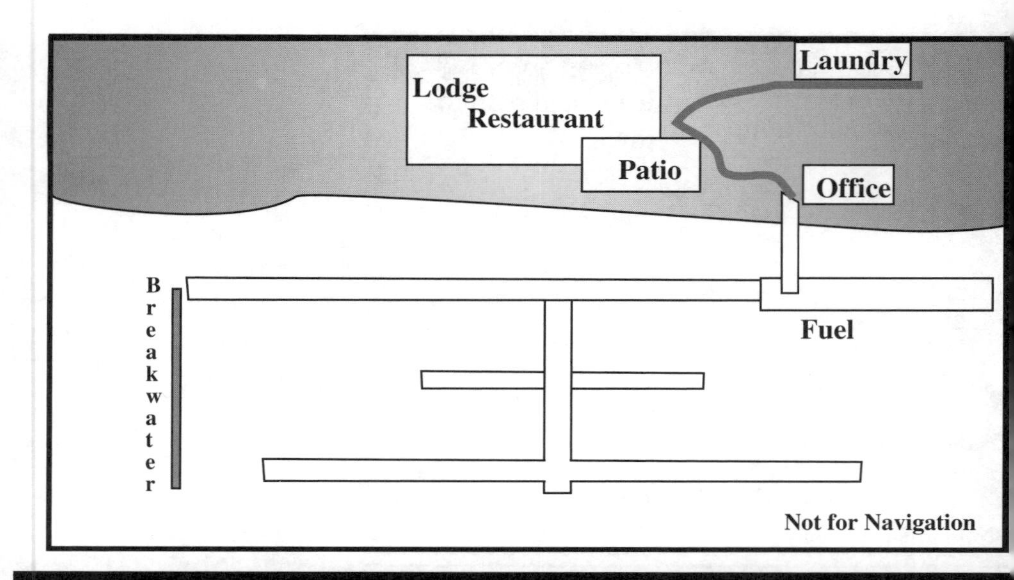

Manana Lodge & Marina

Manana Lodge & Marina

Don and Gail Kanelakos,
Jim and Ruth Bangay
4760 Brenton-Page Road, RR #1
Ladysmith, B.C, V0R 2E0
Phone: (604) 245-2312 Fax: 245-7546
Chart 3310, 3475, 3443, 3463 VHF 68

Marina services:

Fuel: Gas. Diesel. Propane. Service available. Marine supplies. Fishing gear, licences, charts, bait.
Guest moorage, 1400 feet dock space.
Water at dock.
Power at docks: 15. 30 amp to be added.
Laundry, showers, washrooms.

Customer services:

Restaurant. Fine dining. Licenced. Also patio service.
Gift shop. New appetizer bar plus additional patio service.
Cabins, bed & breakfast.
Book ahead in summer.
Public pay phones ashore.
Daily float plane service accessible and stops at marina for pick-up.
Short boat trip to Ladysmith–stores. Stop at government dock opposite/south.

Entertainment.

Cycles free with room rental. Canoes, rowboats. Car rentals. Road access walking or cycling.
Scuba diving arrangements and charters–ask marina for details.
Escape and solitude.

Adjacent facilities:

Excellent bed & breakfast accommodations at lodge.

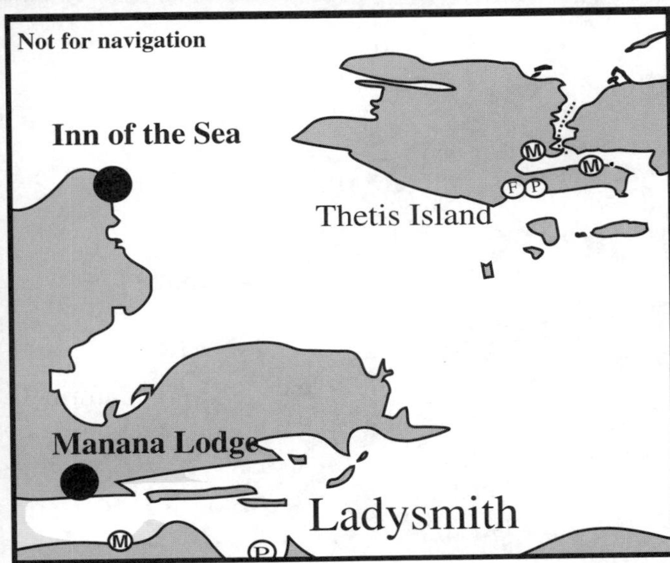

Manana Lodge and marina offers excellent overnight sheltered moorage, fuel, restaurant and many amenities. Inn of the Sea has limited, semi exposed moorage. Check for weather and shallows.

Inn of the Sea Resort

Carol Radloff
3600 Yellow Point Road,
Ladysmith, BC., VOR 2E0
Phone(604) 245-2211 Fax (604) 245-3442
Chart 3310, 3443

Hazard: Reef extends out from the point. Give wide berth and approach from the south-east. Consult chart.

Marina services:

Guest, limited moorage.
Reservations advised.
No water at dock.
Power at docks: 15 amp.
Mooring buoys.
Laundry, showers, washrooms at lodge.

Customer services:

Restaurant. Lounge. Breakfast, lunch, dinner. Licenced. Luxurious shore accommodations. Heated outdoor pool. Road access walking or cycling. Nearby walking trails. Public pay phones ashore.

Entertainment.

Tennis, canoeing, swimming, jaccuzi.

Adjacent facilities:

Excellent bed & breakfast accommodations at lodge.

Marine Parks in the Gulf Islands

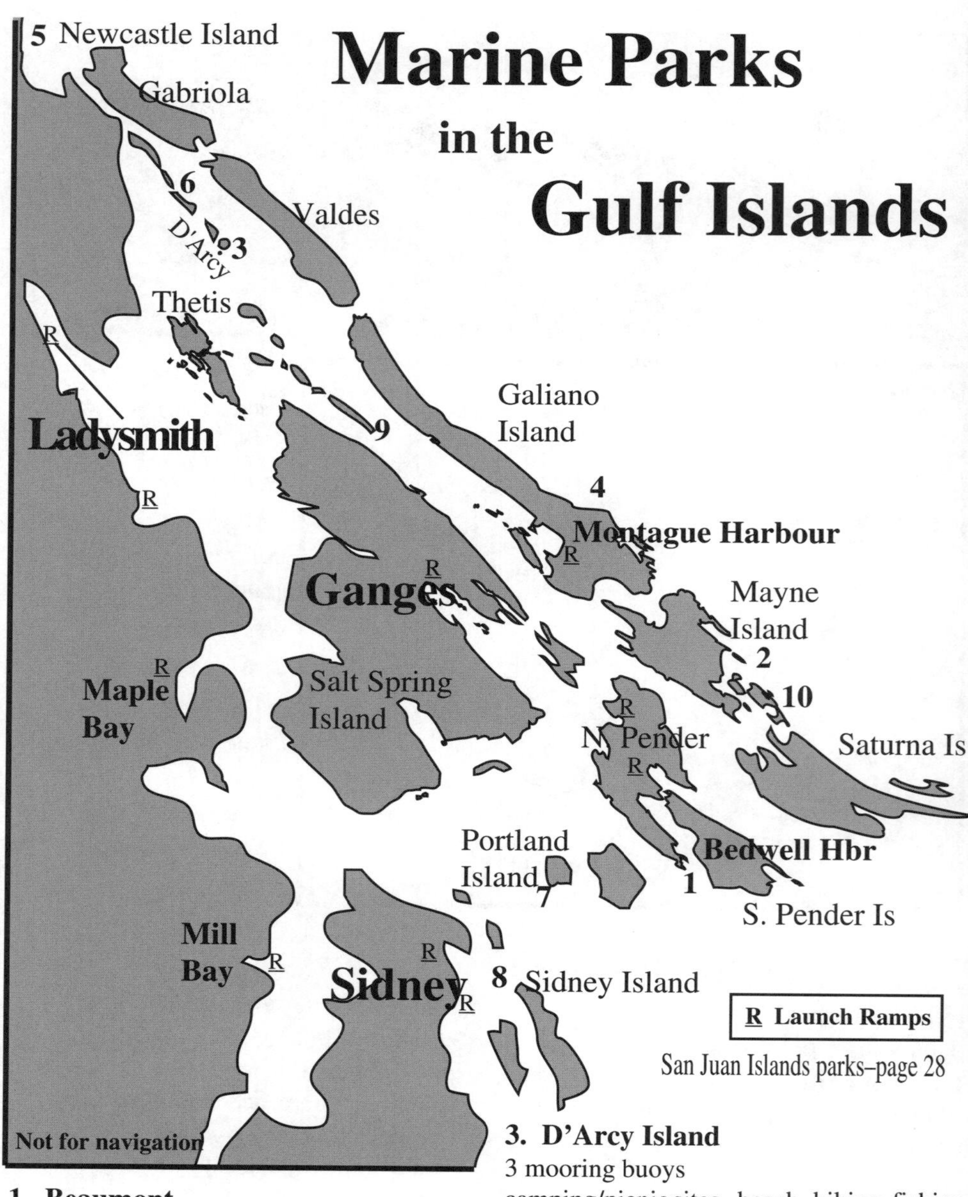

1. Beaumont
All weather anchorage
15 mooring buoys
camping/picnic sites water toilets park host beach hiking.

2. Cabbage Island
10 mooring buoys
camping/picnic sites toilets beach fishing good scuba.

3. D'Arcy Island
3 mooring buoys
camping/picnic sites beach hiking fishing scuba.

4. Montague Harbour
All weather anchorage
Boat and dinghy dock 26 mooring buoys
camping/picnic sites water toilets park host beach hiking
Fishing near Active Pass. Scuba diving in vicinity-best use scuba charter service.

Wallace Island marine park offers good walking trails as well as beautiful views of Trincomali Passage and the adjacent Gulf Islands. Montague Harbour is a popular anchorage with mooring buoys, and boat or dinghy dock. It has extensive walking trails, beaches, a launch ramp and many campsites.

5. Newcastle Island

All weather anchorage
(Some wind conditions occur)
Boat and dinghy docks
camping/picnic sites water toilets beach hiking.

6. Pirates Cove

All weather anchorage
(some wind conditions occur)
Dinghy dock
camping/picnic sites water toilets park host beach hiking.

7. Princess Margaret

Temporary anchorage–overnight only subject to wind forecast.
Camping/picnic sites water toilets park host beach hiking scuba–wreck as artificial reef *GB Church* off east shore.

8. Sidney Spit

35 mooring buoys. Boat and dinghy docks camping/picnic sites water toilets park host beach hiking good fishing in vicinity.

9. Wallace Island

Boat and dinghy dock
camping/picnic sites water toilets park host beach hiking, recommended fishing and scuba in vicinity.
Place of interest.

10. Winter Cove

All weather anchorage
picnic sites water toilets hiking.

The parks included here are those with boat or dinghy docks or mooring buoys. Others, not shown, are popular overnight anchorages or day anchorages.

Anchorages and trails such as those found at Wallace Island are features of the Gulf Islands. The joy of simply being there during the course of any summer is difficult to match. And there is much history to the area which can be uncovered by delving into the origin of some place names.

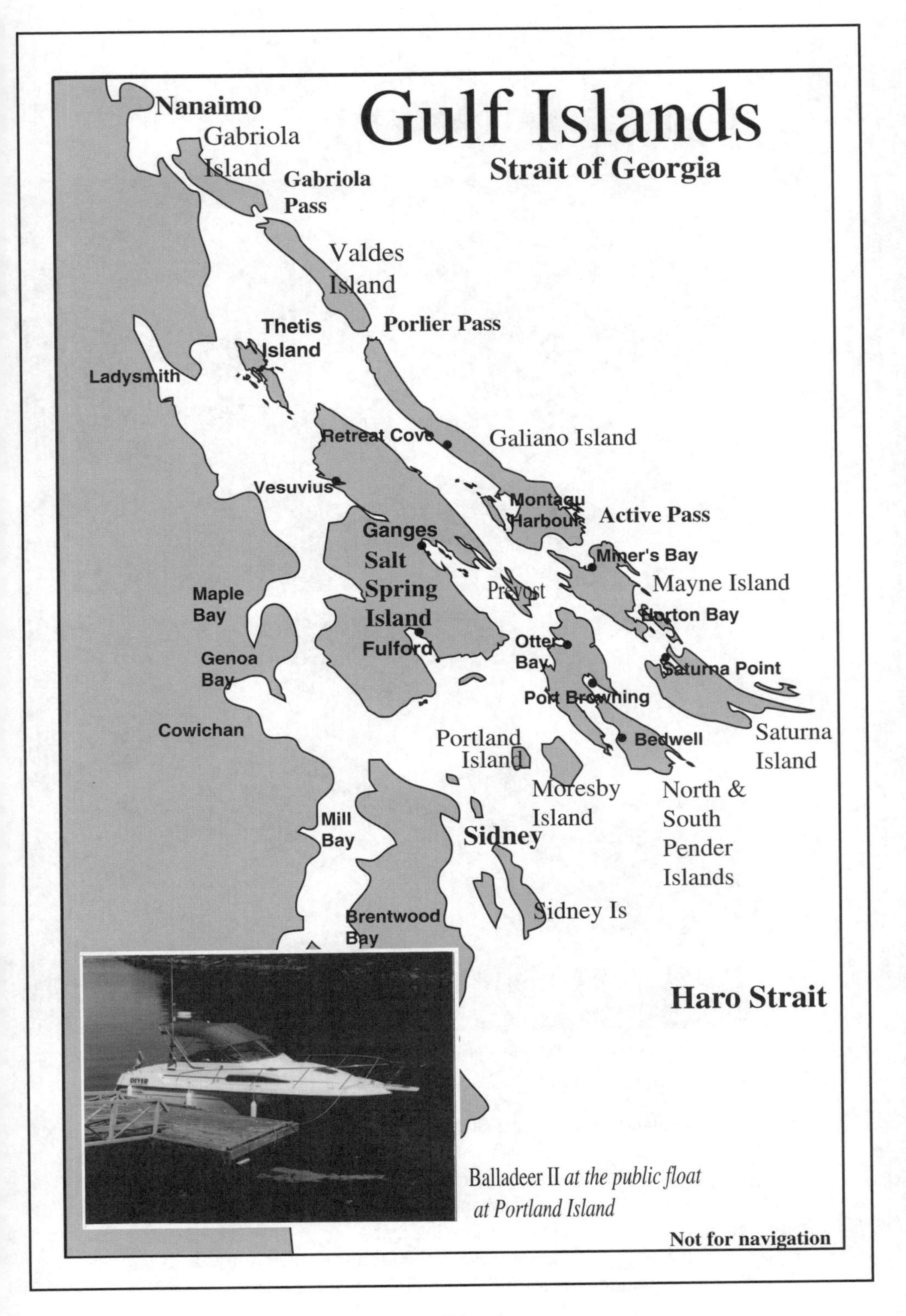

Balladeer II *at the public float at Portland Island*

Gulf Islands

The islands are known internationally for their sandstone formations. The church at Fulford Harbour was built using materials carried to the island in canoes .

The islands in the lower Strait of Georgia known as The Gulf Islands offer many anchoring and mooring alternatives. The map on the previous page shows the main islands which make up the group including islands which offer marinas, moorages and anchorages safe for overnight useage unless otherwise cautioned in the following text.

Salt Spring Island, opposite, is the largest of the Gulf Islands and has most facilities and amenities similar to mainland centres.

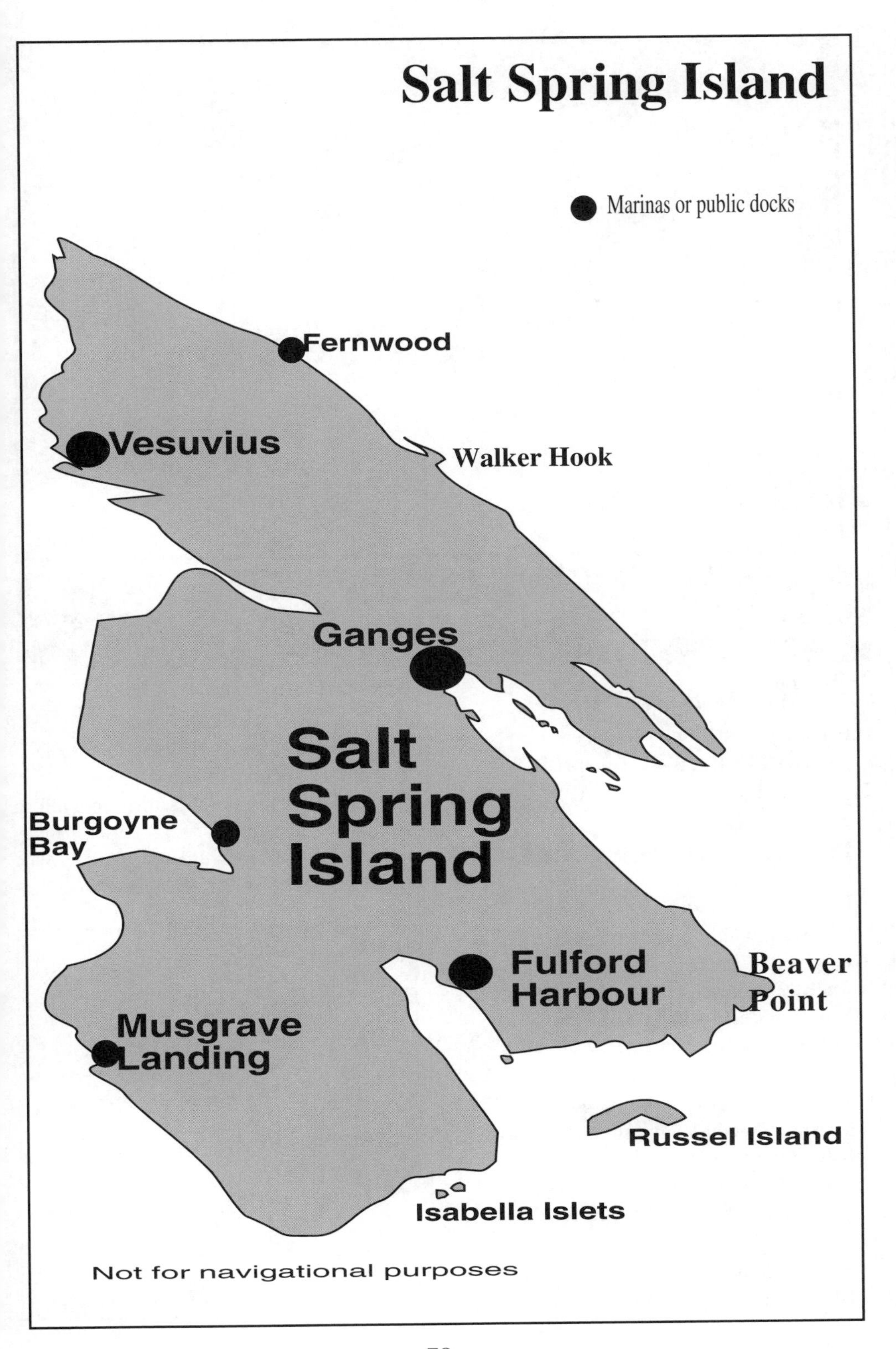
Salt Spring Island
Marinas or public docks
Fernwood
Vesuvius
Walker Hook
Ganges
Salt Spring Island
Burgoyne Bay
Fulford Harbour
Beaver Point
Musgrave Landing
Russel Island
Isabella Islets
Not for navigational purposes

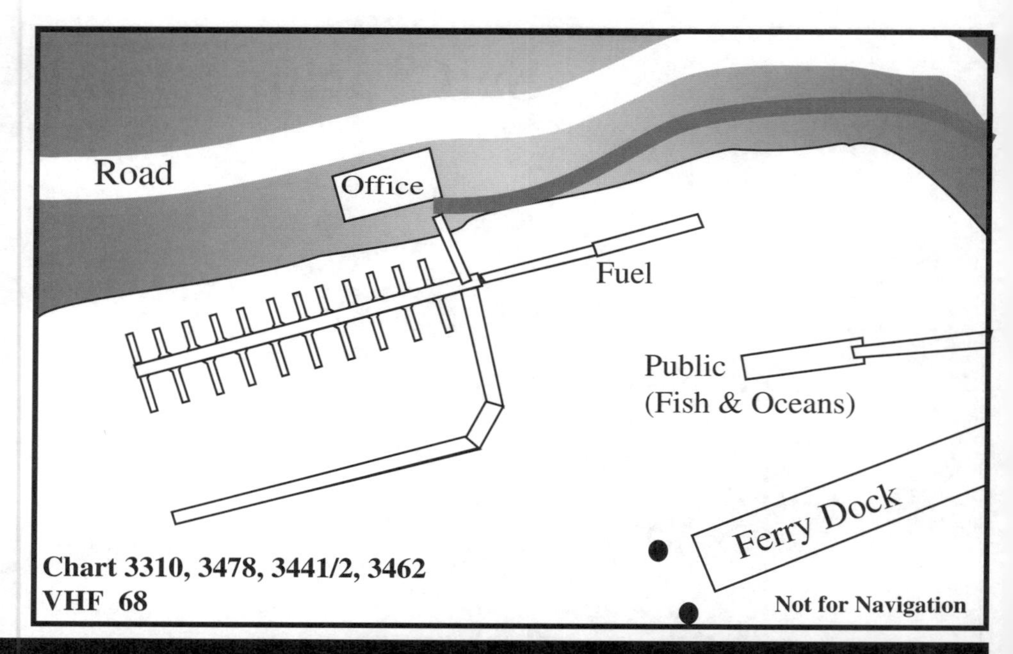

Fulford Marina

Fulford Marina

Eric Manchester and Mona Ferguson
#1–2810 Fulford–Ganges Rd.,
Salt Spring Island,
BC. V8K 1Z2
Phone: (604) 653-9600 Fax: 653-9800

Marina services:

Moorage: Guest and permanent.
Large breakwater float.
Fuel: Gas, diesel, oil.
Water at dock. All slips.
Power at docks: Multiple 30, 20 amp.

Customer services:

Public phone ashore.
Marina office has some supplies, charts, fishing licences and tackle.
Showers, washrooms. Grocery store: souvenirs, office supplies, coffee/deck. Deli. Snacks, light meals.

Entertainment.

Island tranquility. Eagles, herons, otters and seals. Walking, beaches.

Adjacent facilities:

BC Ferries to Sidney. Government docks. Temporary anchorage in bay.
Places of interest: Churches, historic. Fulford settlement–arts and crafts, groceries, restaurants, hotel. Walk to Drummond Park. Private museum of Indian Art–Bob Akerman collection.

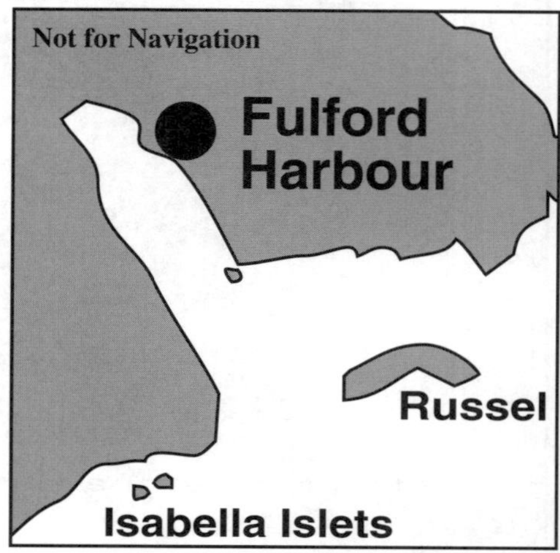

Rodrigo's Mexican restaurant at the ferry landing in Fulford Harbour.

An old fuel pump at what was once a busy garden shop in Fulford Harbour

Public docks:
Fulford Harbour, outer dock
Fisheries & Oceans dock
Phone 537-5711
Chart 3310, 3478, 3441, 3442, 3462
Manager – Reid Collins. Phone 653-4728 •
Float length 36 m
Garbage • Lights • Power • Public phone ashore •
Adjacent ferry to Sidney, restaurants, shops.

Fulford Harbour, Inside breakwater.
Transport Canada dock
Chart 3310, 3478, 3441, 3442, 3462
Manager • Float length 16 m
Public phone ashore •
Not recommended for overnight moorage.

A summer place.

Fulford Harbour is one of those places you may never visit by boat if you aren't prompted to go there for some specific reason. For years I bypassed Fulford Harbour en route between Vancouver and Sidney, thinking there was no point running up a blind inlet in a slow boat. I was wrong. I had missed out on what has since become one of my favourite cruising destinations.

Fulford Harbour has some of the Gulf Islands' most fascinating features and history. The oldest church on the island is located not far from the marina, the historic Fulford Inn nearby and the village at the ferry terminal give this quaint place a character all of its own, making it quite different from other settlements in the Gulf Islands.

Fulford is the start of the highway across Salt Spring from the ferry terminal that carries traffic out of Sidney, and gives travellers and residents access to and from the island's other settlements, Ganges being the major centre.

Summertime sees thousands of visitors passing through the gateway village of Fulford, many stopping at the busy Mexican restaurant, Rodrigo's at the ferry terminal, or Patterson's general store and gas station next door. Throngs of passengers and islanders picking up foot-passengers can be seen almost constantly awaiting ferry arrivals and departures. They sit at tables outside the stores, on the roadway or in their cars. In summer tourists come by bicycle, camper, car and motorcycle and bring with them tents for camping at any one of the many beautiful campsites on the island. Some travellers arrive at Fulford and leave from another ferry terminal, usually Long Harbour, or the other way around.

At the Fulford settlement there is a surprising number and variety of enterprises and services. At the post office you can buy stamps as well as fishing licenses. Not far you can walk into the local craft shop or cross the road and browse in the very well-stocked nursery, eat at Rodrigo's–inside or out on their patio, or check out the goods at the pottery studio, or the knick knack store nearby.

No matter what interests you at Fulford or what other people are up to, waiting for a ferry or just passing through, stopping there even for a brief moment is certain to captivate one by its charm and tranquillity.

Arriving by boat up the harbour, a wide and sometimes windy inlet, one can stop briefly at a small government dock outside the breakwater, or enter behind the breakwater and possibly find a spot at the government dock inside. But moorage is readily available at the Fulford Marina most times of the year. Some summer weekends are busy with visiting yacht club members, but rarely have I dropped in unexpectedly and not easily found moorage. A phone call in advance, of course, will ensure space if you want to make reservations. About 40 slips are available for visitors. The marina operator has a friendly attitude towards boat owners which contributes to a pleasant visit. The docks are well built and well equipped with cleats for secure tie-up, water and shore power with 30 amp service. The marina office at the head of the dock collects moorage and electrical fees and offers showers and laundry facilities too. They serve fuel at their fuel dock located to port en route to the government docks in the lee of the ferry landing.

In winter time some fairly strong winds can assail Fulford, blowing up the harbour from the south east, so monitor the weather channel before planning a trip there out of season. If you do go into the marina and anticipate a storm, make sure you tie up well inside rather than on the outer floats. The docks are subject to a fair amount of movement in a storm. A large log boom has been used as a breakwater during winter. Overnight the Fulford ferry remains at her berth, serving as additional protection to inner sections of the marina.

One of the best attractions at Fulford Harbour is the pleasant surroundings and the ability to go for a quiet stroll ashore. From the marina a path follows the immediately adjacent shoreline and gives access to a tranquil spot under a picturesque gazebo overlooking the marina and the harbour entrance. Following the pathway leads to the island highway which passes tree sheltered tennis courts (take your tennis gear with you and check with the marina) and leads down to the Fulford Inn. Along the way you pass the quaint old St. Paul's church which has an interesting history. It was built back in 1880 by the local population using materials recovered from the remnants of another old church in the Gulf Islands. A stained glass window, the door and a bell were carried

Fulford Marina showing the breakwater dock and offices and store ashore. Fuel and government dock are to the right. Opposite: A view of Fulford Harbour.

from Cowichan to Salt Spring Island by Indian canoe and then hauled overland by an ox-drawn cart on skids.

Once at the Fulford Inn you can stop for lunch or make dinner reservations, or just drop in at most meal times. It's a busy place at times with some Christmas and other holiday meals booked to capacity. The inn, as old and historic as it may appear, however, is relatively new, being the fourth building on its site, the previous three having succumbed to fire. Not far from the Inn is the community hall and another old church, St. Mary's, which was built back in 1894 and, like St. Paul's, continues holding services to this day.

We have visited Fulford in the winter and found some facilities operating at reduced hours. But Rodrigo's is open and busy all year round. The inn and restaurants are excellent places to meet the local islanders. Some of these are internationally famous figures. Salt Spring Island is home to many artists and their work can be seen at local craft stores and galleries on the island.

Beyond the inn on the road to Isabella Point is cosy little Drummond Park where you can sit on the benches or swings and watch the sea birds and other animals that visit the beach. We have seen swans, geese and sheep wandering on the beach and roads in the area. The park has toilets and a playground for children as well as a large rock bearing a native petroglyph. This area was once a popular hunting ground for aboriginal people and middens are apparent in places along the shore.

In the opposite direction, down the harbour shoreline beyond the ferry dock takes you along a winding road to a park area and Indian reserve. The shady pathways that meander all the way down to the harbour entrance make an excellent outing in summertime or sunny days in the fall or spring. Stop along the way and watch the occasional harbour traffic or just sit and enjoy the ambience of the area. Look for eagles, herons, woodpeckers, hummingbirds, kingfishers and many other birds. Across Fulford Harbour you will see the Fulford ferry coming and going and in the distance the mainland ferries running to and from Sidney.

After a long walk or time spent exploring the settlement of Fulford there is little to match the joy of sitting in your boat and watching the activity at the dock or exchanging communications with neighbours while barbecuing or preparing and having a sunset dinner.

Ganges Marina early morning.

Ganges

Ganges is the business centre and hub of the Gulf Islands. It is not only located on the largest of the Gulf Islands but also it has the largest population of all communities in the archipelago. Salt Spring Island residents as well as visitors by boat or by road via the BC Ferries system use Ganges as a shopping and cultural centre.

Activities on Salt Spring Island as well as arts and crafts attract many visitors each summer. The morning craft market held on the waterfront every Saturday morning has become a colourful attraction. The work of local artists can be seen and bought in the several art shops and galleries in Ganges. Shopping at Mouat's historic store provides opportunity to stock up on the items you need for boating comfort, safety and convenience. The many other specialty stores in the town will provide hours of pleasurable shopping or window shopping. And the restaurants are of a variety that will enable you to select from a wide range of menus. One of the top restaurants in BC is located in Ganges.

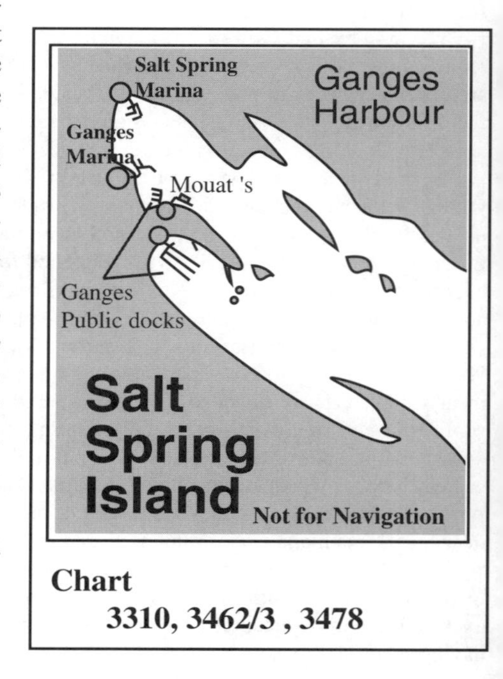

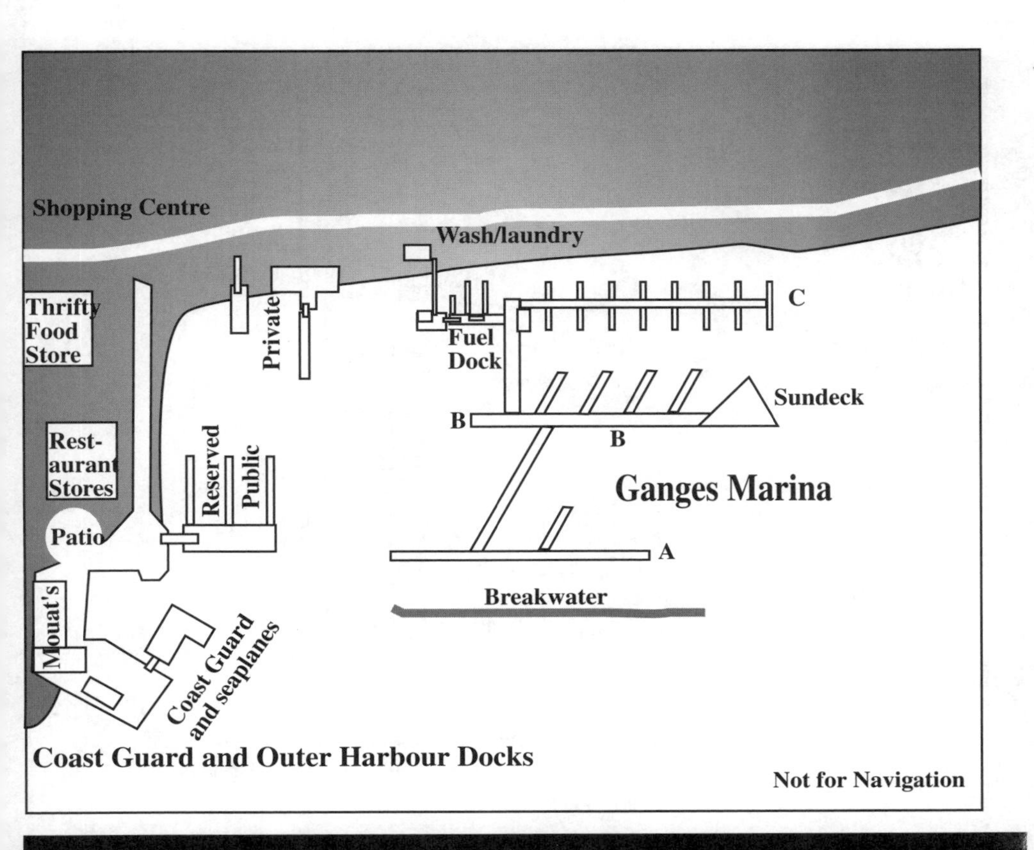

Ganges Marina

Ganges Marina

Bard & Lynda Brown
161 Lower Ganges Road,
Ganges, BC V8K 2T2
Phone: (604) 537-5242 537-5331

Marina services:

Moorage: Guest and permanent. Reservations taken.
Fuel: Gas, diesel, oils–Shell. Other services available.
Water at dock. All slips.
Power at docks: Multiple 30, 15 amp.

Customer services:

Public phone ashore. Marina store has some supplies, fishing licences and tackle.

Laundry, showers, washrooms.
Ice, bait, fishing gear.
Car rentals at marina.

Entertainment.

Ganges Saturday public market.
Arts and art galleries.
Scooter rentals nearby. Walking and cycling on island roads, some nearby waterfront and beachfront access.

Adjacent facilities:

Government docks. Shopping centre. Close to all Ganges facilities. Fresh produce. Bakery. Thrifty store. Restaurants. Anchorages and places of interest. Churches, arts and crafts, groceries, hotels, bed and breakfast.

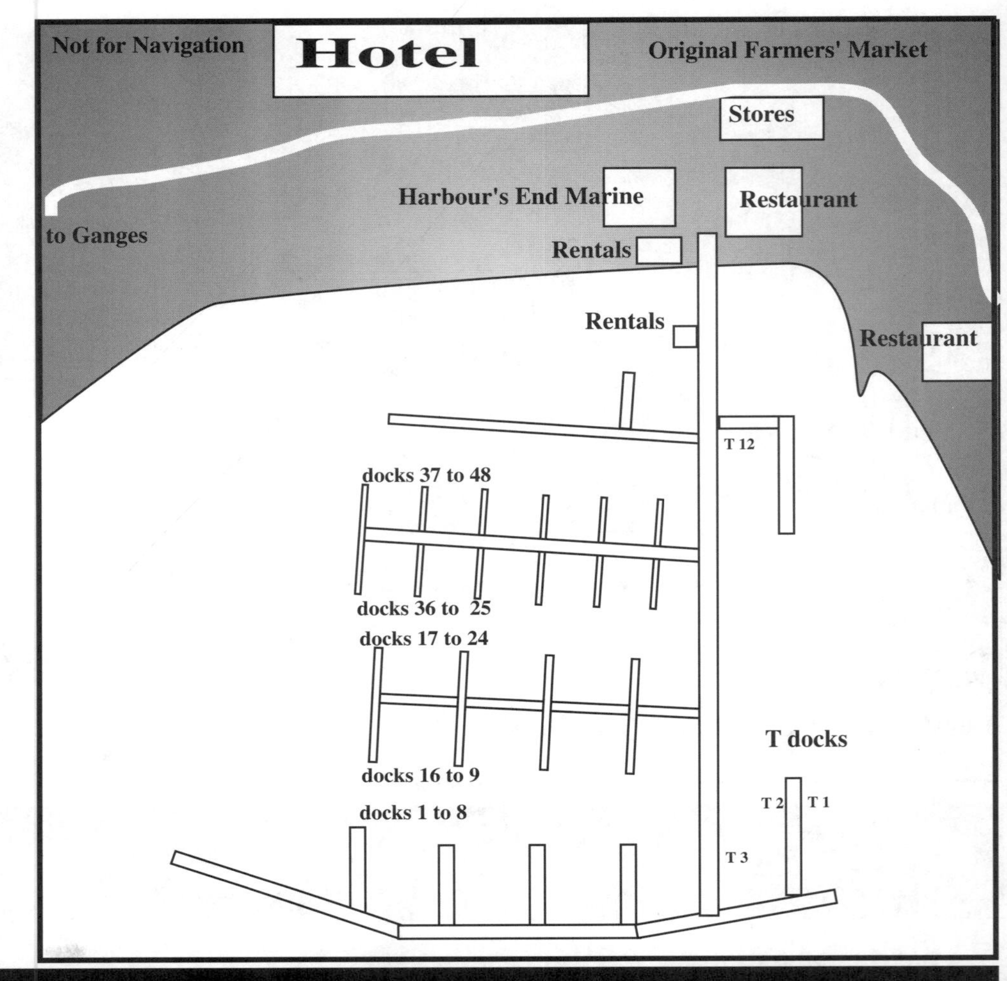

Salt Spring Marina

Salt Spring Marina

Dick Durante. Lesley Cheeseman (mgr)
120. Upper Ganges Rd., Ganges
Salt Spring Island, BC. V8K 2S2
Phone: (604) 537-5810 Pub: 537-5559
Chart 3310, 3462/3, 3478 VHF 68

Marina services:

Moorage: Guest and permanent.
Haulouts, towing and other services.
Water at docks.
Power at docks: Multiple 30, 15 amp.

Customer services:

Restaurant and pub. Public phone ashore.
Marina store has chandlery, fishing licences and tackle. Marine service.*
Showers, washrooms. Grocery store, souvenirs, coffee, ice, bait, fishing gear.
Car rentals at Ganges Marina.

Entertainment.

Ganges Saturday public market.
Arts. Galleries.
Scooter, kayak and boat rentals.

Ganges Marina and Salt Spring Marina from Mouat's Store.

Hastings House restaurant will take reservations and collect you at your boat for a meal that will cost you a lot but provide you a memorable gourmet experience that will be hard to match.

Boat services include temporary stopping if space permits, at the government dock on the north side of the town or in the harbour. Private marinas Ganges Marina and Salt Spring Marina provide overnight and extended mooring with power and electricity at the docks and laundry, showers and toilets on shore.

Salt Spring Marina offers also a large restaurant at the head of the dock and activities such as boat, bicycle and scooter rentals, as well as boat repairs and service. Harbour's End Marine Supply is an authorized dealership for several brands of engines and other equipment and is located at the head of the dock at the marina.

There was an Esso marine station near the north side government dock but it has closed. Fuel is available at Ganges Marina.

Walking on island roads, some nearby waterfront and beachfront access.

Adjacent and nearby facilities:

Moby's Pub. Shopping centre.

Anchorages and places of interest: Churches, arts and crafts, groceries, restaurants, hotels, bed and breakfast.

*** Harbour's End Marine & Equipment Ltd**

Barry Green and Ross Walker

122 Upper Ganges Rd.,

P.O. Box 1440 Ganges,

Salt Spring Island BC. V0S 1E0

Phone(604) 537-4202

Marine repairs, chandlery, service.

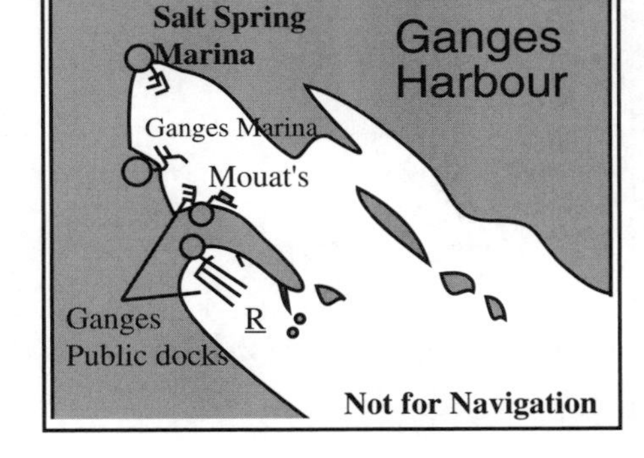

Not for Navigation

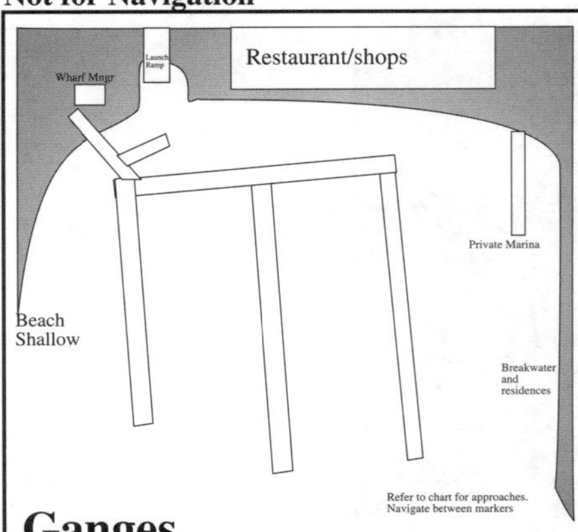

Ganges, Salt Spring Island Public docks.

(Outer dock and Coast Guard)

Transport Canada dock

Float length 24 m
Aircraft Float • Water • Lights • Power •
Public phone ashore •
Adjacent restaurants, shops. Fuel dock adjacent.
Marinas, fuel, services nearby.

Ganges Boat Harbour (Inner Harbour)

Fisheries & Oceans dock

Phone 537-5711

Manager • Float length
326 m
Launch ramp • Breakwater • Garbage •
Waste oil disposal • Water • Lights •
Power • Public phone • Washroom •
Showers •
Adjacent restaurants, shops.

Ganges, (Outer Harbour)

Fisheries & Oceans dock
Manager • Float length 41 m
Garbage • Water • Lights • Public phone ashore •
Adjacent restaurants, shops.

Charts 3310, 3478, 3442, 3462

Restaurant and walk at Ganges overlooking Boat Harbour public docks (Inner Harbour).

Not for Navigation

Fernwood,

Walker Hook, Salt Spring Island
Transport Canada dock
Chart 3310, 3462, 3442
Float length 12 m

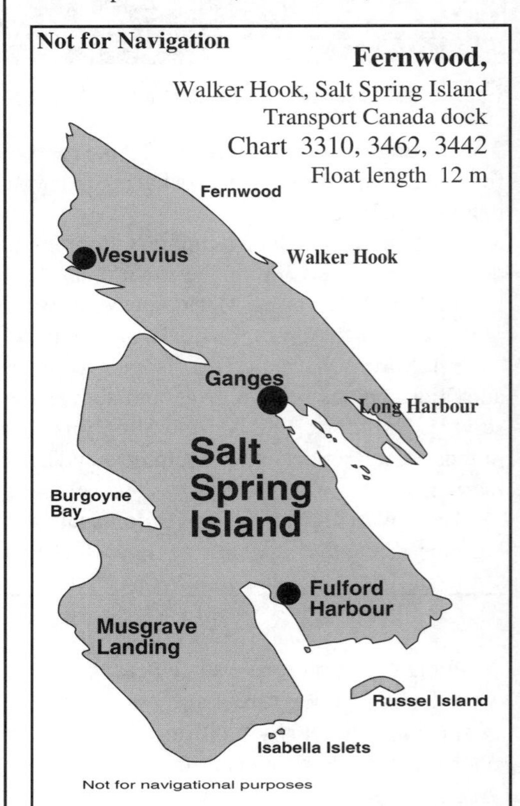

Musgrave Landing,

Salt Spring Island
Fisheries & Oceans dock
Chart 3310, 3441/2
Float length 12 m

Burgoyne Bay

Fisheries & Oceans dock
Phone 537-5711
Chart 3310, 3478
Manager • Float length 10 m

Patio service, restaurants, art, hardware, clothing and many other stores surround historic Mouat's store at Ganges.

Merchants' Market and Farmers' Market on Saturday mornings. One is held on Ganges waterfront, the other near Salt Spring Marina.

Pender Canal, the narrow passage between the Penders was man made to provide an alternative route north to south. At high tide the clearance is 26 feet and at low tide the depth of water is seven feet.

Port Washington had a general store which closed down in the past decade after serving passing vessels since the early 1900s. The floats will accommodate several small to medium sized boats but are exposed to washes from passing ferries and some wind conditions.

One of the few fuel stops in the Gulf Islands is at Bedwell Bay.

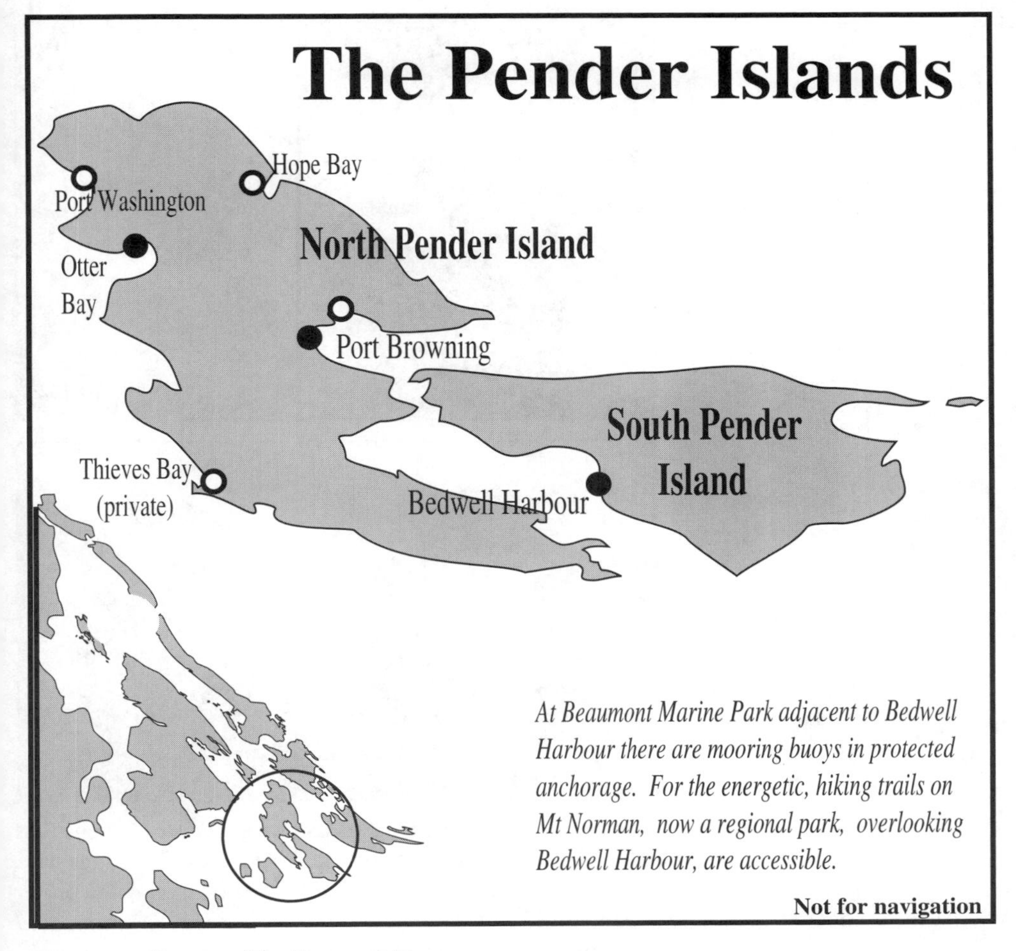

Pender Islands

If there were no islands in the Strait of Georgia other than the Pender Islands we would still be talking about the outstanding cruising on the west coast of Canada. The Pender Islands are blessed with beautiful, unspoilt and charming features and are central to the major group of Gulf Islands, providing moorage, anchorage and safe stops for all boat operators. The main harbour of the Penders is Bedwell: resort, marina and customs stop. It is a major anchorage with an adjacent marine park which ranks highly in popularity among boaters and campers. Up the harbour is one of the most picturesque passages on the entire coast, Pender Canal, which separates North from South Pender and provides access to Port Browning. This port has an extremely sheltered marina which caters to the needs of overnight moorage customers most adequately. Facilities include pub and restaurant, store and swimming pool as well as laundry, toilets and close access to the island's main but small business centre. Here one can shop for groceries, arts and crafts, liquor, real estate, pharmacy items and more. Popular stop is the ice cream and bakery store as well as Saturday Farmers' Market on the property. In late summer look for ripe blackberries on the bushes that line the road ways.

Hope Bay store, another early establishment on the Penders. The floats were more extensive in recent years, serving as an alternate landing for the Otter Bay ferry during strong westerly blows. This is also an exposed dock and best used for short visits. Opposite: A longtime landmark, the marine bar and bistro at Bedwell.

Pender Canal is a narrow passage which curves its way under a low bridge that connects the two Pender Islands. At high tide boats will clear the bridge if they are no taller than 26 feet. At low tides shallow draft vessels have no trouble but a seven foot draft could be a problem. Travel slowly through the canal and be prepared to possibly meet a boat coming from the opposite direction midway through.

A major, but little known attraction on North Pender Island is Hope Bay named after a former postmaster and local land owner, Rutherford Hope. The docks at Hope Bay are minimal and exposed to wind at times making them not the most secure for overnight moorage. There is no power, no water and no services. But on land is the historic Hope Bay Store which in recent years has reopened, closed and reopened under different owners. It served for many years as post office, supply store and provision centre for the islanders living at that end of Pender as well as for passing vessels or those calling from neighbouring areas, such as lighthouse keepers and islanders of nearby islands. At one point it was also a ferry landing. In its most recent reopening the store has taken on a new life of service and character in which owners Carol and Kees Van Der Valk have managed to retain the flavour of the past. It still houses the old post office counter at the back of the store, although this serves more as a museum now as it is no longer in operation. But the cappuccinos are excellent and on a warm, sunny day one may sit on a bench out front and enjoy the ambience of the place.

The docks at Hope Bay are not too extensive but can accommodate several medium sized craft on the outside of the main float for short stays, and another

several on the inside if the docks are clear or if you are prepared to raft alongside other boats. The store has a fascinating array of collectable and unique items and also caters snacks. Next door are arts and crafts stores which sell works of local and other artists.

General stores seem to have enjoyed a heyday in the islands. On North Pender Island is the Port Washington General Store on the west side of the island in Grimmer Bay. It is closed now but served the local people from 1910 until the late 1980s. Washington Grimmer was responsible not only for the names of the settlement and the bay, but also for the mail on Pender in the early years and was involved in bringing the first educator to the island. There is a government float at Port Washington which will accommodate about four medium sized boats at each of two fingers. Some wash comes into the bay from passing ferries and other vessels or from weather conditions from the west.

Up the hill a short distance from the Port Washington store building are several shops on a large property. They sell local arts and crafts and feature jewellery and hand made sweaters, bed clothes and children's fashion. A short distance farther south is the Pender Islands ferry terminal and Otter Bay. Here is another of the Gulf Islands' major ports for recreational boating.

Otter Bay has a fully operational marina with good docks, power, water, laundry, showers and a store which carries a limited amount of stock; some fresh produce, canned goods and frozen foods among other items. The marina office sells fishing licences and can provide information on local island services such as mechanical, towing, bed & breakfast and ferries schedules. It is a convenient spot to leave your boat between weekends and ferry back and forth between Pender and Vancouver Island or the mainland.

There is no fuel available at Otter Bay. The nearest fuel docks are at Ganges, Active Pass, Montague Harbour, Saturna, Bedwell Bay, Fulford or Sidney.

Recently new facilities were installed at Otter bay. These include a new, enlarged store, a large sun deck on top of the breakwater and a swimming pool. A new building was erected recently for laundry, showers and washrooms.

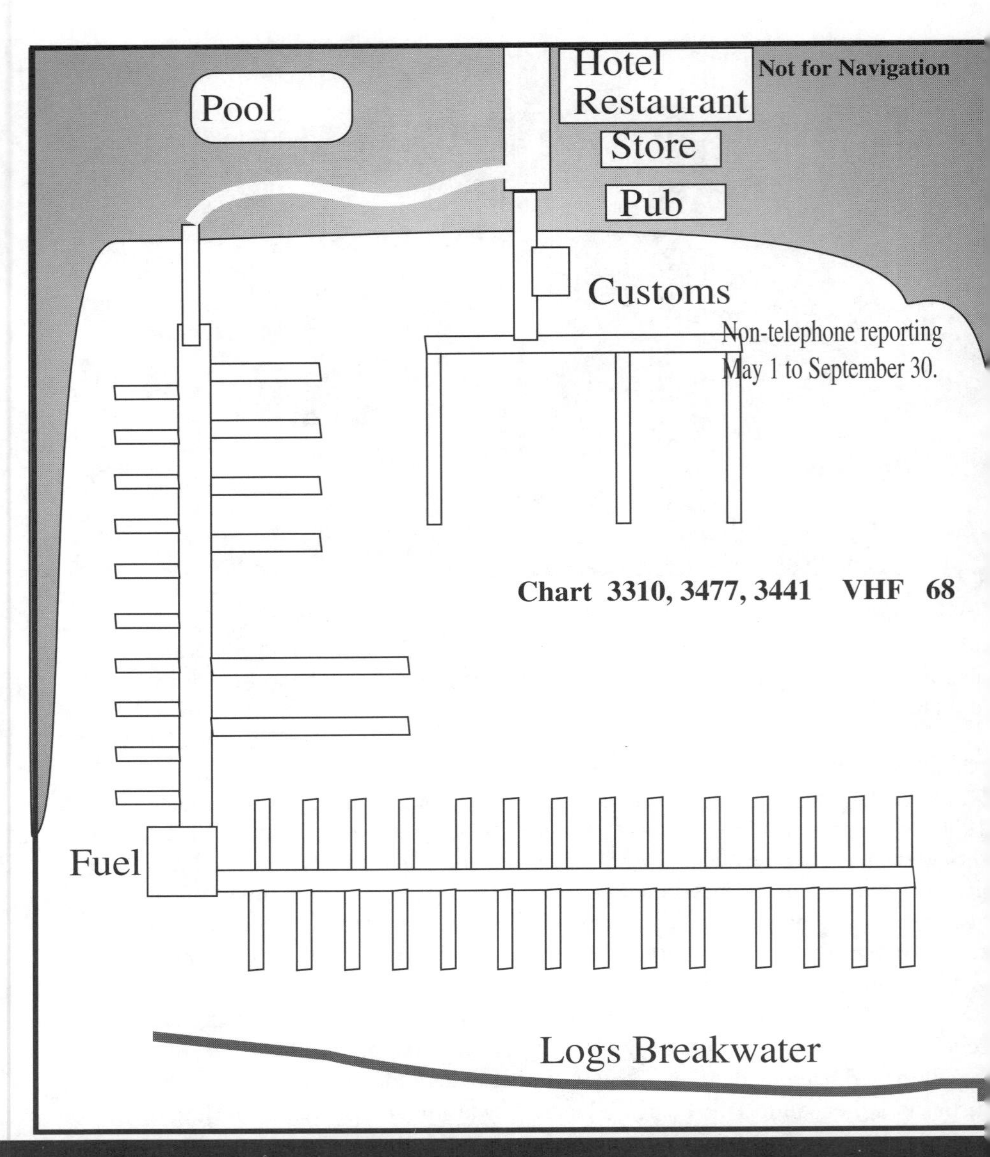

Bedwell Harbour Resort

Bedwell Harbour Resort

Bill James
RR #1 South Pender Island,
BC., V0N 2M0
Phone: (604) 629-3212
Fax: (604) 629-6777

Customs service.
Customs. Phone 629-3363
officials on duty office and other hours.

Marina services:
Fuel: Gas, diesel, ice. Propane. Service.
Moorage. Large marina with mostly transient moorage.

The pool at Bedwell Harbour Island Resort overlooking the marina. Below: The marine pub and patio with general store to the left beneath resort building.

Water at dock.
Power at docks: 15 amp.
Laundry, showers, washrooms.
Tackle shop on dock.

Customer services:

Restaurant. Breakfast, lunch, dinner. Licenced. Also patio service.
Swimming pool. Lodging. General store: Fishing gear, licences, charts, bait. Fresh baked goods. Gifts. Groceries.
Tennis raquets available. Bicycle rentals.
Road access walking or cycling. Nearby hiking trails.
Public pay phone ashore.

Entertainment.

Live music weekends, summer. meals at poolside. Tennis courts. Fireworks on weekends in summertime.

Adjacent facilities:

Play area. Pet area.Beaumont Marine Park. Camping, hiking. Mooring buoys. Nearby Mt. Norman is accessible by trail.

Bedwell Harbour.

This is one of the main American entrances to Canadian waters in British Columbia. It is a busy customs port throughout the summer months July through September. It is essential that visiting vessels clear customs at an official entry port before stopping elsewhere in Canada. And Bedwell is one of the most used entry ports for vessels arriving, including returning Canadians, out of the San Juan Islands or Puget Sound. The facilities at Bedwell are as comprehensive as you will find anywhere in British Columbian waters. The docks are extensive and power and water are available, the latter not for washing boats due to the relative short supply from its on-island source. A fuel dock serves gas and diesel and other marine products and the marina, as part of the shoreside resort, offers access to the swimming pool and other amenities included with one's moorage. Showers, laundry, a general store, restaurant, snack kiosks, and a marine bar and bistro make up most of other facilities. There is a hotel which is popular for visitors arriving by boat or by road via ferries from Sidney or the mainland, as well as town- houses which are home to their owners who mostly use them at weekends.

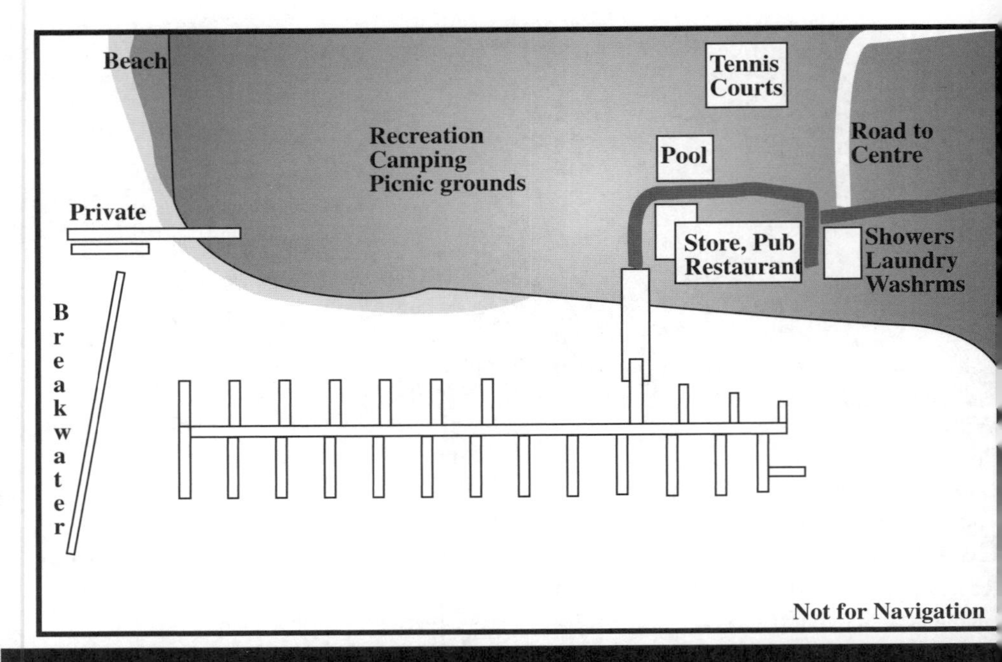

Port Browning Marina

Chart 3310, 3477, 3441/2 VHF 68

Port Browning Marina Resort

Lou Henshaw

General Delivery,
North Pender Island.
BC, V0N 2M0
Phone: (604) 629-3493

Caution: Narrow, shallow Pender Canal if travelling from Bedwell Harbour. Check chart and tides.

Customs service.

Check in at Bedwell Harbour.

Marina services:

General and marine store. Ice, groceries, charts. Fishing tackle, licences, ice, bait, gifts. Moorage. Large marina with permanent and transient moorage.

Water at dock.

Power at docks: 15 amp.

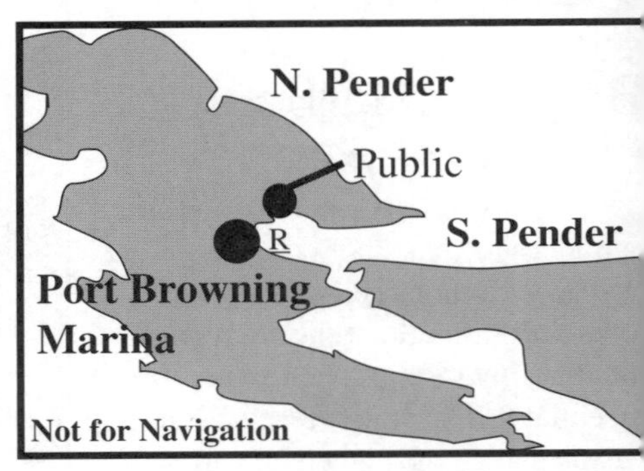

Laundry, showers, washrooms.
Reservations advised summertime.

Customer services:

Pub. Restaurant. Breakfast, lunch, dinner. Licenced. Also patio service.
Swimming pool. Cold beer and wine store at marina.
General store: Fishing gear, licences, charts, bait. Fresh baked goods. Gifts. Groceries.
Road access walking or cycling. Take care

Docks and facilities at Port Browning include pub, store, restaurant, pool and tennis courts. A large expanse of lawn is used frequently in summer for yacht club or group gatherings and regular week-end lamb or pork barbecues.

Farmers' market at nearby shopping complex. (Below)

walking the narrow island road.
Good beach access.
Public pay phones ashore.

Entertainment.

Swimming pool, large lawn, camping.
Tennis, golf, nearby.
Saturday morning early farmers' market at nearby shopping centre.

Adjacent facilities:

Shopping centre nearby: wide range of services, general store, restaurant, liquor, bank, art, gifts, dairy products, bakery, hairdresser.

Browning Harbour (public)
North Pender Island
Fisheries & Oceans dock
Phone 629-3423
Chart 3310
Manager • Float length 27 m
Breakwater
Marina, store, recreation nearby. Port Browning Marina.

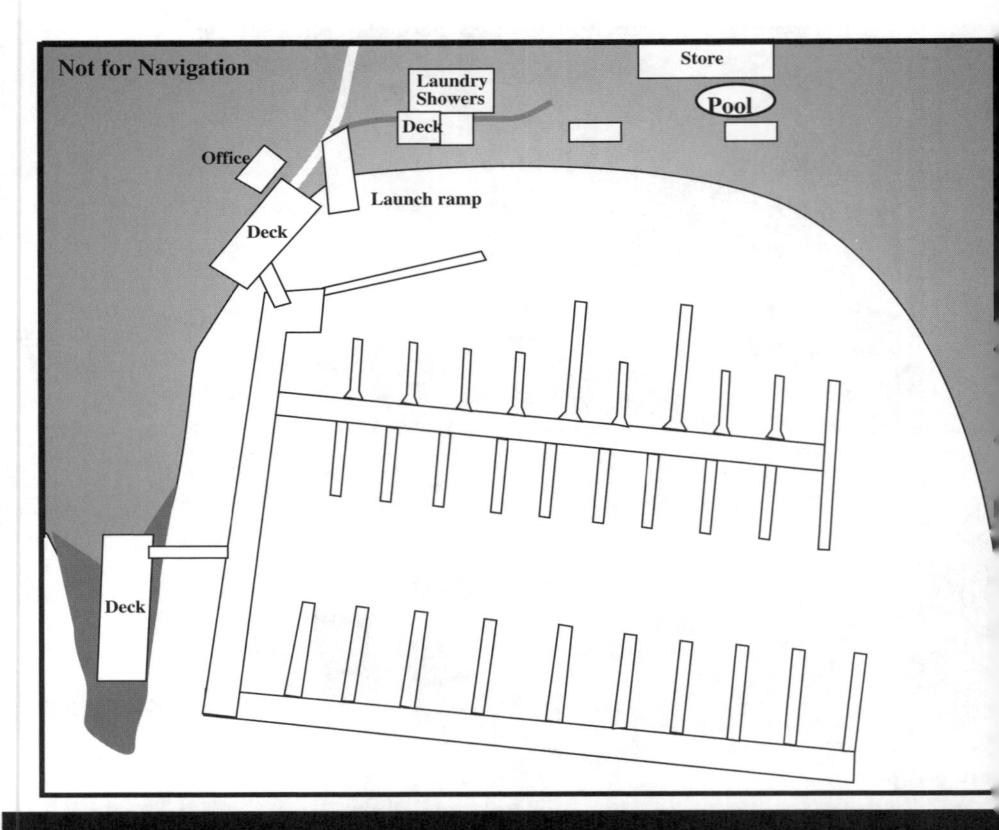

Otter Bay

Otter Bay Marina

Kay and Chuck Spence
General Delivery,
North Pender Island.
BC., V0N 2M0
Phone: (604) 629-3579
Chart 3310, 3441/2 VHF 68
Hazard: Keep clear and to starboard of green spar U 57.

Marina services:

Launch ramp.
Moorage. Large marina with permanent and transient moorage.
Water at dock. Use sparingly please.
Power at docks: 30, 15 amp.
Laundry, showers, washrooms.
Reservations advised summertime.

Customer services:

Store. Gifts, bait, ice, limited groceries
Charts. Fishing tackle, licences.
Garbage disposal.
Road access walking or cycling. Take car
walking the narrow island road.
Public pay phones ashore.
Cabin sleeps 4–5 people.

Entertainment.

Eagles, herons, otters and seals.
Bicycle, boat and kayak rentals.

Early morning at the marina. It is busy in summer months so make reservations ahead of your arrival.

Adjacent facilities:
BC Ferries dock.
Picnic tables, barbecue area.
Gazebo.
Restaurants nearby.
New deck on breakwater at marina.
Golf course–10 minutes walk.

Not for Navigation

Hope Bay

Store

Crafts
Art
Grocery

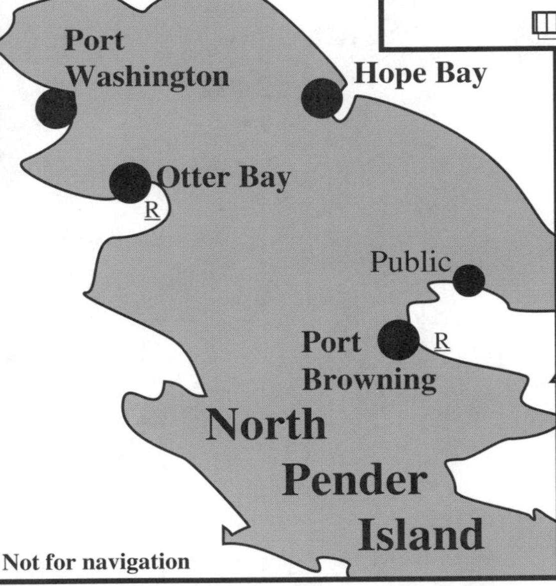

Port Washington,
North Pender Island
Transport Canada dock
Chart 3310, 3442
Manager •
Float length 45 m
Aircraft float •
Public phone ashore •
Nearby arts and crafts.
Walking–island roads.

Hope Bay,
North Pender Island
Fisheries & Oceans dock
Phone 629-4323
Chart 3310, 3477, 3461/2, 3441
Manager •
Float length 69 m
Lights •
Public phone ashore •
Adjacent shops.

Not for Navigation

Old Grocery
Store Closed

Private

Port Washington

Mayne & Saturna Islands

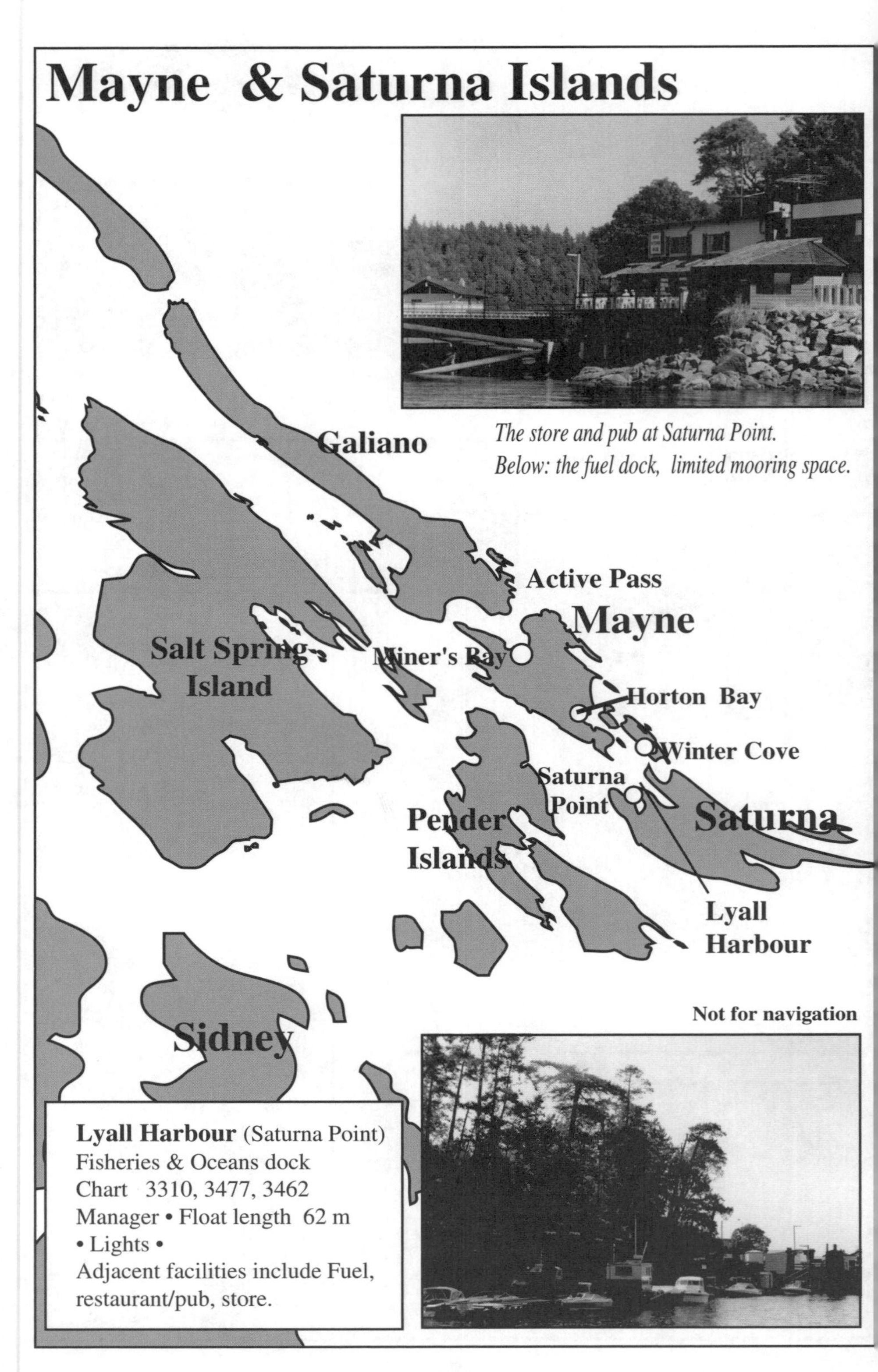

The store and pub at Saturna Point.
Below: the fuel dock, limited mooring space.

Lyall Harbour (Saturna Point)
Fisheries & Oceans dock
Chart 3310, 3477, 3462
Manager • Float length 62 m
• Lights •
Adjacent facilities include Fuel, restaurant/pub, store.

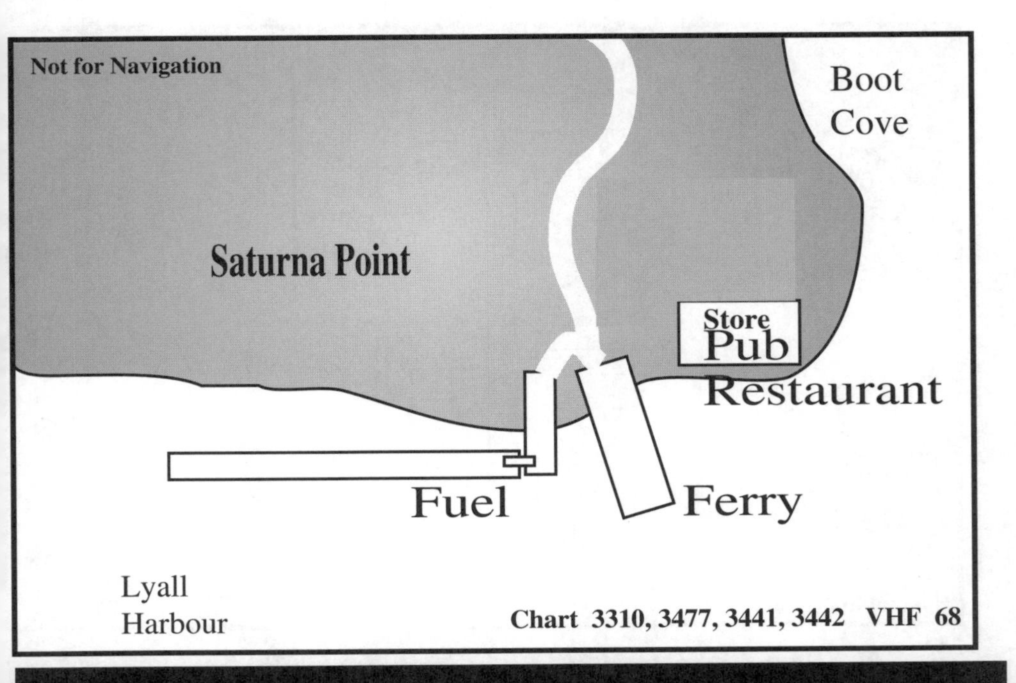

Saturna Point Landing

Saturna Point Landing

& Fuel Dock. Lyall Harbour, Saturna Island, BC. V0N 2Y0
Phone: (604) 539-5725

Harbour Master: Gloria Manzano 539-2229

Marina services:

Government dock. Limited space–mostly drop off/pick up. Not intended for overnight.
Fuel: Gas, diesel, outboard mix, oil.
Public phone ashore.
Store and restaurant ashore. Lighthouse Pub.

Customer services:

Restaurant
General store: fish tackle, hardware, licences, ice, bait. Propane available nearby.
Post office nearby–1 mile

Entertainment.

Annual lamb barbecue July 1st. at Winter Cove. Island tranquility. Eagles, herons, otters and seals.

Adjacent facilities:

BC Ferries. Use caution manouvering when ferry operating.
Anchorages and places of interest:
Winter Cove, Lyall Harbour, Boot Cove.

Horton Bay, Photo, left.
Mayne Island.
Fisheries & Oceans dock
539-2402
Chart 3310, 3477, 3462
Manager • Float length 60 m
Garbage • Lights •

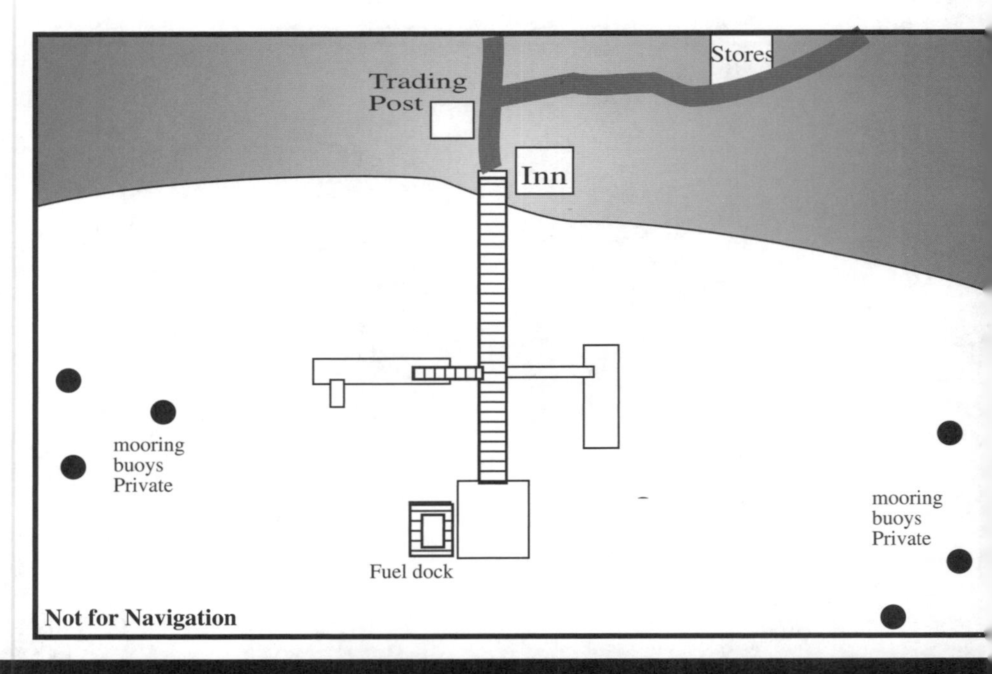

Miner's Bay

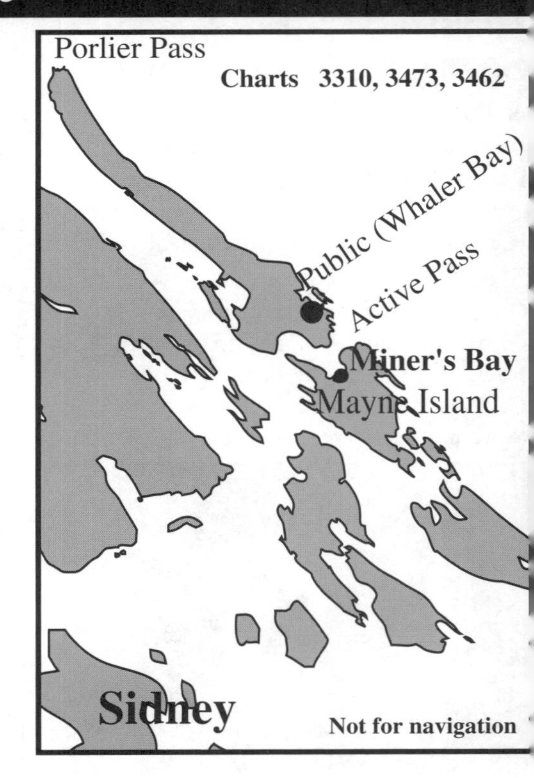

Mayne Island, Miner's Bay

Transport Canada dock
Manager • Float length 37 m
Aircraft float • Lights •

Marine Services:

Fuel • gas, diesel, outboard mix. pop, confectionery. Tackle, bait, propane.
Adjacent restaurants, shops.
Moorage at wharf, slips.
No Water or power on docks.
No laundry–No washrooms.
Taxi service.
Access to settlement.
Near Ferry service–Gulf Islands to Mainland/Sidney.
Churches nearby.
Groceries, stores near.
Accommodation near.
Easy walking on island roadways.
Ferry wash causes some rolling at dock.

The docks at Miner's Bay and the fuel float. This is one of very few fuel stops in the Gulf Islands. It is open seven days a week for fuel. Other marine services are available through the general store on shore.

Active Pass

There is excellent scuba diving in Active Pass. However one has to be mindful of the strong current and tide rips as well as the constantly passing ferries. It is best, therefore, if scuba divers use the services of professional dive charter operators rather than attempt diving the pass off their own private vessels.

Fishing in the pass, and particularly at each entrance to the pass is extremely popular and rewarding. However, here again, one should exercise caution due to the passage of ferries. Fishing vessels are obliged to move aside for approaching ferries. Common sense calls for such action to avoid collision and also to aid the ferries in their tight manouvering in the restrictive passage.

When approaching Miner's Bay for fuel, simply steer directly towards the fuel dock. The water shallows off towards the shore but mooring buoys indicate adequate water in their vicinity. Watch for the swells created by passing ferries and other vessels and wait for them to pass before attempting to dock at the fuel dock or the government floats behind the modest wood piling breakwater.

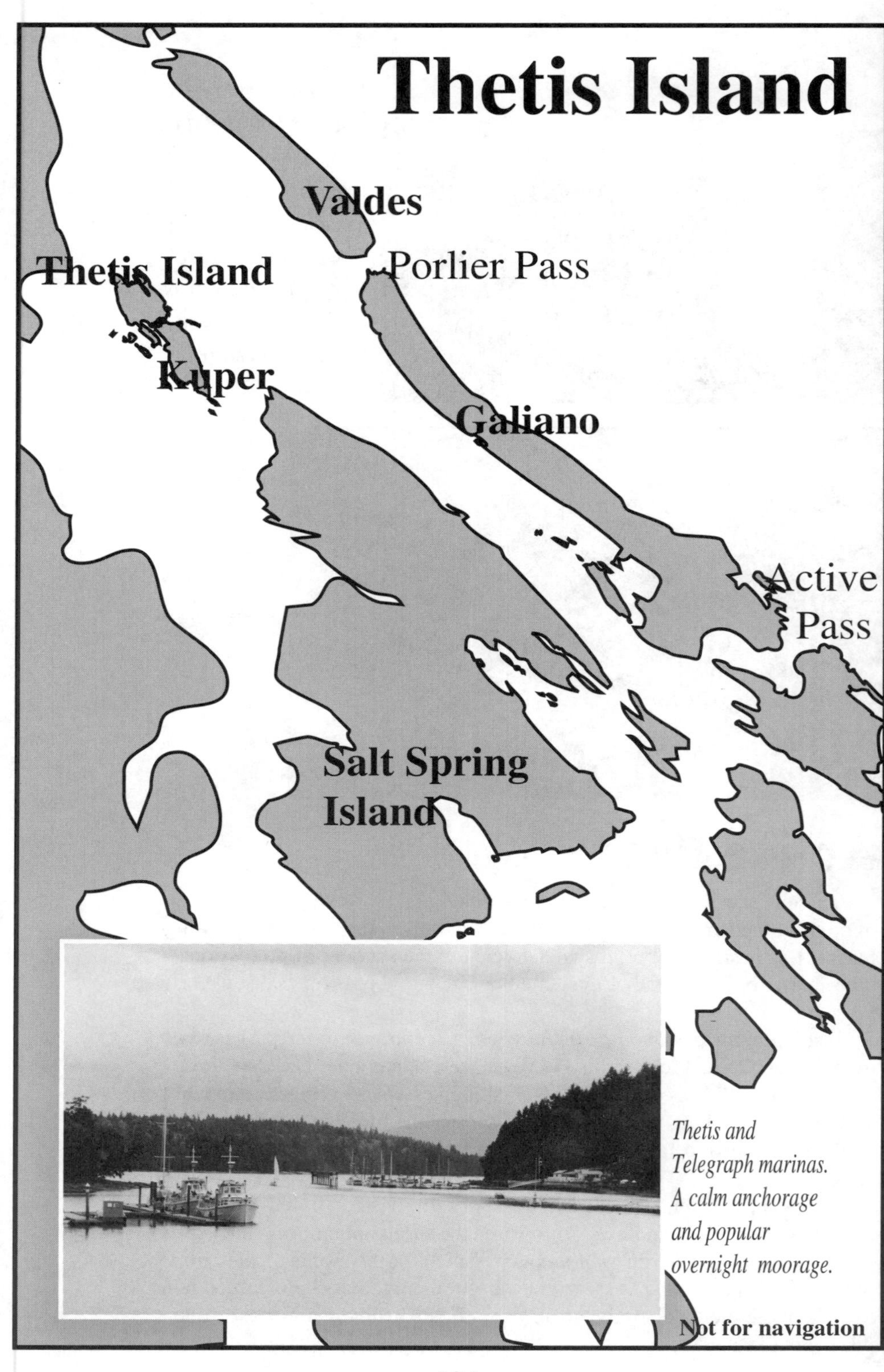

Thetis and Telegraph marinas. A calm anchorage and popular overnight moorage.

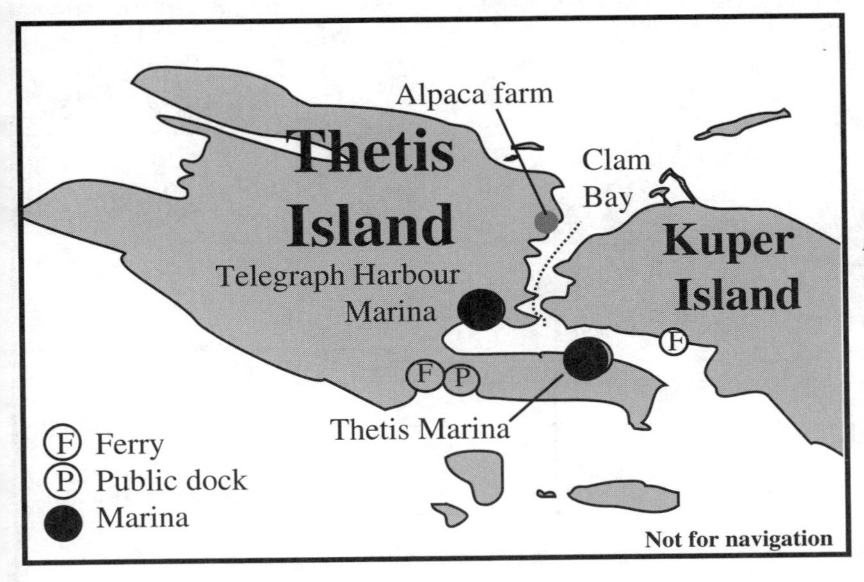

Below: Central location in the Gulf Islands. Moorage at Telegraph Harbour Marina

Thetis Island

There's a waterway in the Gulf Islands that draws boats to the challenge of its shallows. One which lures sailors like the legendary sirens to an ignominious fate of running aground if not onto the rocks, to reach the prize beyond of sheltered anchorage and a fair haven from unexpected squalls and wind. The shallow, narrow passage that separates Thetis Island from Kuper is the eastern entrance to one of the most centrally located and popular anchorages in the Gulf Islands. The canal lets boats through only at medium to high tides and denies passage to all but the tiniest of craft at low tides. It dries at a one foot tide. But despite the quirks and whims of the famous passage, it is the waterway that experienced local cruising yachtsmen associate with Telegraph Harbour. The alternative route into the anchorage at Telegraph, of course, is around the bottom of Kuper or the top of Thetis. If you are coming from a Vancouver Island base and returning to Vancouver Island after a stay at Telegraph, the passage is not an issue. But if you are crossing the Strait of Georgia and entering the Gulf Islands through Porlier Pass then the canal is the preferred access to the sheltered harbour. Choose a high tide to approach the canal or plan a longer, but pleasant detour around one of the islands.

When you arrive in Telegraph Harbour, if you are among the average type of boat owner, the first thing you will do is find moorage, at Thetis Island Marina or at Telegraph Harbour Marina. At the former you may look for the pub, at the latter you will want to moor quickly and head up the dock for one of the delicious old fashioned milkshakes for which

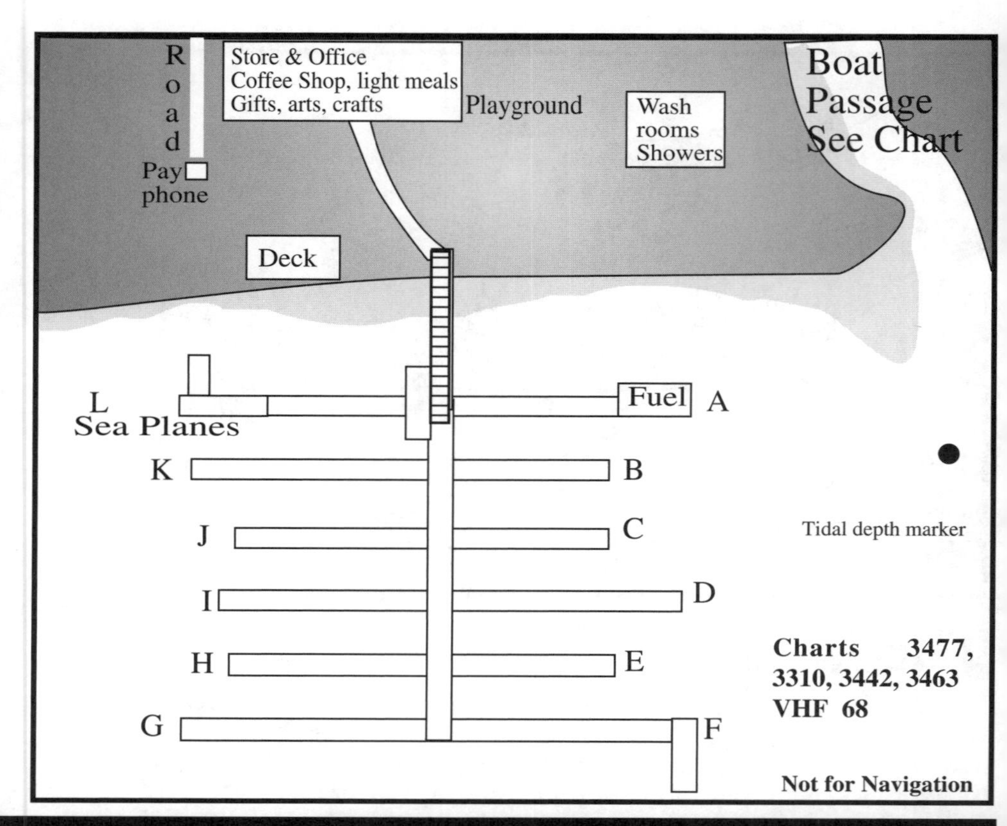

Telegraph Harbour

Telegraph Harbour Marina

John, Jan & Julie Ohman
Thetis Island, BC,
V0R 2Y0
Phone: (604) 246-9511
Fax: (604) 246-2668

Marina services:

Fuel: Gas. Diesel. Oils. Outboard mix. Service available.
Marine supplies. Fishing gear, licences, charts, bait, ice.
Marine repairs available.
3000 feet of moorage.
Water. Limited supply–use sparingly.
Power at docks: 30, 15 amp.
Multiple outlets.

Customer services:

Laundry, showers, washrooms.
Store/coffee shop, some groceries, milkshakes, ice cream, bakery products.
Frozen foods, produce, gifts, arts and crafts, books, snacks. Continental breakfasts and light meals available in store or on patio.
Boating groups book week-end events/rendezvous. Playground.
Picnic/barbecue facilities ashore.
Book ahead in summer.
Nearby church.
Road access walking or cycling.
Some nearby parkland and beach trails.
Scuba diving arrangements and charters –ask marina for details.

the marina store has become famous. Telegraph Harbour Marina is owned and operated by John and Jan Ohman, a most convivial couple who go to great lengths to welcome you and make you feel at home. In fact, so warm is their welcome that we have found ourselves cancelling our continuation plans in favour of just staying at the marina longer than planned. And staying on at Telegraph Harbour is a logical choice considering the advantages of being on Thetis Island. The harbour is very protected from winds and weather and available moorage is usually plentiful even in the busy summer period. In the height of the season, of course, it is advisable to arrive early in the day or, better still, to phone ahead and reserve a mooring spot.

A friendly gathering place at Telegraph Harbour Marina

When rounding Thetis Island the western entrance to Telegraph Harbour is via Preedy Harbour where frequently seals can be seen sunning themselves on the rocks just off Foster Point. Thetis Island Marina juts out into the main passage and posted signs effectively call on boats entering Telegraph Harbour to slow down. Thetis Island Marina, owned and run by Peter Quinn, has a pub and serves meals from a more varied menu than that at Telegraph Harbour Marina. The regular clientele at the two marinas can be quite different, naturally, the pub being more of a social centre and congregating place for those who enjoy the pub atmosphere. Telegraph Harbour Marina is suitable for families and family activities. Facilities at both marinas include moorage, water and power, showers and toilets, fuel and other boat servicing supplies.

Like most of the Gulf Islands water is in short supply on Thetis and boat owners are asked to use only what they need for refilling their fresh water tanks. Garbage is a problem for marinas but they do allow disposal of garbage by moorage customers. The Thetis Island post office is located at Thetis Island Marina. Propane is available on the island and the convenience stores at both marinas carry some souvenirs, charts and books as well as a selection of items for replenishment of boating supplies. Other than these stores at the two marinas there are no shops or shopping centres on the island. However, Chemainus on

---

Public pay phones ashore.
Daily float plane service. Short ferry trip to Chemainus shops and famous murals. Fresh roasted coffee available on island. Enquire.

Entertainment.

Nearby Alpaca hobby farm. Spinning. Knitted goods.
Recreation building. Volleyball, shuffleboard, horseshoes.

Adjacent facilities:

Excellent bed & breakfast accommodations nearby.

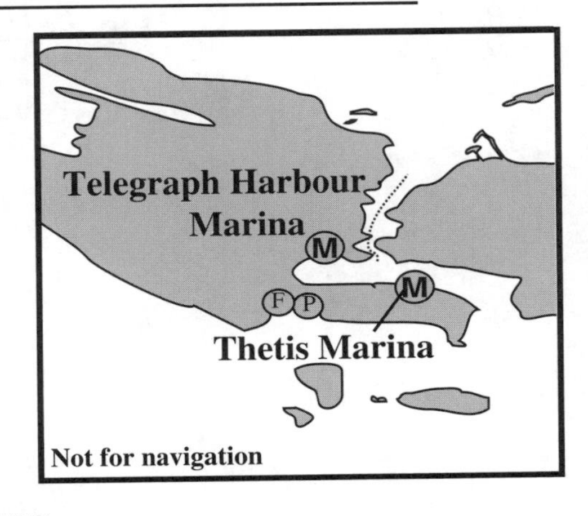

Thetis Marina protrudes into the passage beyond Telegraph Harbour.

Vancouver Island, which is a short ferry ride away, has a selection of stores and restaurants to please everyone. It is worth the ferry ride to stroll around this artistic Vancouver Island centre. The passenger ferry leaves Thetis Island for the short run across Stuart Channel eight times a day.

Not far from Telegraph Harbour Marina is a well-known supplier of fresh roasted coffee—Pot of Gold is open at most times to sell their rich aromatic beans or freshly ground coffee to islanders and visitors alike.

Thetis Island is known for its arts and crafts and not far from either marina is Thetis Island Handicrafts located in a section of a private residence. Crafts on sale represent the works of various islanders and prices are generally more favourable than those for similar items in the cities.

If you enjoy strolling a walk along any of the Thetis Island roads is relaxing and easy without any significant hills and traffic. Or at low tide you can don your boating boots and go beachcombing along the dry but marshy flats of the canal and watch your fellow boat owners trying their luck as the tide creeps out.

At Thetis Island.

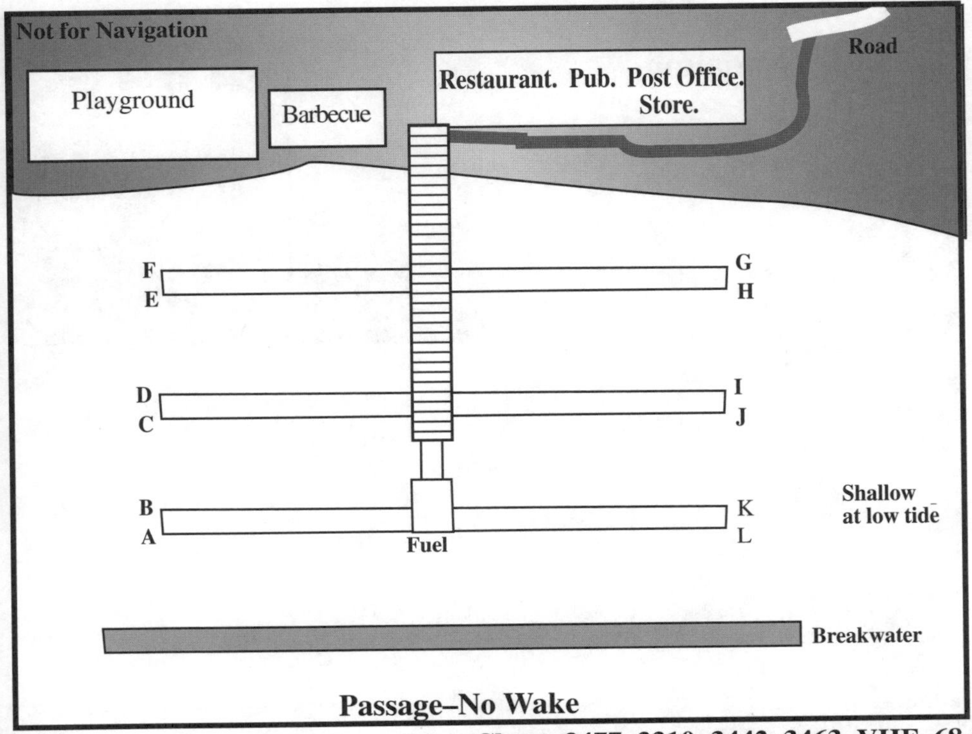

Chart 3477, 3310, 3442, 3463 VHF 68

Thetis Island Marina

Thetis Island Marina and Pub

Paul and Dawn Deacon, Pete Quinn.
Thetis Island Marina
General Delivery, Thetis Island
BC, V0R 2Y0
Phone: (604) 246-3464

Marina services:

Fuel: Gas. Diesel. Propane. Service available. Marine supplies. Fishing licences, charts, bait, ice. Marine repairs available.
Transient moorage.
Water. Limited supply–use sparingly.
Power at docks: 30, 15 amp.
Multiple outlets.
Laundry, showers, washrooms.

Customer services:

Post Office. Store– groceries, dairy treats, ice cream. bakery products. Frozen foods, produce, gifts, arts and crafts, books, snacks.
Restaurant/pub–meals available inside or on large sunny patio.
Boating groups book weekend events/rendez-vous. Playground. Picnic/barbecue facilities ashore. Arrange/book ahead in summer.
Nearby church. Road access walking or cycling.
Scuba diving arrangements and charters–ask marina for details.
Public pay phones ashore and at fuel dock.
Daily float plane service. Short ferry trip to Chemainus shops and famous murals. Fresh roasted coffee available on island. Enquire.

Entertainment.

Island arts and crafts, spinning, knitted goods.
Horseshoe pit, satellite TV. Darts.

Adjacent facilities:

Excellent bed & breakfast accommodations nearby.

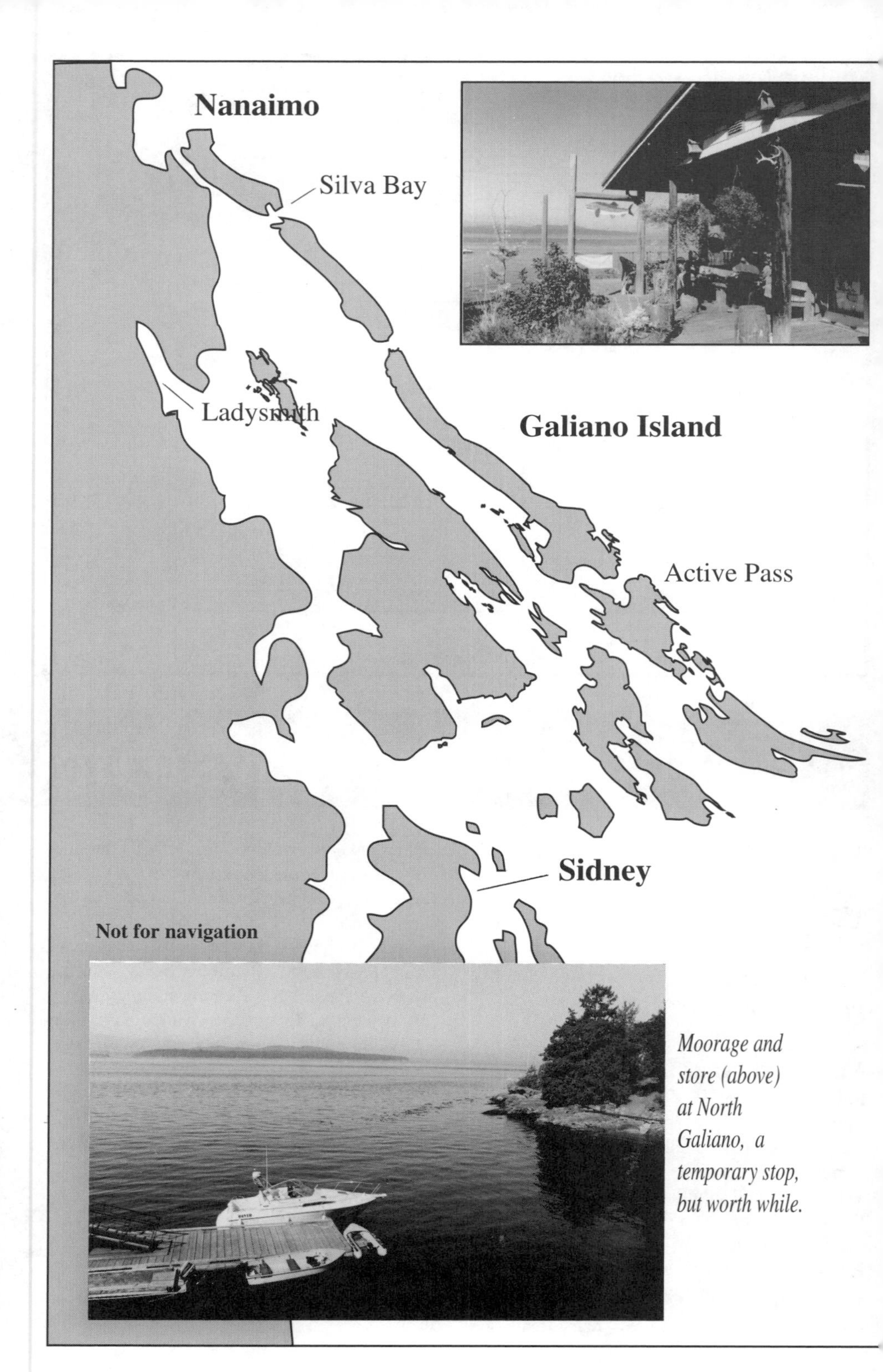

Moorage and store (above) at North Galiano, a temporary stop, but worth while.

Galiano Island

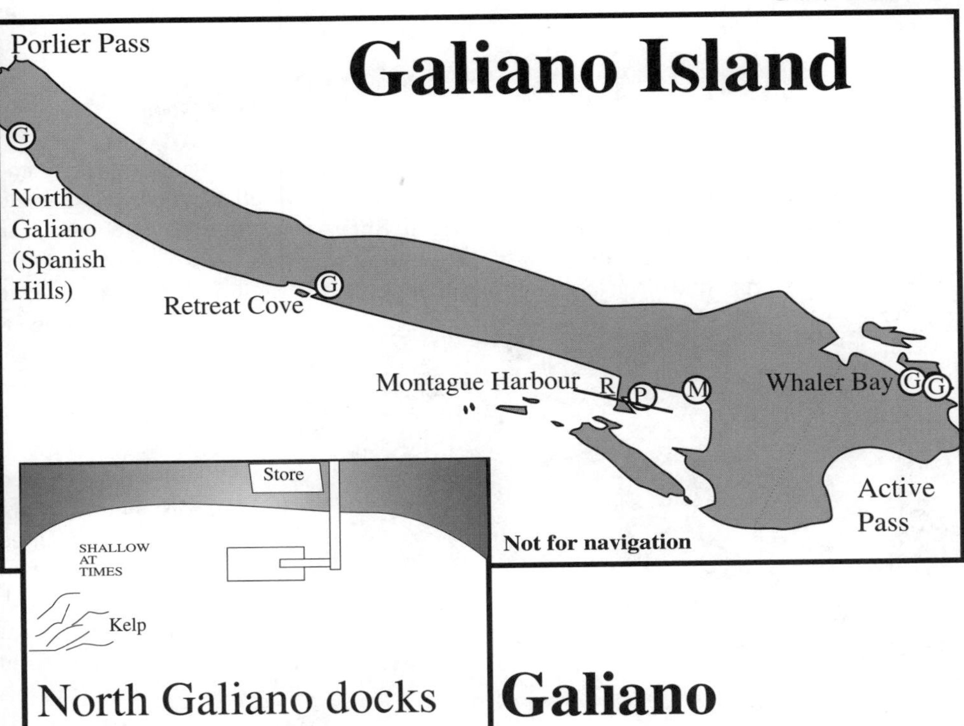

North Galiano docks
Spanish Hills grocery

North Galiano,
Galiano Island
(Spanish Hills)
Fisheries & Oceans dock
Phone 539-2352
Chart 3310, 3443, 3463
Manager • Float length 12 m
Public phone ashore •
Adjacent deli–Spanish Hills Store.

Retreat Cove,
Galiano Island.
Fisheries & Oceans dock
Phone 539-2611
Chart 3310, 3442, 3463
Manager • Float length 24 m

Montague Harbour,
Galiano Island
Transport Canada dock
Chart 3310, 3473, 3462
Manager • Float length 50 m
Adjacent marine park.

Galiano

Montague Harbour Marina

Bob and Rosemary Walker
RR #1 Galiano Island, BC.
V0N 1P0
Phone: (604) 539-5733 Fax 539-2010

Marina services:

Fuel: Gas. Diesel.
Marine supplies. Fishing licences, charts, bait, ice. Marine repairs available.
Transient and permanent moorage.
Water. Power: 30, 15 amp.

Customer services:

Store–Local fresh produce, gift shop, island arts and crafts, books, charts, fishing licences, ice, bait and tackle. meals–light fare.
Expresso bar–sundeck. Sea kayak float.
Road access walking or cycling.
Scuba diving good in Active Pass and nearby reefs. Use charter services. Public pay phone .

Adjacent facilities:

Marine park at Montague Harbour. Mooring buoys and dock. Extensive walks and camp ground, beaches and picnic facilities.

Montague Harbour

Montague Harbour can be quite a busy anchorage in the summertime and although there are numerous mooring buoys as well as a fairly large dock, finding space to tie up can be difficult. But whether you take your chances on moorage in season or visit Montague out of season you will find it a worthwhile place to spend some time. Located near the south end of Galiano Island, Montague opens onto Trincomali Channel and offers a safe haven for boats in all weather conditions. The odd violent storm has caused some discomfort at anchor in Montague but no known dangerous situations have been recorded. The main dock at Montague Harbour is in the waters of the provincial marine park and is operated and maintained by the Parks Department. Moorage is charged for tying up overnight at the dock or on a mooring buoy. Access to the park is from the dock, which provides access to a delightful walk along the beaches or shoreline and the adjacent island. Views up Trincomali are spectacular in sunny weather and many people who have come by road and ferry to camp in the campgrounds also enjoy the scenery and the walking paths.

Fishing in Active Pass is excellent but beware of the ferry traffic. It is illegal to impede the passage of a large vessel underway in designated traffic lanes, and plain foolish too. Watching wildlife in and around the pass, at Montague and across Trincomali in the inlets and bays of Prevost have been a favourite activity of mine and many of our boating friends for many years. Look for eagles, cormorants and river otters.

Other places of interest, moorage and anchorages near Montague include Annette Inlet and Glenthorne Pass at Prevost Island, Long Harbour and Ganges on Salt Spring Island and Whaler Bay on the other side of Galiano from Montague. Prevost Island provides excellent anchoring in shallow water and sheltered coves. Annette Inlet is a large shallow inlet that can accommodate a large number of boats while Glenthorne Pass has a small bay at the end of a narrow passage which will handle several boats swinging at anchor. The passage itself was used at one time for anchoring to a greater extent than in recent times, however some permanently located crab traps and their attendant floats now deter boaters from mooring. The head of the inlet is the preferred anchorage.

Marine bars and bistros, pubs and inns on the waterfront are popular destinations. These at Bedwell (centre), Vesuvius and Active Pass are classic retreats.

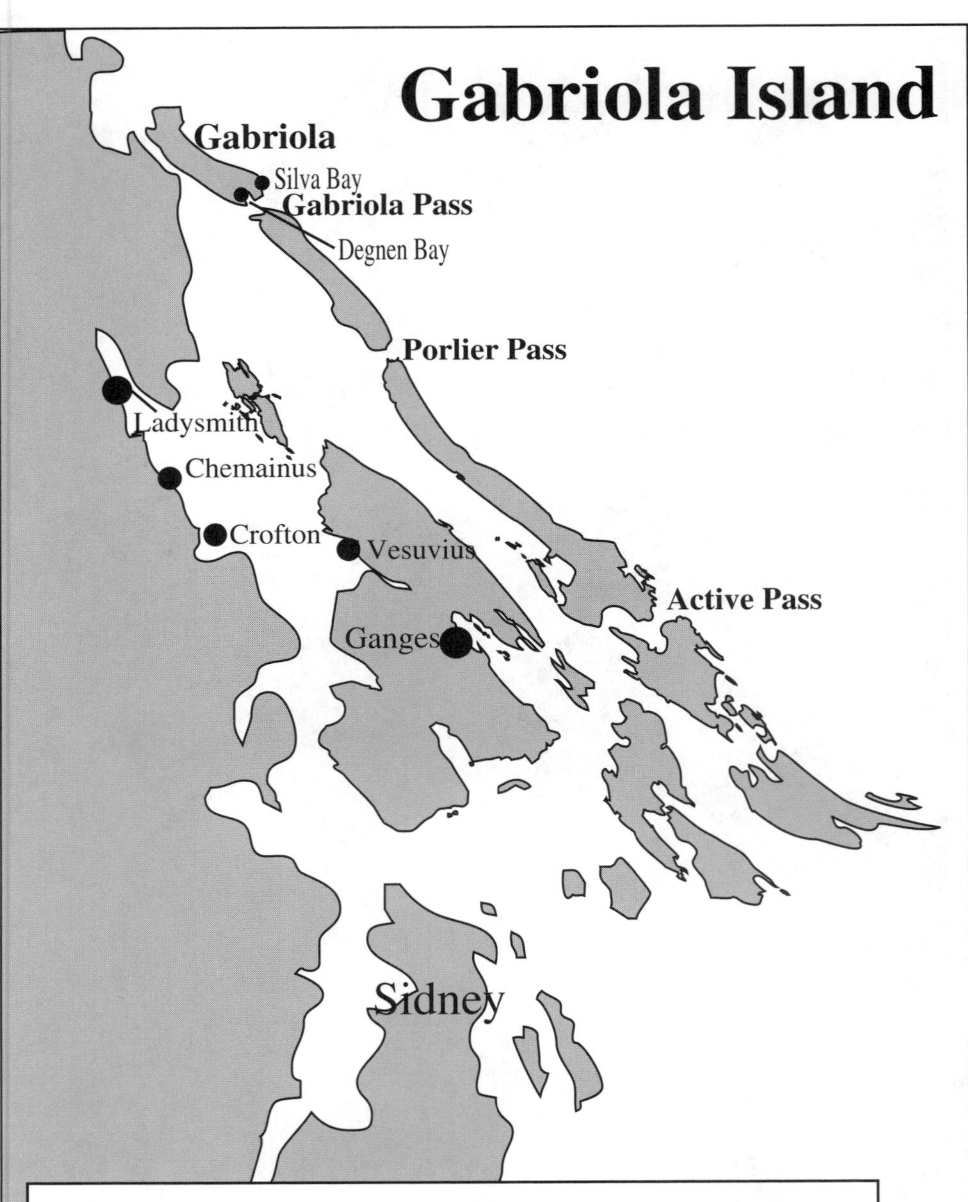

Constant changes have seen Silva Bay Marina open mostly but closed at the time of this writing. The docks may be used and a casual fee is collected but there is no power, water or fuel. These services are available at the two adjacent marinas. Anchoring in the bay is popular but beware of strong northerlies or north-westerlies that tend to howl into the bay at times causing the need for a watch during the night and anchors to drag. Fishing at nearby Thrasher Rock keeps the bay busy throughout summer and quite popular during other months.

Not for navigation

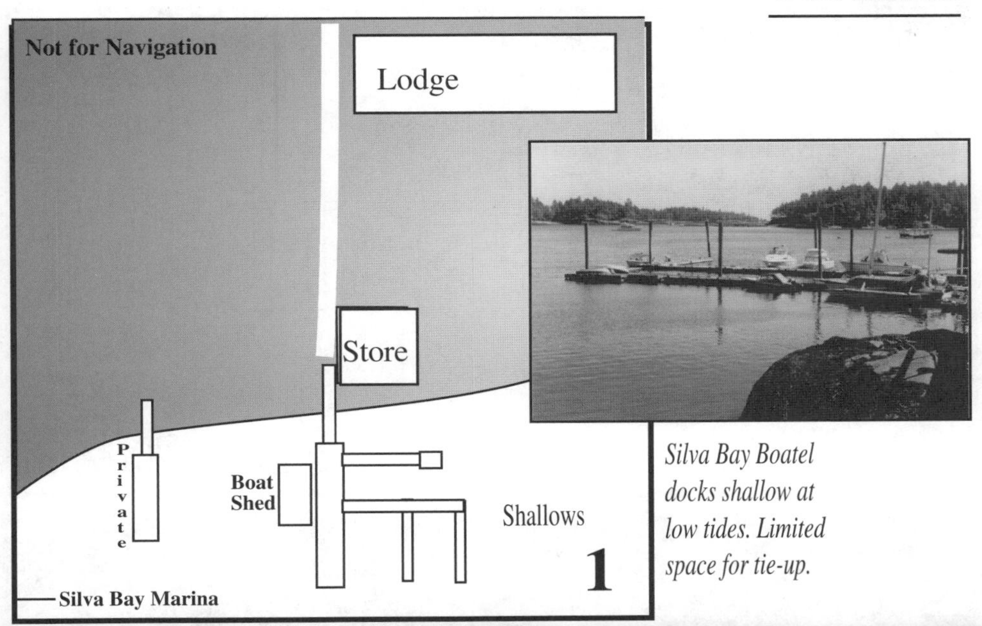

Silva Bay Boatel docks shallow at low tides. Limited space for tie-up.

Silva Bay Boatel

Silva Bay Boatel

Lou and Audrey Leloupe
Silva Bay, Gabriola, BC,
V0R 1X0
Phone : (604) 247-9351

Marina services:

Moorage (limited–mostly small boats).

Customer services:

Grocery store. Fishing licences, bait, tackle, some hardware. Ice, propane. Head depot.

Chart 3457, 3310.

Walking road access.
Good scuba diving in nearby locations.
Public pay phone.

Entertainment.

Fishing charters can be arranged.

Adjacent facilities:

Accommodation in motel. Self-contained kitchenette suites–7 units.

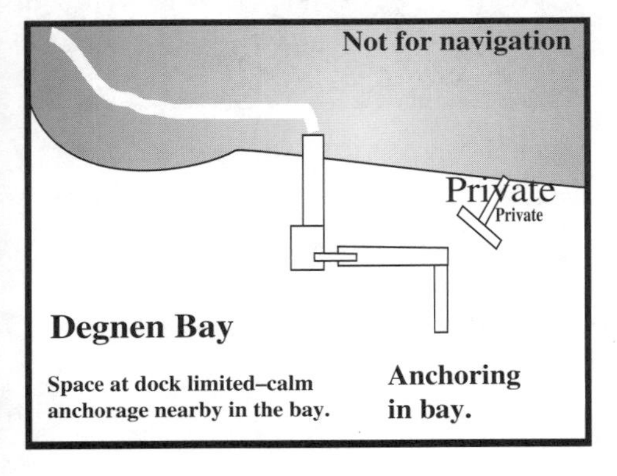

Degnen Bay, Gabriola

Island public dock.
Fisheries & Oceans dock
758-8058
Chart 3310, 3463, 3475
Float length 60 m
Garbage • Lights • Power • Public phone •
Washrooms • Showers •

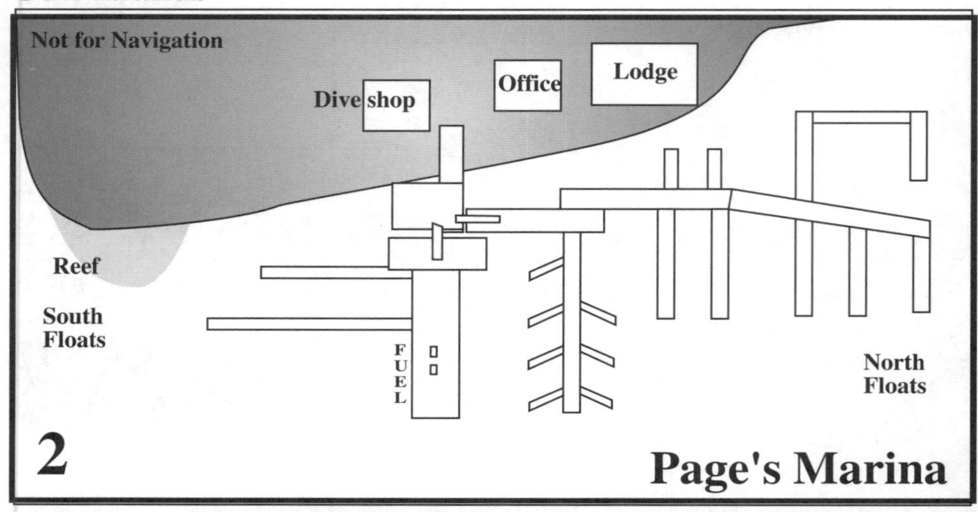

Page's Marina

Page's Marina dock has a large area and easy docking. Located at the end of the passage inside Sear Island. Watch depths at low tide and use a chart when navigating.
Page's has books and art at the office ashore.

Page's Marina

Ted and Phyllis Reeve
Site 30 RR #2, Gabriola, BC, V0R 1X0
Phone: (604) 247-8931
Chart 3475, 3310.

Marina services:

Fuel: Gas. Diesel. outboard oil.
Moorage mostly to 30 feet, some larger.
Water at dock. Limited supply.
Power 15 amp.

Customer services:

Rental cottages. Picnic and campground. Office/store has art, books, etc.
Showers, laundry, washrooms.
Walking road access.
Good scuba diving in nearby locations. Dive shop ashore, rentals, air fills. (Nick Small).
Mobile repairs, service, available.
Public pay phone.

Entertainment.

Fishing charters can be arranged.

Adjacent facilities: Grocery store at Silva Bay Boatel. Fresh fish store.

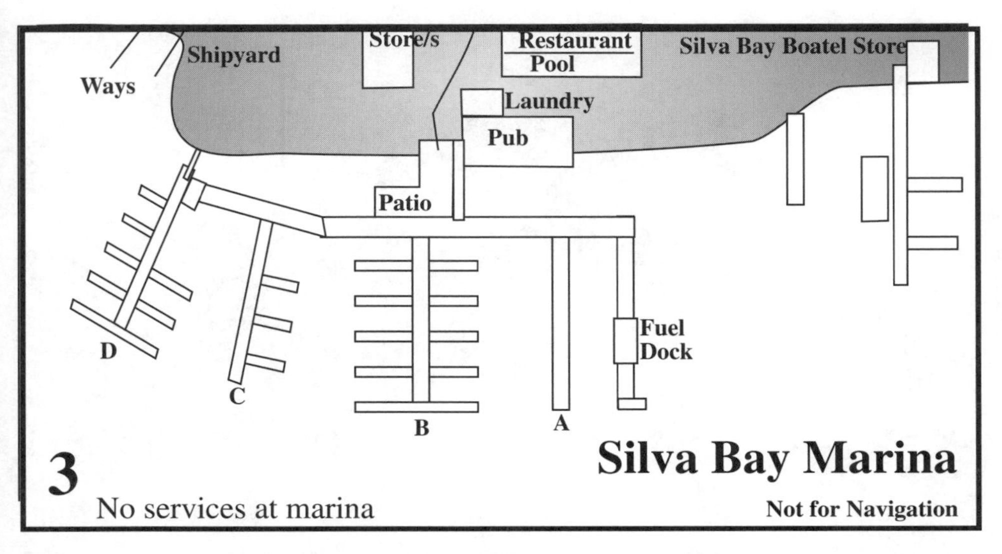
Ways
Shipyard
Store/s
Restaurant
Pool
Silva Bay Boatel Store
Laundry
Pub
Patio
Fuel
Dock
D
C
B
A
3
Silva Bay Marina
No services at marina
Not for Navigation

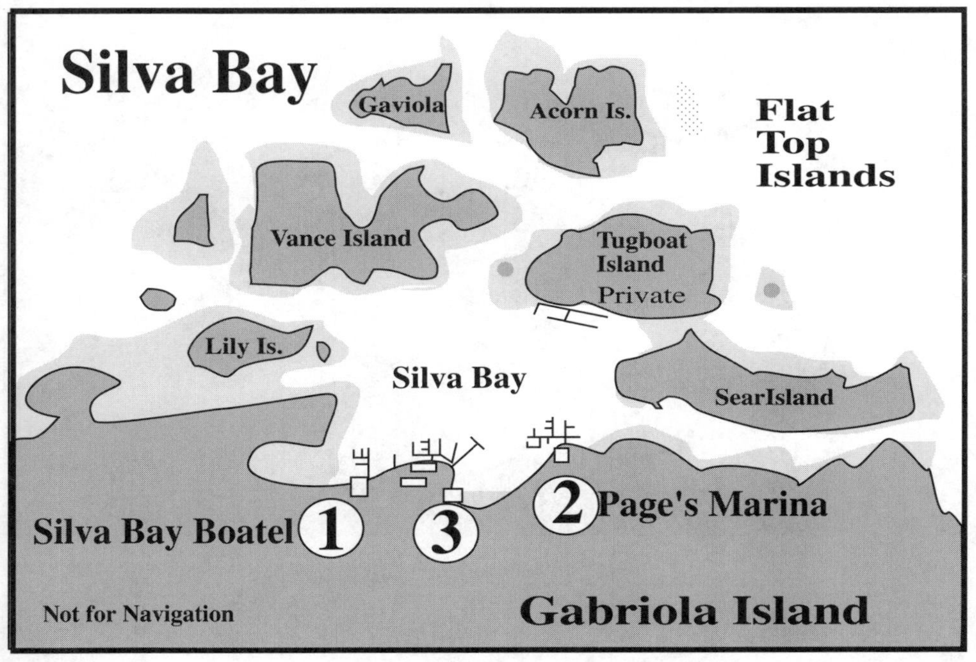
Silva Bay
Gaviola
Acorn Is.
Flat
Top
Islands
Vance Island
Tugboat
Island
Private
Lily Is.
Silva Bay
SearIsland
Silva Bay Boatel
1
3
2
Page's Marina
Not for Navigation
Gabriola Island

Notes:

The Dinghy Dock Pub at Protection Island is a popular stop. The channel inside Newcastle Island has numerous facilities. Newcastle Marine Park docks.

Nanaimo

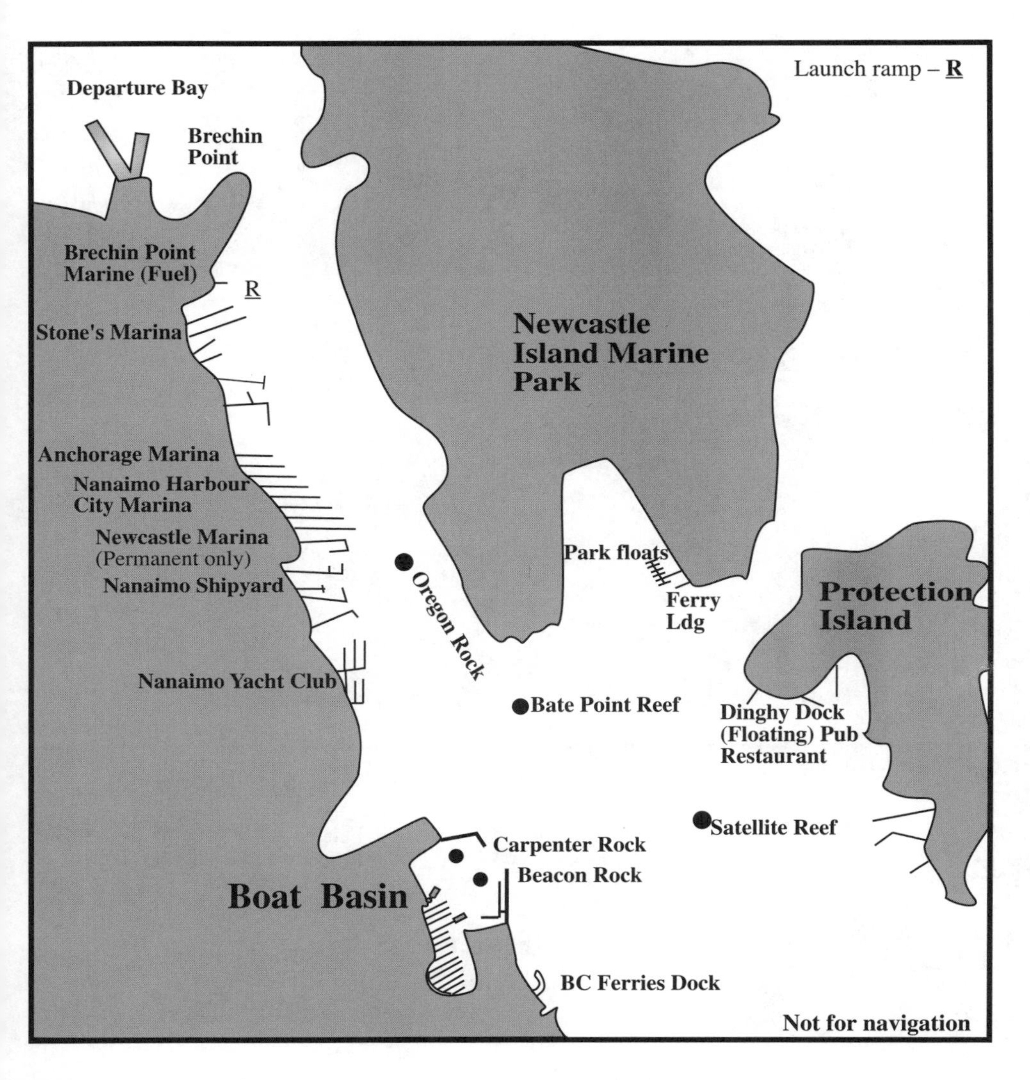

Nanaimo and its nearby islands.

Development of the city of Nanaimo has been fast and furious in recent years. Marinas and docks are plentiful with several having been upgraded substantially. The waterfront has undergone a massive face lift and new restaurants and public areas have evolved. There is a regular ferry service between Newcastle Island Marine Park and Nanaimo and another that serves the famous Dinghy Dock Pub on Protection Island. Their docks accommodate boats but space ashore is shared with the non-boating public.

Anchored boats between Protection Island and Newcastle. Ferry landing in foreground. A fish boat cruises slowly down the channel. No wake speeds are enforced. Mind the shallows in mid channel marked by a piling with a sign indicating correct passage.

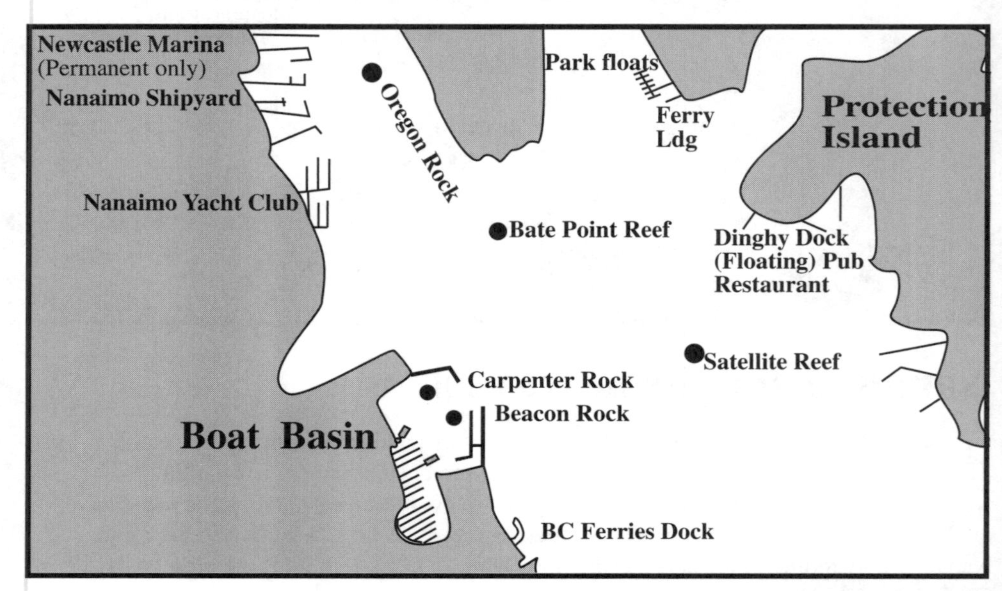

Not for navigation

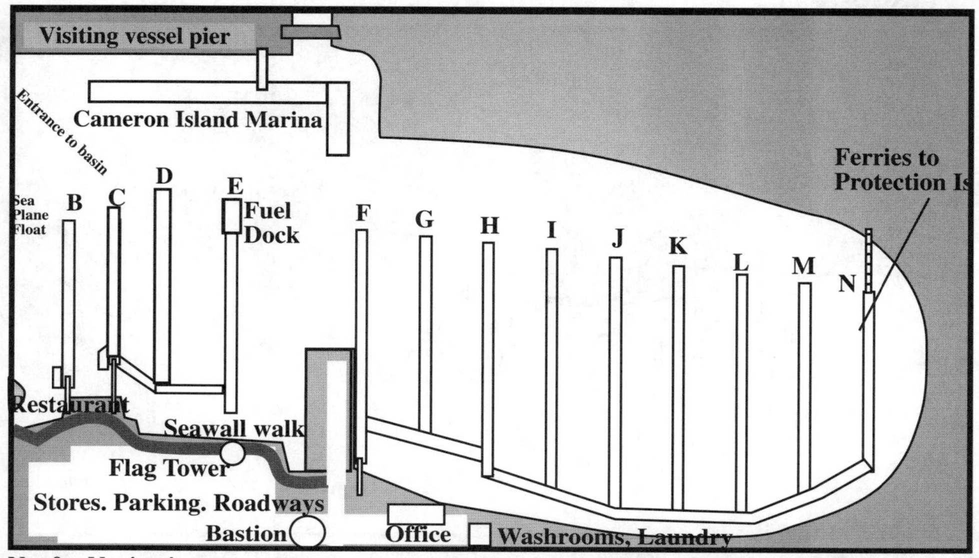

Not for Navigation

Chart 3310, 3463, 3457/8 VHF 67

Nanaimo Boat Basin

Nanaimo Boat Basin

Dick Nickerson
Port of Nanaimo, BC,
Wharfinger (604) 754-5053

Hazard: When proceeding past Oregon Rock use passage on Newcastle Island side, indicated by sign on mid-channel marker. Consult your chart.

Marina services:

Fuel, Petro Canada: Gas, diesel, mixed gas, ice. Service available.
Moorage. Large civic marina with pleasure boat moorage in summer. In winter docks are heavily used by fishermen. Reservations taken for new 600 foot floating breakwater pier for large vessels and adjacent Cameron Island Marina (phone (604) 755-1216 June to August). Hydraulic crane to 500 kg.
Water at dock. **Power**: 15, 20, 30 amp. Also 50 and 100 amp.
Laundry, showers, washrooms.
Sani-station pump out.

Customer services:

Customs/phone 24 hour service.
Downtown Nanaimo at doorstep of marina.
Road access walking or cycling or vehicle rentals. Public pay phones.
Daily float plane service.

Entertainment.

From restaurants, pubs and theatres to arts and crafts exhibits, stores and galleries. Bathtub race every July. Many festivals and activities.

Adjacent facilities:

Walkway, plaza and shops. Shipyards, ways, all marine services. Lighthouse Bistro/Pub. Marinas. Newcastle Island Marine Park –docks, walking trails, camping, picnics, (see Marine Parks on page 74).
BC Ferries to mainland nearby. Walk on ferries to Newcastle or Protection Islands. Protection Island: Dinghy Dock pub. Anchor off and row to dock. Seats about 80 inside and on patio.

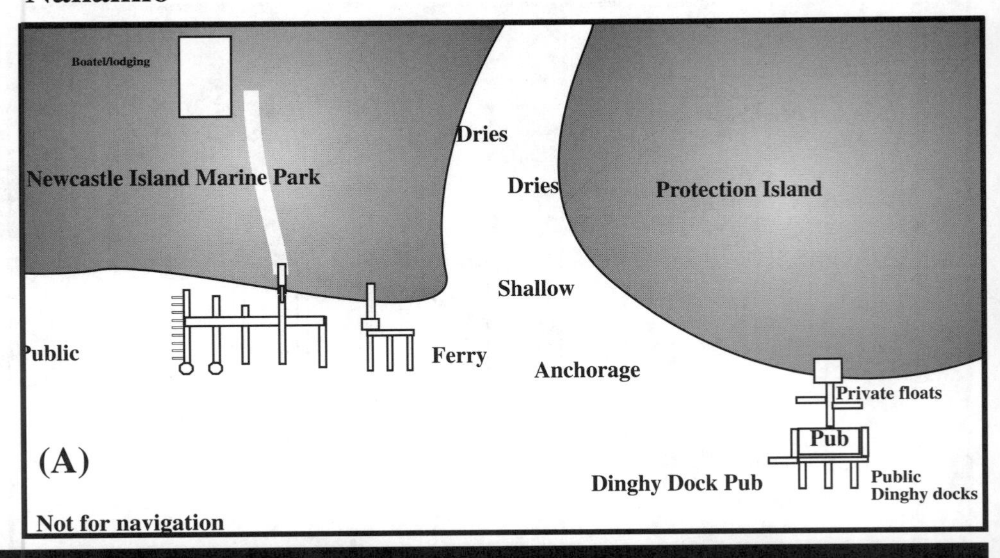

Dinghy Dock Pub

Dinghy Dock Floating Marine Pub

Box 771, Nanaimo, #8 Pirate's Lane,
Nanaimo, BC. V9R 5M2
Phone: (604) 753-2373
Hilda and Bob Banerd
Charts 3457/8 3310, 3463. Call Dinghy Dock Pub on VHF 18A.

Marina Services

Moorage for overnight guests on a limited basis (as space allows). Tie up space for restaurant/pub.

Laundry, Showers. Fine dining. Walking on Protection Island. More moorage and anchoring at Newcastle Island.

Dinghy Dock Pub and Newcastle Island Marine Park (Map A)

The Dinghy Dock Pub has won awards for excellence. It makes a perfect lunch or dinner stop and a limited number of boats will be able to stay overnight. The pub is built on floats and has slips to accommodate eight to ten small to medium sized boats. It is best to anchor out and come to the pub by dinghy. Or, if you are spending the night at Nanaimo take the ferry that leaves regularly from the Boat Basin. Facilities at the Dinghy Dock Pub include showers, laundry and washrooms.

Newcastle Island Marine Park is a short distance away and there are several slips for medium to larger sized boats as well as numerous slips for smaller boats and dinghies. Going ashore at Newcastle Island is a treat, providing lots of treed pathways for hiking, walking or cycling. An interpretive centre functions in summer for the use of students, groups and others interested in the use of the facilities.

The ferry between the Nanaimo Boat Basin and Protection Island leaves the docks hourly, 9:00 am to 11:00 pm.

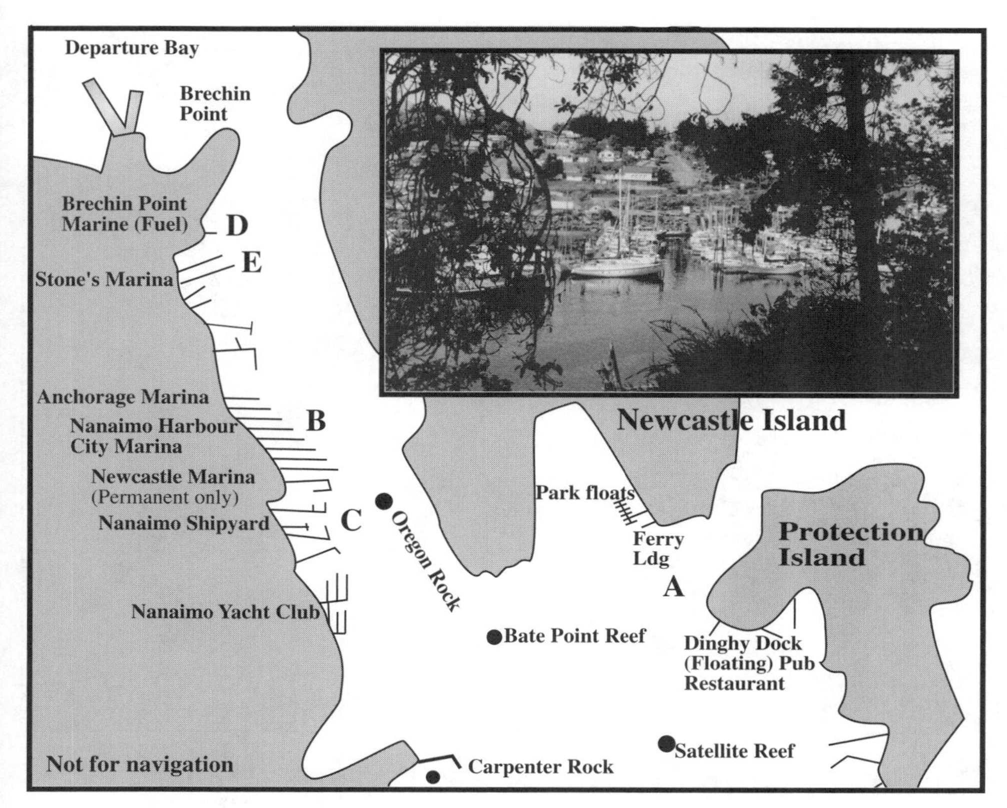

Inset: Nanaimo Harbour City Marina across from Newcastle Island.

Nanaimo Harbour City Marina (B)

Ron and Susan Mielke
1250 Stewart Avenue,
Nanaimo, BC., V9S 4C9
Phone: (604) 754-2732 Fax: 754-7140
Chart 3310, 3463, 3457/8

Hazard: Enter Nanaimo via south of Protection Island.
From the north/Departure Bay watch correct channel when passing the mid channel rock. Passage on Newcastle Island side.

Marina services:

Moorage. Mostly permanent. Haulouts. Repairs, welding. Boatyard. Travel lift.
Water at dock. Ice.
Power at docks: 15, 20 amp
Showers, washrooms.

Customer services:

Downtown Nanaimo near marina. All facilities and services are available.
Road access walking or cycling or vehicle rentals.
Public pay phones.
Daily float plane service.

Entertainment.

From restaurants, pubs and theatres to arts and crafts exhibits, stores and galleries. Bathtub race every July.

Adjacent facilities:

Shipyards, all marine services.
Nanaimo Yacht Club reciprocal moorage.
Marinas.
Newcastle Island Marine Park; docks, walking trails, camping, picnics.
BC Ferries to Vancouver.
Ferry to Newcastle and Protection Island.

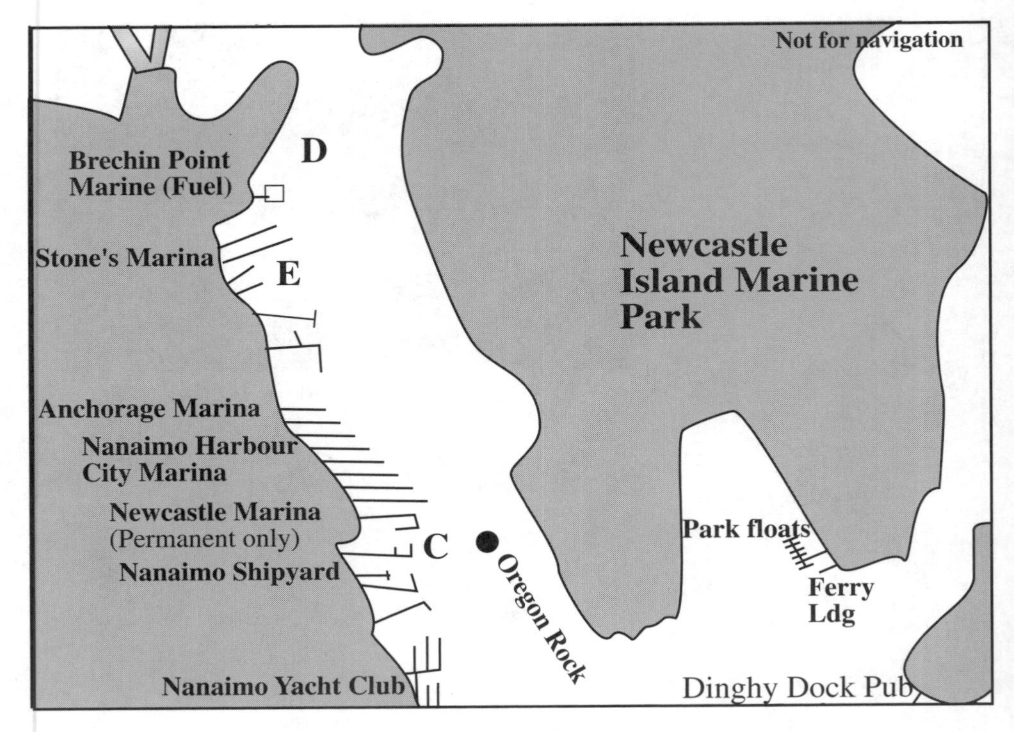

Nanaimo Shipyard (C)

1040 Stewart Avenue
Nanaimo, BC., V9S 4C9
Phone: (604) 753-1151
Fax: (604) 753-2235
Chart 3310, 3463, 3457/8

Hazard: Enter Nanaimo via south of Protection Island. From the north/Departure Bay: use correct channel when passing the mid channel rock.
Passage on Newcastle Island side.

Marina services:

Moorage. Haulouts. Repairs. Vessels to 200 feet.
Chandlery Phone: (753-1244): All boating supplies.
Water at dock.
Power at docks.

Customer services:

Downtown Nanaimo near marina. All facilities and services are available.
Road access walking or cycling.
Vehicle rentals.
Daily float plane service nearby.

Entertainment.

From restaurants, pubs and theatres to arts and crafts exhibits, stores and galleries at Nanaimo. Bathtub race every July.

Adjacent facilities:

Shipyards, all marine services.
Nanaimo Yacht Club reciprocal moorage.
Marinas.
Newcastle Island Marine Park; docks, walking trails, camping, picnics.
BC Ferries to Vancouver.
Ferry to Newcastle Island and Protection Island.

Brechin Point Marina

(D) North of main facilities

Customs, Seaplanes,
Fuel dock:
Diesel, gas, oils, propane.

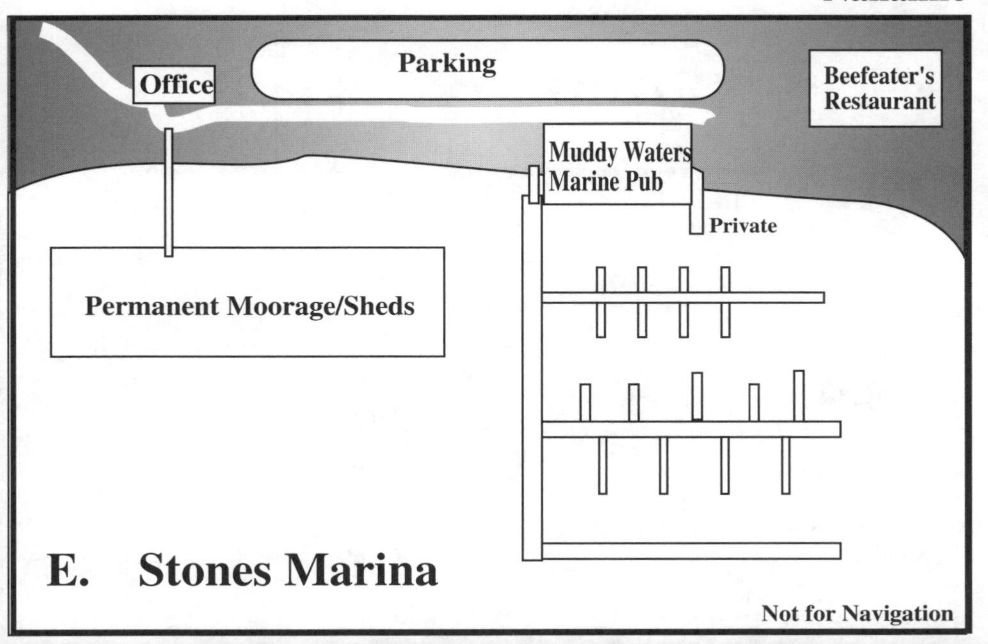

Stones Marina & RV Park

Stones Marina & RV Park. (E)

Mark Stone
1690 Stewart Ave., Nanaimo, BC.
V0N 2H0
Phone: (604)753-4232
Chart 3310, 3463, 3457/8
Location: next to Seaquarium, and near BC Ferries. **Launch ramp adjacent.**

Marina services:

Moorage. Transient in summer months.
Power: 15, 30 amp
Water at dock.

Customer services:

Ice. Laundry, showers, washrooms
Pay phone. Garbage disposal. Store. Tackle, fishing licences, bait. Mobile LPG service. Marine sales. **Pub and restaurant.**
Walking: Road access walking or cycling.

Stones Marina on the left with its pub ashore. Facilities in foreground are adjacent to former public market–now the Seaquarium.

Entertainment.

Nearby access to ferries to Newcastle and Protection Islands.

Adjacent facilities:

Muddy Waters Pub, restaurant and RV Park. Brechin Point Marina fuel dock and sea-plane float–nearby.

Vancouver Area

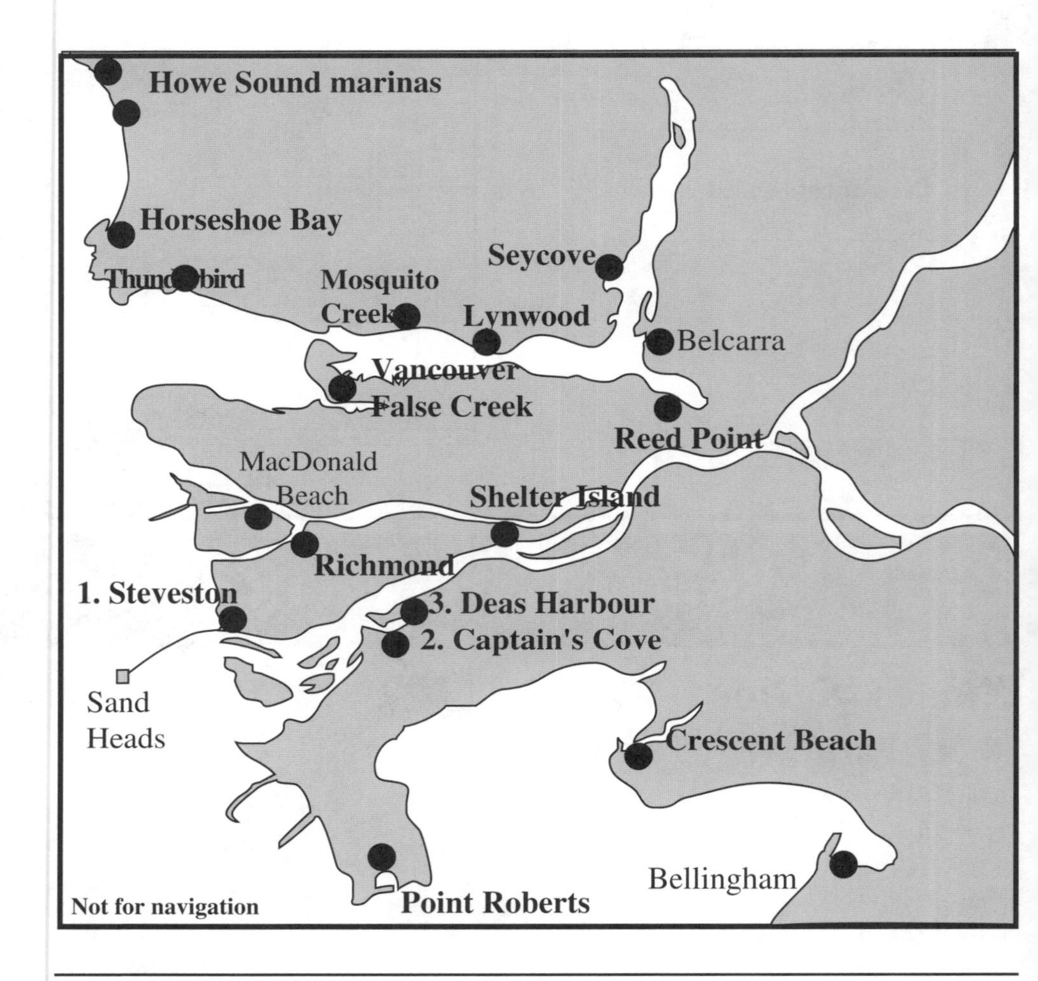

Marinas in the Greater Vancouver area do offer moorage for overnight customers. However, most of them are dedicated to providing permanent moorage and although some have many slips they usually can allocate space only as needed during summer when many of their customers' boats are away. Because of the river estuary and large delta making up most of the area, marinas are located at some off the beaten track locations, such as up the Fraser River. Boat operators in transit from southern ports to places such as the Sunshine Coast and Desolation Sound rarely want to take the time to deviate from their course to an up river marina just for an overnight stop. So there should be some purpose in cruising up the river, either the main arm of the Fraser or the north arm. A fast powerboat will have no trouble accessing some up-river marinas, but slower boats looking simply for an overnight mooring should consider Vancouver's downtown area. There are many attractions down town but consider the farther reaches

1. Steveston.

Near the mouth of the Fraser River.
Fisheries & Oceans dock Gulf of Georgia
Phone 271-6808
Chart 3490, 3601, 3463
Manager • Float length 778 m
Breakwater • Grid • Garbage • Waste oil disposal • Parking • Water • Lights • Power • Public phone ashore • Washrooms • Showers •
Adjacent city restaurants, shops, marine stores, chandleries, repair facilities. Auxiliary Coast Guard. Fuel at three locations
Additional public docks (Paramount) for fishing and commercial vessels.

Crescent Beach

Fisheries & Oceans dock
Phone 536-3403
Chart 3463
Manager • Float length 12 m
Lights •

2. Captain's Cove Marina

Laura Reynolds
6100 Ferry Road, Ladner, BC. V4K 3M9
Phone: (604) 946-1244

Chart 3463

Fresh water moorage at visitor's dock, Water, power. **Fuel:** gas, diesel, engine and outboard oils. Showers, laundry, washrooms. Public phones. Rusty Anchor Pub adjacent. Travel lift 30 ton, repairs, service, storage and workyard, power wash, painting. Launch ramp adjacent.

3. Deas Harbour Marina

Stu Stewart-David
5825 60th Ave, Ladner, BC. V4K 3N3
Phone (604) 946-1251

Chart 3463

Limited moorage (mostly permanent). Some water, power available–15 amp. Public phones. Chandlery , repairs, service. Fiddler's Green restaurant and marine pub. Low bridge beyond Captain's Cove Marina 14' clearance at medium high tide.

---

of the Fraser River. One can cruise all the way up to the Albion Ferry Crossing safely by just staying in mid channel most of the way. It is possible to reach Mission or farther up river with the help of a river pilot. Or turn off on the Pitt River and enjoy a splendid run into Pitt Lake. There is fuel on the Pitt River at **Pitt Meadows Marina** (and launch ramp) at the confluence of Pitt River and the Alouette River.

Entering the Fraser River is safe provided you do so when winds are relatively calm and the tide is right. At about maximum low tide with a northwesterly wind you are well advised to wait. If you are crossing from Active Pass or Porlier, or coming up from the States it is best to not leave the shelter of the closest anchorage or moorage at those spots until the wind drops and the tide slackens. Approaching high tide in calm to light winds is the best time to enter the river. Beware of the shallows off the mouth of the river, especially if you do find yourself running into some wind and waves. It is well marked but the

Crescent Beach Marina (1967) Ltd.

B.J. Chapman
12555 Crescent Road, Surrey,
BC. V4A 2V4
Phone (604) 538-9666 Fax 538-6367
Chart 3463. See map on page 126.
Entrance: Follow markers in long channel through Boundary Bay, using red right returning. Moorage (phone for reservations). Water, power 15 amp. Washrooms, public phones. Fuel: gas, diesel. Ice. Chandlery, bait, fishing supplies. Haulout up to 45' power, 30' sail. Launch ramp.

4. Shelter Island

Terry McPhail
120–6911 Graybar, Richmond,
BC. V6W 1H3
Phone: (604) 270-6272 Fax: 273-6282
Chart 3463 3490
Fresh water moorage (permanent), water, power. Showers, laundry, washrooms. Public phones. Marine hardware, repairs, service. Two travel lifts to 150 tons–vessels to over 130', 30' beam. Workyard for up to 500 boats. Pub, beer and wine store, restaurant adjacent.

5. Bridgepoint Marina

Gary Cross
8831 River Road, Richmond,
BC. V6X 1Y6
Phone (604) 273-8560 Fax: 231-8081
Chart 3490
Fresh water moorage, transient welcome. Water, power, showers, laundry, washrooms. Public phones. Pub, restaurant on site. Sales adjacent. Fuel dock nearby.

6. Delta Vancouver Airport Hotel Marina

Bob Dunne
3500 Cessna Drive, Richmond,
BC. V7B 1C7
Phone: (604) 278-1241 Hotel & Marina
Phone: (604) 273-4211 Delta Charters
Chart 3490
Transient moorage. Water, power.
Public phones. Hotel facilities and services. Restaurant.
Near Richmond city facilities, restaurants and shopping centres.

---

shallows actually extend somewhat beyond the markers, especially around the beacon to the south of the lightship.

Stopping at Steveston is a treat if you find moorage and go ashore. There the variety of shops, cafes and restaurants will keep you busy for hours. However, there is extremely limited moorage for pleasure craft when the fishing fleet is in. One dock has been allocated for pleasure boat tie up, and that is at the outside of the harbour after you pass the two first fuel docks. Other moorage is available by rafting up to a fish boat on the inside of that dock. The harbourmaster can be called at 271-6807 and if there is alternative moorage he will advise you. This is a major commercial port and a good place to fuel up.

Going farther up the river there is Captain's Cove for haulouts, repairs and service as well as some overnight moorage, fuel, ice and a pub, The Rusty Anchor, which serves good meals seven days a week. Beyond Captain's Cove is Deas Harbour beyond the low bridge of Highway 99. Deas Harbour boasts a splendid pub and restaurant at Fiddler's Green with patio service. Another good establishment is the Maritime Restaurant at Shelter Island a little farther up river. Here the currents can be quite strong and tie-up

7. Vancouver Marina

John Short
8331 River Road, Richmond,
BC. V6X 1Y1
Phone: (604) 278-9787
Chart 3490
No transient moorage. Permanent up to 45' open, 38' covered, Water, power. **Fuel:** gas, diesel, stove oil, engine and outboard oils. Public phones. Repairs, service. Restaurant. Near Richmond city facilities, restaurants.

8. Skyline Marina

Dave Shirley
8031 River Road, Richmond,
BC. V6X 1X8
Phone: (604) 273-3977
Chart 3490
Shipwrights. Some transient moorage, water, power–15 amp. Fuel (nearby): gas, diesel, stove oil, engine and outboard oils. Public phones. Repairs, service, chandlery nearby. Nearby Richmond city facilities, restaurants.

● Quayside Marina

900 Quayside Drive,
New Westminster. V3M 6G1
Phone (604) 520-1776
Fax (604) 520-5645
Limited visitor moorage. **Water. Power.**
Hotel, restaurant, public market.

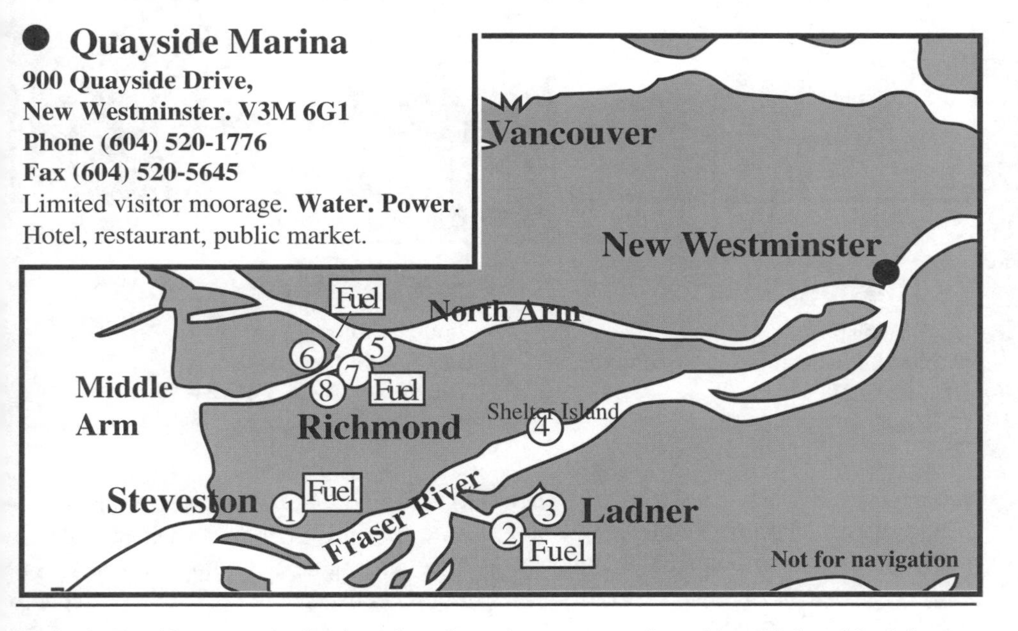

limited. But if you need a haulout for a large boat or a workyard in which to block it up Shelter Island can provide the necessary facilities.

You could cruise on to New Westminster and back out to the Strait of Georgia by going down the north arm of the Fraser. Part way down you will come to Richmond's marinas just after passing under Knight Street bridge and Oak Street bridge. Fuel is available at Vancouver Marina just beyond the swivel bridge on the Middle Arm. There is another fuel dock as you continue down the river, directly beneath the newer Arthur Laing bridge.

A stop worth considering for a lunch hour or pleasant day in the sun is MacDonald slough which opens to the south as you pass down-river of MacDonald Beach. It is a shallow slough but with a fairly constant and adequate depth. There are log booms to tie up alongside and one can observe a variety of water fowl that inhabit the area. At the mouth of the North Arm is a tiny cove called Boat Basin or Coward's Cove. It is where mariners sometimes sit and wait for a change in conditions before venturing out into the Strait. Here again, log booms serve for tying up, or it is safe to anchor. The breakwater and nearby Wreck Beach are popular among naturalists.

Vancouver area

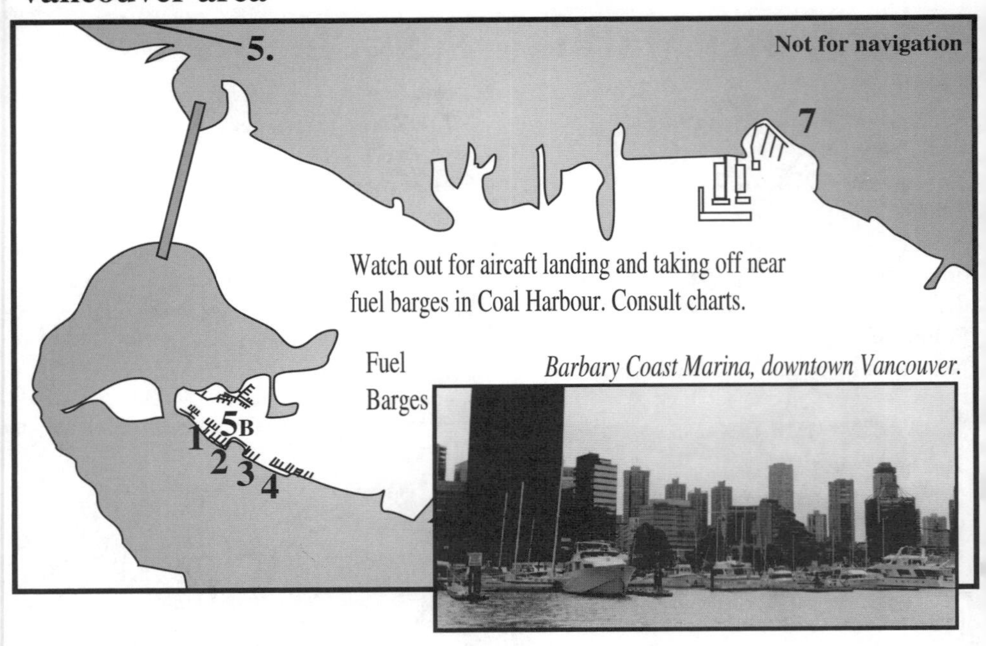

Barbary Coast Marina, downtown Vancouver.

1 Harbour Ferries

Cindi Armstrong
#1 North foot Denman, Vancouver, BC., V6G 2W9
Phone: (604) 687-9558

Moorage, water, power 15, 20, 30 amp. Fuel (nearby): gas, diesel, stove oil, engine and outboard oils. Washrooms. Public phones. Chandlery, repairs, service, nearby. Located next to Stanley Park and charter vessel basin.

2 Westin Bayshore Marina

Jane Boddy
1601 West Georgia, Vancouver, BC. V6G 2V4
Phone: (604) 682-3377

Moorage to approx 100 feet, Water, power 30, 50 amp. Fuel (nearby): gas, diesel, stove oil, engine and outboard oils. Hotel facilities incl: showers, laundry, washrooms, health club, spa, pool. Public phones. Chandlery, repairs, service, nearby.
Near city centre, restaurants, facilities.

3 Coal Harbour Marina

John Nicholls
Box 5. 466 Cardero, Vancouver, BC, V6G 2W6
Phone: (604) 682-6841 Fax: 682-3834

Moorage. Cable vision. Water, power 30 amp 50 amp. Fuel (nearby): gas, diesel, stove oil, engine and outboard oils. Washrooms. Public phones. Chandlery, repairs, service, nearby.

Nearby city centre, restaurants.

4 Barbary Coast Yacht Basin

Scott Hoffman
1601 West Georgia, Vancouver, BC, V6G 2W6
Phone: (604) 669-0088

Guest moorage as available, Water, power to all needs (20, 30, 60, 110, 220). Fuel (nearby): gas, diesel, stove oil, engine and outboard oils. Showers, laundry, washrooms.

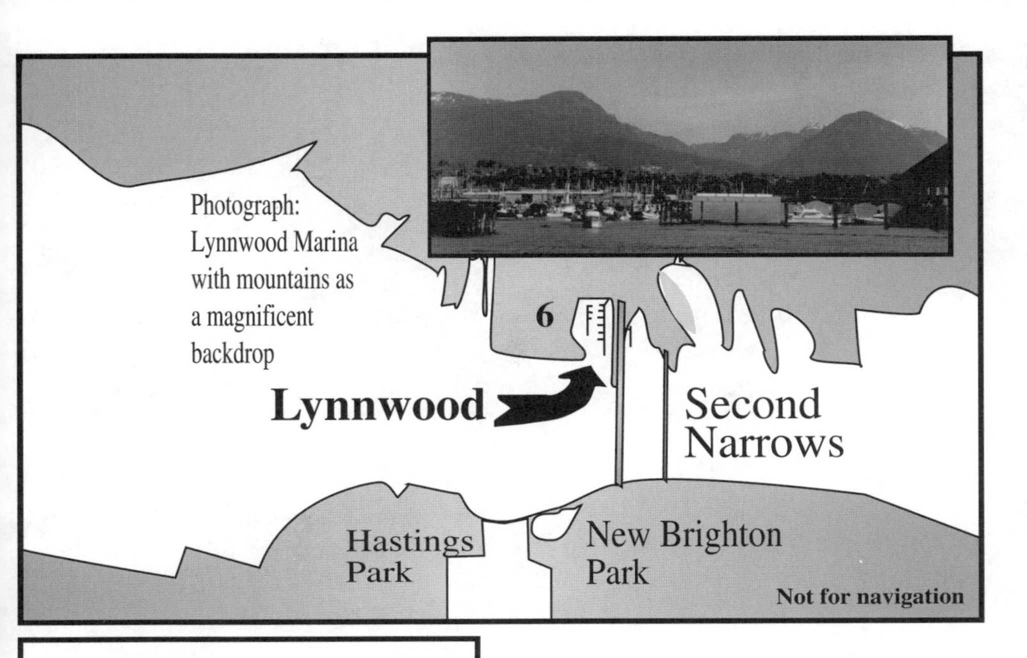

Use charts 3311, 3495

Public phones. Chandlery, repairs, service, nearby.
Nearby Vancouver centre, restaurants. Adjacent seaplane services.

5 Thunderbird Marina

5776 Marine Drive, West Vancouver, BC, V7W 2S2
Phone: (604) 921-7434
Charts 3311, 3534, 3481

Limited moorage, water, power. Fuel dock (nearby): gas, diesel, stove oil, engine and outboard oils. Public phones. Marine store, tackle, bait, fishing licences, repairs, service. 25 ton travel lift for boats to 51 feet. Workyard, storage.
Also downtown Vancouver moorage: **(5B) Bayshore West Marina**. Guest moorage, water, power, phones. Near hotel and downtown amenities.
Near Stanley park.

6 Lynnwood Marina

Roger Gibson
1681 Columbia, North Vancouver, BC. V7J 1A5
Phone: (604) 985-1533

Moorage, water, power. Ice, bait, fishing tackle, licences. Washrooms. Public phones. Chandlery, repairs, service. Painting, storage and work yard, 60 ton travel lift to boats 70' by 18' size.
Restaurant. Services.

7 Mosquito Creek

Bill Williams
Ft Forbes Ave., North Vancouver, BC. V7L 4J5
Phone: (604) 987-4113

Moorage, water, power, fuel: gas, diesel. Washrooms. Public phones. Marine supplies, repairs, service. Crane. 35 ton travel lift.
Nearby North Vancouver centre, restaurants, all facilities.

Reed Point Marina, has fuel and will usually find a slip for overnight guests.

Pelican Bay Marina

Michael Jensen
1253 Johnston Vancouver, BC. V6H 3R9
Phone: (604) 683-7373 Dock: 682-7454

Chart 3311

Moorage, water, power. Showers, laundry, washrooms. Public phones. Hotel facilities available to moorage customers. Dining. Spa. TV cable, phone hookup.
Boat lift and all services available on Granville Island (685-6924) 15 ton capacity.

Heather Civic Marina

600 Stamps Landing,
Vancouver, BC.V5Z 3Z1
Phone (604) 874-2814

Chart 3311

Moorage (mostly permanent), water, power. Showers, laundry, washrooms. Public phones. Pub adjacent, restaurants nearby. City shops and facilities nearby. Park, water-front paths adjacent.
Boat lift.

In Vancouver you have the alternative of an overnight in False Creek or Burrard Inlet. False Creek offers limited transient moorage. The Granville Island Hotel is the best bet with all hotel facilities including spa and dining, phones and cable TV at your boat. On the other hand the government dock near the entrance is large and offers the basics, provided you can find room. If the fishing fleet is away and they usually are to a greater extent in summer months, you should have little difficulty finding a slip. On the north side of False Creek, near the entrance is the False Creek Yacht Club and opposite is Granville Island. If you find a spot to stop at the limited time dock, you will be able to enjoy the entertainment and fresh produce market. Restaurants and pubs, nearby stores and facilities offer a variety of activities and entertainment. There are mooring buoys east of Granville Island. These are designated for use only by visiting offshore cruising yachts–a reciprocal arrangment of the Blue Water Cruising Association.

In Burrard Inlet the marinas are obvious and easy to locate after rounding Brockton Point and passing the fuel barges. Call any one of them and you will find a place to moor for the night possibly longer and this will give you the opportunity to visit downtown Vancouver within easy walking distance.

However, if you wish to be away from the city, continue down Burrard Inlet and find your way to Indian Arm or Port Moody. At Port Moody Reed Point Marina will find you an overnight slip if you call ahead or pull into the fuel barge. If you prefer to anchor out overnight go up Indian Arm to Bedwell Bay and drop anchor. It's a sheltered anchorage and rarely do northerly winds disturb an overnight sleep, excepting in winter when the wind blows into the bay more frequently.

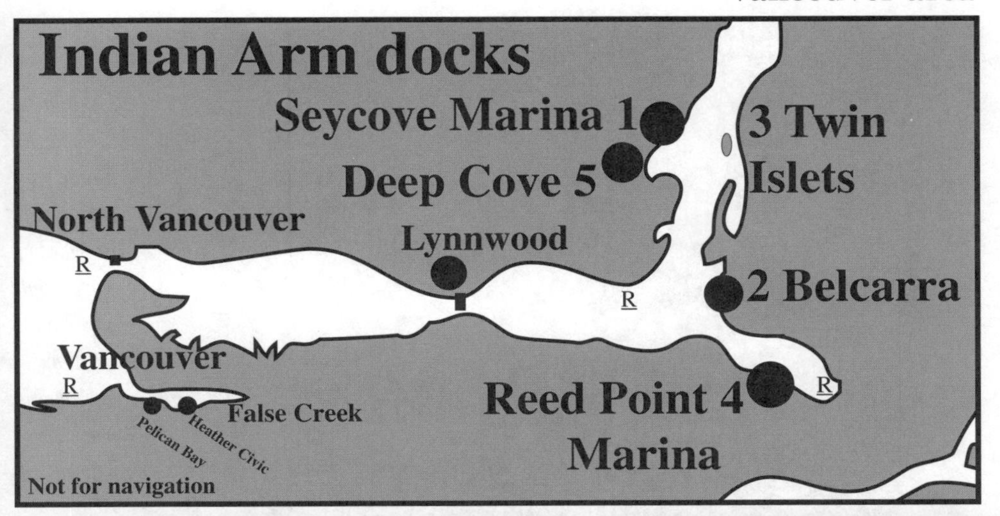

Indian Arm

1 Seycove Marina

K.J. Kim
2890 Panorama Drive, North Vancouver, BC. V7G 1V6
Phone (604) 929-1251

Chart 3495, 3435, 3311

Moorage to 70 feet, water, power 15 amp, fuel: gas, diesel. Washrooms. Public phones. Chandlery, mobile repairs, service.
Nearby Deep Cove village, restaurants.

2 Belcarra Park

Burrard Inlet
Indian Arm
Parks Board park and floats.
Small dock mostly used for recreational fishing. Kiosk serves snacks, light meals.

3 Twin Islands

Indian Arm

Boat dock (dinghy).
picnic sites water toilets hiking fishing scuba

4 Reed Point Marina

David Harris
850, Barnet Highway,
Port Moody, BC, V6H 1V6
Phone (604) 931-2477
Chart 3311, 3435
Marina services:
Fuel: Gas, diesel. Stove oil. Ice, water. Snacks. Bait, fishing licences. Overnight moorage, power 20 amps. 30 ton travel lift, Summer moorage for trailerable boats. Dry storage and work yard. Hamburger stand. Public phone, washrooms. Marine supplies, service repairs.
Yacht sales and service. Lee's Marine–sales, service.

5 Deep Cove,

Burrard Inlet Indian Arm
Transport Canada dock
Phone 757-9331
Chart 3311, 3495
Manager • Float length 44 m
Lights • Small village of Deep Cove has restaurants, groceries and other services.
Adjacent: Deep Cove Yacht Club.

The lightship at Sand Heads, unmanned it provides no wave height information. Caution is advised for mariners entering the river.

Steveston near the Fraser mouth is a sheltered stop but with very limited moorage. California sealions gather at the river mouth in March or April.

Crossing the Strait

If you are journeying from the Gulf Islands to Howe Sound or the Sunshine Coast, you will probably find Silva Bay your best point of departure, simply because of its relatively close proximity to Vancouver. The closest landfall across the Strait is the entrance to the north arm of the Fraser River at Point Grey. If you travel up the river you will find moorage and fuel at Richmond. Some swift currents in the river when the tide is falling can make manoeuvring at docks tricky so exercise caution. Tugs travelling up and down the channel cause large washes. Be cautious when crossing over them.

Farther up the river is the confluence of the north arm with the main arm of the Fraser and New Westminster. There are possible stops at New Westminster such as at the public market but the currents mostly keep boats from an easy docking and when you have docked there is no easy access ashore. But up the Fraser to Pitt River you pass under a very low bridge to Pitt Lake. If you have a smaller, fast boat and decide to do this trip check chart #3062 and ensure you can pass beneath the bridge. Mind the shallows and stick to the chart. Fuel is available at the confluence of the Pitt River and the Alhouette and the marina may be able to accommodate a small boat overnight. There are pleasant temporary anchorages in Pitt Lake and one marina located on the south western shore. Winds come up suddenly and the lake can be quite uncomfortable if you are anchored in the wrong place.

Top: A serene waterway up the Fraser at Ladner. Above: The coast guard hovercraft running along the Fraser River.

Had you entered the Fraser via the main arm you would have passed the Sandheads Lightship. Hopefully you monitored the weather and checked the tides, for a passage of the river mouth at the wrong time can be dangerous.

From Silva Bay to Vancouver Harbour or Howe Sound is the shortest crossing of the Strait other than between the lightship at Sandheads and Porlier Pass. Howe Sound is known for its excellent moorage in close proximity to Vancouver.

Howe Sound

Bracketted between Horseshoe Bay and Gibsons Landing, a score of coves, bays and anchorages welcome the yachtsman on Bowen, Gambier and Keats Islands. All have absorbing histories, but the main attractions today are astounding scenery, nearby fishing, and the quick escape from the city.

Cruising to Howe Sound for the week-end is highly possible for boat owners of almost any sized vessel moored in and around Vancouver, regardless of most weather conditions. The well-known "Squamish" wind which rips down the Sound at times ought not to be overlooked. Shelter from the Squamish is best found in lee anchorages such as Centre Bay on Gambier Island or Snug Cove on Bowen.

Going ashore at Snug Cove is like stepping onto a welcome mat at the door of Bowen Island. Land speculation seems to be the greatest industry, along with tourism, on Bowen Island. At one time a certain amount of whaling was done in the vicinity, especially in the waters around Worlcombe Island. The earliest settlers on Bowen were loggers but it didn't take long before they were homesteading and others were beginning to trek to it for summer weekend vacations and later day tripping aboard the Union Steamships for picnics, or pouring in for a weekend of swimming, dancing, hiking and a variety of sports activities.

Early this century and right up until boating came within the reach of most people, hordes

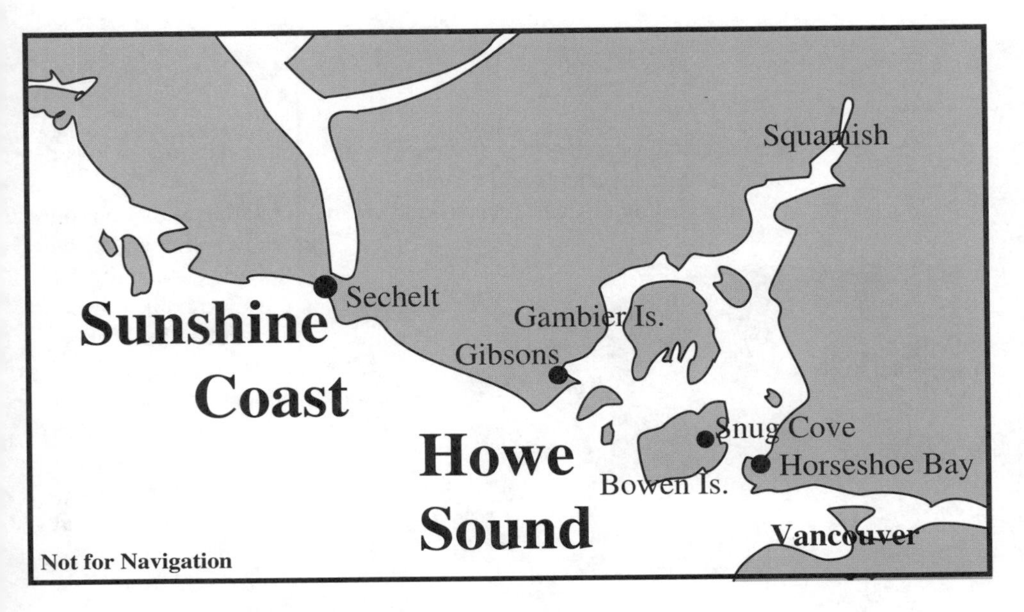

of holiday makers used the steamships leaving Vancouver at the foot of Columbia for Snug Cove on Saturdays. Eventually this "group" activity faded out as people took to doing their own things with their individual pleasure boats.

Union Steamships had put up a hotel, the Bowen Island Inn, which offered "magnificent vistas of mountains and sea." It offered visitors full course luncheons and dinners served in the "Sea-View" dining room. Moonlight cruises were offered aboard the *Lady Alexandra* and dancing aboard that vessel and at the Bowen Pavilion, was all part of the fare. A brochure put out by Union Steamships, in appealing to the public to make capital of the island's natural and other attractions, aptly describes Bowen's appeal: "... Lovely walks amidst glens and streams ... through woodland trails that will take you to many beauty spots such as Lake Killarney, Trout Lake and Mount Gardner Park. On top of all this you get the restful one hour cruise each way . . . around Point Atkinson into Howe Sound, a typical British Columbia fjord of incomparable beauty, . . . towering mountains and wide sweep of sheltered sea."

A cruise around the lower reaches of Howe Sound could easily end at Snug Cove, even if one has designated that only as a first stop on a weekend's cruising itinerary encompassing Bowen, Keats and Pasley for example.

We strolled along the Deep Bay road and forgot about time. The sun had broken through the thin veil of cloud and shone brightly on the peaks of Mount Strachan and Black Mountain looming over Horseshoe Bay opposite. It was easy, looking at the holiday and permanent cottages nestling among the trees and lush vegetation, to understand what motivated a deep interest among early as well as present day visitors and settlers to Bowen Island.

For the visiting boatsman, Snug Cove is a shelter in most weather although it can become a little uncomfortable in a bit of an easterly winter blow. For specific information on Snug Cove and other facilities at Bowen Island refer to the British Columbia Small Craft Guide. For those who like anchoring overnight caution should be taken not to drop the hook over submarine cables, nor to obstruct the path of the Bowen Island ferry.

If you want some good reading on the history of Bowen Island and the people who have come and gone and given places on the Island their names get a copy of Irene Howard's *Bowen Island 1872 -1972*. She has drawn in it a fascinating word picture of the island's past and present and through it one is more easily able to relate to the rest of lower Howe Sound, its islands and people.

Gibsons Landing and Keats Island are major boating attractions on the western side of the Sound, especially for those who like to get together with other boat owners or go ashore and either picnic or camp at the Marine Park in Plumper Cove or visit the small town stores and facilities at Gibsons.

From a sleepy, quaint town with occasional comings and goings of the ferries, Horseshoe Bay has turned into a busy hub of travelling activity. Sewell's Marina, top, and the ferry to Bowen Island landing at Snug Cove, above.

As a marine park, Plumper Cove on the west side of Keats attracts large numbers of boats each sunny weekend in summer. Its picnic and camping grounds are made much use of and its shady walks in the woods are popular. Views from the cliffs adjacent to the picnic and camping ground are magnificent and one can sit for hours just watching the boats cruise by or take in a colourful sunset over the opposite shore.

A cruise down Collingwood Channel could include a temporary stop at Mount Gardner Park, where there is a government float and some protection from the weather in the lee of Hutt Island.

Bowen Bay and Tunstall Bay are the large indentations on the west side of Bowen. Here it is possible to anchor and row ashore for some beachcombing. Tunstall Bay was the site in the early days of an explosives factory and the creek which runs into the bay appropriately bears the name Explosives Creek.

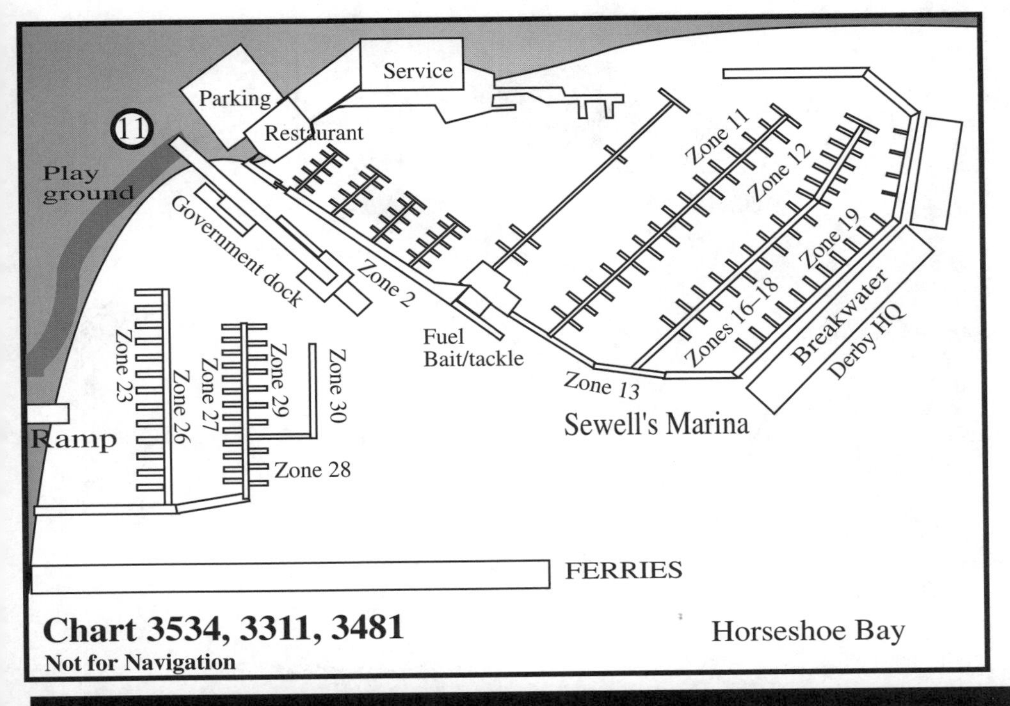

Sewell's Marina

Sewell's Marina

Derek Rendle
Dan Sewell
6695 Nelson West Vancouver, BC.
V7W 2B2
Phone: (604) 921-3474

Marina Services

Moorage
Fuel: gas, diesel, stove oil, engine and outboard oils.
Water
Power–15, 20, 30 amp.
Washrooms nearby. Public phones, launch ramp. Chandlery, repairs, service, fishing charters, licences, bait, tackle, rentals. Restaurants, Horseshoe Bay village adjacent–many services available.

11 Horseshoe Bay,

West Vancouver
Transport Canada dock
Chart 3534, 3526, 3311, 3512
Manager • Float length 64 m
Lights • Power • Adjacent restaurants, shops, ferries to Vancouver Island and the Sunshine Coast via Langdale/Gibsons.

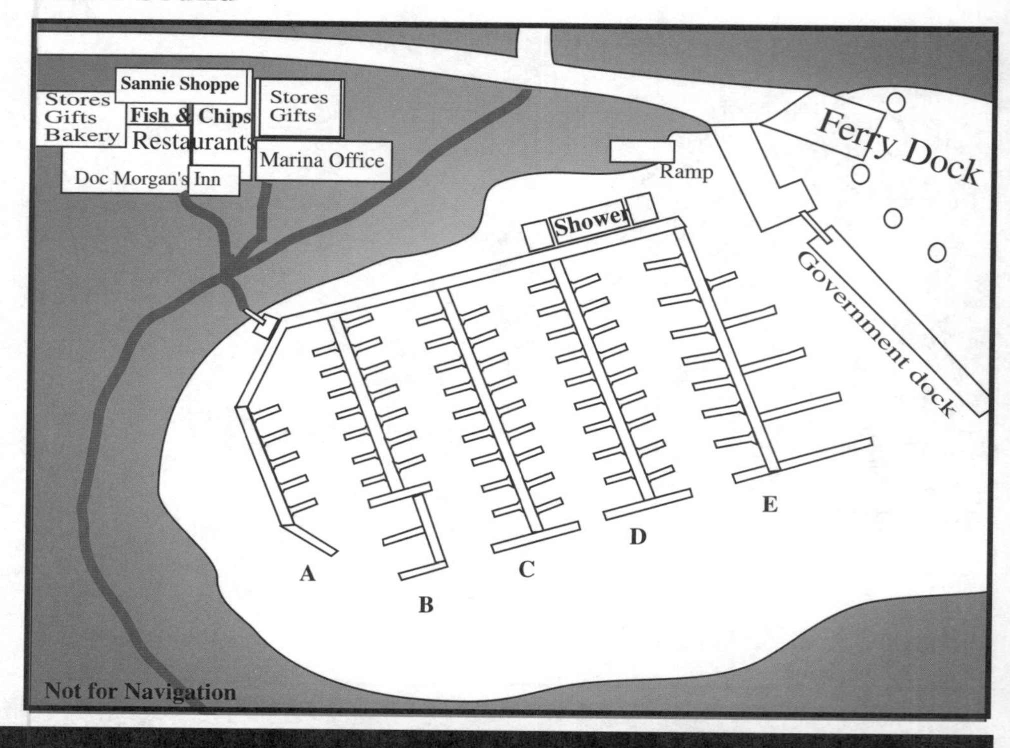

Union Steamship Co. Marina

Union Steamship Co Marina–Snug Cove

Rondy and Dorothy Dike.
P.O. Box 250
Bowen Island, BC, V0N 1G0
Phone: (604) 947-0707
Fax: (604) 947-0708
Chart 3534, 3311, 3526, 3481, 3512
VHF call 68
Hazard: Easy entrance.
Watch for ferry operations.
Shallows near beach beyond marina docks.

Marina services:

Moorage: 170 slips. Maximum to 220 feet.
Water at dock.
Power at docks: 50, 30 amp.
Showers, public phones, washrooms.

Customer services:

Chandlery. Boating supplies. Gifts, novelties, charts, snacks. Fresh produce, frozen foods, pharmacy, liquor, tackle, bait, hardware, ice and most supplies–at marina or in village. Restaurants, pubs, art and crafts stores, bistro, bakeries, health food and gift and specialty stores.

Entertainment.

Annual summer events include live entertainment, (pub Saturday nights),
Bowen Island parade and festival (Saturday prior to Labour Day). Dog Days of Summer (First Saturday in August).
Walking roads and trails on island. Crippen Regional Park has many trails and walks. Including 600 acres surrounding Snug Cove and marina.

Adjacent facilities:

BC Ferries to Horseshoe Bay. Crippen Regional Park. Picnic ashore. Walking trails. Killarney Lake in Crippen Park area. Anchorage in Mannion Bay (temporary).

Balladeer log 1984–*The old general store building was being shifted from its street front location to a site a short distance back from the road. It seemed some development is being planned for the settlement of Snug Cove here on Bowen Island. It had been a general store, in fact on a previous visit we had gone inside and inspected the sparse array of goods on the shelves, squeaked across a creaking wooden floor and chatted to the storekeeper.* It was not long before the store was closed to make way for change. Today the building serves as a post office and offices for the Greater Vancouver Regional District. The library which was housed in it for some years was moved recently to the main street in Snug Cove.

Snug Cove

Fast becoming one of the busiest boating centres on the coast, Snug Cove has been developed into a high profile marina and boating haven. Its multi slip dock facility with some 400 slips catering to boats up to well beyond 100 feet in length. The government dock that serves as a breakwater will dock about ten more boats depending on size. The ferry from Horseshoe Bay lands right alongside the government dock. Its wake and wash from the substantial propellers causes a tide-like stream that washes against boats moored to the dock so caution should be exercised when coming or going as well as when tying up–be sure to secure your boat adequately before leaving it for a walk up to the stores or the park and lake nearby.

The walk through the park is an easy one with well worn pathways as is the stroll up to Killarney Lake. Hiking around the lake is also not too taxing, unless you choose to do so in the middle of summer. Lots of shade helps reduce the discomfort in summertime and the cooler weather out of season does the same. Follow the trail up through the park, along the paved road a short distance to the right and then pick it up again for the stroll to the lake.

The village at the ferry landing is simply known as Snug Cove. Here there are several gift, handicraft and souvenir stores (a favourite of mine is The Sannie Shop) as well as refreshment establishments which include the Whirling Dervish, a light meals and coffee shop, excellent cappuccino and latte. A bakery next door serves coffee to go along with any of the freshly baked bread and pastries available. The long-established restaurant at the lower end of the stores has been serving a variety of simple meals for many years and the newer restaurant in the main Union Steamship landing building now offers a wide selection at mealtimes.

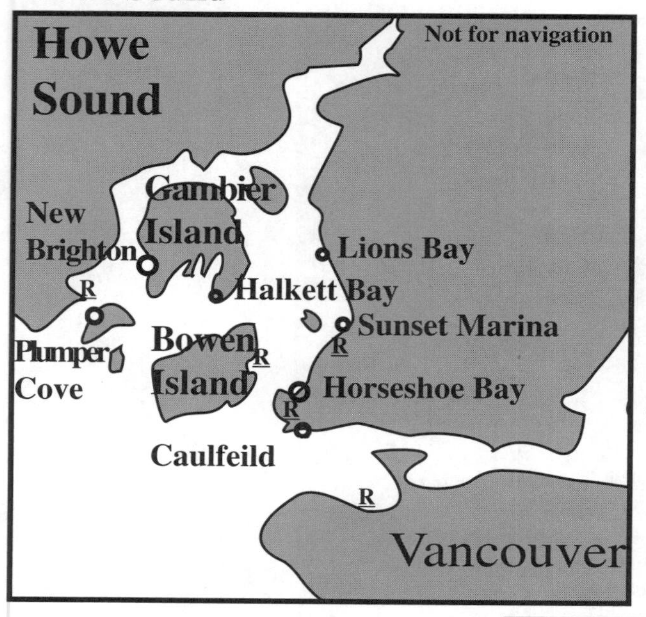

Opposite Page, Top: The general store near the New Brighton dock. A favourite stop for a light snack, groceries or ice cream cone. Bottom: The docks at Plumper Cove

Lions Bay Marina

Ken Wolder
Lions Bay, West Vancouver,
BC. V0N 2E0
Phone: (604) 921-75109

Chart 3311, 3526, 3586

Moorage, water, power at fuel dock.
Fuel: gas, engine and outboard oils. Washrooms. Public phones. Launch ramp, store–marine supplies, ice, snacks, fishing licences, bait.
Closed Tuesdays and Thursdays

Sunset Marina

Sue Rauter
34 Sunset Beach, West Vancouver, BC. V7W 2T7
Phone: (604) 921-7476

Chart 3311, 3526, 3586

Wet and dry moorage, water, power at gas dock. **Launch Ramp, marine store.**
Fuel: gas, engine and outboard oils. Tackle, fishing licences. Washrooms. Public phones. Repairs, service, power wash. Tackle, bait, ice. Restaurant. Parking.

12 Caulfeild
West Vancouver Fisheries & Oceans
Chart 3311, 3526, 3463 Float length 16 m Lights • Garbage • Water •

Bowen Island Marina

Norma and Dennis Dallas
RR #1, A-1, Bowen Island,
BC V0N 1G0
Phone: (604) 947-9710

Chart 3311, 3526, 3586, 3534 VHF 16

Marina located to starboard on approaches to Snug Cove, just before ferry landing. Limited transient moorage.Reservations. Moor alongside main dock (marked).
Fishing licences, bait, tackle.
Hazard: Ferry dock alongside. Watch operations and propeller turbulence from vessels while at dock.

Parks in Howe Sound

Halkett Bay
All weather anchorage
(some wind conditions)
Dinghy dock,
camping sites, toilets, hiking.

Porteau Cove
Temporary moorage
Buoys mark location of artificial reefs.
camping/picnic sites, water, toilets, beach,
scuba diving (wrecks as artificial reefs).

Plumper Cove
All weather anchorage
(some wind conditions).
8 mooring buoys, Boat docks,
camping/picnic sites, water, toilets, beach.
hiking. Fishing nearby at the Cut.

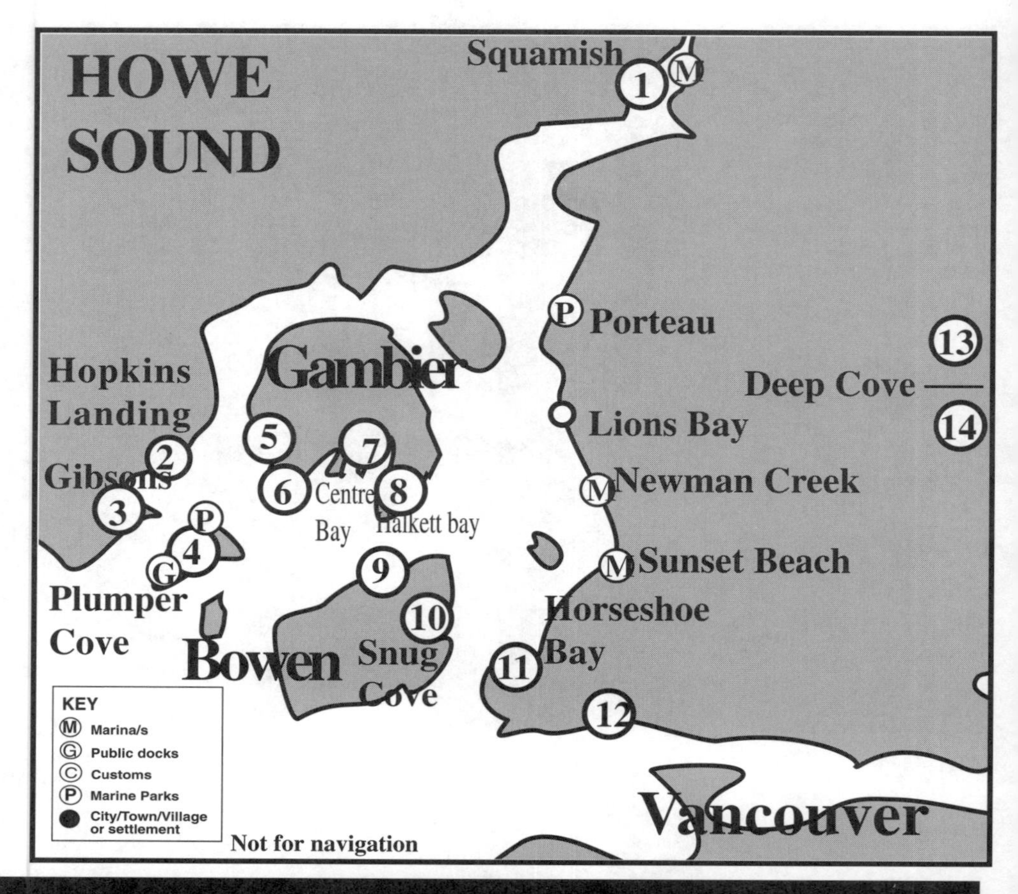

Howe Sound Public Docks

1 Squamish,

Fisheries & Oceans dock
Phone: (604) 892-3908
Chart 3311, 3534, 3526
Manager • Float length 118 m
Garbage • Water • Lights • Power • Public phone ashore • Near city restaurants, shops, churches, services and facilities. Yacht club may allow some transient moorage.

2 Hopkins Landing,

Transport Canada dock
Chart 3311, 3526, 3512
Manager • Float length 17 m
Lights •

3 Gibsons,

Fisheries & Oceans dock
Phone: (604)886-8017
Chart 3534, 3311, 3526, 3512
Manager • Float length 407 m
Launch ramp • Breakwater • Aircraft float • Garbage • Waste oil disposal • Water • Lights • Power • Public phone ashore • Near by restaurants, shops. Gibson's Marina adjacent.

4 Keats Island,

Transport Canada dock
Chart 3311, 3526, 3512
Manager • Float length 15 m
Water • Lights •

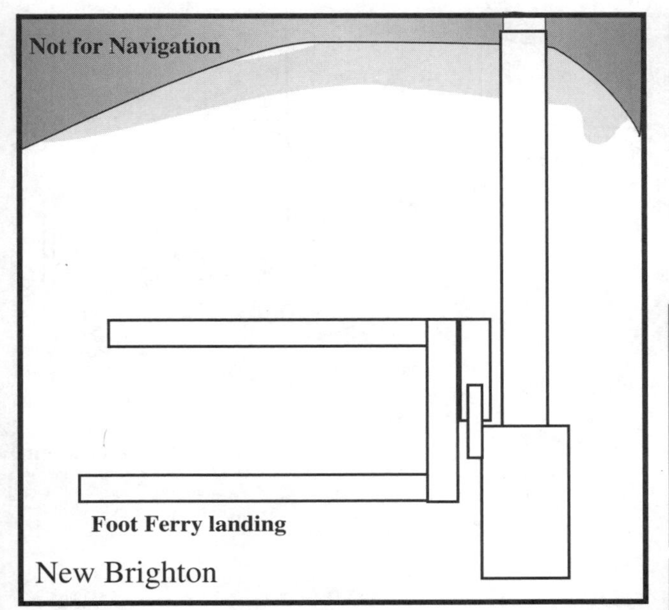

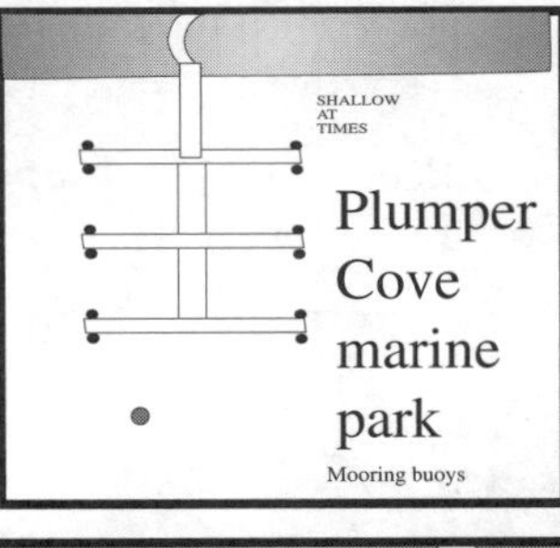

5 New Brighton,
Gambier Island
Transport Canada dock
Chart 3311, 3526, 3512
Float length 120 m •
Lights • Public phone •
Walking–island roads.
Nearby store.
Ferry service to Langdale/
Gibsons

6 Gambier Harbour,
Gambier Island
Transport Canada dock
Chart 3311, 3526, 3512
Float length 30 m
Lights • Showers •

7 Port Graves,
Gambier Island
Transport Canada dock
Chart 3310, 3512, 3526
Manager • Float length 10 m

8 Halkett Bay,
Gambier Island
Transport Canada dock
Chart 3311, 3526, 3512
Float length 17 m
Adjacent marine park

9 Mount Gardner Park,
Bowen Island
Fisheries & Oceans dock
Chart 3311, 3526, 3512
Float length 17 m

10 Snug Cove,
Bowen Island
Transport Canada dock
Chart 3534, 3311, 3481, 3512, 3526
Manager • Float length 105 m
Garbage • Lights • Power •
Public phone ashore •
Washrooms ashore •
Adjacent Union Steamship Marina.
Near village arts and crafts, bakeries, restaurants, shops.
All services.
Ferry to Horseshoe Bay.

Notes:

Gibsons. Transport Canada dock
(604) 886-8017 Manager • Float length 804 m
Breakwater • Water • Lights • Power •
Public phone ashore • Near restaurants, shops.

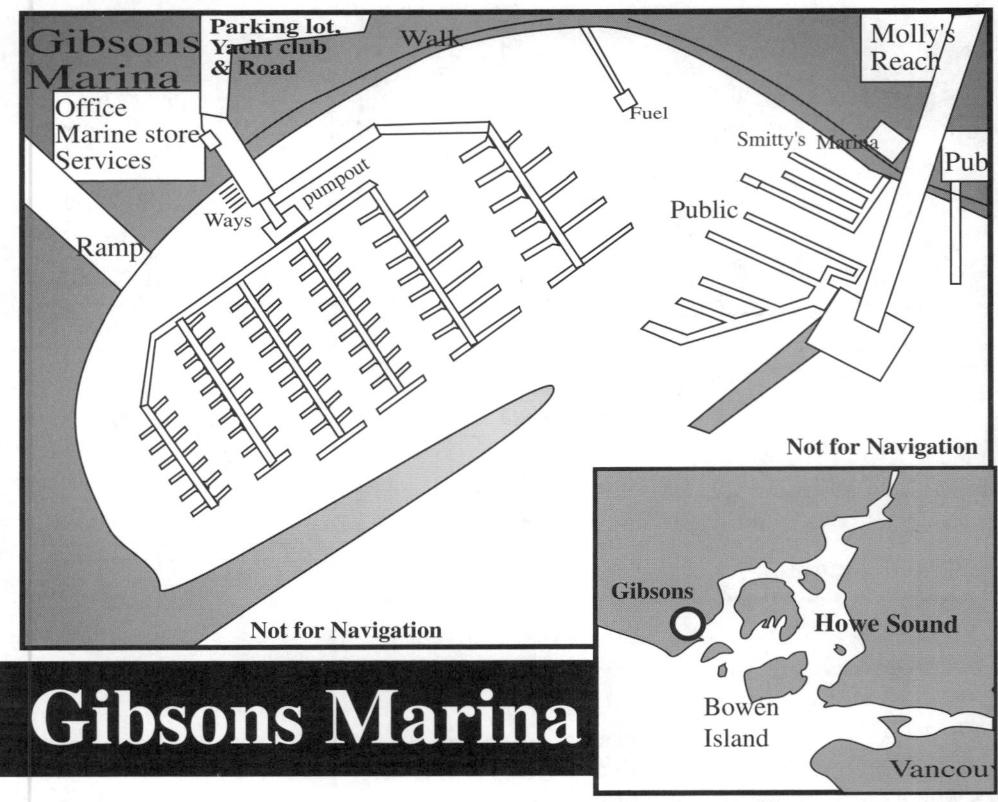

Gibsons Marina

Art McGinnis
P.O. Box 1520, Gibsons,
BC, V0N 1V0
Phone: (604) 886-8686
Fax: (604) 886-8686
Charts 3534, 3311, 3526, 3512 VHF 68

Marina services:

400 permanent and transient berths. Dock A – main visitor dock.
Water at dock. Many outlets.
Sani-station (pumpout).
Power at docks: 15 amp at all slips.

Customer services:

Laundry, showers, washrooms.
Marine supplies at chandlery/marina office.
Fishing gear, licences, charts, bait, ice, repair accessories, bank machines. gifts, arts and crafts, books, snacks.
Nearby church/es multi-denominational.
Post Office: Walk to stores in village, also pharmacy and other necessities.
Scuba diving at Sechelt up the Sunshine coast. Ask for information.
Public pay phone ashore.
Walking: Road access walking or cycling. Waterfront walk, partial around bay. Walk, cab or bus up to main shopping centre.

Entertainment.

Fishing excellent at The Cut a short run from marina.
Rental bicycles. Scooters. Museum, local stores. Art galleries.

Adjacent facilities:

Fuel: Gas, diesel, oils. Outboard mix.
Service, haul-outs.
Marine repairs available–mechanic on call.
Marine and boat equipment sales.
Launch ramp.
Vehicle rentals.

The floats at Gibsons Marina are higher than average, sturdy and well-equipped with water and power.

Right: A view of Gibsons Landing government docks from Molly's Reach location of TV's Beachcombers fame. Gibsons Marina in the background.

Gibsons to Squamish

Gibsons today is a busy community of residents, transient ferry travellers, business people and boat operators docking their craft at Gibsons Marina. This large facility is one of the biggest and best of its kind in local coastal waters. It provides all services required by mariners from the chandlery store at the head of the dock to nearby repair facilities. The marina offers power and water, showers and laundry, fish cleaning, bait, tackle and accessories. In the waterfront village of Gibsons Landing there are stores, restaurants, a pub, post office, pharmacy, museum and supermarket. A very handy delicatessen is located near the marina for excellent specialty items and a sit down cup of tea or coffee. Craft and art stores have become a major attraction.

From Gibsons to Squamish takes you either up the eastern shore of Howe Sound, where you can see numerous waterfront homes or small settlements, or up the western side with its islands and passages. One of the major landmarks on the steep-sloped eastern shore is Britannia Beach with its scarred hillside from former mining operations.

The passage up the western shore passes from Gibsons via New Brighton on Gambier, privately owned club facilities of Thunderbird Yacht Club and Burrard Yacht Club at Ekins Point and McNab Creek opposite.

Upper Howe Sound

It's remarkable the number of times one cruises into Howe Sound, around the top of Bowen Island, beyond Gambier and out again without as much as stopping to explore some of its coves, anchorages and accessible shores. Upper Howe Sound has much to offer the cruising enthusiast who wants to get away from the crowds during summer or get a closer view of the snow peaks of the Coast Range in winter. Well, most winters anyway. It's easy in the early part of summer to take advantage of the long daylight hours on a Friday evening, perhaps and cruise off to an overnight spot in the lower reaches, spend the night and then set off early for a cruise farther up.

You might cruise to Squamish, passing Anvil Island after a night in Centre Bay, West Bay or one of the marinas at Gibsons, Snug Cove or Horseshoe Bay. The magnificent surrounding scenery reshapes itself as new dimensions come within sight.

The chill of the grey weather was dissipated with the appearance of the sun and patches of blue sky through the high cloud ceiling. Anvil Island loomed up ahead and we steered slightly towards it passing Pam Rocks and Christie Islet, the latter hosting its usual rookery of seals. We reached Britannia Beach and circled the local moorings, the only wharf we could find in the area. We cruised across to Woodfibre and strolled as far as we could in the vicinity of the landing. It was sunny, just then, and the walk allowed us to get a better look at the surrounding terrain. But we were restricted to a relatively small area before encountering what appeared to be private property.

Squamish is an interesting destination up Howe Sound. Here one can tie up against a log boom and spend a weekend in total oblivion of the rest of the world. Or put in at the government wharf after negotiating the logboom littered waterway up to the town. And spend some of the evening in Squamish. There was a time when a ferry service operated between Vancouver and Squamish. It carried passengers during the week to meet the Great Pacific Eastern Railway which linked Squamish with Williams Lake and Quesnel. The road to Prince George, built in 1952, however, reduced the traffic on the railway line and hence on the ferry, resulting in its demise.

McNab Creek is a suitable place for going ashore in search of beachcombing or quick hiking trails. It also affords shelter from some of the wind conditions that

Squamish

occur in the area, and anchorage for overnight or daytime stops.

In the 1920s the government tried to get homesteaders interested in settling at McNab Creek but the effort failed. Loggers moved in to claim the available timber and eventually made off leaving their cabins to fall into disrepair. Since those days several new structures have appeared as well as a dock used by Canadian Forest Products.

Travelling south from McNab Creek you pass Port Mellon to reach New Brighton which has a large float area. However, sea conditions and weather can make this a rather uncomfortable shelter especially in winter.

Moorage in Squamish

The Squamish Yacht Club has moorage alongside the public marina. There is often adequate room to tie up at the public docks and sometimes a yacht club member will invite you to stop for a while at their facilities, provided there is room. Many mariners tie up to log booms in the area but be careful not to hinder any work in progress if you do. Stop and enquire at the Yacht Club if the government docks are full. *Above: A view from the public docks alongside the Squamish Yacht Club (opposite).*

The entrance to the Sound is not much more than half an hour away from Vancouver in a slow boat. It is 10 miles wide at the entrance, has something like 14 main islands and extends northward more than 20 miles. The only serious condition that could disrupt a pleasant weekend's cruising in Howe Sound is a Squamish wind that blows up an unpleasant sea, but this is not common during summer.

Marina and roads at New Brighton. This is an excellent place to visit, accessing the general store pictured on page 143. The water taxi stops at the outer dock so look for space on the inside. Unfortunately there is not much space nor is it frequently available. The small dock at Gambier or the slightly larger one at West Bay, around the south tip of the island, provides limited moorage and a good walk across to New Brighton.

Sunshine Coast

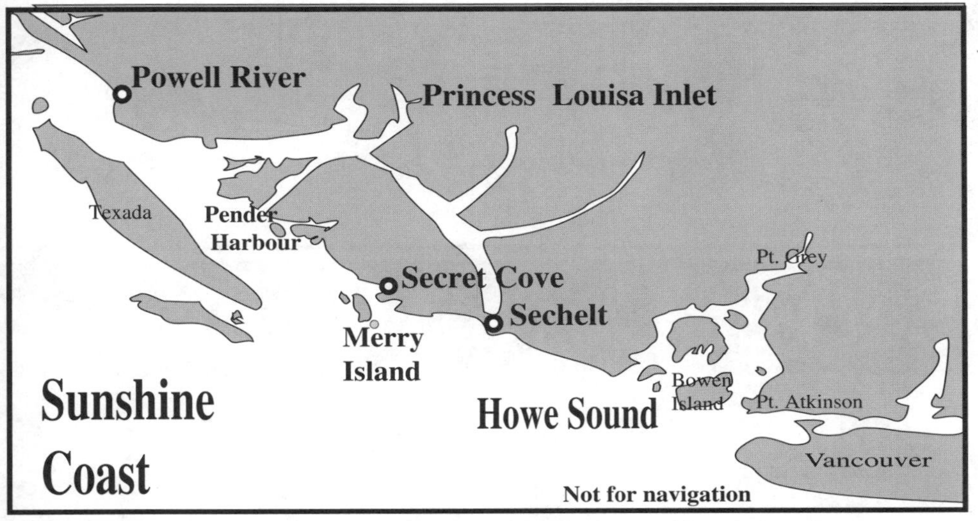

Merry Island is an area where weather can provide a lasting good impression of leisurely boating up the coast, or a terrible memory of wishing you had never left home. Careful planning and monitoring of the weather channels will help you enjoy the cruise in safety and comfort.

The sight of the lighthouse standing loftily above the island is a feast of visual delight. In the foreground are kelp beds and rocks protruding above a shiny warm blue surface on a mild summer day. Slowly slipping by at reduced speed produces a tranquillity to be enjoyed by all. Recreational fishermen in small boats gather off the island for good salmon catches, their boats adding to the colourful scene of this major landmark on the BC coast. Beyond Merry Island we cruise into the sheltered coves and bays of the Sechelt Peninsula having passed Sechelt proper a few miles to the south and Halfmoon Bay as we continue towards Secret Cove.

A smart crew will not pass dock lines to someone on shore until the skipper is good and ready. Spectators who are eager to assist often are inexperienced and will pull on the bow line, throwing the skipper's manouvres totally out of control. It is best only to pass someone ashore a line connected amidships, and only when it is really necessary, such as when wind or current are pushing the boat away from the dock.

Smuggler Cove provides cosy anchorage after passing through Welcome Passage, with Secret Cove offering anchorage or moorage at one of several marinas. Secret Cove Marina has fuel and supplies to meet every need, moorage with power and water and access ashore. Hotels nearby provide accommodations for travellers and meals for a break from the galley. Mechanical services, moorage and fuel are available also at Buccaneer Marina.

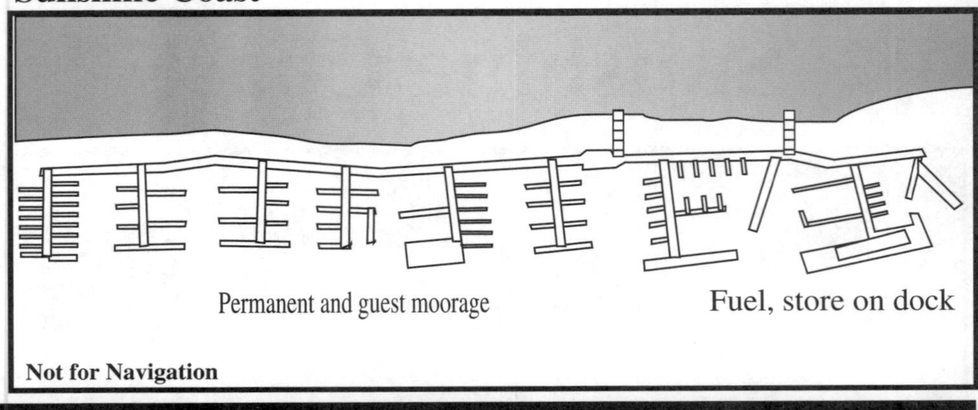

Secret Cove Marina

Secret Cove Marina

Gerry and Deborah Haag
Box 1118 Sechelt,
BC, V0N 3A0
Phone: (604) 885-6037
Chart 3535, 3311, 3512

Marina services:

Fuel: gas, diesel, oil, live bait, ice,
150 berth permanent and transient docks.
Water at dock. Many outlets.
Power at docks: 30, 15 amp.

Customer services:

Hotel access: pool, spa, restaurants.
Showers. Washrooms. Fish cleaning tables, picnic tables, garbage disposal for moorage customers only. Marine supplies at chandlery. Fishing gear, licences, charts, bait, ice, electronics, repair accessories, books, gifts, arts and crafts, snacks. Fax service. General store. Public pay phone ashore.

Walking: Road access walking or cycling. Cab or bus up to main shopping centres.

Entertainment.

Fishing excellent a short run from marina. Rental bicycles. Scooters.

Adjacent facilities:

Golf. Swimming

Rough water refuge between Secret Cove and Howe Sound at Thelma Park just south of Sechelt on Indian reserve.

Secret Cove,

Fisheries & Oceans dock
Chart 3311, 3535, 3512 Manager •
Float length 44 m • Lights • Power •
Public phone •
Adjacent marinas, lodges, provisions, fuel, repairs, service.

Halfmoon Bay,

Sunshine Coast
Transport Canada dock
Chart 3311, 3512
Float length 26 m • Lights •

Sechelt,

Sunshine Coast
Fisheries & Oceans dock
Chart 3311, 3512
Manager • Breakwater •

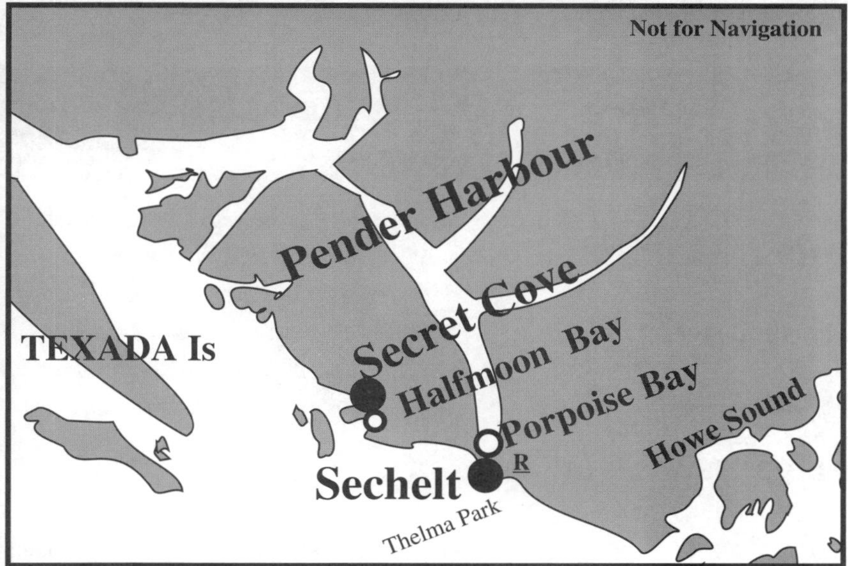

Pictured above: The store on the docks at Secret Cove Marina.

Porpoise Bay, Sechelt

Fisheries & Oceans dock
Phone 885-1986
Chart 3310, 3512
Manager • Float length 132 m •
Launch ramp • Grid • Aircraft float •
Garbage •

Water • Lights • Power •
Public phone ashore •
Adjacent restaurant, hotels, dive store, nearby shops.
Excellent scuba diving in vicinity.
Charters. Rentals.

Buccaneer Marina

Buccaneer Marina

Bob Mercer
RR 1 Halfmoon Bay
BC, V1Y0
Phone: (604) 885-7888
Fax: (604) 885-7824
Chart 3311, 3535, 3512 VHF 68

Buccaneer Marina does not advertise moorage for guests but rather has slips for permanent customers. Many keep their vessels at the marina year round and travel by road to use them to access the fabulous fishing areas nearby. The marina is known for its repairs, service, fuel and marine supplies.

Marina services:

Haulouts. Fuel: gas, diesel, oil, live and frozen bait.
Marine centre and store. Sales & service. Parts and repairs. Mercury service.
Permanent moorage and repair dock. Water and power at dock.

Customer services:

Boat rentals.
Fishing gear, licences, charts, bait, ice, propane, groceries, snacks.
Hull repairs, steam cleaning, bottom painting.
Post Office: At store.
Public pay phone ashore.
Walking: Road access walking.

Entertainment.

Fishing excellent a short run from marina.

Adjacent facilities:
Moorage, Secret Cove Marina. Accommodations, Lord Jim's Lodge (604) 885-7038, and Jolly Roger Inn (604) 885-7184.
No overnight guest moorage.

Sandy Beaches, Sheltered Coves

The focal point on the Sunshine Coast on the Vancouver side of Pender Harbour is Secret Cove with nearby Smuggler Cove and Buccaneer Bay. It's a total distance of about 40 miles from Vancouver so that even with a slow boat it is an easy run. Ideal for a day's fishing in the vicinity, especially just north of Thormanby Island and at Tottenham Ledge — most popular fishing grounds for local anglers, and visitors too.

The entrance to Secret Cove is at the southeast end. It dries at low tide at the north-west side which can look deceivingly navigable at high tide. The lee of Turnagain offers sheltered anchorage for those who prefer to remain untethered during the night. Secret Cove measures about a mile in length and is about a quarter of a mile wide with two navigable arms at the eastern side. Secret Cove Marina with its new extensions and its well-stocked floating store and fuel station is a busy place in the summer. The marina has a lot to offer and many docks for overnight moorage. The store on the docks sells groceries, fishing tackle and most items that cruising people look for when they are out cruising.

There are private floats in the southern arm and Buccaneer Marina occupies a significant area in the other. At this marina, owned and run by the Mercer family, repairs and servicing are available as well as gas, diesel fuel and small boat launching (for those who choose to arrive by road the marina operators will put trailerables in the water with a four wheel drive). Many property owners on Thormanby Island across Welcome Passage maintain boats in Buccaneer Marina permanently and park their cars on the Mercers' property when they take off to their island homes at week-ends. Getting in and out of these arms is regarded by some as tricky, but this is not really the case if one follows a chart carefully and takes heed of the various markers.

If you have any doubt about navigation in this area a good book to use is the B. C. *Small Craft Guide.*

The Jolly Roger Inn and Lord Jim's Lodge at Secret Cove offer hotel accommodations, restaurant and other luxury facilities for those who need a break from boating.

The Union Steamship ferry that plied the coast from Vancouver to Pender Harbour used to call at many stops on the way and these included Halfmoon Bay and Sechelt. The boats that called in Secret Cove, however, were mainly commercial or occasional pleasure boats— sometimes carrying groups of weekending holidaymakers, most of whom made their destination the golden sands of nearby Buccaneer Bay.

Romantic as the name "Buccaneer Bay" may sound it does not stem from any historic facts concerning pirates and buried treasure, but rather from a race horse in the 1860 Derby held at Epsom in England. The name was given by Captain Richards who was surveying the area at the time and it appears he and his men were quite influenced by the Derby because other names, including Merry Island, Thormanby, Welcome Passage and Epsom Point have similar origins. The horse, Thormanby, belonging to J.C. Merry (Merry

Island) won the race while one of the favourites went by the name of Buccaneer.

The area was settled by immigrants from Europe and back east, and researching the history of places such as Gibsons, Roberts Creek and many others one could unearth a wealth of interesting information concerning early days on the Sechelt Peninsula. The new settlers were responsible for clearing land to build homes and church or community halls, schools and government wharves. They planted the lands and were responsible for the beginnings to the Peninsula Highway, which incidentally reached Sechelt from Gibsons and Langdale as early as 1912, Halfmoon Bay in 1930 and Pender Harbour in 1936.

Smuggler Cove hides from Welcome Passage behind the rocky breakwater that is Wilbraham Point and whose entrance is practically due south of Pender Harbour and less than a mile out of Secret Cove. Smuggler Cove (not Smuggler*s*) Marine Park is one of the best anchorages on the coast. Its narrow entrance, dotted with rocks and tiny islets, is almost deceiving to the uninitiated. Make sure you are in the right channel as you enter.

To reach Buccaneer from Smuggler Cove it is wise to travel all the way around the buoy at the northern edge of Tottenham Ledge. Down into the Bay the expansive stretch of golden sand lures you on until you are in among the many other boats, sail and power, anchored and rafted within a short row of the beach.

Picnicking or just strolling on the beach as well as dipping in the cool water are the favourite ways to enjoy this area in Buccaneer Bay. The beach, which divides North Thormanby Island from South Thormanby, extends up to Vaucroft beach on the west side of the bay. There is a public wharf which provides limited berthing space in 18 feet of water. For overnight anchorage the most suitable place for small craft is on the opposite shore at Water Bay which opens off the east side of Gill Beach. Another overnight anchorage could be found in the lee of Surrey Islands just off the northern end of South Thormanby Island.

Make certain your children are wearing life jackets around the water, and particularly on marina docks.

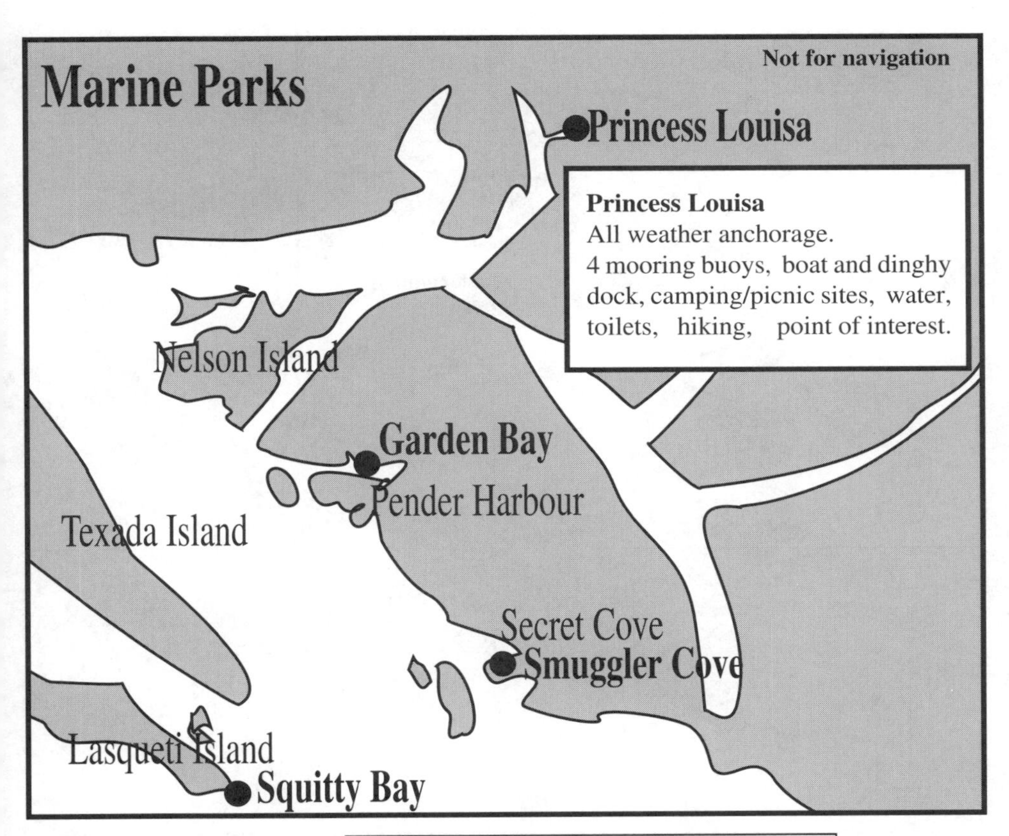

Garden Bay
All weather anchorage.
Dinghy dock,
(Adjacent marinas),
picnic sites, toilets, park host, beach, hiking.
Nearby good fishing and good scuba diving.

Smuggler Cove
All weather anchorage, camping sites, toilets, park host, hiking, Fishing in vicinity.

Squitty Bay
All weather anchorage (limited room and some wind).
Boat dock, picnic sites, water, toilets. Good fishing in vicinity.

Some vessels visit Princess Louisa early in the season to capture the loneliness and tranquillity of the place. Short days and long cool nights provide a brisk but refreshing atmosphere to this unique park.

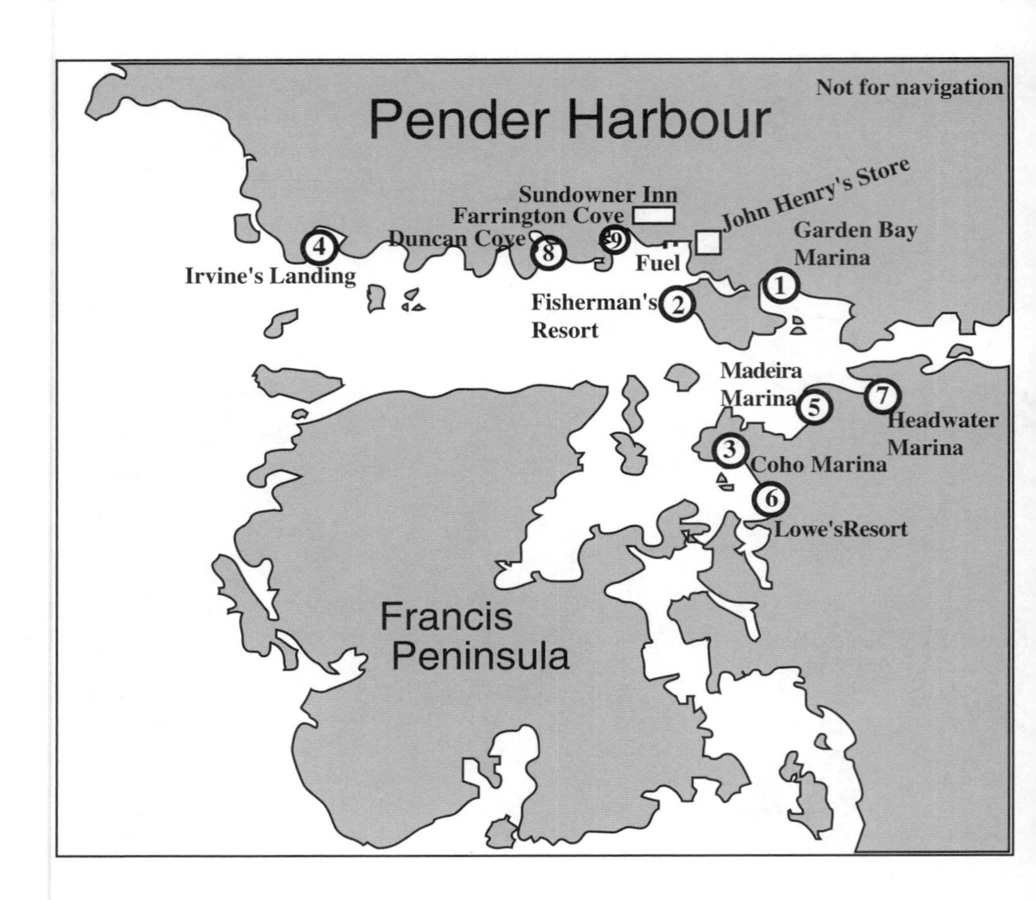

Pender Harbour

Aside from its scenic value, which is considerable, Pender Harbour has long attracted yachtsmen as a base for fishing and supplies, well away from the cities, yet readily accessible for a weekend.

When the wet days of winter are over and the sunshine of summer draws myriad boats back into the water, that new but enigmatically familiar urge for adventure spurs on the enthusiastic yachtsman to dig out his charts and begin to plan his weekend cruising.

While it is probably every boat owner's dream to put into some hitherto unknown and unexplored inlet—such a luxury is not for most weekenders out of Vancouver or Vancouver Island. For them, rather, a destination that will prove among the most appealing is bustling but strangely alluring Pender Harbour.

The scenic attractions of Pender Harbour are many and varied along the inlet's jagged 32 miles of shoreline, but many eyes may be blinded to this by the busy development along the shores.

The weekending boat-owner heading for Pender is mainly attracted by the fishing to be done there. The waters around Pender are well-known for their yield of lingcod, salmon, and various species of rockfish. Or one can enjoy the inlet just lying at anchor in one of the many sheltered coves or putting into a marina and exploring some of the local shore-side attractions.

It's usually a quick trip in a fast power boat and on a good day it can be done in under two hours out of Vancouver. But it can also take a day if you linger over some of the engaging distractions en route, including nosing into Halfmoon Bay, one of the stops usually missed on any cruise up the Sunshine Coast. Halfmoon Bay was once the halfway stop for the Union steamships carrying tourists to Pender.

The government wharf there, however, offers limited moorage and poor shelter from any severe weather.

Approaching Fisherman's Resort in Hospital Bay, with John Henry's fuel dock and facilities in the background. Garden Bay Hotel Pub and restaurant on waterfront.

In 1929 the Union Steamship company vessels were doing the run to Pender from Vancouver three times a week. The trip would take anywhere from five to 10 hours—and getting back home entailed an indefinite wait on the wharf, often throughout a hot afternoon and sometimes into the evening, for the boat to arrive. In those days Irvine's Landing at the entrance to Pender Harbour was the terminal dock for travellers. From the earliest days of settlement until the 1930s when the Sechelt Highway reached the area, Irvine's Landing was one of the main centres of growth and activity.

It was about that time that other centres began springing up to cater to the many visitors and new land owners who began to pour into the area. Places such as Pope's Landing and Donnely's Landing on the Francis Peninsula and Madeira Park were established or began coming into their own. And the Union ships included them in their stops.

Entering Pender Harbour after rounding Francis Peninsula, pass between Martin Island to port and Charles and William Islands to starboard. Irvine's Landing is situated in the tiny cove called Joe Bay immediately beyond Henry Point on the northern shore of the inlet. Joe Bay takes its name from Portuguese Joe Gonsalves, who with his son-in-law, owned the first two buildings at Irvine's Landing, the hotel and the saloon.

Today the favoured overnight stops include Irvine's Landing, Fisherman's Marina, Garden Bay Hotel and Marina, Madeira Marina and Coho Marina. People stopping at the government docks at Madeira Park may walk over to Lowe's Marina for a shower or to use the other facilities such as laundry. Their marina is basically dedicated to regulars and permanent moorage and the diehard fishing enthusiasts who operate from there year round.

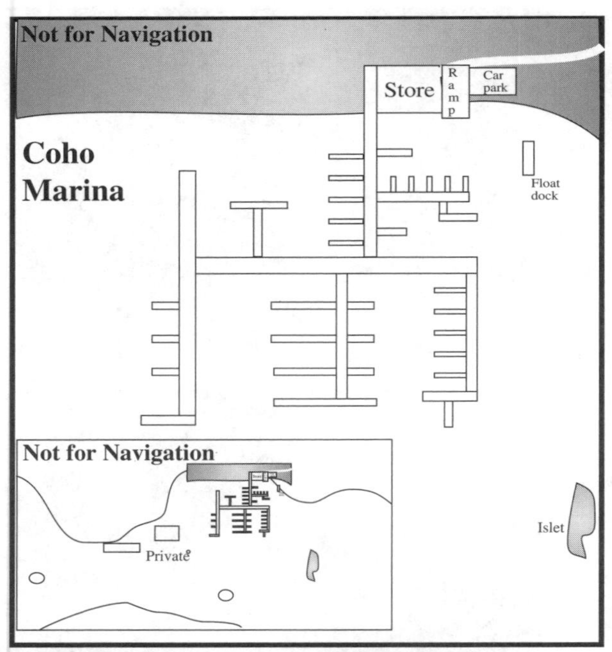

The one-time hospital at Hospital Bay is now a lodge and caters to dining and overnight lodging guests. Yachts tying up at marinas in Hospital Bay and Garden Bay will not be far from the facility. Coho Marina is across Pender Harbour from Hospital Bay and if a dinner is planned at Hospital Bay there should be ample dock space at the government float. Temporary tie up of a dinghy for the purpose of using adjacent restaurant or store facilities should be no problem at most marinas. Just advise the operators of your intentions and get their permission.

Coho Marina

Overlooking Lowe's Marina (no overnight moorage), with Coho Marina in the background.

(3)

Coho Marina Resort

Gordie and Nichole Standal
P.O. Box 160 Madeira Park BC
V0N 2H0 Phone: (604) 883-2248
Chart 3512, 3535, 3514 VHF call 68

Hazard: Rocks in bay–marked by beacons. Consult charts.

Marina services:

Moorage. Launch ramp.
Water at dock. Ice. **Showers.**
Power at docks: 15 amp.

Customer services:

Fishing tackle, licences. Marine hardware.
Washrooms. Campsites, trailers.

Nearby church/es: multi-denominational.
Public pay phone ashore.
Walking: Road access walking or cycling.

Entertainment.

Scuba diving and fishing excellent a short run from harbour.

Adjacent facilities:

Nearby stores/shop centre.

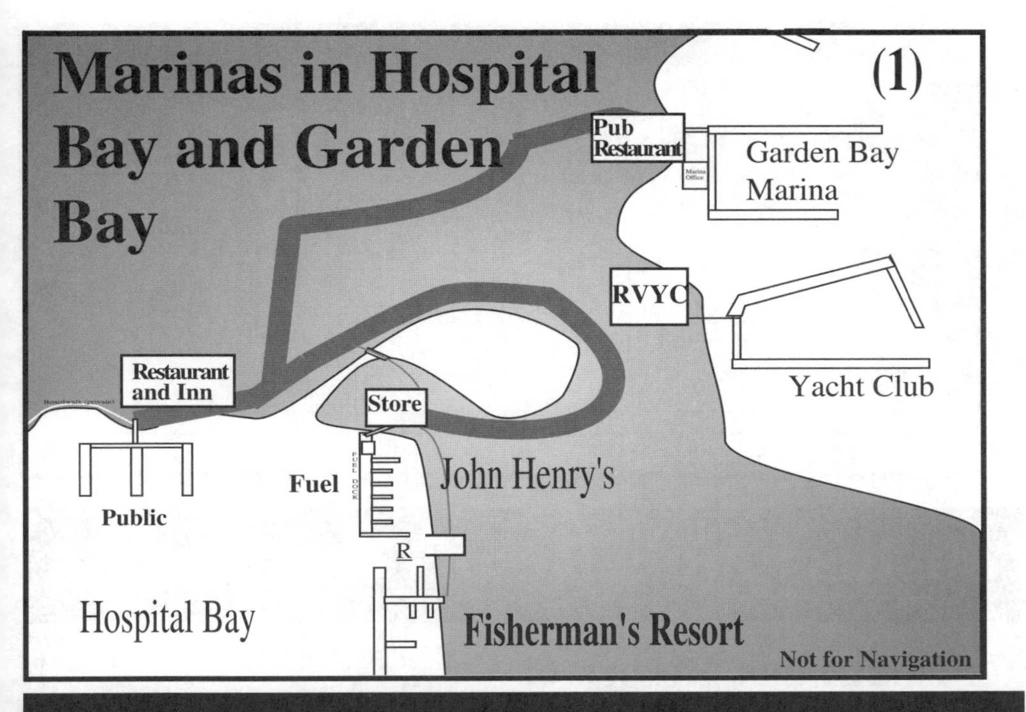

Garden Bay Hotel & Marina

Chart 3535, 3311, 3512 VHF 68

Garden Bay Hotel & Marina

Ron Johnston & Marita Jonkela
P.O. Box 90, Garden Bay,
BC, V0N 1S0
Phone: (604) 883-2674

Marina services:

Fuel: at John Henry's Marinas in Hospital Bay. Gas, diesel, stove oil, outboard fuel, propane. Tackle.
Moorage. Water at dock.
Power at docks: 30 amp, 15 amp.

Customer services:

Fine dining at waterfront restaurant. Pub.
Fishing charters. Air charters.
Laundry, **Washrooms.**
Gift shop and art gallery.
Nearby church/es. Post Office:
Scuba diving arrangements and charters–ask marina for information.
Public pay phone ashore.

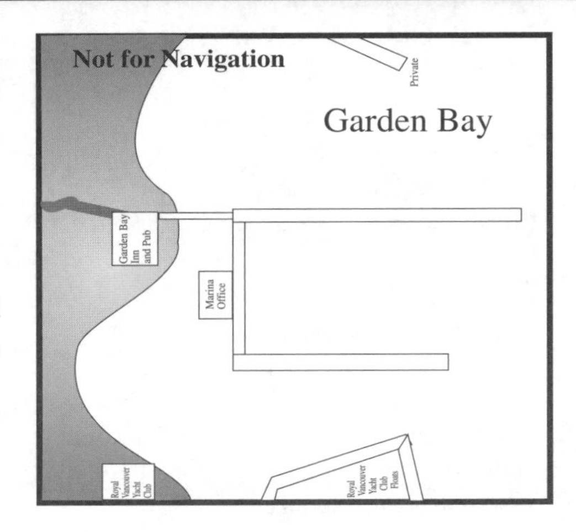

Walking: Road access walking or cycling.

Entertainment.

Fishing excellent a short run from harbour.

Adjacent facilities:

Nearby–fuel dock, liquor agency, restaurants, anchorage.

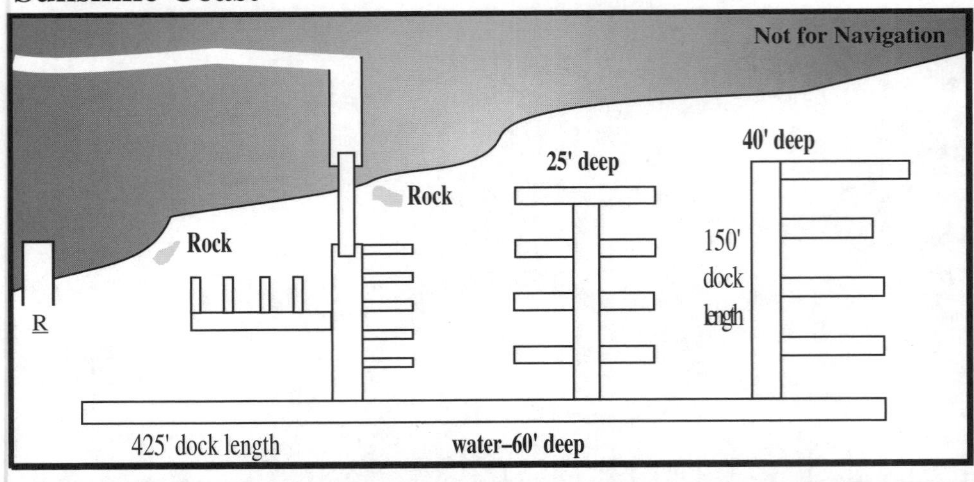

Fisherman's Resort & Marina

Fishermans Resort & Marina (2)

Wally and Susan Nowik
Box 68 Garden Bay
British Columbia, V0N 1S0
Phone: (604) 883-2336

Marina services:

Moorage. Launch ramp.
Power at docks: 30, 15 amp.
Water.

Customer services:

Laundry, showers, ice, bait.
Waterfront cottages. Public phone ashore.
Marine charts, books. Fishing gear, licences.
Nearby church/es: multi-denominational.
Scuba diving arrangements and charters –ask marina for details.
Walking: Road access walking or cycling.

Entertainment:

Fishing is excellent in general area out of Pender Harbour. Consult fishing guides.

Adjacent facilities:

Groceries at John Henry's general store. Also, post office, liquor, restaurants.

Chart 3535, 3311, 3512 VHF call 68

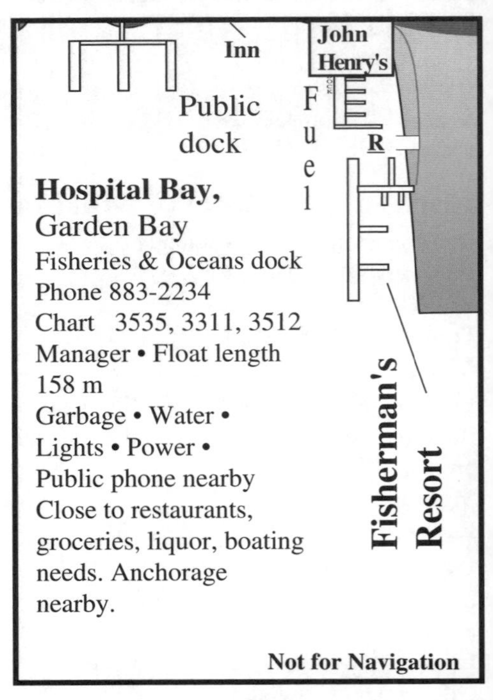

Pharmacy and other necessities at store. Sundowner Inn Restaurant. Phone: 883-9676. Public marina. Anchorage (in Garden Bay). Fuel at Irvine's Landing or John Henry's.

A view over the bay from Sundowner Inn includes John Henry's fuel dock in the foreground and Fisherman's Resort beyond. The marina, busy in the early part of summer.

Irvine's Landing with fuel dock and space for overnight moorage.

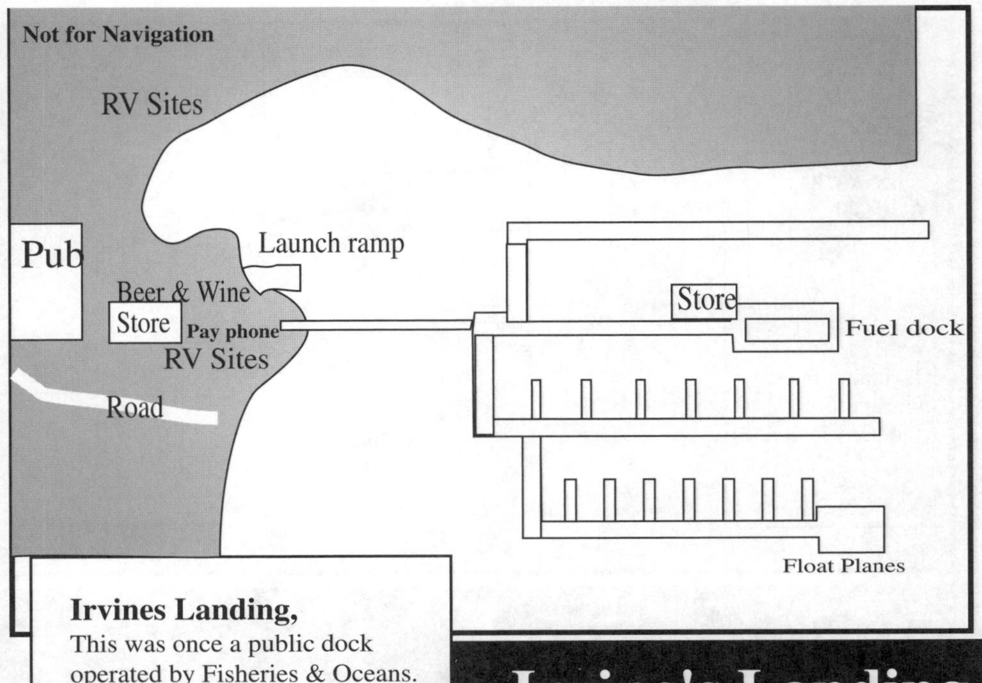

Irvine's Landing

Irvines Landing,
This was once a public dock operated by Fisheries & Oceans. It is located at the entrance to Pender Harbour and offers guests moorage, fuel, groceries and many of the needs of cruising mariners, as well as the many sports fishing enthusiasts who frequent the facility. It has a pub style restaurant and patio service.

Irvines Landing (4)

Marina & Pub

Wayne Macdonald
RR #1, Irvines Landing Road,
Garden Bay, B.C. V0N 1S0
(Phone: 604) 883-2296 (docks).
Phone: 883-1145 (Marina & Pub)
Chart 3535, 3311, 3512

Marina services:

Fuel: gas, diesel, outboard mix. Transient moorage.
Power. 30, 15 amp. **Water.**

Customer services:

Irivne's Landing Pub. Dining. Patio service. Wine & beer store. Groceries. Tackle, charts, live and frozen bait.
Showers, Washrooms. Pay phones.
Excellent fishing nearby. Guides.
Fish freezing. Fish cleaning stations (2). Boat rentals–guided or unguided. Marina conveniently located at entrance to harbour.

Entertainment.

Walks, hiking–parks and roads. View points. Animal and marine life.

Adjacent facilities:

Launch ramp. Newly renovated. Fishing charters.

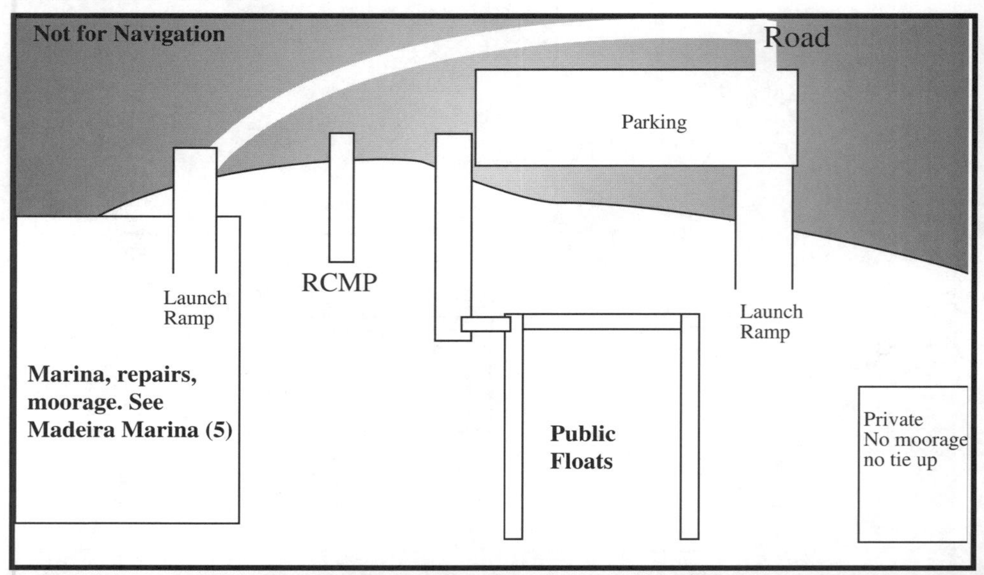

Madeira Park

Madeira Marina (5)

Karen Reid and Rick King

P.O. Box 189 Madeira Park, BC. V0N 2H0

Phone: (604) 883-2266

Chart 3512, 3535, 3514

Location: next to Madeira Park public docks and ramp.

Marina services:

Moorage. For customers at lodge, and adjacent RV park, also service customers. **Water** at dock. Ice. No power at docks.

Customer services:

Marine store and supplies, fishing tackle, licences, ice, freezing.

Walking: Road access walking or cycling.

Entertainment.

Scuba diving and fishing excellent a short run from the harbour.

Adjacent facilities:

Public dock. Nearby supermarket, post office, bank, pharmacy, restaurant.

Madeira Park,

Pender Harbour
Fisheries & Oceans dock
Phone 883-2234
Chart 3535, 3311, 3512
Manager • Float length 196 m
Launch ramp • Aircraft float • Garbage • Waste oil disposal • Water • Lights • Power • Public phone • Nearby restaurants, shops.

Duncan Cove Marina (8)

Albert Hull

4686 Sinclair Bay Road, Madeira Park, BC. V0N 1S0

Phone: (604) 883-2424

Fax: 883-2414

Chart 3512, 3535, 3514

Showers, laundry, washrooms.

Ice, **water, power.** Groceries, fishing tackle, licences, garbage disposal, rental boats. Walking.

Top: A popular stop right at the entrance to Pender Harbour, at Irvine's Landing for fuel, bait and restaurant, plus overnight moorage. The fuel dock at John Henry's. The docks at Garden Bay Hotel (Above, right).

Headwater Marine (7)

Pender Harbour
Gunboat Bay, B.C. V0N 2H0.
Phone: (604) 883-2406
Chart 3535, 3311, 3512 VHF 73

Marina services:

Transient moorage.
Power. Water.

Entertainment.

Walking on roads. Animal and marine life.

Adjacent facilities:

Fishing charters. Anchorage nearby–consult local chart.

Lowe's Resorts (6)

Davenia and Reg Morton
Box 153, Madeira Park, BC.
V0N 2H0
Phone: (604) 883-2456
Chart 3535, 3311, 3512

Moorage. Limited–primarily for lodge customers. Boats to 28/30 feet.
Manager–Larry Curtis.
Water, power.

Customer services:

Showers, washroms, tackle store, snacks.
Fishing charters.
Accommodation. Boat rentals.
Fishing and dive charters.
Shops nearby.

Note: Moorage guests at Madeira Park or other transient boat crews are welcome to use coin operated laundry and showers at this marina.
Access is by way of an easy walk from Madeira Park public docks.

Above: Bathgate Marina docks and store with laundry and showers in building on left.
Left: Docks and fuel float at Bathgate Marina.
Below: Public docks at Egmont.

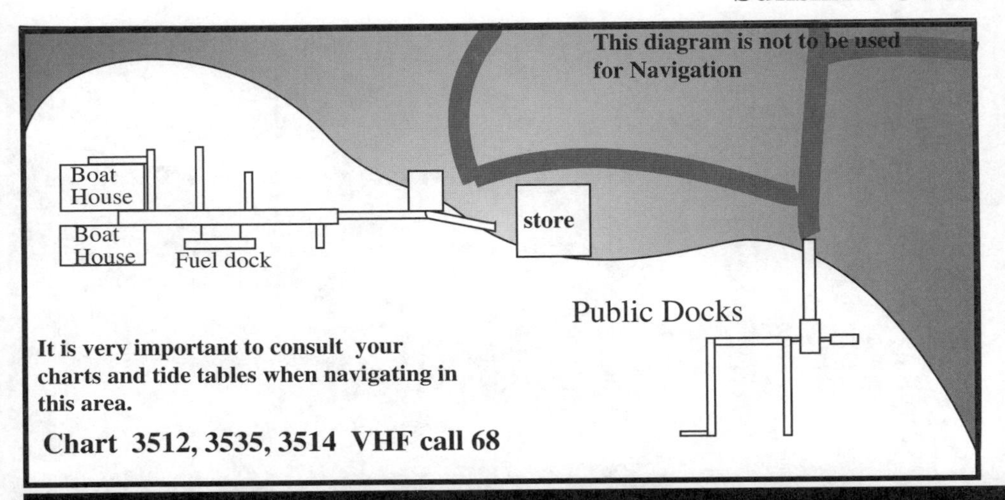

Bathgate Marina & Public Dock

Bathgate General Store & Marina

Doug and Vicki Martin
Egmont BC V0N 1N0
Phone: (604) 883-2222

Hazard: Drying reef in middle of bay on approaches to fuel dock and another off the government dock. Check your chart.

Marina services:

Fuel: Gas, diesel. Propane, kerosene, stove oil, naptha.
Moorage.
Water at dock. Ice.
Power at docks: 15 amp.

Customer services:

Liquor agency. Grocery store–fresh meat and vegetables. Fishing tackle, licences. Water taxi service.
Washrooms, showers, laundry.
Boat, cabin, video and VCR rentals.
Nearby church.
Scuba diving. Charters–ask at marina store for details.
Public pay phone ashore.

Walking: Road access walking or cycling. Nearby hiking trails. Trail to the Sechelt Rapids viewpoint in the Skookumchuck Provincial Park.

Entertainment.

Scuba diving and fishing excellent a short run from harbour.

Adjacent facilities:
Public dock. Access stop before trip to Princess Louisa Inlet.

Egmont Public dock

Fisheries & Oceans dock
Phone 883-9243
Chart 3512, 3535, 3514.
Manager • Float length 145 m
Aircraft Float • Garbage • Waste oil service • Lights •

Egmont Marina at the Back Eddy Pub in Egmont. Opposite: Launching at the ramp adjacent to Royal Reach Marina.

Egmont Marina

John and Margaret Mills
General Delivery,
Egmont, BC V0N 1N0
Phone/fax: (604) 883-2298
Tollfree 1 800 626-0599
Chart 3311, 3512 .

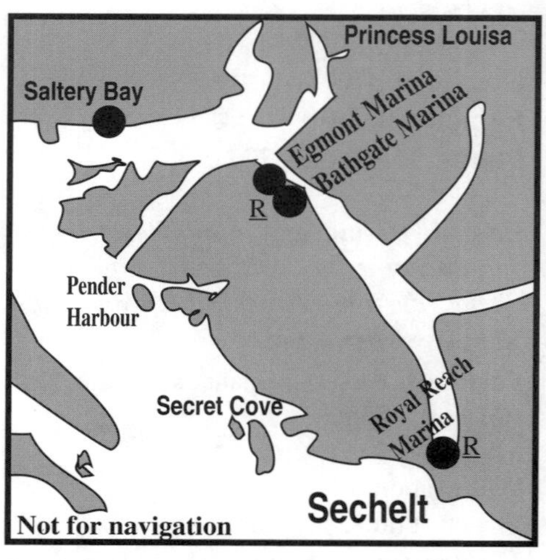

Marina services

Moorage.

Fuel: gas diesel,oils, two stroke oil, live/frozen bait at fuel dock. Power 15, 30amp.

Potable water. Ice, bait, tackle, fishing licences, book exchange, groceries.

Laundry, showers, washrooms. public phone ashore
rental boats available.

Entertainment.

Backeddy Marine Pub, summer long-weekend live entertainment. Pool table. Nearby trails to Skookumchuck rapids.

Adjacent facilities:

Restaurant, diver air station.
Dive and fishing charters.
Launch ramp. Campground–22 sites with power. View cabins.
Kayak lessons and rentals.
Mountainbike rentals.

Royal Reach Marina

Royal Reach Marina and Motel

Joe Mandocdoc
Porpoise Bay BC
Phone: (604) 885-7844
Chart 3311, 3512

Marina services

Moorage.
Power 15 amp. Water.
Ice at marina and motel. Laundry, showers, washrooms at motel and ashore.

Entertainment.

Sechelt nearby has numerous centres, shops and facilities.

Adjacent facilities:

Pub, dive shop, Venture Airways–regular/ scheduled flights.

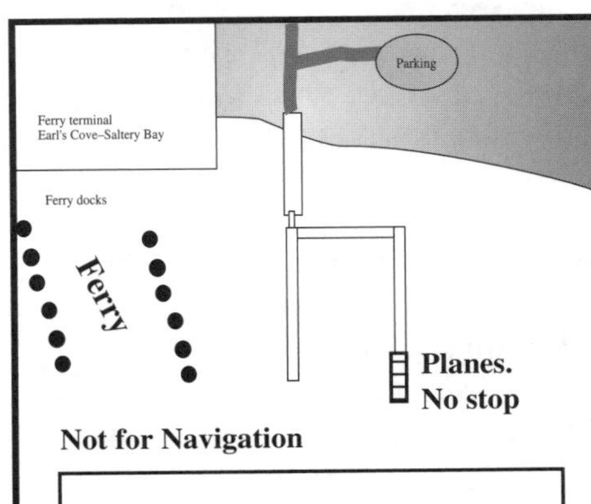

Saltery Bay,

Sunshine Coast
Fisheries & Oceans dock
Phone 487-9541
Chart 3514
Manager • Float length 133 m
Garbage • Lights •
Adjacent ferry dock–Egmont, Sunshine Coast.

Not for Navigation

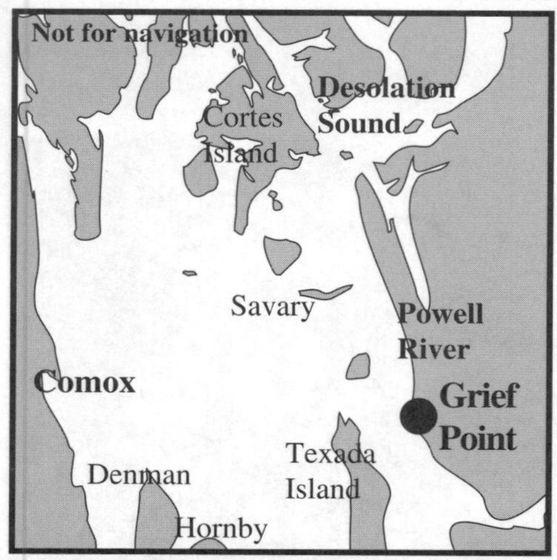

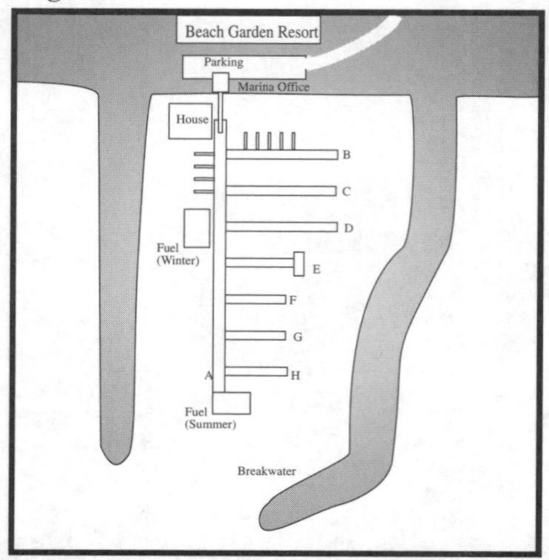

Beach Gardens Resort

Beach Gardens Resort

Dr Cam Hobson
7074 Westminster Ave,
Powell River, BC. V8A 1C5
Phone: (604) 485-7734 Resort 485-6267
Fax (604) 485-2343
Chart 3311, 3513 VHF 68

Marina Entrance.

At breakwater just south of Grief Point.

Marina services:

Petro Canada **Fuel:** Gas, diesel., oil. ice, live bait. Mechanic and services available from local and nearby marine operators and facilities can be arranged.
Moorage: Large permanent marina with limited overnight moorage slips. Reserve.
Water at dock. Multiple outlets.
Power at docks: 30, 20, 15 amp. Multiple outlets.
Laundry, Showers, Washrooms.

Customer services:

Hotel with full facilities. Sauna, pool. Cold wine and beer store.
Grocery store, post office and tackle shop nearby.
Nearby church/es. Fine dining restaurant in the hotel. Pub open 7 days a week.
Walking trails or road access. Some beachfront walks.
Fishing charters. Dive shop nearby, air, rentals. Scuba diving arrangements and charters–ask hotel for details.
Public pay phones ashore.

Entertainment.

Canoe Room marine pub.

Adjacent facilities:

Tennis, golf, nearby.

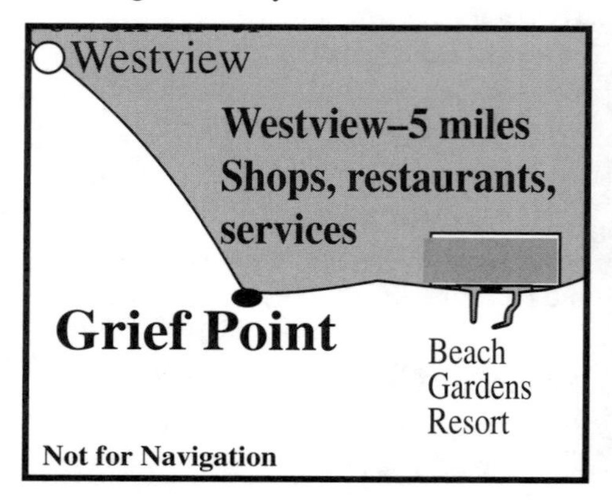

Beach Garden Resort is one of the most popular stops on the Sunshine Coast.

The hotel/resort complex became a favoured stopover for cruising mariners in the mid 1970s when management at the hotel pursuaded government to build a breakwater in front of their property. The breakwater was finished and later extended to accommodate resident boat owners in need of moorage. It became also a major stop for mariners en route to Desolation Sound. Monitoring the weather conditions at Grief Point has been made easy by the inclusion some years ago of Grief Point as a weather reporting station. The existence of Beach Gardens Resort at Grief Point provided the staffing required to observe and report current conditions.

At the marina is a good place to be during strong wind conditions. Northwesterlies blow up some vigorous seas off Grief Point. Often seas will run in the opposite direction too. Rough conditions from either direction usually mean a calmer sea in the lee of Grief Point and a short run around the very tip of Grief Point means a brief spell in the waves before shelter behind the Beach Gardens breakwater. At extreme low tides the entrance becomes quite narrow and the depth, especially close to shore is reduced.

Each year scores of boats stop over in search of recreation at the spa, the fine cuisine for which the hotel restaurant has become famous and the tranquil setting of the facility. Fishermen and other vacationers fly into the area to spend time at Beach Garden Resort or out fishing with one of the regular fishing charter operators based at the marina.

In summer time the fuel dock is located at the entrance to the marina and in winter it is moved closer towards the shore for protection from the swells that wash around the end of the breakwater. Some year-round marina tenants means that not all dock space is available for transient moorage and it is best to check with the dock manager before tying up. In boating season a full time staff working the docks will be awaiting your arrival. It is also best to check in by phone or call on VHF prior to your arrival. Reservations may be made well in advance or at the last moment depending on available space.

The next stop for fuel and moorage after Grief Point is Westview a few miles north en route to Powell River, Lund and Desolation Sound. Fuel is available south at Pender Harbour.

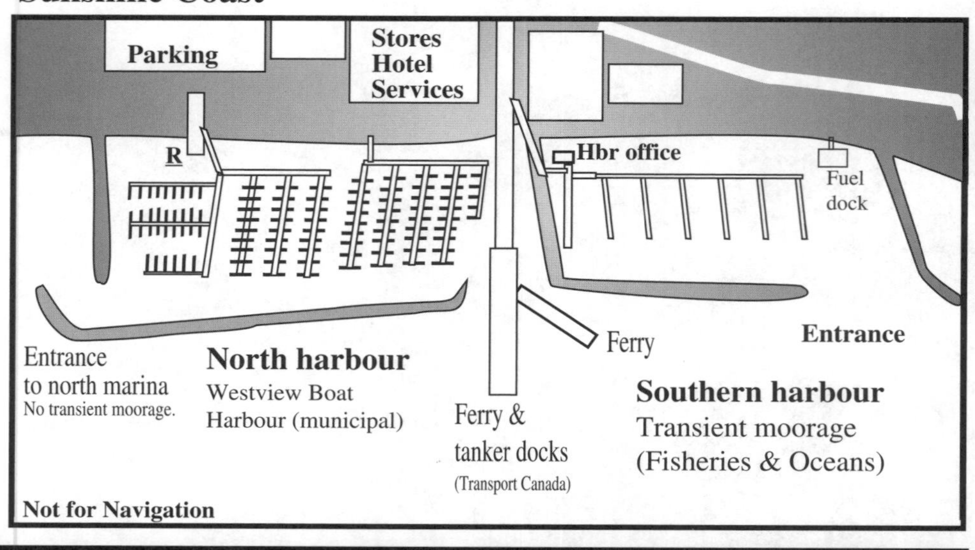

Powell River (Public docks)

Westview (north) Boat Harbour

Transport Canada dock/Boat Harbour
Phone 485-5244 **(no transient moorage)**
Chart 3311, 3563, 3514
breakwater and marina
Launch ramp • Water • Lights • Power •
Near ferry landing, city restaurants, shops.
Fuel dock nearby: Gas, diesel, outboard mix, naptha, water, ice. (in South harbour)
Fuel dock phone: (604) 485-2867

Blubber Bay

Texada Island

Transport Canada dock
Chart 3311
Float length 13 m
Limited facilities and moorage.
Best for overnight at Westview on Sunshine Coast shore opposite.
Facilities also at Powell River.
Marina at Beach Garden Resort.

Powell River South harbour

Transient moorage
Fisheries & Oceans dock
Chart 3311, 3563, 3513
Manager–Jim Parsons **(604) 485-5244**
• Float length 625 m
Breakwater • Grid • Garbage • Waste oil disposal • Water • Lights • Power • Public phone • Washrooms •
Near city restaurants, shops, hotels. Enter southern marina via fuel dock.
Fuel dock. Inside breakwater. Gas, diesel. Outboard mix. Ice.
All services and facilities. Propane, fishing tackle, marine supplies nearby. Most located at north harbour. Also up town.
Ferries adjacent to Comox, Vancouver Island and Texada Island.

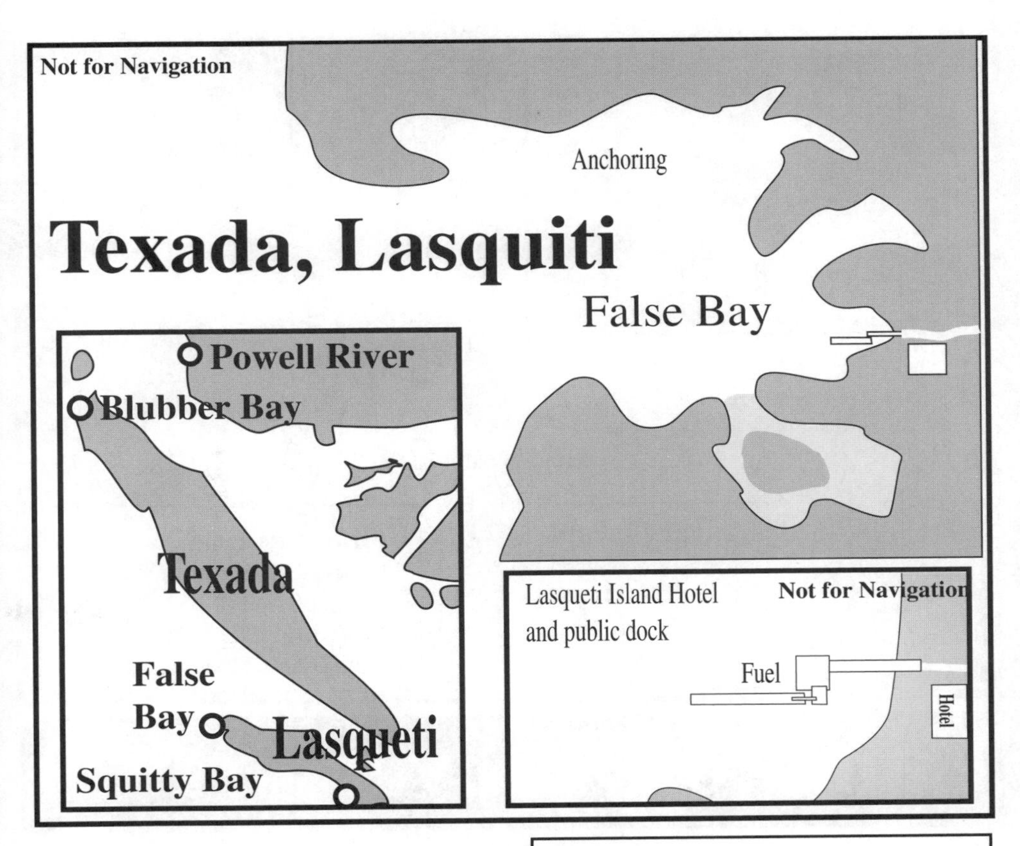

Lasqueti Island Hotel & Resort (Public docks)

Michael Oltarz
Lasqueti Island, BC,
V0R 2J0
Phone: (604) 333-8846
Chart 3512, 3513, 3536

Marina services:

Fuel: Gas, diesel. Stove oil. Ice at local store. **Moorage** (limited) at nearby government dock. **Water** at dock.

Customer services:

Hotel with facilities including jacuzzi, gym, convenience store. Showers. Public phone. Washrooms. Restaurant–licensed.
Walking road access. Fishing and boat charters. Good scuba diving in nearby locations. Public pay phone.

False Bay

Lasqueti Island
Transport Canada
Chart 3536, 3512, 3513
Float length 36 m • Aircraft Float • Garbage • Lights • Power •

Squitty Bay

Lasqueti Island
Fisheries & Oceans dock
Chart 3512
Float length 47 m • Garbage • Walking, trails, island roads.

Entertainment.

Bike rentals. Fishing charters available.

Adjacent facilities:

Anchoring at end of bay–see local chart.

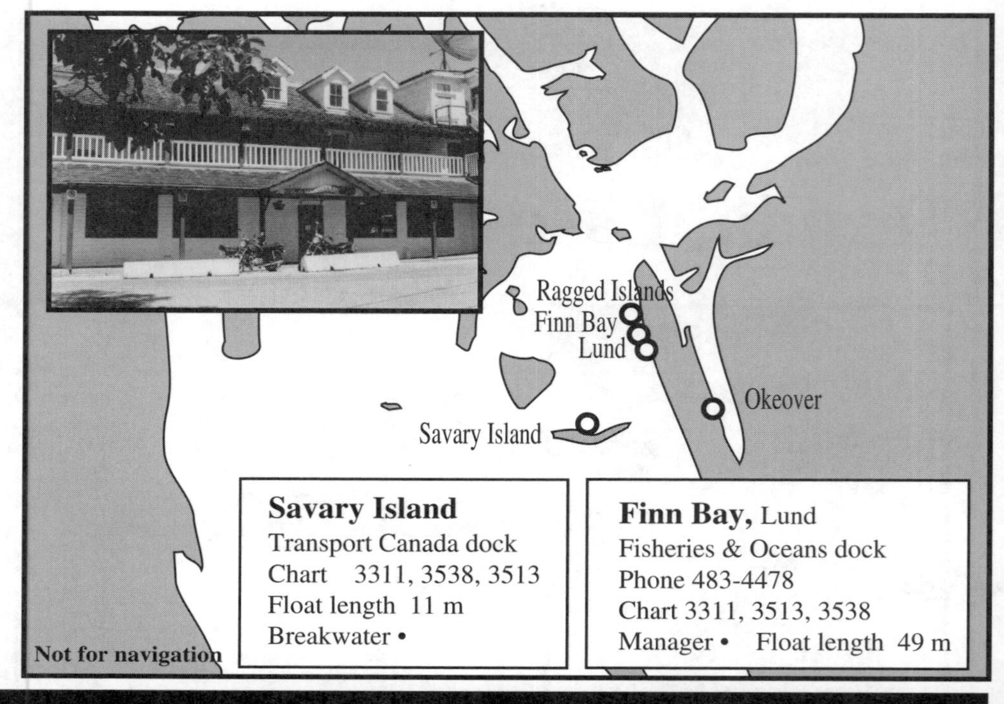

Lund to Okeover

Lund Public Marina

Public docks

Phone: (604) 483-3199.

Chart 3311, 3538, 3513 VHF call 73

See Government docks.

Marina services:

Fuel: Gas, diesel, **showers, laundry,** ice, propane.

Mechanic and services available.

Emergency towing. Ways, engines. Service.

Customer services:

Hotel with restaurant, pub and other facilities. General store, groceries, tackle, marine supplies. Charts. Some hardware. Liquor agency.

Nearby church/es. Restaurant. Pub open 7 days a week.

Walking trails or road access. Some beachfront walks.

Fishing charters. Dive shop, air, rentals. Scuba diving arrangements and charters– ask hotel for details.

Public pay phones ashore.

Adjacent facilities:

Stores, hotel.

Lund Marine & Diesel

Box 73, Lund, BC

V0N Z9O

Phone: (604) 483-9002

Fax: (604) 483-4914

Lund Hotel

Lund Auto and Outboard

The Lund Hotel, opposite inset, is a landmark for mariners and road travellers. Above, the marina has a recently upgraded breakwater, entrances south and north. Left: Seafood shop on the wharf and many other facilities in and around the hotel.

When there is a lot of traffic at a marina for fuel or other services and you have the choice of moorage, it is best to select a spot out of the way of the action. If you can find space only close to the coming and going vessels, drop fenders over the exposed side of your boat in case another vessel needs to come alongside, which sometimes happens unintentionally, especially in windy or strong current conditions.

Okeover Inlet (Arm)
Fisheries & Oceans dock
Phone 483-2218
Chart 3559, 3538, 3513
Manager • Float length 35 m
Breakwater • Lights • Power •
Public phone ashore •
Near restaurant.

Lund, Sunshine Coast
Fisheries & Oceans dock
483-4711
Chart 3311, 3513, 3538
Manager • Float length 204 m
Launch ramp • Breakwater •
Garbage • Waste oil disposal •
Water • Lights • Power • Public phone •
Adjacent Lund Hotel, restaurants, shops.
Marine services. Fuel, supplies.

Lund is an interesting place, existing as the last town on the Sunshine Coast road. It has an historic hotel and numerous facilities including antique store, watersport and dive shop, grocery store selling a fair selection of marine hardware, a fresh seafood shop and an adjacent marine service centre and chandlery catering year round to the commercial and fishing trade. It's also a busy fuel stop before entering Desolation Sound. However there is a lesser known fuel stop at the Copeland Islands just a few miles north. Ragged Islands Marine has a pricing structure that makes you pleased to have stopped there for fuel.

Ragged Islands Marine

Ragged Islands Marine

Wendy and Derek Cox
P.O. Box 22
Lund BC. V0N 2G0
Phone: (604) 438-8184
Chart 3538

Marina services:

Moorage: Overnight limited space.
Fuel: Gas, diesel, oil.
Water, snacks. Gifts.
Fishing tackle, licenses.

Customer Services:

Accumulate fuel points for lower prices.

Adjacent facilities:
Ragged Islands Marine Park. Anchoring. This is the entrance to Desolation Sound.

Ragged Islands Marine docks can accommodate a couple of boats overnight. The store has some snacks and supplies. It is a good fuel stop.

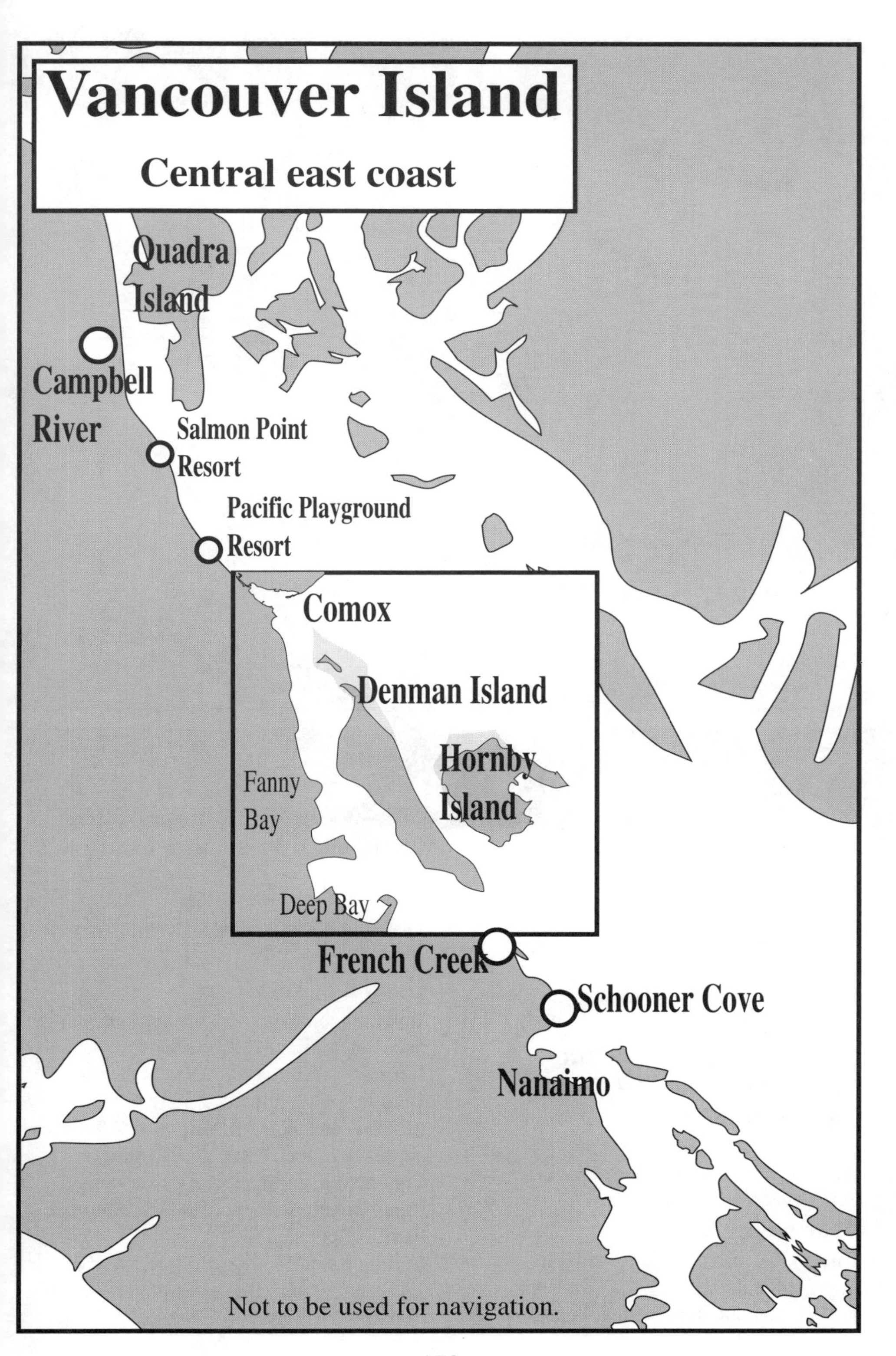
Vancouver Island
Central east coast
Quadra Island
Campbell River
Salmon Point Resort
Pacific Playground Resort
Comox
Denman Island
Hornby Island
Fanny Bay
Deep Bay
French Creek
Schooner Cove
Nanaimo
Not to be used for navigation.

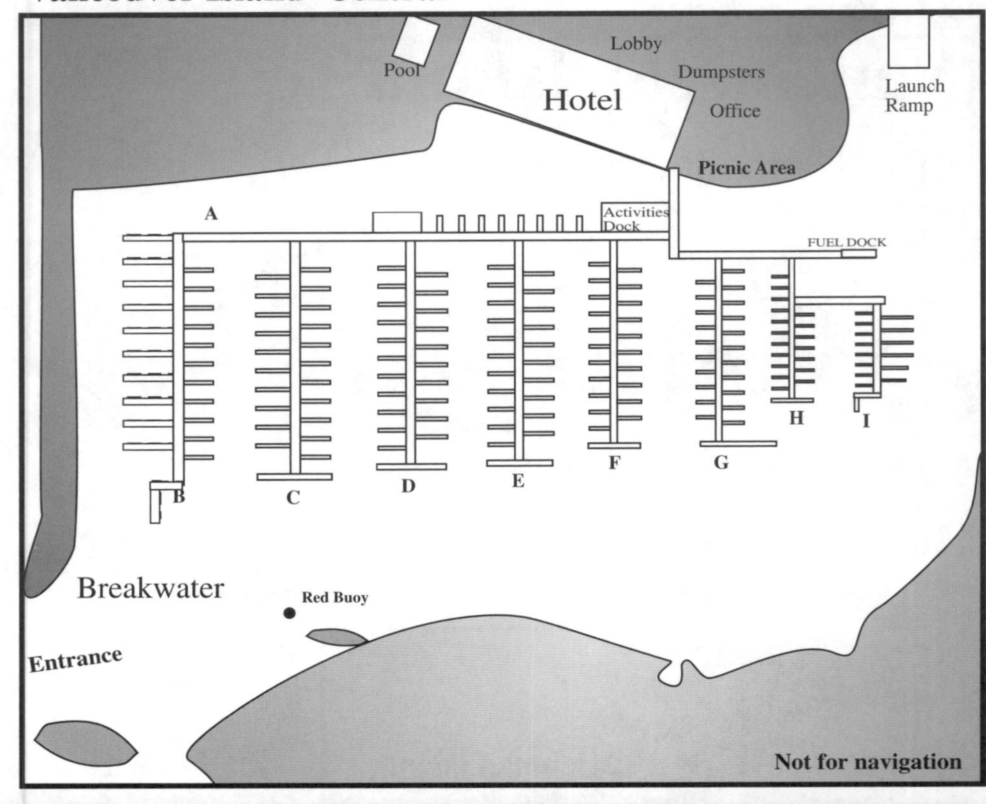

Schooner Cove Resort

Chart 3512, 3459, VHF call 16 & 73

Schooner Cove Resort

Hotel & Marina

Murray Hamilton
Box 12, Schooner House,
3521 Dolphin Drive,
Nanoose Bay, BC, V0R 2R0
Phone: (604) 468-7691
Fax: (604) 468-5744

Hazard: Drying rock in entrance to marina. Pass marker to port and keep close to floats.

Marina services:

Fuel: Gas, oils, service available–can be arranged at dock.
400 permanent and transient berths.

Water at dock. All berths.
Power at docks: 30, 50, 15 amp. All slips.

Customer services:

Hotel, accommodation, restaurant, lounge, pub. Fine dining. Coffee shop
Laundry, Showers, Washrooms.
Outdoor pool, hot tub. Public phones.
Marine supplies, fishing gear, licences, charts, bait, **ice,** books, gifts, snacks.
Cold beer and wine store. Bakery.
Nearby church/es**:** multi-denominational.
Post Office:
Courtesy shuttle to post office, banks, groceries. Scuba diving arrangements and charters–ask marina for details.

Schooner Cove is in one of the most beautiful settings on the coast. Nearby golf courses and developments have turned the area into a prized piece of real estate, and the adjacent waters into prime fishing and scuba diving destinations. The hotel marina office is adjacent to restaurants and other facilities, including marine supplies.

Walking: Road access walking or cycling. Nearby parks.
Entertainment.
Fishing excellent near marina.
Rental bicycles. Horseback riding, nature walks.
Adjacent facilities:
Courtesy shuttle to golf at Fairwinds 18 hole course, bare boat charters and fishing charters. Group facilities.
Launching ramp. Picnic area overlooking marina.

From Nanaimo go along the coast to Campbell River with a stop possible at Schooner Cove, one of the largest and finest facilities anywhere with hotel and all amenities including golfing nearby, good fishing and excellent scuba diving. Farther north up Vancouver Island's east coast is Comox with a vast set of docks, private and public. Des Reid Marina or Blackfin next door, with lots of transient moorage and restaurants ashore, a park and nearby stores and other facilities along with events such as Nautical Days each

August will keep you entertained and enthused about the stop-over. En route to Campbell River you may decide to stop at a government dock and the ones at Deep Bay and French Creek are substantial, or try for space at Pacific Playgrounds Marina or Salmon Point Resort.

Fanny Bay,

Fisheries & Oceans dock
Phone 335, 2513 Chart 3513
Manager • Float length 42 m
Breakwater • Grid • Power •

Deep Bay,

Public docks. Large, protected marina near Hornby and Denman Islands.
Chart 3513

Ford Cove, Hornby Island.

Fisheries & Oceans dock
Phone 335-2169
Chart 3527, 3513
Manager • Float length 86 m
Breakwater • Grid • Garbage • Waste oil disposal • Water • Lights • Power • Public phone • Washrooms •

Denman Island

Fisheries & Oceans dock
Chart 3527, 3513
Float length 24 m
Launch ramp • Breakwater •

French Creek,

Fisheries & Oceans dock
Phone 248-5051 1 977-4725 toll free
Chart 3512, 3513
Manager • Float length 804 m • Ramp • Breakwater • Grid • Garbage • Waste oil disposal • Water • Lights • Power • dry storage • rentals • repairs • moorage • public phone • ice • gas • adjacent restaurants, shops. Seafood store–prawns, crabs. Foot ferry to Lasqueti. Coast Guard station. Launch ramp.

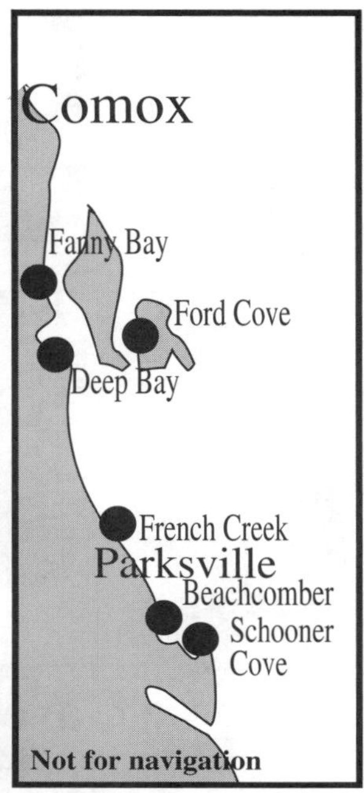

Above: Schooner Cove Marina.
Left: Beachcomber Marina, a relatively unknown stop, but mainly permanent moorage. Anchor in bay.

Beachcomber Marina

Beachcomber Marina

Bill Loewen
RR #1 Box 21, Beachcomber
Nanoose Bay, BC, V0N 3A0
Phone/Fax: (604) 468-7222
Chart 3459, 3512
Hazard: Enter marina through channel markers. Reef extends between breakwater and port buoy. Consult chart.

Marina services:

Fuel: gas, diesel, ice (in summer).
Permanent and limited transient docks.
Water at dock.
Power at docks: 30 amp.

Customer services:

Summer: Snacks, pop.
Walking: Road access walking.
Adjacent facilities:
Launch ramp.
Anchorage across bay behind log booms.

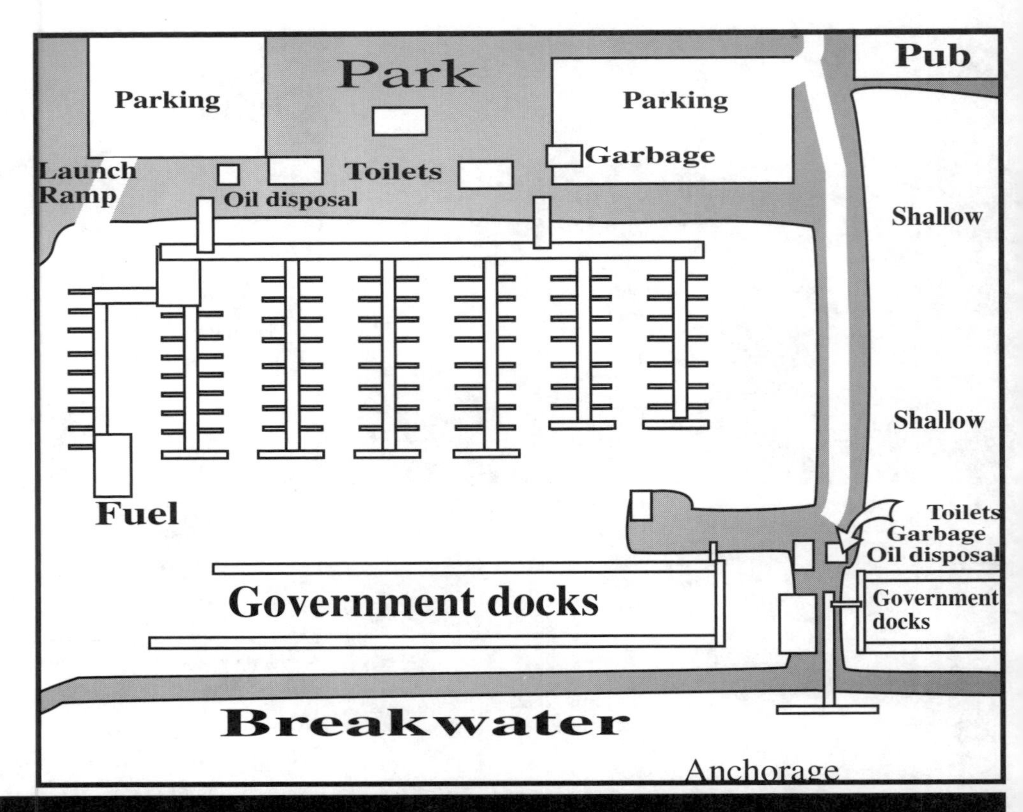

Blackfin Marina

The Blackfin Pub & Marina

Dave Desmeules
132 Port Augusta St,
Comox, BC, V9N 8G7
Phone: (604) 339-5030 (pub)
Phone: (604) 339-4664 (marina)
Fax: 339-3022
Charts 3527, 3513 VHF call 68

Marina services:

Fuel: Gas. Diesel. oils, outboard mix. Ice.
Moorage: Boats up to about 45 feet.
Water at dock.
Power at docks.

Customer services:

Laundry, Showers, Washrooms.
Restaurant and pub.
Scuba diving arrangements and charters–ask hotel for details. Public pay phone.

Entertainment.

Town pier–pleasant for walking.
Nautical Days celebrated every August.
Picnic facilities at Marina Park.
Rental vehicles.

Adjacent facilities:

Charters. Desolation Sound Yacht Charters. Golf, Shopping centre, liquor store, post office. Public dock. Garbage disposal. Canadian Armed Forces base. HMCS Quadra camp at Goose Point.

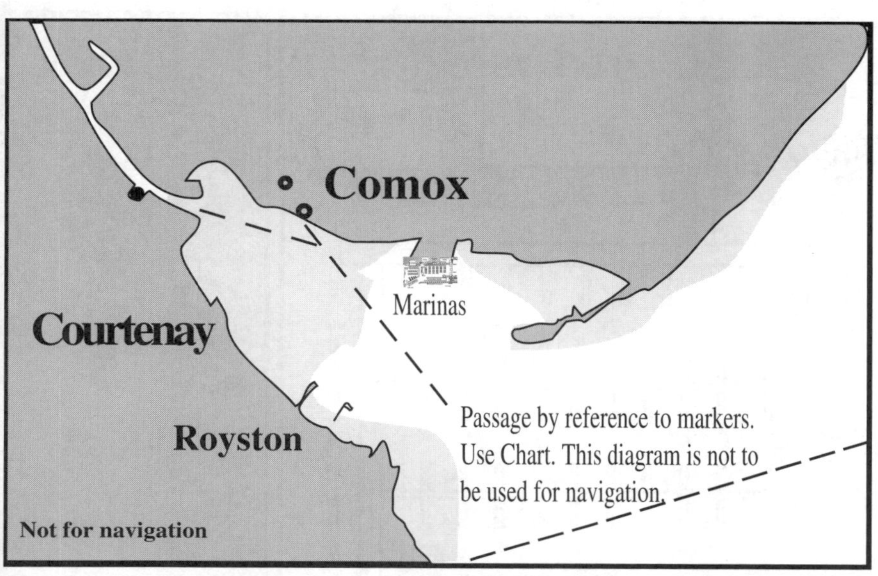

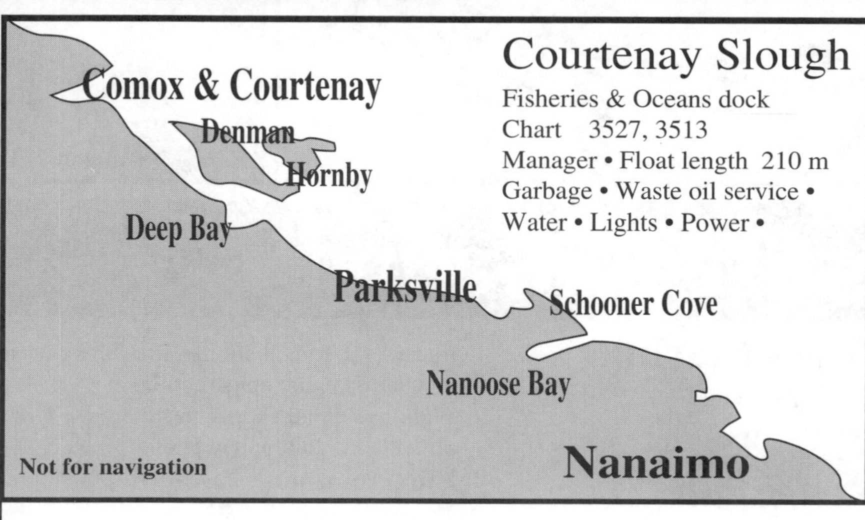

Courtenay Slough

Fisheries & Oceans dock
Chart 3527, 3513
Manager • Float length 210 m
Garbage • Waste oil service •
Water • Lights • Power •

Comox

Fisheries & Oceans dock
Phone 339-6041
Chart 3513, 3527
Manager • Float length 340 m •
Breakwater • Grid • Garbage • Waste oil service •
Water • Lights • Power • Public phone
• Washrooms •

Ferry to Powell River departs from Comox.

Comox
Royston

Fisheries & Oceans dock
Chart 3527, 3513
Manager • Float length 140 m
Waste oil service •

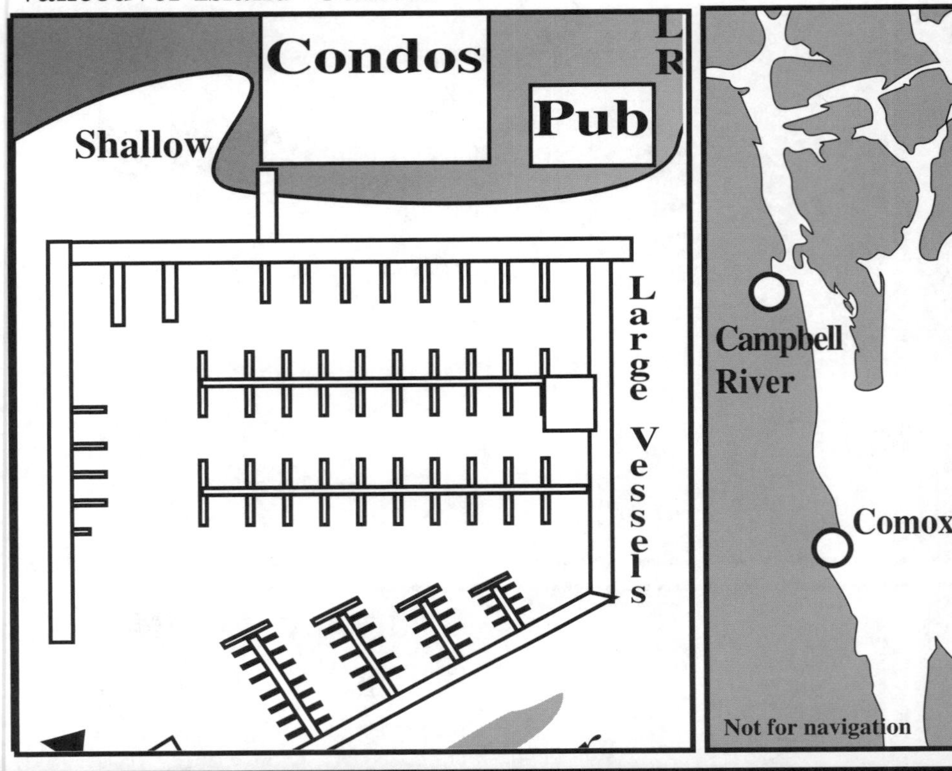

Des Reid Marina

Des Reid Marina

Margaret and Des Reid
1805 Beaufort Ave.,
Comox, BC, V9N 1R9
Phone: (604) 339-4566
(604) 339-6153 (marina)
Fax: (604) 339-3022
Charts 3527, 3513

Marina services:

Moorage: Transient and permanent. Boats to all sizes.
Water at dock.
Power at docks: 50, 30, 15 amp.
Hydro-hoist available.

Customer services:

Laundry, Showers, Washrooms. Ice. Restaurant. Lunch, dinner. Plus breakfast at new motel under construction.
Walking: Road access, nearby park. Town of Comox. Public pay phone.

Entertainment.

Town pier–walk.
Nautical Days celebrated every August.
Picnic facilities at Marina Park.
Rental vehicles available.

Adjacent facilities:

Charters. Desolation Sound Yacht Charters. Golf, shopping centre, liquor store, post office. Motel suites (under construction for 1994/1995). Yacht club. Excellent view and location. Public dock. Garbage disposal. Canadian Armed Forces base. HMCS Quadra camp at Goose Point. Ferry to Powell River departs Comox.

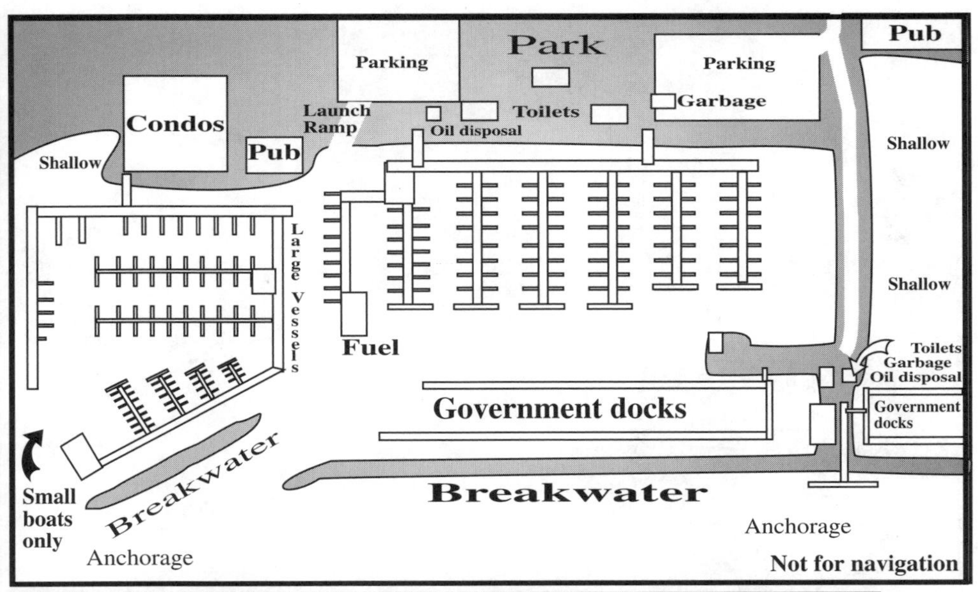

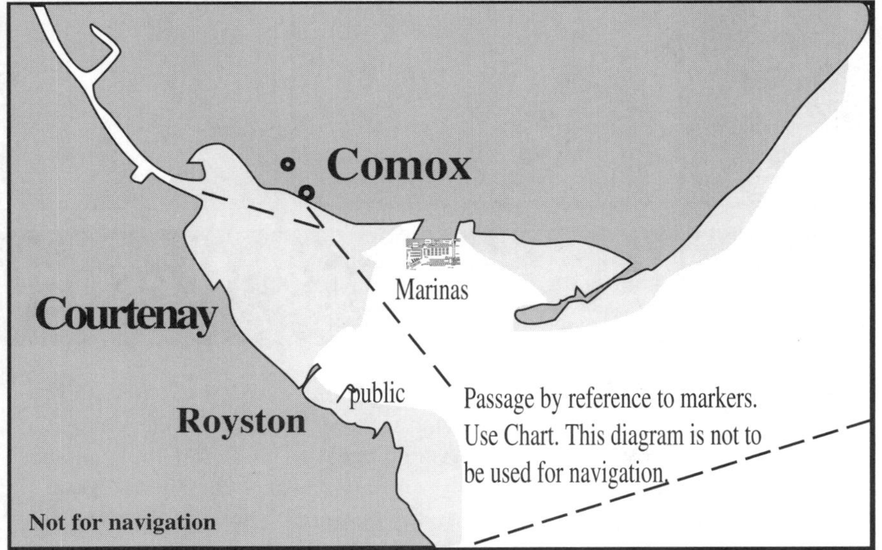

Comox Municipal Marina

Moorage for small boats & a few large slips.
Phone: (604) 339-2202 Ask for Marina.
Water, power, garbage disposal.
Public phone. Used oil disposal.
Fishing pier and promenade.
Adjacent anchorage.
Hazard: drying flats to north in harbour near pier
Chart 3599. 3527

Courtenay Slough Marina

Limited moorage for small boats.
Phone: (604) 338-8124.
Water, power, public phone.
Hazard: Shallow river. Depths allow boat with shallow draft only–about 4 feet. Check chart. 3599.
Walking: Uptown Courtenay.
Public pay phone.

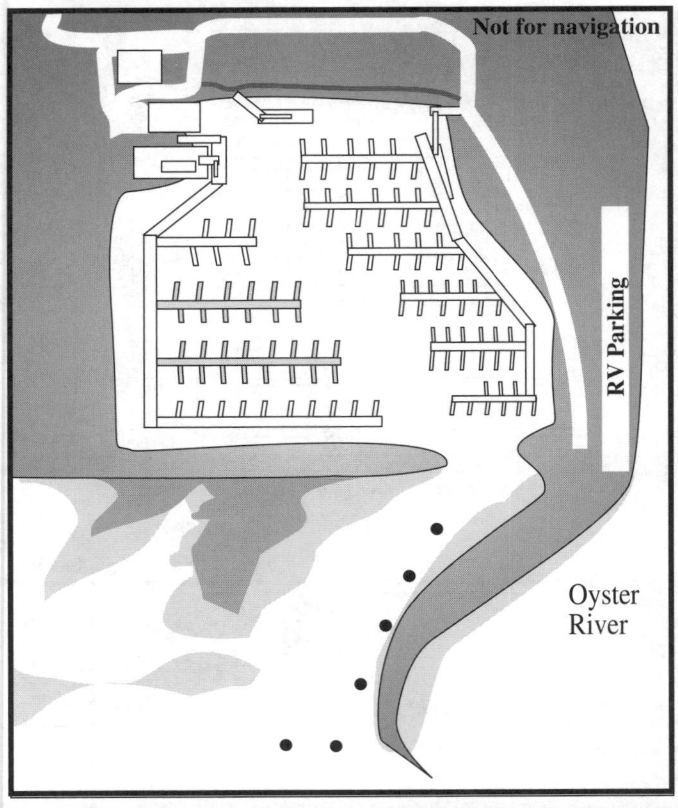

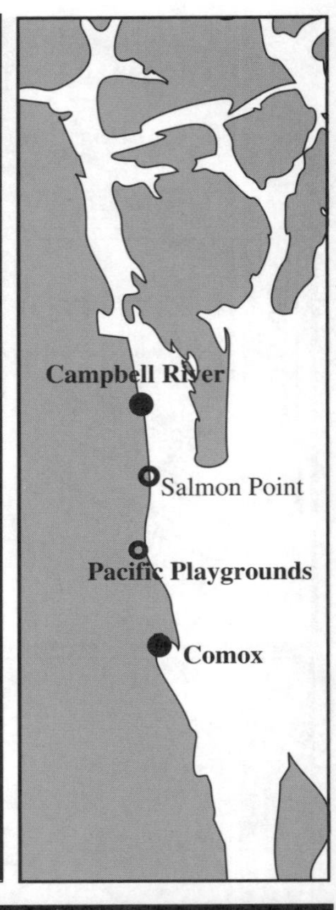

Pacific Playgrounds Resort

Pacific Playgrounds Resort

Bob Nissen
9082 Clarkson Drive,
Black Creek, BC. V9J 1B3
Phone: (604) 337-5600.
Chart 3527, 3513 (Alongside Oyster River Mouth.)
Hazard–Channel may be entered at 4 foot (plus) tides. Follow pilings.

Marina:

Moorage. Sheltered basin. Numerous slips to 40 feet.
Fuel: Gas, diesel. **Water, power**–30 amp.

Services:

Marine store: Supplies, tackle, charts, fishing licenses, groceries. public phone. Resort facilities including heated pool, grassy play area. **Showers, laundry, washrooms.** Garbage disposal.

Entertainment and nearby facilities:

Golf, mini-golf, driving range, tennis, hiking roads and trails. Stores and restaurants. Scenery, sunsets and eagles. Nearby beach walks, bird watching. Fishing: guides available.

Pacific Playgrounds Resort with its open water entrance. Its approaches are clearly marked.

Nanaimo to Campbell River.

This coastal section is not well known to mariners from Vancouver and mainland points south. Most boats cruising to DesolationSound and beyond travel out of Washington State and the Lower Mainland of British Columbia via the Sunshine Coast. Mariners from Victoria and Sidney tend to favour the Vancouver Island side and therefore know the coastline better.

After leaving Nanaimo, one can stop at Schooner Cove for a few nights of rest and recreation, knowing that golf is just a short courtesy bus ride away, or that there are some excellent roads and trails to walk. The salmon fishing out of Schooner Cove is excellent and the scuba diving surprisingly good, with such locations nearby as Mistaken Island and Sangster. There are resorts along the way that cater emphatically to sports fishing and these include Pacific Playgrounds on the Oyster River and Salmon Point Resort approaching Campbell River.

Typically these resorts cater to RV campers and lodge guests, but they also welcome overnight mooring guests who have full acces to their many resort facilities. After even one day of boating it is relaxing to climb into a spa and unwind, better still after several days. Or to stretch one's legs on shoreside nature trails, on the tennis courts or the golf courses available. Guides are available for fishing and this is a good idea if you really want to catch salmon.

As you travel up this coast you have the option of stopping at places such as Deep Bay, Nanoose, Fanny Bay, French Creek and across at Hornby or Denman Islands. These islands are beautiful and the waters that surround them worthy of slow cruising by just for observation and sightseeing. Flora Islet attract boatloads of scuba divers in search of the famed six-gill sharks that dwell in the near shallows. These creatures are rarely seen in BC. They are encountered frequently by divers at Hornby Island although seldom if ever by others. Dally around the islands while water conditions are calm but look for protected overnight moorage at Vancouver Island shorline marinas when the wind is up. Ford Cove on Hornby is the only hope of shelter in an adverse blow. Dock space is limited and anchoring out may not provide a comfortable night's sleep. If you have a shore boat visit the lighthouse keeper on Chrome

Vancouver Island Central

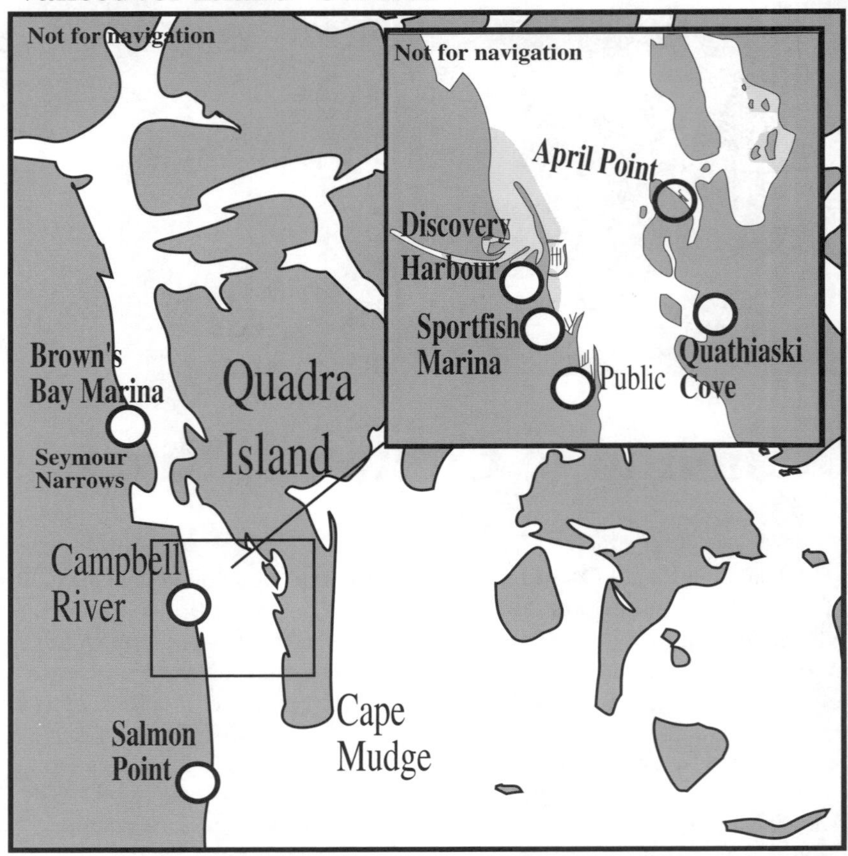

Island and look for the petroglyphs on a rock face just below the lighthouse. Many artists live on Hornby and if you can reach the island centre you are bound to find some excellent works of art by local people.

Entering Campbell River you pass Cape Mudge on your starboard side but be mindful of the tides and winds as a huge sea can occur off Quadra Island when conditions are stormy or just windy at maximum current velocities. The currents in the passage can be strong and treacherous too so take care to keep out of the most current swept areas if you are running in a slow boat. There are numerous mooring options in Campbell River, from the government docks at Quathiaski Cove or in Campbell River with their limited or typical public facilities to a night aboard tied up to the docks of April Point Fishing Lodge on Quadra or Brown's Bay Marina just beyond Seymour Narrows. There are large marinas such as Discovery Harbour or the Discovery Marina alongside the ferry dock for Quadra. This latter facility is operated by the Discovery Inn and the large Sportfish Centre located there offers many facilities as well as fuel, charter fishing and scuba excursions. Campbell River is renown for its outstanding scuba diving and several operators are located there to cater to the needs of visiting divers.

Anchoring in Gowlland Harbour offers overnight protection from most wind and current conditions.

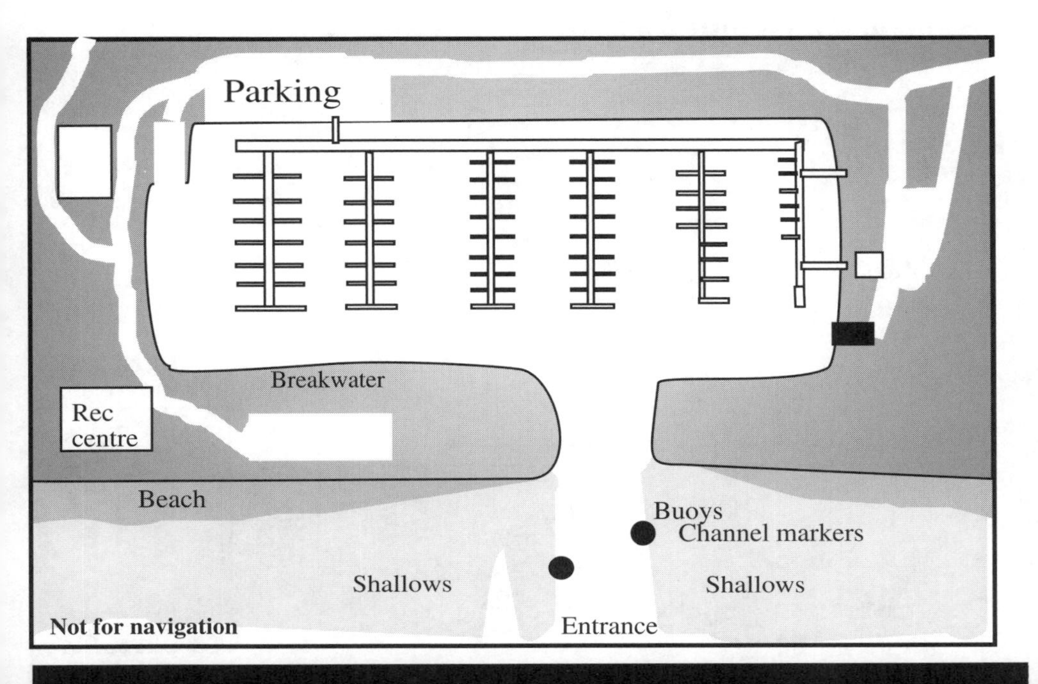

Salmon Point Resort

Salmon Point Resort

2176 Salmon Point Road,
BC. V9H 1E5
Phone: (604) 923-6605

Chart 3527, 5313

Hazard: Narrow channel into marina .Shallow. Proceed between floats off breakwater. Call–ask marina for entrance guidance.

Marina:

Sheltered moorage for up to 200 small boats (to 26 ft.).
Fuel: Gas, limited water, power. Phone.

Services:

Resort with many amenities–for resort, moorage and RV guests. Restaurant. Hot tub, heated pool.

Nature trails, tenting. Laundromat. Restrooms, showers.
Fishing guides and charters. Garbage disposal. Fish freezing and packaging.

Entertainment and nearby facilities:

Golf, mini-golf, driving range, tennis, hiking roads and trails. Stores. Scenery, sunsets and eagles. Nearby beach walks, bird watching. Fishing.

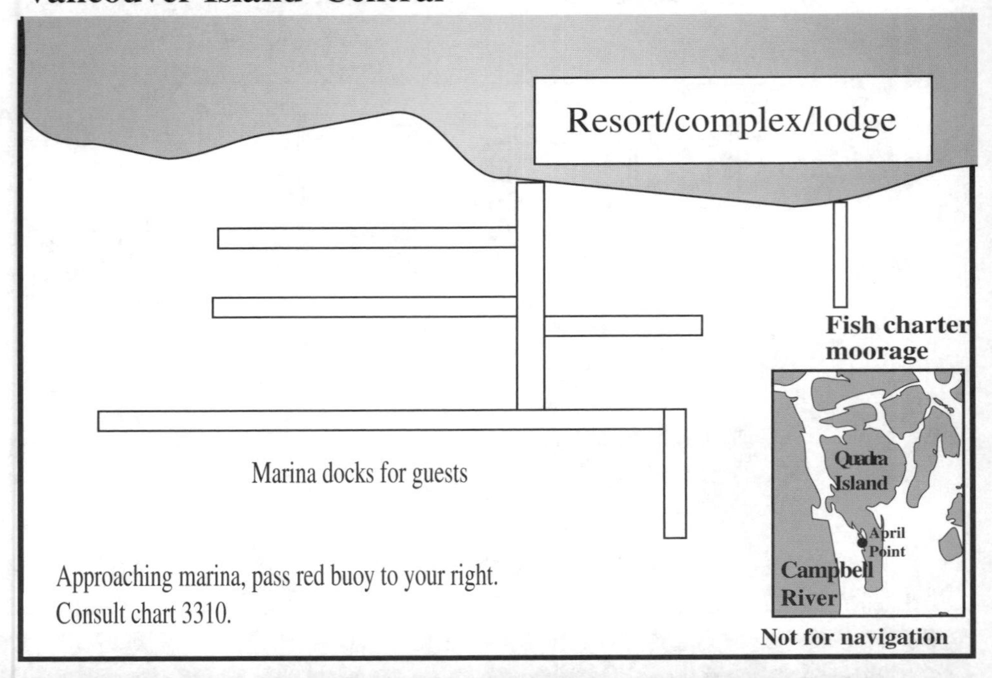

April Point Marina

April Point
Fishing Lodge
Resort & Marina

Eric & Warren Peterson. Joy Peterson.

P.O. Box 1, Campbell River,
BC. V9W 4Z9
Phone: (604) 285-3621 (lodge)
285-2222 (marina) Fax (604) 285-2016
Charts 3310, 3540, 3539, 3463 VHF 73

Marina services:

Fuel: Gas, diesel, oil. **Ice**, live bait. Mechanic and services on site. Fibreglass repairs. Outboard motors sales/service.
Moorage. Large permanent marina with overnight or extended moorage available. Reservations recommended in mid summer.
Water at dock. Multiple outlets.
Power at docks: 20, 30, 50 amp. Multiple outlets.
Laundry, showers, washrooms.

Customer services:

Lodge with full numerous amenities.
Fishing guides and charters.
Restaurant. Breakfast, lunch, dinner. Open 7 days a week.
Coffee shop. gift shop.
Nearby church/es.
Walking trails or road access.
Some beachfront walks.
Scuba diving arrangements and charters–ask lodge for details.
Public pay phones ashore.
Scooter rentals. Taxi service.
Accommodations at lodge and bungalows.
Limousine to airport. Taxi service.

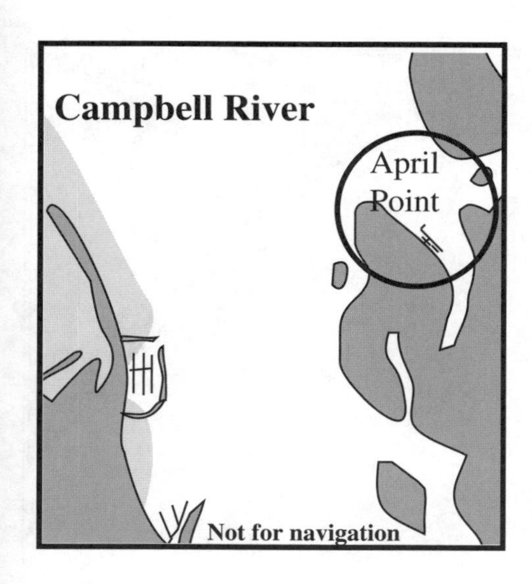

Campbell River is a busy place. There are resorts at this international sportfishing playground that cater solely to fishermen, offering guided salmon fishing and tournaments. Some offer no transient moorage while others have an open door to overnight boating stops. The velocity of water surging through Seymour Narrows just north of the town makes for interesting navigation, even dangerous so be mindful of tides and current, especially when venturing through the narrows or around the bottom of Quadra Island and its infamous Cape Mudge during gusty winds and swift moving waters.

Fuel up at Campbell River or across the way at Quathiaski Cove, or just beyond Seymour Narrows at Brown's Bay, because you may not find fuel too conveniently for a while if you are going north. Unless you turn off to Blind Channel and head into Desolation Sound. Blind Channel not only has fuel but also an excellent restaurant, general store and other facilities including a liquor agency. Fuel is available also at Heriot Bay on the east side of Quadra Island as well as at Gorge Harbour, Manson's Landing and Refuge Cove.

Entertainment.

Barbecue on Saturday nights.
Cable television.

Adjacent facilities:

Kenmore Air regular flights.
Liquor, grocery, arts and crafts and other stores including post office nearby.
Hiking trails at Rebecca Spit Provincial Park on Quadra Island.
Also walk island roads, trails and beaches.
Indian Museum and Cultural Centre.
Philips Marine. Fax (604) 285-2407

Notes:

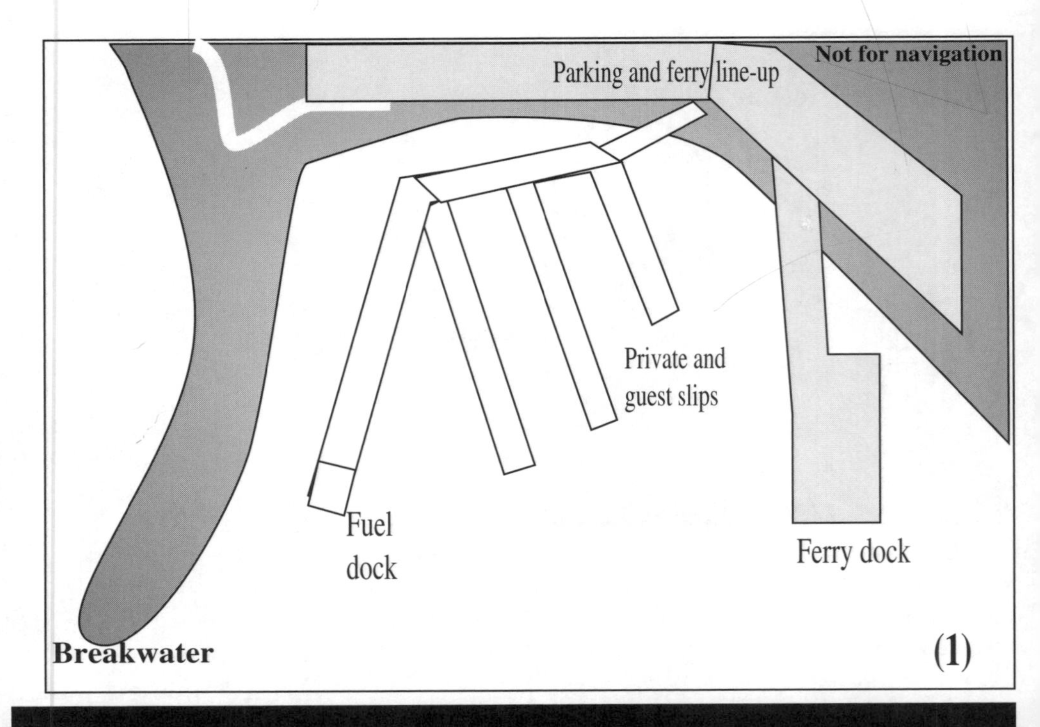

Sportfish Centre

1 Discovery Marina Sportfish Centre

Paul MacKay. Ernie Johnson (manager)
9775 Shopper Row, Campbell River, BC. V9W 2C5
Phone: (604) 287-4911
Chart 3540, 3539 VHF call 73

Marina services:

Campbell River Chevron Marine Station (Dave Facey)
Campbell River,
BC. V9W 6Y4
Phone: (604) 287-3319
Fax: (604) 287-8767
Chart 3540, 3539 VHF 73
Fuel: Gas, diesel, stove oil, outboard mix, sani-dump. **Moorage.** 2700 feet docks.
Power: 15, 20, 30 amp. 50 amp/220 volt.
Water. Garbage disposal.
Dockside marine services.

Customer services:

Laundry, showers, ice, bait.
Public phone ashore.
Marine charts, books, fishing gear, licences, boat supplies.
CNG, kerosene and stove fuels.
Light refreshment (snacks).
Nearby church/es: multi-denominational.
Walking: Road access walking or cycling.

Entertainment:

Scuba diving arrangements and charters–ask marina for details.
Fishing excellent in general area .
Fishing charters, boat rentals.

Adjacent facilities:

Restaurants. Ferry adjacent.
Restaurants and all services–location in centre of town.

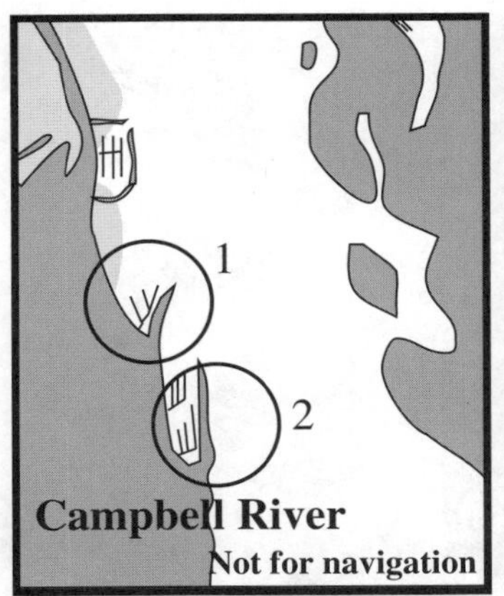

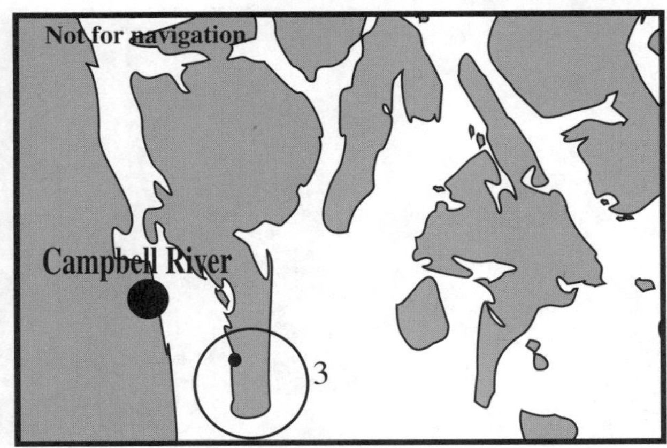

2 Campbell River

Fisheries & Oceans

Phone 287-7931
Chart 3540, 3539
Manager • Float length 1033 m
Breakwater • Grid • Garbage •
Waste oil service • Water • Lights •
Power •
Public phone • Washrooms •
Showers •
Fuel • Gas, diesel, CNG, stove oil.
Ice, bait, tackle, charts.
Campbell River town adjacent.
Also ferry to Quadra Island.

3 Cape Mudge

Fisheries & Oceans dock
Phone 285-3622
Chart 3540, 3539
Manager • Float length 60 m •
Breakwater • Marine Ways •

Notes:

Discovery Harbour Marina is a large marina with new docks and a vast breakwater. It is on aboriginal native land and is operated by the local native Indian band. On the opposite shore is Cape Mudge. The view over the breakwater is looking south. Note the substantial and roomy concrete docks which provide secure tie up.

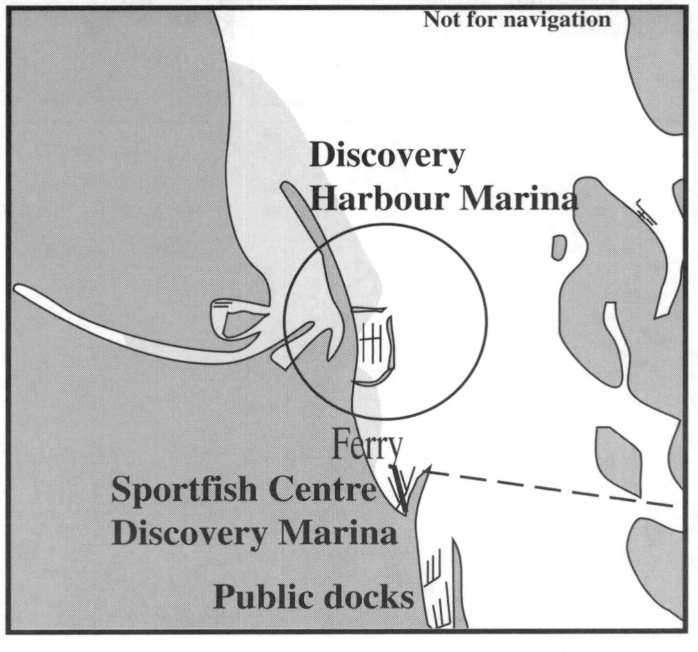

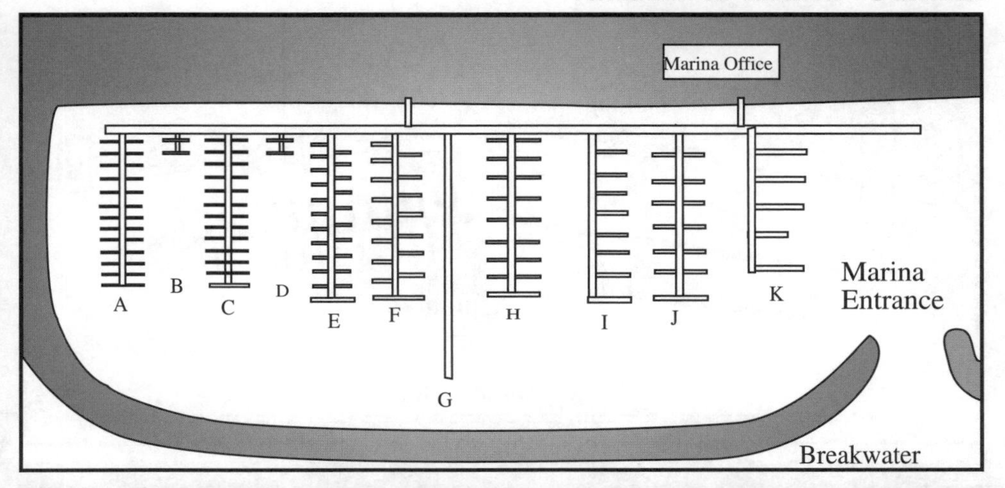

Discovery Harbour Marina

Discovery Harbour Marina

1400 Weiwakum Road,
Campbell River BC. V9W 5W8
Phone: (604) 287-2614
Fax: (604) 287-8939
Chart 3540, 3539
VHF call 73
ask for Discovery Harbour Marina

Marina services:

Fuel: gas, diesel.
Moorage: 150 berths for transient moorage. Boats to 100 feet and over.
Power at docks: 15, 20, 30, 50, 100 amp.
Water.
Dockside marine service can be arranged.

Customer services:

Laundry, showers, ice, bait.
Public phone ashore.
Nearby churches: multi-denominational in Campbell River.
Walking: Road access walking or cycling. Vehicle rentals in town.

Dock A is for 18 foot boats, B is for 20, C & D for 24, E & F for 30, H is for 36, I and J are for 40 and K for 100 footers.

Entertainment:

Scuba diving excellent in area. Strong tidal currents, use local dive operators as guides. Fishing excellent in general area.

Quathiaski Cove,

Quadra Island.
Fisheries & Oceans dock
Phone 624-2244 Fuel dock: 285-3212
Chart 3540, 3539
Manager • Float length 195 m
Launch ramp • Garbage • Waste oil disposal •
Lights • Power • Public phone •
Adjacent–Shipyard, **Fuel dock**: Diesel, gas, outboard mix, water, propane, oil.
Shops nearby. Adjacent ferry to Campbell River.

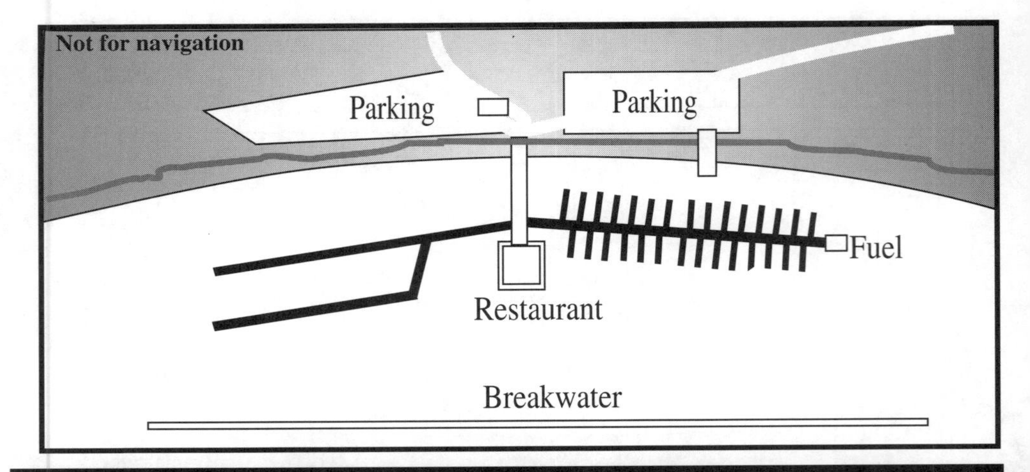

Brown's Bay Marina

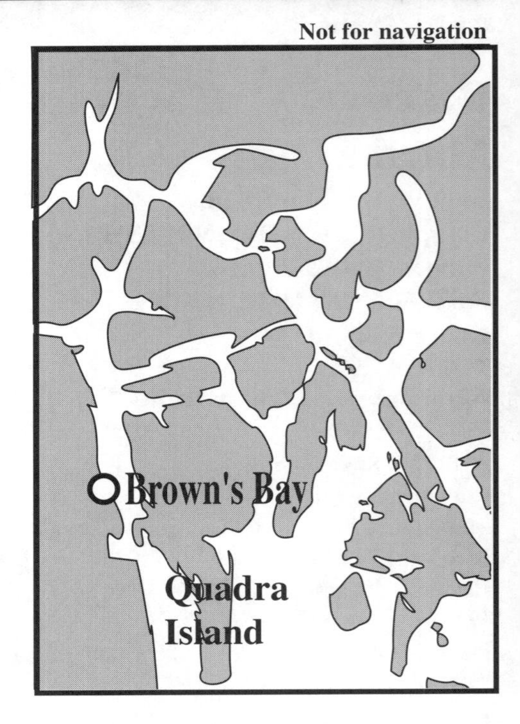

Browns Bay Marina

Jim and Julie Camp
Box 668 Campbell River
BC, V9W 6J3
Phone: (604) 286-3135 Fax 286-0951
Chart 3540, 3513

Marina services:

Fuel: Petro Canada. Gas, diesel, oils. Propane. Oil change facility.
Moorage. 1800 feet transient dock. Boats to over 100 feet.
Power at docks: 30, 20, 15 amp.
Water. Ice. Garbage disposal.

Customer services:

Bed and breakfast accommodation.
Laundry, showers, ice, bait.
Public phone ashore.
Store. Marine charts, tackle, licences, foul weather gear.
Floating restaurant/cafe.
Outstanding scuba diving at Campbell River and vicinity. Boat rentals. Fishing. Wildlife viewing. Guides available.
Walking: Road access walking or cycling.

Entertainment:

Fishing excellent in general area near harbour.

Adjacent facilities:

Ripple Rock RV Park–many facilities.

Entering Desolation Sound

Refuge Cove Store, a busy stop in the summer months.

Once in Desolation Sound you will not be stuck for fuel because there is a full service fuel stop at Refuge Cove. This facility is a centre for all boating needs to serve the cruising mariner. It has liquor, fresh produce, groceries, frozen foods, books, charts and more. The crafts shop and the hamburger stand on the property above the marina make an excellent place to wander or sit in the sun and enjoy the ambience of being out boating.

Desolation Sound is an excellent place to anchor for days on end in the summertime. From the many coves and bays of Grace Harbour or Prideaux Haven to Pendrell Sound and Walsh Cove, or Roscoe Bay, Theodosia Inlet, Van Donop Inlet and Squirrel Cove to name a few, one can find the ideal place to set up home aboard for a few days or play musical moorages and move from one to the next as one spends a summer vacation in this warm water oasis in BC. Move early in the day to avoid difficulty in finding a place to drop anchor in some of the busier bays.

To the west is Heriot Bay and Drew Harbour with its anchorage behind Rebecca Spit. Good fishing near this area has many boat owners flocking to the area every year. Go up to Surge Narrows from Heriot Bay, or cross over and spend the rest of your vacation at Gorge Harbour, one of the most sheltered large bays in the area, with a fine marina and excellent restaurant to keep you in comfort for the length of your stay. There is fuel at Gorge Harbour, a store, all facilities plus petroglyphs on the sheer rock face at the entrance. In the vicinity you may want to stop in for a stroll at nearby Whaletown. Dock space is limited but you may plan to have guests stay at Whaletown's cottages while they enjoy some time boating with you.

Desolation Sound and vicinity

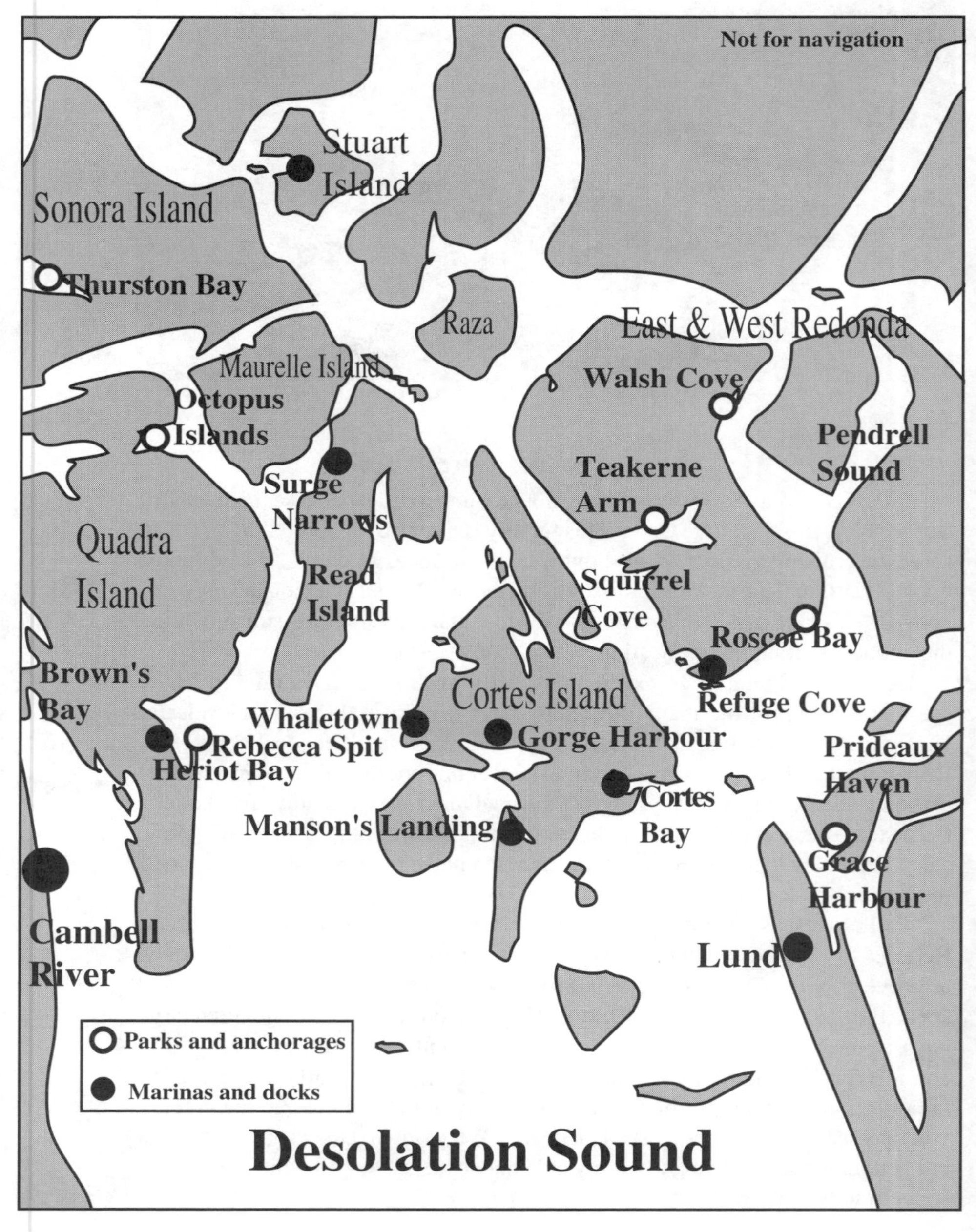

A lovely spot in the Octopus Islands

Parks

Rebecca Spit
All weather anchorage.
(Some sections exposed to wind conditions at times).
Picnic sites, water, toilets, beach, hiking, good fishing in vicinity.

Roscoe Bay
All weather anchorage
camping, toilets, hiking.

Octopus Islands
All weather anchorage
Fishing in vicinity
scuba diving nearby.

Teakerne Arm
Dinghy dock
Hiking fishing.

Thurston Bay
All weather anchorage
Recommended fishing.

Pictured above: One of the most tranquil marine park anchorages is at the Octopus Islands at the north-east corner of Quadra Island.

Copeland Islands
camping sites, toilets, park host, beach, good fishing and scuba in vicinity.

Walsh Cove
All weather anchorage.
Good fishing in vicinity.
Petroglyphs on rock face at north of cove.

Manson's Landing
Boat dock
picnic sites, toilets, beach, hiking, fishing.

Owen Bay

Transport Canada dock
Chart 3538, 3541
Manager • Float length 9 m

Evans Bay,

Read Island
Transport Canada dock
Chart 3538, 3541
Float length 18 m

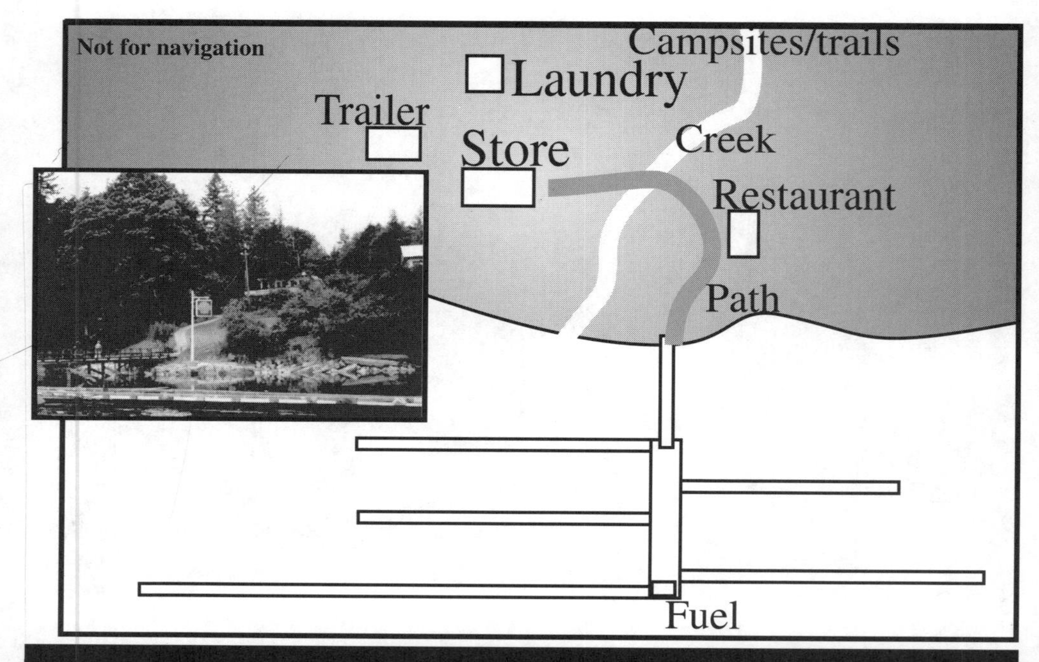

Gorge Harbour Marina

Gorge Harbour Marina & Resort

Glen and Verlie Carleton
P.O. Box 89 Whaletown,
BC. V0P 1Z0
Phone: (604) 935-6433
Chart 3538 VHF 73 CB 18

Marina services:

Fuel: Gas, diesel, oil.
Moorage: Guest moorage.
Water at dock. Multiple outlets.
Power at docks: 30, 15 amp.
Multiple outlets.

Customer services:

Grocery store. Fishing licences, bait, tackle. Ice, books, gifts charts, propane.
Laundry, showers, washrooms.
Public pay phones ashore. Boat rentals.
Private rooms with showers and baths. Good scuba diving nearby. Charters. Fish cleaning station.

Entertainment.

Walking. Excellent campground access and walking. Trail to roadway.

Adjacent facilities:
Restaurant–breakfast, lunch and dinner.
Fine dining–restaurant on premises.
Arts and Crafts nearby.
Campground. RVs

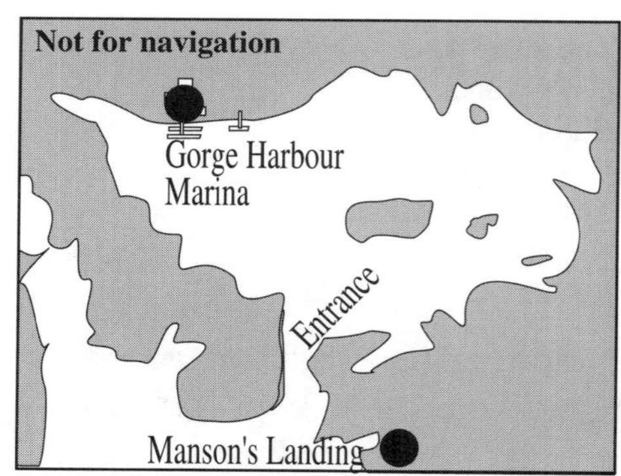

The entrance to Gorge Harbour is narrow and subject to current. There are petroglyphs on the rock face to port. Opposite inset: Gorge Harbour Marina.

Manson's Landing

(and Squirrel Cove)
(604) 935-6361
Irvine and Doreen Redel
Joanne Prestley
Chart 3311, 3538 VHF 73

Hazard: Exposed to westerly winds. Shallows on north approaches.
Marina services:
Limited moorage at government dock.

Customer services:
Groceries. Public phone. Bakery goods and fresh produce, milk, frozen foods, ice, water, tackle, bait, charts.
Toys, arts and crafts. Gifts.
Entertainment.
Hiking. Island roads. Beaches. Lagoon.
Adjacent facilities:
Marine Park. Beaches.

Whaletown

BC V0P 1Z0
(604) 935-6562
Hazel and George Frost
Chart 3538

Hazard: Rock near government dock. See chart 3538.
Marina services:
Limited transient moorage at public dock..
Customer services:
Post office. Deluxe waterfront cottage–two bedrooms. Sundecks, kitchens. Store: Groceries. Public phone. Bakery goods and fresh produce, milk, frozen foods, ice, water, tackle, bait, charts. Novelties. Gifts.
Entertainment.
Hiking. Island roads. Swimming. Scuba diving, fishing, canoeing, bird watching.
Adjacent facilities:
Ferry to/from Quadra.

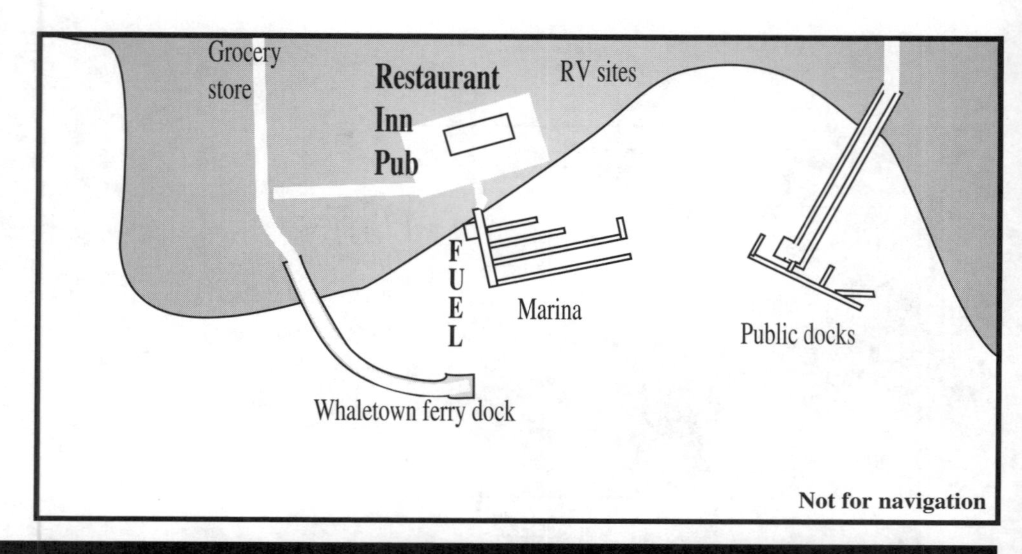

Heriot Bay Inn

Heriot Bay Inn

Tom and Julia Pearson
P.O. Box 100 Heriot Bay,
BC V0P 1H0
Phone: (604) 285-3322
Fax (604) 285-2708
Chart 3538/9 VHF 73

Marina services:

Fuel: Gas. Diesel. Oil. Propane.
Moorage, repairs, service available.
Water at dock. Multiple outlets.
Power at docks: 30, 15 amp.
Fish cleaning station.

Customer services:

Restaurant, pub. The Logger & The Fisherman. Patio service. Grocery store. Fishing licences, bait, tackle.
Propane, ice, books, gifts charts.
Laundry, showers, washrooms.
Public pay phones ashore. Boat rentals. Private rooms at Inn. Cottages. RV Park Fishing, sight-seeing charters. Good scuba diving nearby.

Entertainment.
Historic Heriot Bay Inn and its classic pub. Walking–roadway and some beach access. Also at Nearby Rebecca Spit.

Adjacent facilities:
Large grocery store and mini shopping centre–delivery to boats. Arts and crafts. Campground. RVs. Government dock. Anchorage at Drew Harbour inside Rebecca Spit, Rebecca Spit Marine Park.

Heriot Bay,

Quadra Island
Fisheries & Oceans dock
Phone 285-3958
Chart 3538, 3539
Manager • Float length 204 m
Launch ramp • Garbage • Lights • Power • Public phone •
Near marina–inn, ferry to Cortes Island,

Rebecca Spit Marine Park, shops.

Heriot Bay Inn caters to boating. It has lodging, restaurant, marine bar, a spacious marina, store and fuel.

Heriot Bay

Rich in history and charm, this cruising destination offers convenient provisions, ideal fishing conditions, and a compelling atmosphere.

If you are heading north during your summer cruise and stop en route at Heriot Bay, chances are you will remain right there for the rest of your holiday.

If you are fond of beachcombing, or strolling along country lanes, nearby Rebecca Spit and the immediate environs of Heriot Bay provide ample opportunity. If lounging on a sunny veranda appeals to you then you may get no farther than the sun porch at the Heriot Bay Inn. Indeed, this charming hostel evokes an ambience of a long-gone era. One writer described the Inn of Edwardian Times:

> *The beer parlour still flourished, offering relaxation to weary loggers and fishermen, but a gentler clientele was served by the remainder of the elegant rooms. There were 19 bedrooms and an upstairs dance hall, as well as a wide veranda on the second floor, used for summer dances. In this era –circa 1912!, hanging flower baskets decorated the lower veranda, which served as a tea-room, and young girls clad in white uniforms waited on the guests. There was an aviary of rare canaries, and oldtimers say a pet seal was kept in a pool behind the hotel.*
>
> *(Doris Anderson)*

The Inn today is still the centre of attention. For most visitors to Heriot Bay it is the focal point of the history of Quadra Island. The present building–several hotels over the years have occupied the same location–has a pub and restaurant, so yachtsmen can splice the main brace or dine out a short stroll up from their boats. The Inn provides float space, and offers fuel and basic provisions, mainly catering to the needs of fishermen who come from all parts of this continent, many religiously every year. The Inn also maintains a popular and spacious recreation vehicle campsite. The history of Heriot Bay is detailed in Bill Wolferstan's cruising guide, **Desolation Sound,** and in Doris Anderson's **Evergreen Islands.**

The store and waterfront with docks at Manson's Landing. Opposite: Cortes Bay public dock, the wharfinger and a regular visitor to the bay.

The Heriot Bay Marina is one of the few stops in the area where you can dispose of garbage. The fuel dock carries gasoline, diesel and engine oils as well as fresh water. Up at the Inn there are laundry and shower facilities. The 500 feet of mooring space is easy to access and is not subject to heavy current action. A marine facility at Quathiaski Cove, on the west side of Quadra, is equipped to do servicing and repairs.

Using Heriot Bay as a base, one can either spend time at the marina or at the adjacent government dock or at anchor in the lee of Rebecca Spit in Drew Harbour. Joyous summer experiences can include fishing and swimming or sunset strolls along the seaside paths of the A-class park that extends the length of the Spit. From your tender, you can troll or mooch the east side of the spit or several other nearby hot spots. A short walk up the main ferry road you will find a large and well stocked supermarket with adjacent coffee shop and craft stores.

Heriot Bay is located at the gateway to the Octopus Islands. A short run through Surge Narrows takes you to that increasingly popular summer cruising destination with fascinating inlets, bays and coves to explore en route. You are also close to Cortes Island and a Whaletown visit or a run down through Uganda Passage, which divides Cortes from Marina Island.

The nearby entrance to Gorge Harbour is a magnificent gateway of sheer rock on one side and wooded incline on the opposite shore. Indian petroglyphs can be found on the rock face of the north side. There is a restaurant with a fine reputation located inside Gorge Harbour. It is open and busy with boat crews and locals during the summer season. A small supply store on the marina property carries a variety of groceries and supplies. A more substantial store is located south of Gorge Harbour at Manson's Landing. It carries a wide variety of goods including fishing gear, groceries, hardware and some marine supplies.

Fishing and scuba diving in the general area are popular pastimes. Fishermen who visit the area frequently know the location where red snappers abound, and the size of some of the catches indicates a bonanza. The salmon caught on the Drew Harbour side of Quadra Island are not quite as impressive as those landed at Campbell River, but neither is the size of the tide rip.

One could easily leave one's boat tied up at Heriot Bay or at anchor in Drew Harbour and take the quick ferry ride across Sutil Channel to Cortes Island for a day's excursion. It is not recommended that you leave an anchored boat unattended, particularly where the anchorage is subject to large tidal changes and wind conditions.

The ferry lands at Whaletown and the road system on Cortes is ideal for more quiet country strolls. At Cortes there is a fascinating Bed & Breakfast near Cortes Bay government dock. Ask the dock manager to make reservations for you at Wolf's Bluff Castle where Karl will make pancakes, eggs and bacon for groups seated at the long tables in the very rustic building that resembles a castle. Then visit the dungeon and turrets on a self-guided tour.

If you anchor in Squirrel Cove to the north of Cortes Bay in July and August try Bill Rendell's fresh baked goods, especially his cinnamon buns. He has the little cabin in the centre of the east shore of the cove to starboard after entering the spacious bay.

When travelling from Lund to Heriot Bay via the west side of Marina Island refer to Canadian Hydrographic Service Chart 3565 or the Desolation Sound Chart Book number 3312 to avoid the shallows off Sutil Point and Marina Reef. They are marked by buoys, but be cautious. Running up through Uganda Passage on the east side of Marina Island is a pleasant alternative and don't fear the narrow waterway. It is well marked, but again follow your chart carefully and maintain a course to the correct side of the buoys and channel markers.

The public dock in Cortes Bay. No private marinas are open to public use. A Seattle yacht club owns the major marina in the bay. It is for the exclusive use of members. Opposite: Squirrel Cove anchorage and going ashore for cinnamon buns.

Many anchorages, few marinas

Facilities in Desolation Sound are scattered through and around the islands that comprise this lovely, popular cruising destination. Most replenishment stops are located west of Refuge Cove while Refuge is the main centre of supply to Desolation Sound. From Stuart Island in the north one could travel straight down Lewis Channel and stop in at Refuge Cove, or go west and take the options of Heriot Bay, Gorge Harbour, Whaletown, Manson's Landing or Squirrel Cove. To the south from Stuart Island is Lund with its mainland community and facilities comprising hotel, store and all services. In the central and eastern sections of Desolation Sound are the numerous anchorages and coves that most tend to favour for their stay. West of Refuge there are even more beautiful spots to anchor and shelter from winds and weather.

Refuge Cove

Located in the heart of Desolation Sound, this facility has been catering to pleasure boaters as long as there has been pleasure boating on the coast. Owners Colin Robertson and Pat Lovell welcome yachtsmen warmly to their 2000 odd feet of dock space. Overnight moorage is secure and available with electricity, water and services includings fuel, ice, propane, groceries, fresh produce, liquor and post office. Adjacent to the store a small kiosk offers hamburgers, chips and other light food preparations. A bake shop and gift shop alongside offer coffee and treats on a cosy sundeck. As a small island community the residents ask that no garbage be left at the dock.

Squirrel Cove

Government dock and store offering groceries, fresh produce, ice, fishing gear and bait, licences. There are telephones at the head of the dock as well as garbage disposal bins. Owners Irvine and Doreen Redel also own Manson's Landing store which is run by their daughter Joanne Prestley.

Manson's Landing

This exposed stop has a government dock with limited space, usually fully occupied by local and fishing boats.

Enquiries should be made to the store at the head of the dock. Supplies available from the store include some automotive, groceries, produce, ice, fishing tackle and licences.

Gorge Harbour

The facilities at Gorge Harbour provide all one needs for a prolonged stay at the marina. The shoreside restaurant is excellent and the marina owners, Glen and Verlie Carleton, are friendly and courteous. Newly installed fuel tanks means a reliable fuel supply.

Whaletown

The store at Whaletown has ice, propane, groceries, produce, fishing gear, licences and much more for passing mariners. The post office is located nearby. There is limited space at the dock, which is protected from weather almost always. A rock in the bay is well marked, as is the one at the entrance.

Heriot Bay

Owners Tom and Julie Pearson offer lodging at Heriot Bay Inn, dining in the lounge and on the terrace. The pub has a classic island atmosphere. The marina offers moorage, fuel, water and power and other amenities, while groceries and produce are at the supermarket a short walk up the road.

Nearby anchoring is available at Drew Harbour in the protection of Rebecca Spit. Some windy conditions occur and boats most sheltered will be those tucked into the curve at the end of the spit. A drying area occurs half way along the beach so mind the depth when anchoring.

Below: A coastal treat is a Sunday breakfast at Wolf's Bluff Castle, complete with dungeon, racks and torture cell. Tranquil anchorage in Cortes Bay, but the wind can blow quite strong at times. Map shows location of dock and castle.

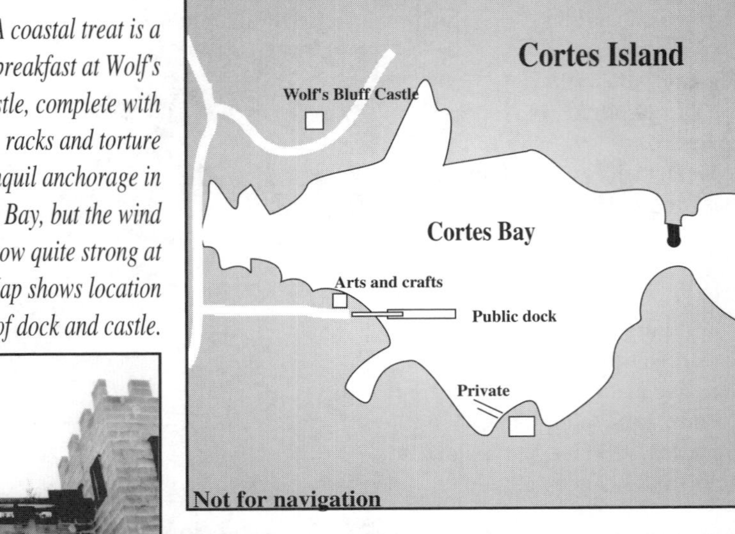

Cortes Bay.

The dock is wide and sturdy although not anchored at the deep end. It is controlled by a wharfinger and shared with local residents owning pleasure and commercial craft. Space is limited and many yachtsmen favour anchoring out in the bay. Cortes Bay is windy and often appears to be more wind-swept than the waters outside. In the mornings groups of boat owners will walk up the road for a substantial logger-style breakfast at Wolf Bluff Castle Bed and Breakfast, a fairytale structure with an old Europe rustic atmosphere complete with dungeon, built by the owner/chef Karl Triller, on a secluded two-and-a-half acre homestead property. No pets or smoking allowed inside the castle. Wharefinger Bill Brown lives in his house at the head of the dock. Ask about the craft stores nearby. In the opposite end of the bay is the Seattle Yacht Club which was once a popular marina serving the general boating community.

Squirrel Cove

(Manson's Landing)
(604) 935-6327
Irvine and Doreen Redel
Joanne Prestley
Chart 3555, 3538 VHF 73

Marina services:

Temporary moorage at government dock.
Garbage drop. Showers, laundry.

Customer services:

Groceries. Public phone. Bakery goods and fresh produce, milk, frozen foods, ice, water, tackle, bait, charts. Propane.
Liquor. Gifts. Marine supplies.

Entertainment.

Hiking. Island roads. Beaches. Lagoon.

Adjacent/nearby facilities:

Squirrel Cove Marine Park. Anchorage.
Squirrel Cove's bakery–Bill Rendall.
Anchor in cove and use dinghy dock in front of Rendall's cabin (central east side of cove).
Arts and crafts shop.

Cortes Government Dock

Cortes Island
Bill Brown (Wharfinger)
Chart 3555, 3538

Hazard: Entering bay–keep rock and day marker at entrance to starboard (passage south of marker).

Marina services:

Moorage at government dock. About 200 feet of dock, wide and solid. Windy at times in bay.
Power at dock: 15, 20 amp.
Garbage disposal.

Customer services:

Public phone. Arts and craft store on shore.

Entertainment.

Hiking. Island roads. Tour and breakfast at Wolf's Bluff Castle–Reservations: wharfinger.

Adjacent facilities:

Yacht club station. Anchorage.

Bill Rendall prepares delicious cinnamon buns and other baked goods at Squirrel Cove.

Squirrel Cove Bakery

Bill Rendall
Box 6 Squirrel Cove
Manson's Landing P.O.
BC. V0P 1K0
Chart 3555, 3538

Dinghy dock only. Squirrel Cove.
Anchor off and row ashore for fresh baked bread and cinnamon buns.
Open summer vacation months only.

> ## Squirrel Cove,
> Cortes Island. (public dock)
> Fisheries & Oceans dock
> Phone 935-6529
> Chart 3555, 3538, 3312
> Manager • Float length 60 m
> Garbage • Lights • Power •
> Public phone ashore •
> Store on shore–provisions, propane.
> Anchorage in Squirrel Cove.

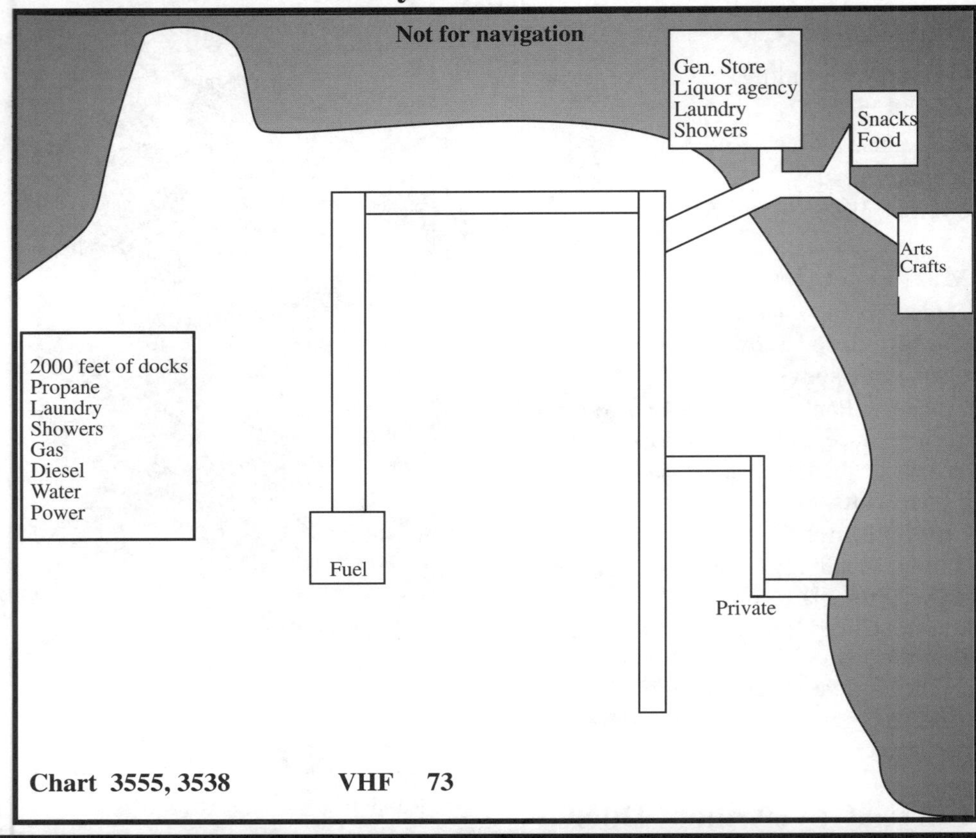

Refuge Cove

Refuge Cove

Colin Robertson & Pat Lovell
Refuge Cove, BC V0P 1P0

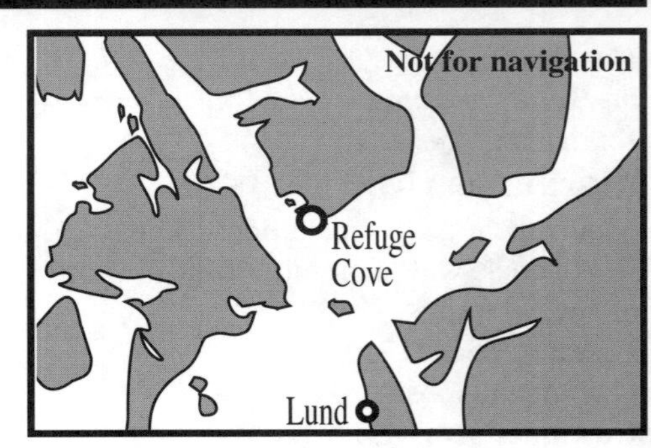

Marina services:

Fuel: Gas. Diesel, oil, propane.
Moorage: Government dock and private. Overnight moorage. 2000 feet of docks.
Water at dock. Multiple outlets.
Power at docks: 15 amp.

Customer services:

Laundry, showers, washrooms. Propane, ice, books, gifts charts, Grocery store, post office. Liquor. Public pay phone ashore.

Adjacent facilities:

Gifts, arts and crafts, coffees, hamburger kiosk.

Above: looking onto the docks at Refuge Cove from the patio of the coffee shop next to the general store. L: Among the many anchorages in Desolation Sound, Grace Harbour is close to facilities and sheltered from wind and weather.

Desolation Sound as Gateway

En route to all parts of Desolation Sound, Refuge Cove is a busy stop during the brief summer season. It affords replenishment of everything from fuels (including propane) and fresh water to liquor, fresh produce, bread, meat and groceries. Charts, books and a limited selection of clothing are also sold at the store, as well as ice and fishing supplies. The store is built on a barge and positioned high and dry above the high-water mark. It and the fuel dock are run effectively to accommodate the heavy traffic of the short summer season and survive the balance of the year.

One of the burdens of summer is the threat of fire when forest conditions are very dry. Water shortages are sometimes threatened but seldom occur. The lake that drains into Refuge Cove is the supply of domestic water and the local population sometimes finds it difficult to prevent transient people from misusing it. The dock does, however, have adequate water for conservative use with outlets at various points for mooring customers.

It amazes me that Captain Vancouver wrote of the entrance to Desolation Sound as having a very inhospitable general appearance, especially considering he was there in the month of June. He may have encountered bad weather and was becoming depressed as suggested by Lester Peterson in **Raincoast Chronicles First Five.** Yachtsmen entering Desolation Sound from the direction of Lund via the Copeland Islands are usually awed by the beauty of the islands and waterways. They also often encounter what Captain Vancouver must have discovered—when the tidal streams from north and south meet around Kinghorn Island, turbulence can be quite strong.

If Captain Vancouver needed to encounter some semblance of the type of civilization from which he had come in order to restore his equanimity, then it is a pity Refuge Cove had not yet been established as a trading centre in Desolation Sound. If he had not been in need of provisions, then he could have accommodated himself with a shower or used the laundry facilities. Or he might have been able to browse through the souvenir and arts and crafts shop near the store. He would not, however, have been able to dispose of *Discovery's* garbage at Refuge Cove. To do so he would have had to cross to Squirrel Cove on the opposite shore of Lewis Channel, where a dockside disposal bin is located. But Captain Vancouver could have saved himself much anxiety in his search for safe overnight anchorage by tying up *Discovery* along any section of Refuge Cove's 2000 feet of berthage, although the 530-ton *Discovery* would have left little room for the rest of us. Or he could have anchored in the northernmost bay of the Cove just near the Refuge Lagoon outlet.

To some yachtsmen, Walsh Cove may be just another ordinary anchorage at the perimeter of Desolation Sound. It is, however, a particularly pleasant and significant anchorage.

Located at the upper reaches of Waddington Channel—which separates East and West Redonda Islands—Walsh Cove is ideal for laying over at night prior to a run up Toba Inlet or a jaunt to Big Bay from Desolation Sound. It is a corner away from the main holiday traffic in the more central anchorages of summer's most popular sound. It is not far from the supply store at Refuge Cove, and close to the warm summer waters of Pendrell Sound. Much of the traffic, therefore, arrives late in the day and leaves early in the morning, which means that arriving yachts should experience no trouble in finding a spot to anchor.

Walsh Cove, tucked into a steep rocky nook on the west side of Waddington Channel, is sheltered by the tiny Gorges Islets. Their protrusion above the water a short distance off the northern sweep of shoreline almost totally encloses the cove, protecting it from most winds (strong northerly winds can find their way in!), and the wash of yachts cruising by. An adequate channel allows only small vessels to slip in and out of the anchorage safely on the inside of the islets. The islets themselves are separated by a

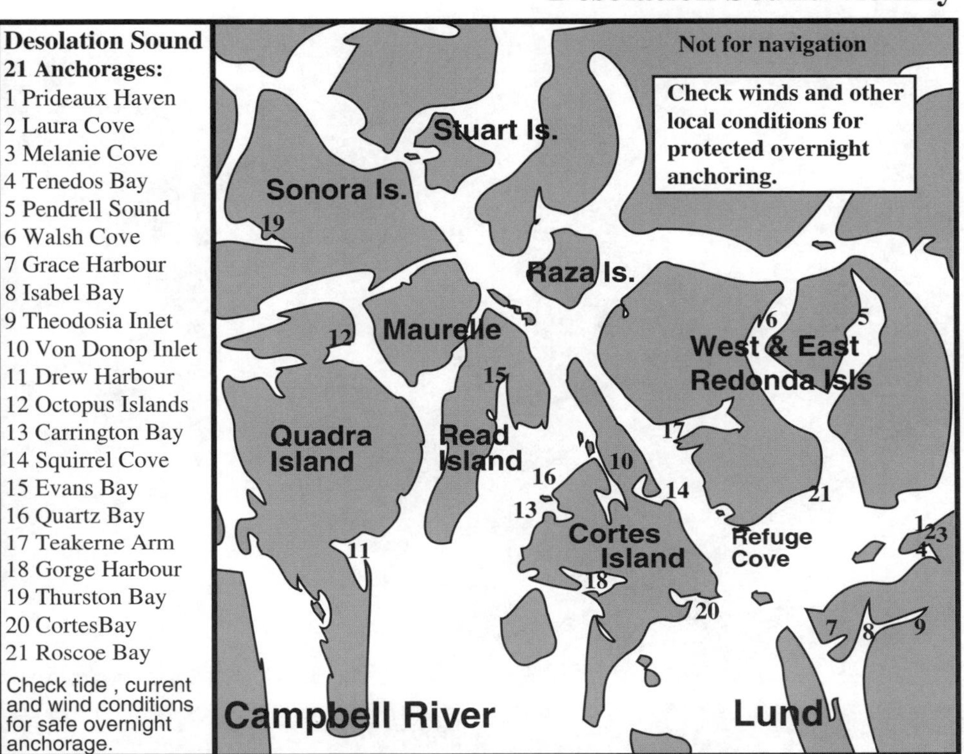

shallow, partially drying channel and a natural pool which attracts snorkellers and swimmers in summer. The water there reaches comfortable temperatures, although it's never quite as warm as nearby Pendrell Sound.

It is easy to become sidetracked in the vicinity of Walsh Cove or en route to a particular destination. Ovemight prawn traps set in about 40 fathoms on the east side of Waddington Channel opposite Allies Island may yield a return sufficient to enjoy a meal or at least a nice appetizer. A short distance up Toba Inlet's northwest shoreline there is a magnificent, high waterfall cascading down the rock face of the shore.

In 1792 the Spaniard Valdes, just leaving the inlet after exploring it to its head, encountered the British about to enter and advised them not to bother going up. "It goes nowhere," I imagine the Spaniard saying. It was definitely not the northwest passage that he knew was the main objective of the British expedition.

At Waddington's narrow entrance there are two sets of pictographs located at Butler Point opposite the north side of Gorges Islets.

Walsh Cove may appear to be incidental to the various places in the vicinity—Prideaux Haven, Roscoe Bay, Pendrell Sound, Toba Inlet and Refuge Cove—but the point is it is central to them all, and not far from Redonda Bay. For many years Redonda Bay was considered, as is Big Bay on Stuart Island today, to be the gateway to the north through the rapids of the Yucultas.

Big Bay Marina

Big Bay Marina Resort

Bruce and Kay Knierim
Chart 3543
Big Bay P.O. Stuart Island,
BC V0P 1V0
Phone: (604) 286-2003, 286-8107

Hazard: Shoal in centre of Bay especially near public dock. Currents.

Marina services:

Fuel: Gas. diesel, oil.
Moorage, outboardmotor repairs & service.
Honda dealer.
Water at dock.
Power at docks: Limited: 15 amp.
Power at marina is being upgraded.
Fish cleaning station.

Customer services:

Restaurant, pub. Breakfast, lunch, dinner.
Patio tables.
Store. Fishing licences, bait, tackle, ice, groceries, frozen foods, fresh bread, books, charts, gifts, video movie rental. Coffee, expresso, latte.
Laundry, Showers, Washrooms.
Public pay phones. Cottages.
Fishing charters. Guides. Good scuba diving nearby.

Entertainment.

Walk in coastal trails. View fast, tidal Arran Rapids.
Games room at resort.

Adjacent facilities:

Pub, restaurant. Government dock.
Post office. Seaplane landing and mooring.

Big Bay lodge, marina and fishing camp, a place to stay, refuel, replenish supplies, charter a fishing guide and much more. There is also a dock nearby for overnight moorage at the Wheelhouse pub, a popular local night spot., or at the adjacent public dock.

The fishing is good and you can wait for the tides to change for an easy passage through Dent and Green Point Rapids.
Walk to the Arran Rapids for a thrilling spectacle of tidal currents at maximum flood and ebb tides.

At Big Bay you will find fuel and moorage as well as an excellent dining facility and a large, newly rebuilt general store. The sport fishing out of Big Bay is outstanding. If you have the time include a day out fishing with a guide. Leave your boat at the dock and go out in one of their fishboats. You may simply sit on the patio and sip expresso and watch the comings and goings of transient boats, or walk along the two mile trail to watch the rushing waters of the Arran Rapids. In Big Bay mariners are advised to enter and leave with caution, noting the shallows near the shore facilities. Consult your chart and watch for kelp–a summertime marker for the reef. The perfect way to end your busy day in Big Bay is dining at the Eagle's Wing restaurant in the main building of the lodge.

Big Bay
Not for navigation
Barber Passage
Stuart Island
Big Bay Resort & Marina (Fuel)
Wheelhouse Pub
Public dock
Gillard Islands
Big Bay Marina
Fuel

Shoal Bay Lodge

Shoal Bay Lodge
P.O.Box 818 Campbell River,
BC. V9W 6Y4
David and Kevan McLean
Phone: (604) 286-6016 Fax 286-1936
(Cell–Shoal Bay–286-2697)
Victoria phone: (604) 598-4432

Marina services:
Transient moorage. Government dock. Water.

Customer services:
Restaurant. Dining. Patio service, Groceries. Tackle, bait, charts.
Laundry, showers, washrooms.
Excellent fishing nearby. Guides.
Boat rentals–guided or unguided.
Accommodation–sea kayak rental packages.
Water taxi access. Flights.

Chart 3543 VHF 73

Entertainment.
Hiking trails. Logging roads. View points along a network of paths. Animal and marine life. Eagles.

Adjacent facilities:
Canoeing. Kayaking. Day trips in adjacent waterways. Includes Thurston Bay Marine Park. Rentals. Picnic area.

Shoal Bay.

East Thurlow Island
Fisheries & Oceans dock
Phone: 287-8233
Chart 3543
Float length 76 m

At Shoal Bay a government dock with fairly generous moorage provides overnight accommodation for several large or additional smaller boats. The grounds of the lodge are pleasant for walking and the facilities include restaurant and store. The lodge offers rental of kayaks and boats along with guides and fishing charters.
The floating lodge below is in Cordero Channel–known internationally for fine dining and successful fishing charters.

Cordero Lodge

Doris & Kellie Kuppers
General Delivery
Blind Channel P.O.
BC. V0P 1B0
Phone (604) 286-8404

Marina services:
Transient moorage.
Customer services:
Restaurant–Fine dining.
Lodging–up to eight guests.
Fishing: Boats–guided or unguided.
Entertainment.
Sunsets and views. Animal and marine life. Bears and eagles.
Adjacent facilities:
Cordero Islands anchoring.

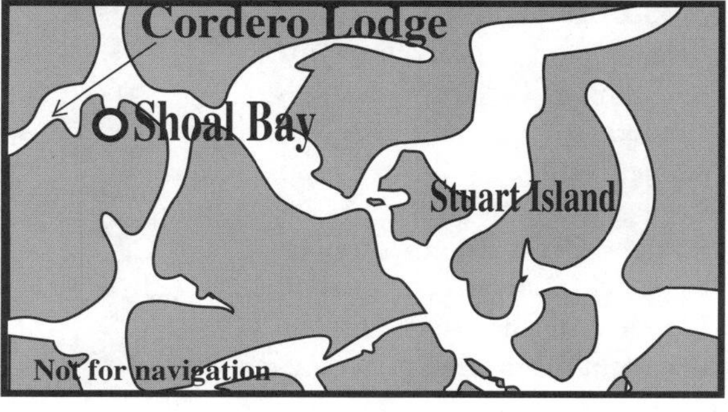

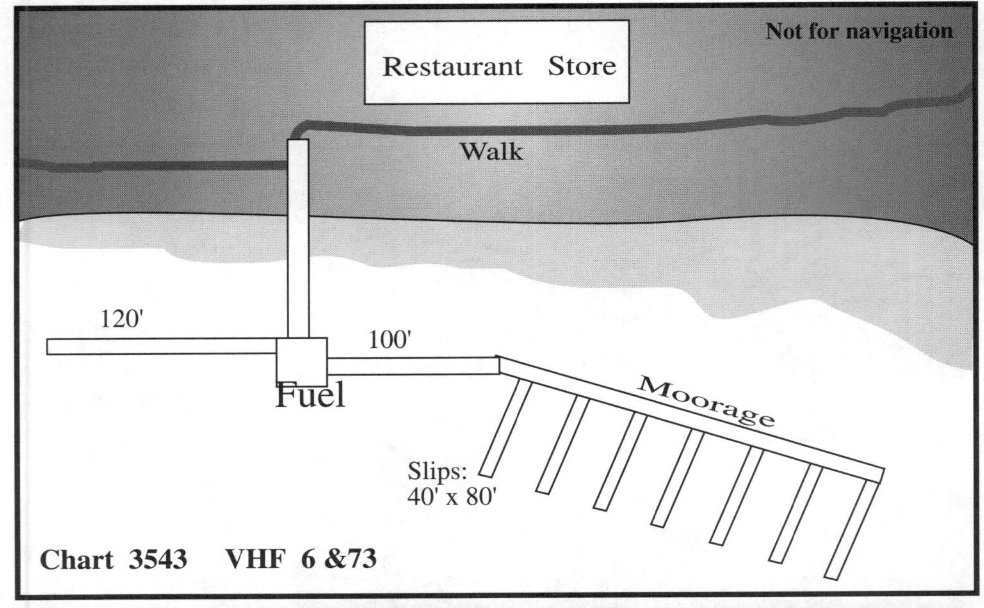

Blind Channel

Blind Channel Resort

Philip Richter
Blind Channel BC
V0P 1B0
Phone (604) 286-8112

Marina services:

Moorage: Transient moorage.
Fuel: Gas, diesel, propane.
Water at dock. Ice.
Power at docks: 20 amp

Customer services:

Restaurant in June and Labour Day.
Fine dining. Patio.
Groceries. Postal drop. Public phone(Satellite). Bakery goods, bread, fresh produce, milk, frozen foods, ice, tackle, bait, charts. Fax service.
Laundry, showers, washrooms.
Liquor. Arts and crafts. Gifts.
Excellent fishing and prawning nearby.

Entertainment.

Hiking trails. Logging roads. Several view points along a network of paths. See the huge "Thurlow" Cedar tree. Incredible sunsets and views. Animal and marine life. Eagles. Dock are wide and embellishments are fascinating. Additional facilities planned 1995.

Adjacent facilities:

Scheduled flights. Picnic area.

The stop at Blind Channel has been a favourite among mariners for many decades.

The Richter family continues to cater to the needs of passing and visiting vessels with fresh produce, baked goods and excellent cuisine.

Blind Channel

Three generations of Richters are busy around Blind Channel when guests are moored at their docks. This long-established marina in one of the coast's busy waterways has evolved over the years to become a well maintained and contemporary facility for cruising yachtsmen. Philip's parents, who established the marina still live and work at the property. Annemarie usually finds time to chat with guests in the restaurant while Edgar was quite involved at the time of writing with planning and preparing for the next addition–a lodge facility. Philip does stints in the store while his wife, Jennifer, can be found preparing bread and other baked delectables for the store and restaurant. The marina offers moorage, fuel, water, propane and 110 volt shore power at the dock. The services include showers, laundry, ice, liquor agency, store and post office.

Nature lovers and hikers will be kept busy for days hiking trails that have been established by a large logging and sawmill company on West Thurlow Island. These trails are designed to show the features of a second growth forest and it just happens that they begin about 300 meters from Blind Channel Marina. There are three different trails, one to a spectacular viewpoint overlooking Mayne Passage and East Thurlow Island, a second to the Big Cedar, a tree with a diameter of 16 feet, via a forest of 80 year old second growth and the third through a thinned western hemlock stand that was naturally established in 1964. The final segment of this trail descends through 100 year old second growth.

Across Cordero Channel, a few miles from Blind Channel is Cordero Lodge which offers outstanding cuisine, and a place to stop overnight. It has limited space for boats and usually requires advance reservations for moorage and dinner. Owned and operated by Reinhart and Doris Kuppers, this immaculate facility has been a stopping place for those in the know for many years.

Beyond the Western Gate
It's all still there, north of Desolation

Along the waterways of Queen Charlotte Strait, Kingcome Inlet and Tribune Channel I felt as though I could look down over the world of Vancouver Island and Desolation Sound far below. There the sets of turbulent rapids free the upper waters from their mountainous reservoir channels to flow and surge into the valleys of Desolation, Georgia Strait and ultimately Juan de Fuca as well as over the northern tip of Vancouver Island into the open Pacific. Currents running swiftly tug at kelp beds lining the shore, carry flotsam rapidly by, ripple and eddy, sometimes forming fascinating whirlpools.

Our first stop beyond Desolation was to have been Owen Bay in Okisollo Channel. But a slight miscalculation took us through Hole-in-the-Wall at more than half its full flooding speed of 9 knots, and so we headed into Octopus Marine Park for the night. And we were glad of our slight error. Octopus is an anchorage in another world.

Many voyagers to the waters beyond Desolation Sound set out initially in fear of the awesome rapids: the Yacultus, Dent and Green Point Rapids. *Sailboating writers made me fearful of the rapids until the first time I navigated them.* Many boat owners never even plan to take in those waters during their years of cruising—perhaps because of a subconscious dread of the rapids and swirling narrows sometimes conjured up by the works of some experienced writers. But there is no need to fear the rapids north of Desolation Sound; just respect them. Respect them and work closely in conjunction with the tide and currents tables. With a hull-speed power boat following the advice of sail boaters makes sense, but a fast powerboat will carry you through at many times when you would wait in a slow boat. However, caution must be observed no matter what boat you have. Rapids and tide rips are dangerous and navigating fast flowing channels at maximum or near maximum currents is foolish and can be disasterous.

We passed through one set of rapids in the Yacultus area, stopped at Stuart Island, smack in between Yacultus and Dent, and waited for the following slack before continuing and passing through the second set. In between we hiked along the island trail to Arran Rapids to watch them run at full flood.

The Arran Rapids, one of the most carefully respected in the area, pour through a narrow channel and on a full ebb create a massive whirlpool at the southwestern end. *It was a moderate flood that we saw, and no problem, boats large and small passed through in either direction. However, they were all high speed planing powerboats ranging from 13 ft Boston Whalers to 28 or 30 ft Sportsfishermen. One fish boat with a 12 knot speed capability ran through with the flood with no apparent concern.*

The channels, straits and sounds beyond the Yacultus are a cruising yachtsman's paradise. They are relatively desolate, environmentally clean, aesthetically unspoilt and naturally quite undisturbed. There are fish, river otters, mink and eagles. We saw many, many bald eagles. And one gigantic golden eagle. There are dolphins, orcas, bears and deer. Some of these are quite elusive.

Cruising out of Johnstone Strait at Alert Bay, it was convenient to transit Blackfish Sound, pass around Swanson Island into the entrance of Knight Inlet and off to port around Midsummer Island, up Retreat Passage to the most isolated, beautiful cove in the world at the north end of Bonwick Island. We anchored and set off in the dinghy to drop traps in the hopes of crab for dinner. Success. We went ashore and dug clams for chowder. And this prompted an urge to get on with some fishing. Spring salmon were running and in no time at all we hooked a couple of small ones — but eight pounds is plenty. We had prawns too—fished out of 45 fathoms off Minstrel Island.

Buildings at Karlukwees, a classic aboriginal native village on the coast of British Columbia. A totem lies near the water's edge at the Mamalilaculla village site.

We had intended to conclude our northward passage with a run up to the head of Kingcome Inlet of ***I Heard the Owl Call My Name*** *fame, but heavy, inclement weather kept us in Cypress Harbour opposite its mouth until time simply ran out and we had to begin the 'downhill' run back towards Vancouver. On a future trip we went up the river in an inflatable as far as Kingcome Village. But the time sitting out the weather was not wasted. We went out of Cypress to look for salmon and —the thrill of catching a big one is hard to equal.*

Indian villages are as exciting as the very names of the islands on which they are located or the channels that serve them. Arrow, Indian and Village Channels, Village, Owl and Midsummer Islands all conjure up romantic notions of history. The now deserted village of Mamililaculla (in the past few years members of the local band have cleaned up the ancient village and welcome vistors each summer for a fee towards the maintenance and upkeep of the property) and Karlukwees have about them an air of pressing history.

We made our way to Mamililaculla after anchoring near its disused jetty by hiking along the rocky shore to the beach in front of the deserted village. The path from the jetty has been cleared and can now be used to reach the historic site.

I wrote on my first visit to Mamaliliculla: *Sitting on a low ledge overlooking Native Anchorage, grey, weathered houses sit forlornly looking across the water. Long grass and weeds grow up around woodwork, porch steps, ancient longhouse frames. Totems, horizontal and fallen, slowly yield to the decay of time and elements. A gentle breeze flaps ragged cloth in window frames, or torn plastic used for temporary coverage since the village's abandonment—signs of recent overnight visitors.* Pathways, homes, community and mission halls were fast succumbing to the encroaching foliage. A sad confirmation of the prophetic accounts of Ms. Wiley Blanchet in her **Curve of Time.**

At Karlukwees a former government maintained dock that would accommodate several boats overnight falls to decay. Permission to go ashore at local villages must be obtained from the U'mista Cultural Centre in Alert Bay. (604) 974-5403.

At Minstrel Island there is fuel, a restaurant, accommodations, showers, laundry and a store where liquor is available as well as a variety of groceries. In Lagoon Cove behind Minstrel Island is Lagoon Cove Marina, another stop where fuel and some services are available. In the upper reaches of the cruising waters farther north, there is a post office, store, arts and crafts and other facilities at Echo Bay. More services for mariners are available at Greenway Sound and at Sullivan Bay or Shawl Bay near the mouth of Kingcome Inlet. Greenway Sound has an outstanding restaurant on its floats and boasts such luxuries as a hairdressing salon and a dog walk. And the fishing in those far reaches is outstanding.

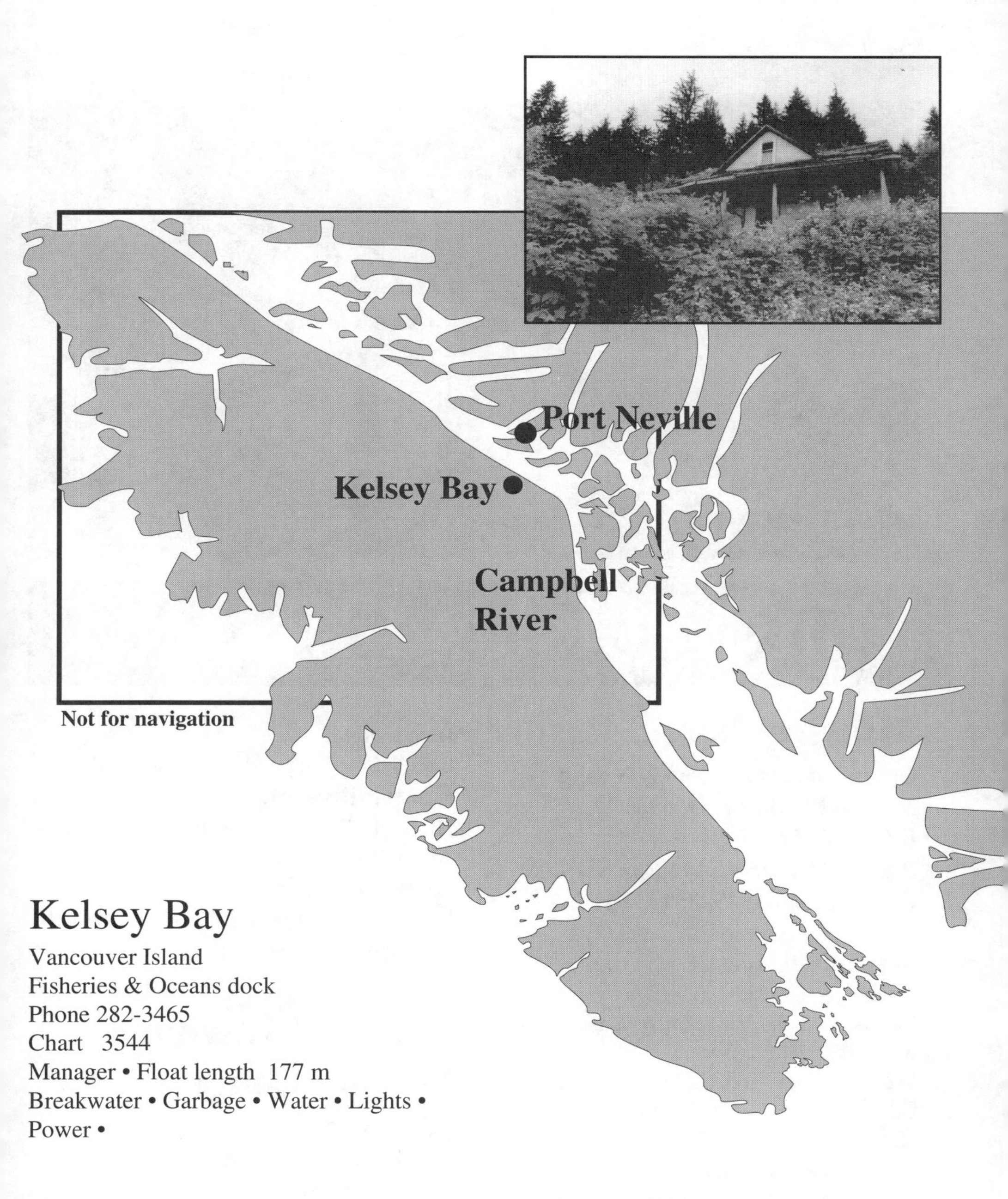

Kelsey Bay

Vancouver Island
Fisheries & Oceans dock
Phone 282-3465
Chart 3544
Manager • Float length 177 m
Breakwater • Garbage • Water • Lights • Power •

Kelsey Bay

Vancouver Island
Transport Canada dock
Chart 3544
Manager • Float length 31 m
Breakwater • Water • Lights • Power •

Port Neville

Johnstone Strait
Transport Canada dock
Chart 3564, 3545
Float length 34 m
Lights • Power •

Minstrel Island Resort

Minstrel Island Resort

Grant Douglas and Sandy Young
Minstrel Island P.O. 69,
B.C. V0P 1L0
Phone (604) 268-8444 Fax Service,
Chart 3564, 3545, 3515 VHF 6 & 73

Marina services:

Moorage: Transient moorage.
Fuel: Gas, diesel, stove oil, propane, aviation fuel.
Water at dock. Ice. Garbage disposal.
Power at docks: 30, 15 amp.
12,000 lb dry dock.

Customer services:

Restaurant. Pub. Accommodation in resort rooms and cottages.
Groceries. Postal drop. Public phone (Satellite). Cold beer. Bakery goods and fresh produce, milk, frozen foods, ice, tackle, bait, charts.
Laundry, Showers, Washrooms.
Boat rentals.
Excellent fishing and prawning nearby.

Entertainment.

Hiking trails. Incredible sunsets and views. Animal and marine life. Bears and eagles.

Adjacent facilities:

Regular scheduled flights. Boardwalk. Wheelchair access up ramp. Hiking trails. Picnic area.

Forward Harbour Fishing Lodge

Al and Mary McAvoy
RR #3, Site 340, C-8
Courtenay, B.C. V9N 5M8
Phone (604) 268-8444 Fax Service,
Chart 3544 VHF 6 & 73
Marina services: Water, Moorage.
Laundry, showers, washrooms, restaurant.
Fishing licences, guides, hiking, walking.
Local interest: petroglyphs.

The docks at Minstrel Island and at Lagoon Cove are protected from most wind and weather. Lagoon Cove Marina is located on the west side of East Cracroft Island.

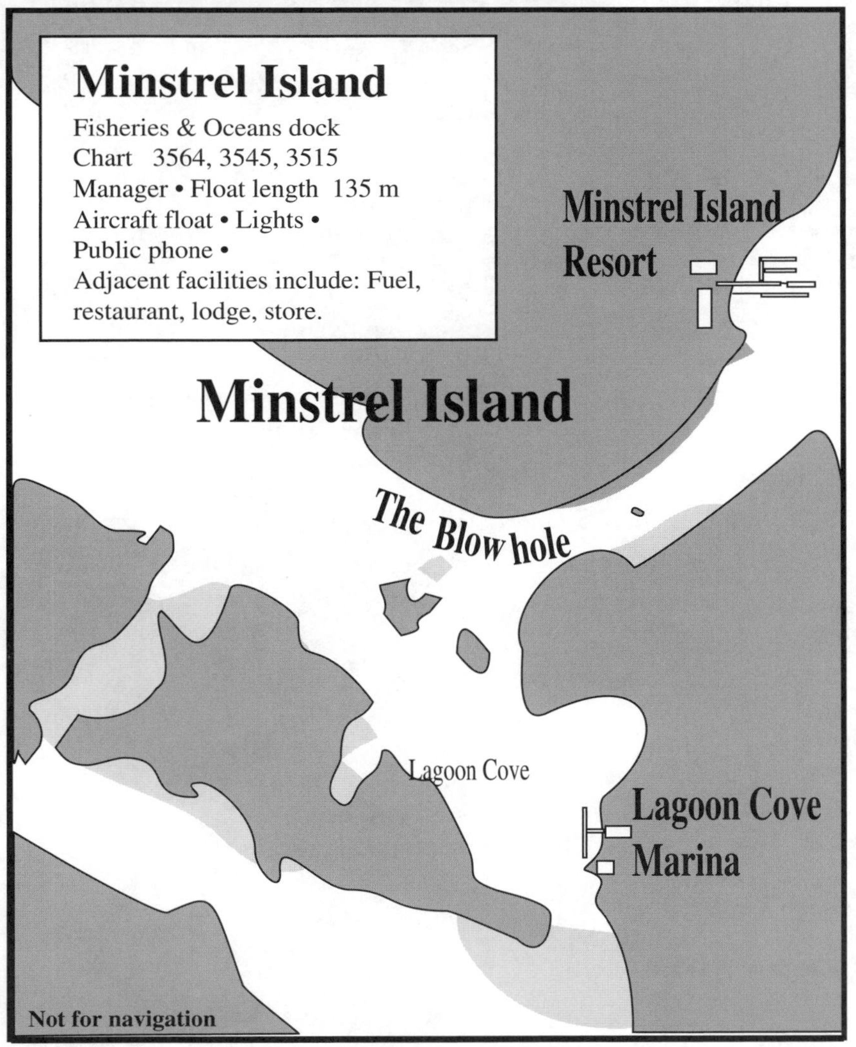

Lagoon Cove Marina

Lagoon Cove

Bill and Jean Barber
c/o Minstrel Island P.O.
British Columbia.
Chart 3545 VHF 73

Marina services:

Moorage: Transient moorage.
Fuel: Gas, diesel, propane.
Repairs, haulouts.
Water at dock.
Power at docks.

Customer services:

Groceries.
Laundry, showers, washrooms.
Boat rentals.
Excellent fishing and prawning nearby.

Entertainment.

Hiking trails. Sunsets and views. Animal and marine life. Bears and eagles.

Adjacent facilities:

Hiking trails.

Not for navigation

Minstrel Island

Lagoon Cove Marina

Many people have chosen to anchor in Lagoon Cove over the past, but with secure docking and the associated peace of mind when the wind is up it is worth while stopping at the marina.

There are showers, laundry, additional accommodation and the friendly greeting of owners, Bill and Jean Barber. Former owners accumulated an incredible collection of marine and other hardware, enough to start a museum. Some have been discarded but many items remain in a work shed deck area planned for conversion to a patio coffee shop.

Doug Pemberton Photo

Telegraph Cove Marina

Telegraph Cove Marina

Gordie and Marilyn Graham.
Janet Lanthier
Telegraph Cove, BC. V0N 3J0
Phone: (604) 928-3131
Marina: (604) 928-3131
Chart 3546

Marina:

Moorage: Transient boats as available. Moorage mostly reserved for resort clients.
Fuel: gas, oil.
Launch ramp.

Customer Services:

Fishing resort, accommodations, camping RV parking. Gifts. Fine art. Arts and crafts. Cafe. Some groceries. Bait, ice, snacks. Fishing tackle, licenses.
Telephone.

Entertainment:
Excellent scuba diving. Whale watching. Marine and bird life. Fishing charters and guides.

Adjacent facilities:

Stubbs Island Charters

Jim Borrowman,
Bill & Donna McKay.
Box 7, Telegraph Cove,
BC. V0N 3J0
Phone: (604) 928-3185 VHF 10

Customer Services:
Gifts. Fine art. Arts and crafts.
Groceries–limited selection.
Whale watching, day trips.
Scuba diving charters.
Accommodation. Cabins on boardwalk.

Launch ramp alongside the marina at Telegraph Cove

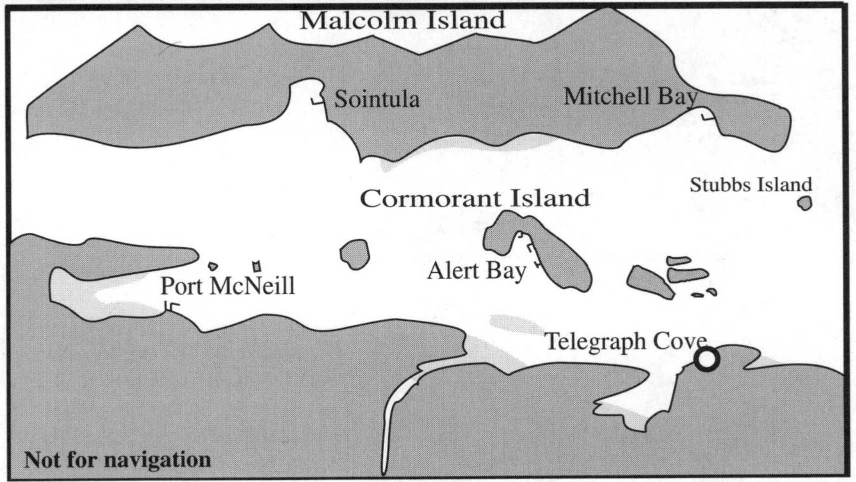

Indian Villages and Telegraph Cove

Telegraph Cove is one of the most picturesque spots on the BC coast. Each of its quaint buildings, which stand on a boardwalk supported by ageing pilings, has a story of its own and today are a reflection of life on the coast in the earlier part of this century. The marina at Telegraph Cove today serves as a base for seasonal sportsfishermen who trailer in their runabouts and more serious fishing rigs from other parts of the province as well as Alberta and the United States. Boats cruising by stop in to visits and to replenish minor supplies. A steady flow of non-boating visitors each year descends on the village to set out on whale watching or scuba diving excursions.

Trailered boats coming into Telegraph Cove by road find moorage at the marina overnight and move out in the early hours of the morning for the excellent fishing in Blackfish Sound. Those less energetic and seeking idyllic cruising take off for the numerous tranquil anchorages that abound, or the historic Indian villages that have been immortalized by writers and visitors in past decades. Mamaliliculla and Karlukwees are nearby native villages which I recall visiting in the mid seventies and at which time they appeared to have been long since abandoned. Today I realise they had not been abandoned that long ago, especially considering the decay and reclamation of the undergrowth and vegetation that has taken place between my earlier visits and more recent years.

Telegraph Cove was little more than a sawmill for many years since its settlement by Mr A.M. Wastell 100 years ago. In the early part of this century salmon fishing prompted the construction of a saltery at the settlement. Other industries grew from the lumber and fishing interests, attracting labour and settlers and turning the sawmill settlement into a coastal village. In 1911 the federal government installed a telephone station at the cove to connect the north end of Vancouver Island with Campbell River. The second world war brought the cove's telephone and telegraph cable system into operation as a communications relay centre. For many years accessible only by water, today an unpaved road runs to the cove from the main Island Highway connecting the northern towns of Port McNeill and Port Hardy to the rest of the world.

Remnants of bygone activity and population in Bones Bay near Minstrel Island.
A quiet anchorage in a corner of Potts Lagoon.

In more recent times tourism has played a large role in the significance of Telegraph Cove. The revelation that some of the world's best scuba diving is possible within a short boat ride of the cove has brought many visitors from all parts of the world to view the abundant marine life at nearby sites such as Stubbs Island and Plumper Rock. Among the diving enthusiasts to have visited the area are Jacques Cousteau and underwater cinematographers Al Giddings and Stan Waterman who were among those responsible for the subsea footage in James Bond movies, The Deep, Jaws and many more. National Geographic Magazine has done major editorial features on the area which included large underwater colour photo spreads by staff photographer David Doubilet. Working with these personalities were individuals who have established a new objective for the existence of Telegraph Cove; Bill McKay and Jim Borrowman who run a charter boat service catering to divers, sightseers and whale watching groups. Whale watching is one of the major industries at Telegraph Cove. People travel from all areas to see killer whales in the wild, and Bill and Jim not only take visitors to see whales but also offer an interesting and comprehensive running commentary on the habits, histories and behaviour of the whales.

Telegraph Cove comprises a marina with office and a parking lot for patrons in a small compound adjacent to the ring of private houses on pilings at the water's edge. At the entrance to the cove from the upper central reaches of Johnstone Strait a small dock offers brief moorage to take on fuel. Adjacent to this dock is a transient moorage area for those who wish to gain access to the boardwalk for a short spell of shopping. Just at the top of the ramp is a post office and store where souvenirs can be purchased or where arrangements can be made for sightseeing, whale watching and scuba diving. Another store offers groceries and some hardware as well as a variety of art and crafts. The whale watching/scuba diving operators also offer accommodations in several of the old houses which have been refurbished and equipped for guests. Summertime is a busy period for whale watching with the season peaking through July and August. In winter, spring and fall scuba diving comes into its own and regular groups of divers make use of the facilities and the two whale watching boats to access the legendary dive sites nearby. Visiting dive charter boats also operate in the area using Telegraph Cove as a base during the diving season.

By private boat, charter boat, excursion or whatever other means, there are many outstanding attractions not far from Telegraph Cove. These include beautiful moorings and anchorages in the nearby island groups such as the Plumpers on the edge of Weynton Passage, access ashore at abandoned and historic native villages and coastal settlements with excellent fishing, wildlife viewing and just simply cruising among some of the most beautiful of the BC coast islands, inlets and waterways.

If anchoring overnight in nearby sheltered waters be careful to check on the effects of tide, current and wind before settling in. It is tempting to anchor in the Plumper Islets. A small cove is formed between two of the larger islets which almost join at the northern end. A local diving club has moored a raft in the middle of the cove and this appears suitable for tying alongside. At higher tides and during tidal changes the water tends to rip through the northern passage causing quite a current through the Plumpers. If you tie up to the raft use the right side entering the cove from the direction of Telegraph because the current is milder than on the left. Or anchor between the raft and the island to starboard.

Make sure to stern tie as well. Unless winds accompanied by high tides are expected this may be a secure overnight anchorage. It affords spectacular sunset views across towards Telegraph Cove where some moorage is available at the marina and where it is advisable to stay overnight if a strong wind is forecast. There are many other anchorages that are larger and safer nearby, specifically in the back of Hanson Island, Harbledown Island and up Baronet Passage at places like Potts Lagoon, Bend Island and Clio Channel.

Now you are in historic native Indian territory. Visting the deserted villages of Karlukwees sand Mamalilaculla is just a short distance from nearby anchorages. The villages have temporary anchorages or dilapidated dock space and overnight stays are not generally recommended. Go ashore, look around but leave everything as you found it. Nearby Minstrel island offers safe and secure overnight moorage and the opportunity to replenish fuel, groceries and provisions to continue your cruise. Access to these areas from Telegraph Cove is easy and close, but be careful with your navigation as some passages are narrow and strewn with rocks and reefs. Use a large scale chart.

The Indian villages of Mamalilaculla and Karlukwees have long been a favourite stop among cruising yachtsmen. Often shrouded in swirling fog, drenching drizzle or heavy cloudy overcast, an atmosphere of history and the presence of spirits of the past lingers in these villages, pervading the ambience of the shamble of houses, tangle of bushes and decayed ritualistic and ceremonial structures. A tilted totem pole peeked jauntily from between the branches of the heavy bushes on a previous visit.

Huge longhouse beams and several horizontal totems fought off the encroaching grasses and weeds, brambles and berry bushes. When Wylie Blanchet (**The Curve Of Time**) visited the area in the 1920s there were people living there and she mused over her prediction that it would not be long before the villages would be abandoned. She was right. But today visitors will find efforts in place to restore historic testimony to what was once a thriving community.

It's a pity that historic Minstrel Island has long since seen the last minstrel show in its grand community hall that once served as an entertainment centre for the area with patrons coming in from nearby Bones Bay (cannery) or from logging installations and camps up Knight Inlet or adjacent waterways.

One of my favourite sightseeing excursions in the area is to Alert Bay, which might well have been the destination when deciding to make a stop at Telegraph Cove. A visit to Alert Bay should include a hike to the spectacular and almost unheard of Gator Gardens located atop the hill behind the radio station. It is reached by a signposted and fairly easy walk up the backroads.

Going in the opposite direction out of Telegraph Cove is Robson Bight, on the east side of central Johnstone Strait. It is here that killer whales congregate in summer and where mating takes place. For years boats would chase the orcas around this area for close views, or stand drifiting in the bight for the occasion when the whales would inquisitively come up to the boats and give the crews a close encounter. Chasing of orcas became a problem and in recent years controls have been applied to limit the access by boats to the habitat of the killer whale population. Cruising anywhere in the vicinity of Telegraph Cove, upper Johnstone Strait, Blackfish Sound and adjacent waters, could present an opportunity to see killer whales in the wild. Eagles abound too. Often you will find the large birds sitting high in the trees overlooking Baronet Passage, especially on Cracroft Point just off Johnstone Strait where many fishermen try for big salmon in the current swept pass. The eagles will select a boat in what they seem to claim as 'their' territory and when an undersized or unwanted fish such as a quilback or other rockfish is thrown back the eagles will swoop down to claim it as their prize. Other eagles tend to respect their neighbour's territory and not dash in to compete for the free meal, as perhaps would the seagull population.

The public dock at the far end of Alert Bay

Although many places become lost to history, thankfully quaint, picturesque Telegraph Cove remains standing as a thriving community, shelter from the storms of Johnstone Strait, centre for whale watching, scuba diving and sportsfishing and most importantly as a classic historic site that represents a most colourful and important segment of British Columbia's past.

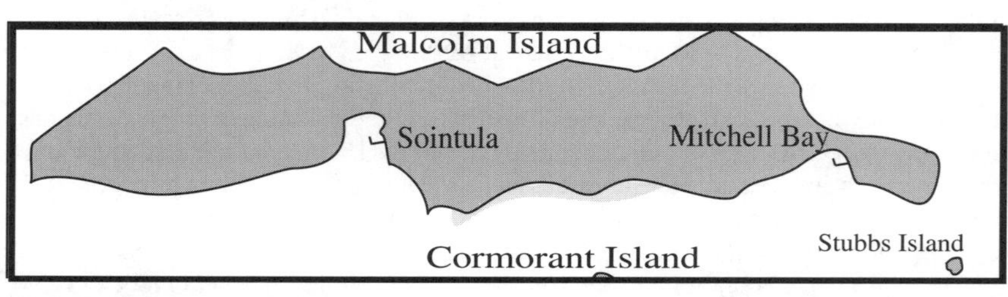

Sointula,

Malcolm Island
Fisheries & Oceans dock
Phone (604) 973-6544
Chart 3546
Manager • Float length 745 m

Malcolm Island Inn Phone: (604) 973-6366

Breakwater • Aircraft float •
Garbage • Water • Lights • Power •
Public phone •
Near stores and facilities.
Ferry to Port McNeill, Alert Bay.

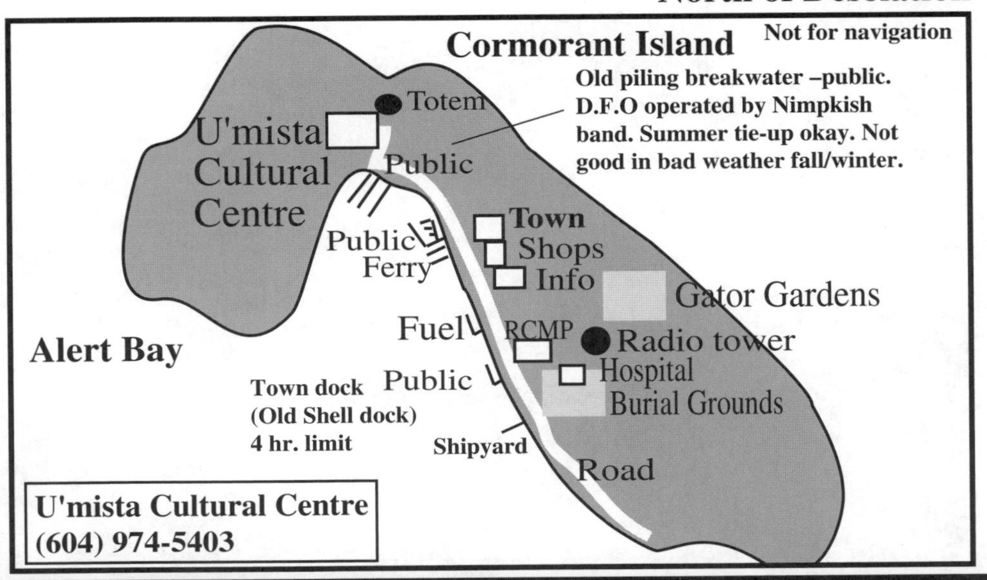

Alert Bay

Alert Bay Boat Harbour

(604) 974-5251 res. 974-5727 office.
Government dock.
Chart 3546 VHF 73
DFO (Fisheries) VHF 78

Marina services:

Transient moorage.
Power. Water.

Customer services:

Restaurants. Dining.
Groceries. Tackle, bait, charts.
Garbage disposal.
All services at village of Alert Bay.
Accommodations, meals.
Credit Union (bank machine). 974-5527.

Entertainment.

Hiking trails and roads. Gator Gardens, an anachronism–Florida's Everglades come to BC. On the hill above the town. Animal and marine life. Excellent scuba diving nearby.

Adjacent facilities:

Paved airstrip (2800 feet).
Marine services: Alert Bay Save On Fuels 974-5411. Alert Bay Shipyards 974-5446. Alert Bay Travel Info Centre 974-5213

ALERT BAY

Fisheries & Oceans dock
Phone 974-5727 res: 974-5251.
Chart 3546
Manager • Float length 533 m
Breakwater • Aircraft Float • Garbage
Water • Lights • Power • Public phone •
Walking–Gator Gardens on the hill.
Waterfront roadway. Waste oil service*

Transport Canada dock
Chart 3546
Manager • Float length 61 m
Launch ramp • Water (on wharf only) •
Lights •
* *Best to return used oil to fuel stations.*

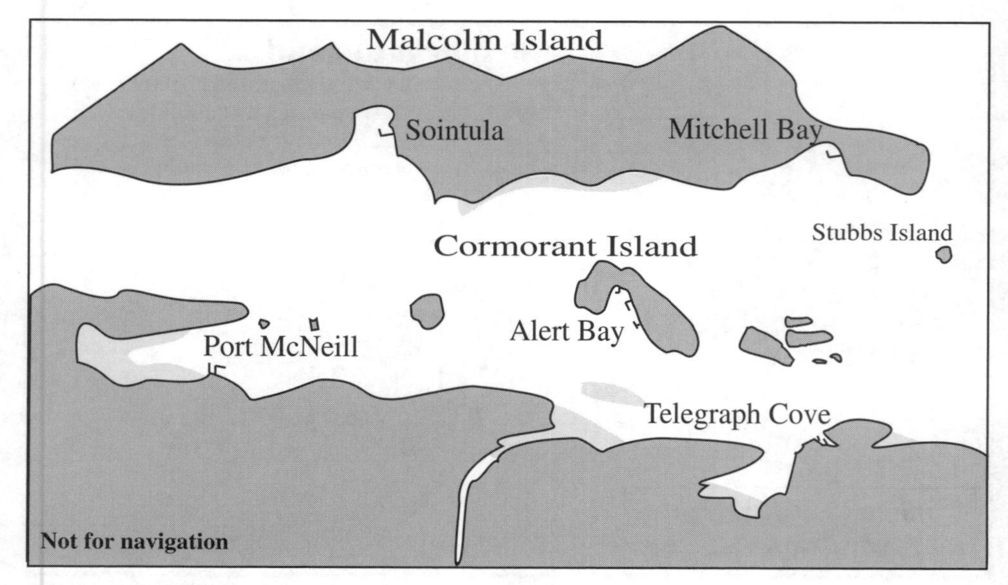

Port McNeill Boat Harbour

Port McNeill, BC.
Phone: (604) 956-3881
Harbour Manager
Chart 3546, 3548 VHF 73

Marina:

Moorage: Extensive sheltered docks.
Fuel: Gas, diesel. Oils. Aviation fuels.
Oil disposal. **Water.**
Power: 30, 15amp.

Services:

Garbage disposal. Tidal grid.
Churches–multi-denominational.

Entertainment:

Walkway on breakwater. Uptown facilities–hotels, restaurants, shops, services. Vehicle rentals. Flights.

Adjacent facilities:

Ferry to Sointula, Alert Bay.
Marine repairs–adjacent and nearby Marinas/fuel barge. Also offering ice, showers, snacks and pop,

---

Opposite: Well known gateway to burial ground at Alert Bay and the lesser known Gator Gardens atop the hill near the radio tower.

Alert Bay

Alert Bay attracts mariners as a stop for replenishment and an opportunity to go ashore for some exercise as they travel en route to points north or home again. For many Alert Bay is a final destination on their northward travels. Whatever the reason for stopping at Alert Bay surprisingly few people seem to know of the existence of Gator Gardens. This very name may well indicate that this attraction is somewhat misplaced here in British Columbia. In name and character it is more like something you would expect to stumble across on a tour of Florida. It is a marshy, swampy glade complete with large still pools of water afloat with the massive leaves of various forms of vegetation and sprouting large sprays of skunk cabbage. Wooden walkways have been erected across the park to allow access for easy walking and viewing. The most prominent feature of the park is its incredible trees which appear to have been struck by lightning at one time. These massive trees are broad and tall and mostly scarred and craggy with eerie looking branches and cracks and splits appearing as though they were the inspiration for the tale of Sleepy Hollow. And the surprising thing is that the entire park is not where you would expect to find it, down near sea level, but rather up on top of the hill overlooking Alert Bay. From the government marinas of Alert Bay to Gator Gardens is a good uphill walk to the back of the residential area overlooking the bay. There are several routes, marked here and there by signs indicating the way. All routes end up alongside or near the transmitter station and entrances to the Gardens, although not well marked, will eventually lead you to the wooden planked walk through the glades.

Alert Bay boasts the once tallest totem pole in the world. It is located a short walk up the hill behind the U'umista Native Indian Cultural Centre which is on the shore adjacent to the government docks north of town.The museum at the cultural centre is well worth a visit. Among other interesting items it has on display segments of the exhibits that were shown at Expo 86 in Vancouver.

You may be lucky when visiting Alert Bay and experience some rare calm, sunny weather. If not you should watch the currents and sea conditions that sweep around the northern channel en route to Port Hardy or the open northern reaches of Johnstone Strait. In windy conditions it is usually possible to sneak around the bottom end of Malcolm Island and through the rocky channels and islets in the area. We once took shelter for two days in the Plumper Islets while the wind raged. It is not really a suitable anchorage for more than a temporary stop because the current rips through quite fast especially at high tides.

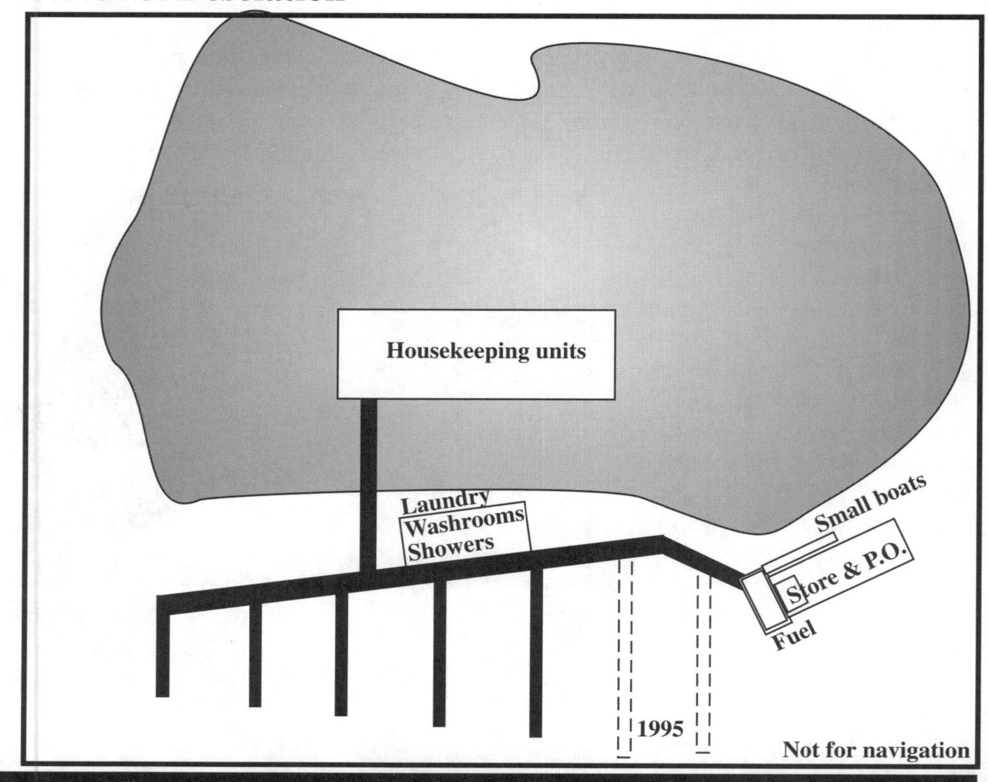

Echo Bay Resort

Echo Bay Resort

Bob & Nancy Richter

Simoom Sound P.O.,

B.C. V0P 1S0

Phone: (604) 949-2501

Fax (604) 949-4911

Marina services:

Transient moorage. Reserve in peak season–July, August. Open three days per week in winter.

Fuel: Gas, diesel, kerosene, oils, propane. **Water** at dock. Ice.

Power at docks: 30, 15 amp.

12,000 lb dry dock. Haulouts boats to about 23 feet.

Customer services:

Groceries. Post office. Public phone. Beer.

Charts 3515 VHF Ch 73

Bakery goods and fresh produce, milk, frozen foods, ice, tackle, books, charts, film, and gifts. Six housekeeping units.

Laundry, showers, washrooms.

(For overnight guests.)

Boat and motor rentals.

Excellent fishing and prawning nearby

Block and party ice.

Entertainment.

The main dock is a part of the former Lake Washington floating bridge. Hiking trail and park access. Incredible sunsets and views. Animal and marine life.

Adjacent facilities:

Regular scheduled flights. Local arts and crafts shops and artists. Nearby anchorage and public float. Marine park.

Right: View out of Echo Bay with Echo Bay Marina on the left, public dock in the foreground.
Top: A nearby, scenic waterway.

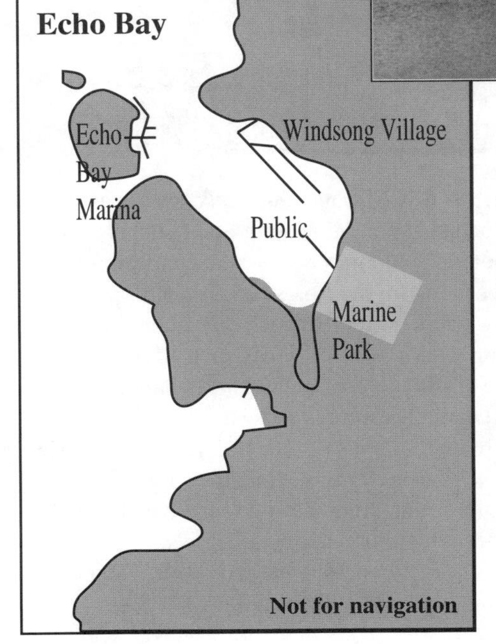

Echo Bay

History and commerce converge at Echo Bay. It is a hub of activity drawing summertime travelling boaters, whale watching tourists out of Telegraph Cove, sportfishing groups from near and far and a constant flow of local people from neighbouring logging camps and fish farms to pick up and drop off their mail and replenish some of their grocery needs. The lodge on the island at the entrance to the cove, for that's all that Echo Bay is—a tiny sheltered cove, caters to a steady flow of itinerant visitors in for a few days of fishing or stopping by in their boats for a spell in the area. Fuel and moorage with

Windsong Sea Village with its spacious docks, rental cottage and arts and crafts shop.

Parks	Gilford Island	Kingcome
Echo Bay All weather anchorage Boat dock, camping sites, water, toilets..	Fisheries & Oceans dock Chart 3515 Float length 60 m Aircraft float •	Transport Canada dock Chart 3515 Float length 55 m Windy and exposed.

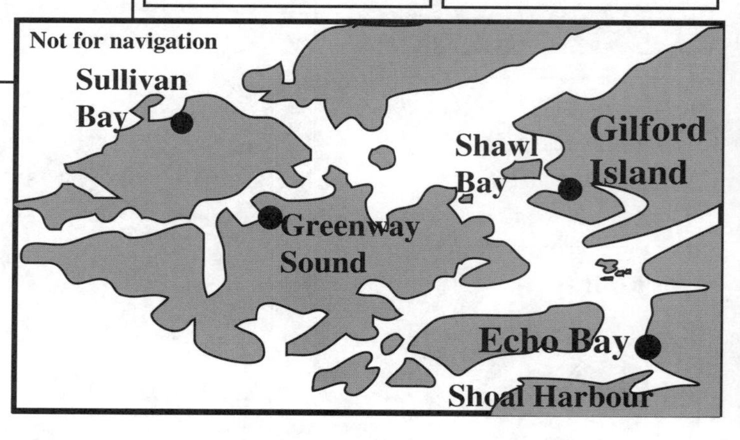

power and water are available from Echo Bay Marina which also serves as post office and store. A marina on the opposite shore, Windsong Sea Village Resort, has large floats which will accommodate a good number of boats and offers moorage for seaplanes too. A small building on the floats proclaims that it is an ultralight aviation centre. This marina offers no fuel or dockside electricity but has a delightful craft shop representing works of local artists such as Alexandra Morton, Yvonne Maximchuck, natives from the nearby Gilford Island Village and the proprietor herself, Muffin O'Donnell.She and her husband James offer adventure tours and have float cabin rentals. James O'Donnell, a pilot with Air Rainbow, one of two regular airlines serving Echo Bay, is an ultra light flying enthusiast in his spare time away from piloting commercially, and has developed a new amphibian aircraft which has been demonstrated at air shows.

There are several talented artists living in the area and their works can be seen at their private studios or the craft shop at Windsong.

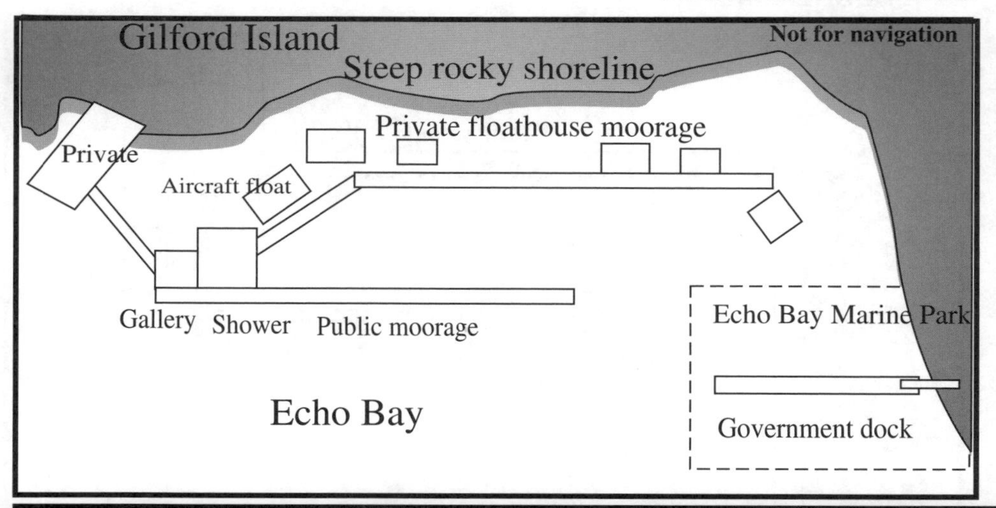

Windsong Sea Village

Windsong Sea Village, Echo Bay.

Charts 3515 **VHF Ch 73**

Muffin and James A O'Donnell
Box 1487, Port McNeill
B.C. V0N 2R0
Phone: (604) 956-4005
Ph/Fax 956-4080

Marina services:

Moorage: Transient moorage. Floatplanes No services.

Customer services:

Arts and crafts store. Fine art.
Floating cabin rental.
Floathouse moorage available.

Entertainment.

Hiking trail and marine park access. Incredible sunsets and views. Animal and marine life.

Adjacent facilities:

Regular scheduled flights. Marine park and trail. Local artists live in vicinity. Their work is available. Nearby anchorage and public float

Good anchorage is available in Shoal Harbour immediately southwest of Echo Bay. It does receive some wind but the worst of it can be avoided by tucking into the western bay. Not too far as it becomes quite shallow farther in.

Excellent fine art may be purchased at Echo Bay and some nearby waterfront cabins. Posted signs indicate stops where one can look at artists' work.

Notes:

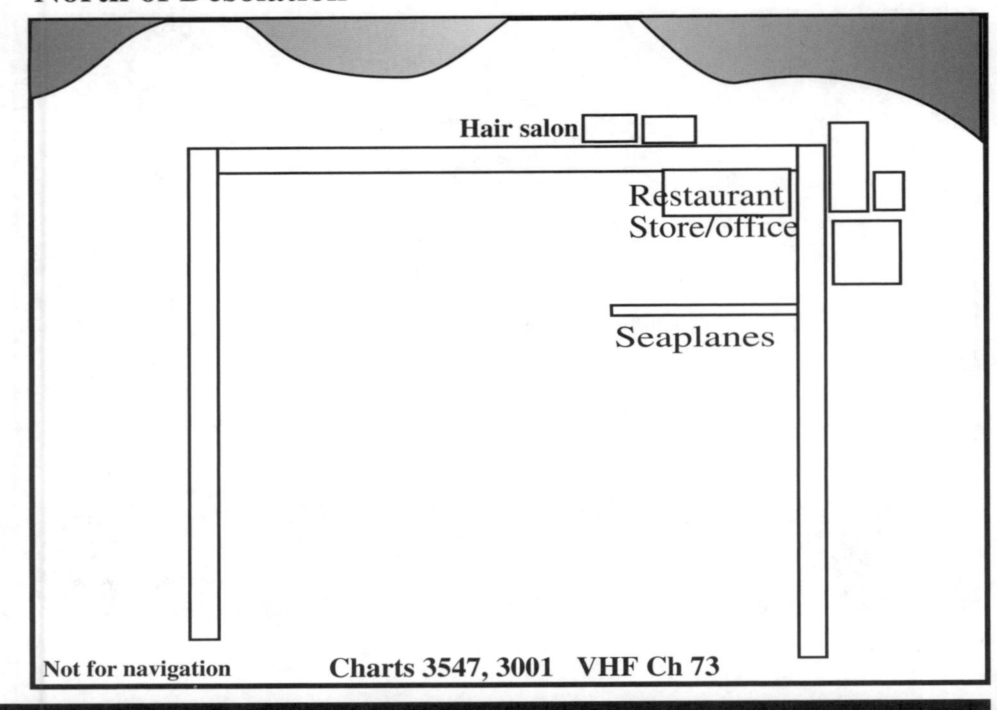

Greenway Sound

Greenway Sound Marine Resort

Tom and Ann Taylor
P.O. Box 759 Port McNeill, BC.
V0N 2R0 (Also at 19924 Aurora Ave. North #54 Seattle Wa. 98133–off season)
1 800-800-2080 Ch 73

Marina services:

Moorage: Large permanent marina with plenty of transient moorage at up to 2,700 feet of red carpeted dock. Good for power walking. Reserve dock space in peak season. **Garbage** disposal (for mooring customers).
Water at dock.
Power at docks: 50, 30, 15 amp. 110 plus 220 shore power available.

Customer services:

Restaurant. All meals. Licensed.
Breakfast, lunch, dinner. Food and beverages. Groceries, post office and liquor. Bakery goods and fresh produce, milk, frozen foods, ice, tackle, books, charts, film, and gifts.
Laundry, showers, washrooms.
Post Office. Public phone.
Boat sitting.
Excellent fishing and prawning nearby.
Block and party ice.
Hair/beauty salon, barber shop.

Entertainment.

Take-out food–pizzas, baked goods, snacks. Book exchange. Hiking trail and lake access. Incredible sunsets and views. Animal and marine life.

Adjacent facilities:

Regular scheduled flights. Supplies shuttled in from Vancouver Island by fast boat. Nearby anchorage.

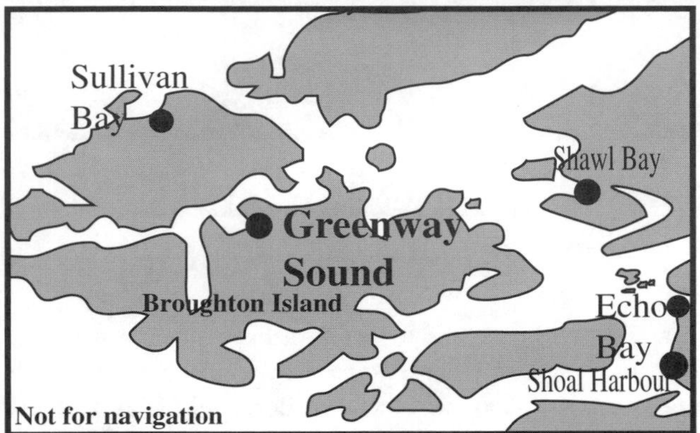

Top: An aerial view of Greenway Sound Marine Resort. Nearby, a hiking trail leading to a lake has been established. It is being maintained by the resort in conjunction with the forestry company that provided the trail. Right: Restaurant and marina.

Shawl Bay

Chart 3515 VHF 73

Brown's Marina, Shawl Bay

Edna Brown
c/o Simoom P.O.
British Columbia V0P 1S0

Marina services:

Moorage: Transient moorage.
Some provisions.

Customer services:

Power, water.

Entertainment.

Animal and marine life.
Entertainment/picnic float.

Adjacent facilities:

Water dock–located in adjacent bay. Water in good supply but use sparingly during summer.

Shawl Bay and Greenway Sound

Shawl Bay is a busy place during the summer season. Many regular boating friends and customers of the people who own and operate the cosy marina at the southern corner of the bay return each year or periodically to tie up at the spacious docks. These docks and the structures on them comprise the Brown's Marina operated by Edna Brown and her sister Johanne along with Edna's son Gary. Brother Alf Didriksen has run a logging camp in the bay for many years and the family's hospitality is legendary among fishermen, loggers and pleasure boats alike. The docks are in good repair and a large floating platform has been cleared for moorage customers to come ashore and relax, socialize and perhaps set up their own barbecue or picnic. The store offers ice and a smattering of provisions but the water supply is copious.

The floats and store on the dock at Shawl Bay and the nearby water supply. In mid-season mariners are asked to use it sparingly.

At a nearby float a hose and a sign declare the availability of water with a request for conservative use. The stop is referred to by the owners as The Watering Hole.

In 1985 Tom and Ann Taylor opened their floating resort at nearby Greenway Sound. The bay where their lodge is located is large and the docks extensive totalling one half kilometer in total length. They are laid out in a wide square with a finger pointing into the square near the far corner where the facilities are located. These facilities set the floating resort apart from others in the area. The store is part of a restaurant with an airy, clean kitchen that serves up mouth-watering dinners, wholesome lunches—hamburgers, chili, sandwiches, salads, excellent clam chowder and ice cream in waffle cones— and splendid breakfasts.

The moorage is typically busy with large visiting yachts, especially from the USA, some of which remain during summer and have owners and their friends fly in for brief or extended visits.The resort literally gives arriving boats the red carpet treatment, from the smiling attendance of young dock helpers to the full length coverage of the floats with red indoor/ outdoor carpet. It is not unusual to see boat crews walking the docks for their daily exercise. Walk the length of the floats three times and you have walked about a mile. Another walk that is being favoured at the park, is a nearby area ashore that has been designated as parkland by the ministery of forests. A dinghy float and ramp are being installed jointly by the Taylors and the ministry, and moorage customers or anyone who calls in the area will have access to the park. A path from the ramp leads up to the lake a short distance up the mountainside.

The resort offers fly in service from points south including Seattle (Tacoma, Renton, Anacortes), Campbell River, Vancouver and Victoria. The store carries produce including fresh and frozen foods, books, charts, tee-shirts and hats. In separate buildings attached to the adjacent docks are laundry and shower facilities as well as a hair and beauty salon and a book exchange library. The docks are serviced with water and 110 volt shore power. The resort stands by on channel 73 and is equipped with regular telephone service. It is possible to reach Alert Bay on VHF for BC Tel radio operated service and cellular is within close reach with the likelihood that it will provide full coverage at the dock soon.

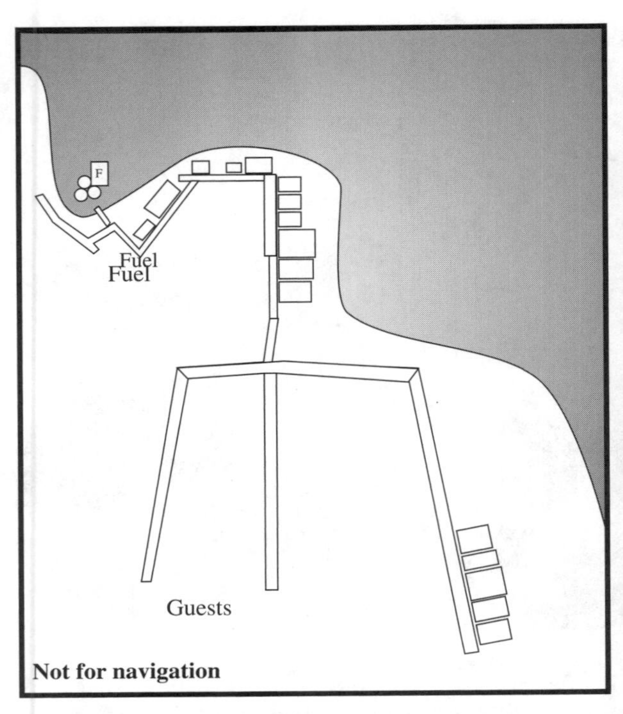

Sullivan Bay Resort

Sullivan Bay Marine Resort

Pat Finnerty and Lynn Whitehead
Sullivan Bay, BC. V0N 3H0
Phone: (604) 949-4905

Chart 3547 VHF Ch 73 and 16

Marina services:

Fuel: Gas, diesel, oil. Aviation fuel.
Propane, ice, bait.
Mechanic and services at Vancouver Island towns and ports.
Moorage: Large permanent marina with plenty of transient moorage at up to 4,000 feet of dock. Reserve in peak season.
Water at dock. Plentiful.
Power at docks: 50 , 30, 15 amp.
110 plus 220 shore power available.
Laundry, showers, washrooms.

Customer services:

Cold beer available.
Post office. Public phone.
Groceries, post office and liquor. Bakery goods and fresh produce, dairy products, frozen foods, ice, tackle, and souvenirs.
Smokehouse.
Boat sitting.
Excellent fishing and prawning in vicinity.

Entertainment.

Library, TV lounge, playground and novel building structures, street names on docks.

Adjacent facilities:

Regular scheduled flights. Private floating homes village.

Views of Sullivan Bay Marine Resort with its floating sidewalks, permanent moorage client residences and itinerant visitors.

Sullivan Bay has long been known for its remote but popular location on the BC coast. It has served for many years as an air traveller's focal point and as a final destination or layover point for mariners.

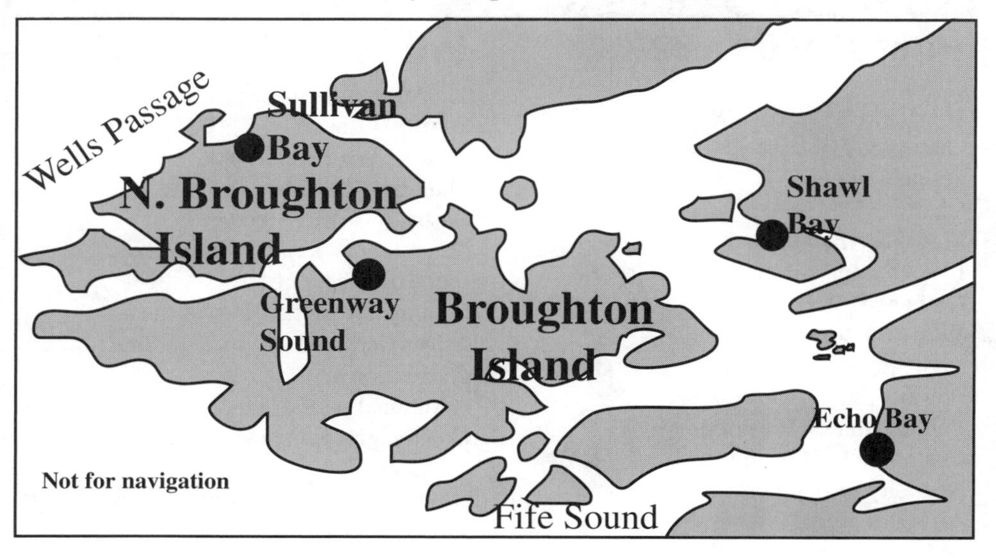

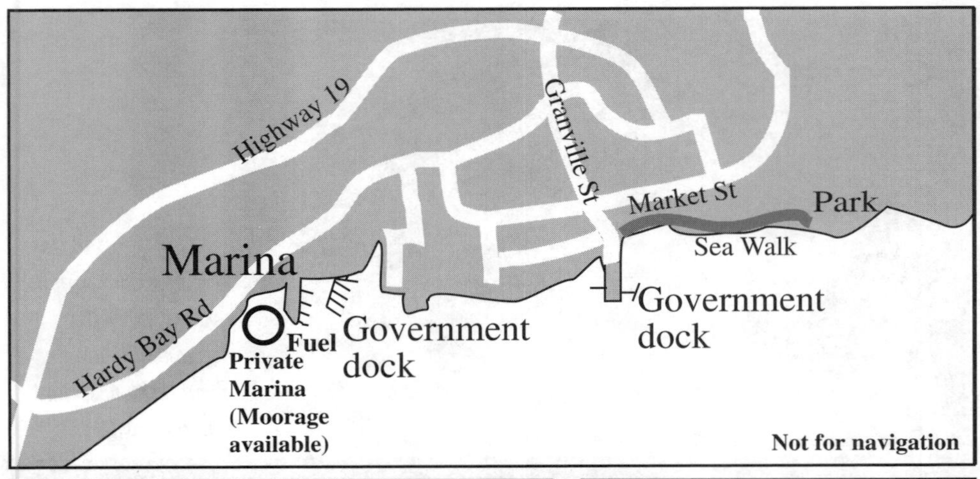

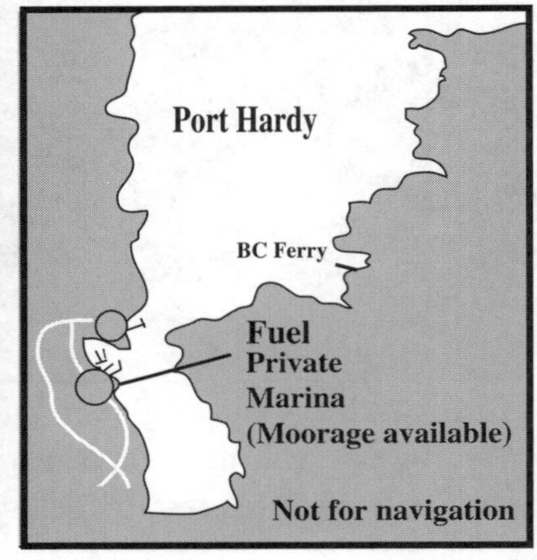

Port Hardy

(Inside breakwater)

Oceans & Fisheries
Phone 949-6665
Chart 3548, 3605
Manager • Float length 574 m
Launch ramp • Breakwater • Grid •
Garbage •
Waste oil disposal • Water •
Lights •
Power •
Public phone • Washrooms •
Customs • Fuel nearby •
Near city restaurants, services, shops.
All services and facilities in Port Hardy and local marina.
Ferries nearby for northern route.

Port Hardy

Transport Canada dock
Phone 949-6665
Chart 3548, 3605
Manager • Float length 30 m
Garbage • Water • Power •
Near city restaurants, shops. Excellent scuba diving nearby.
Enquire at dive facilities in town.
All services and facilities in Port Hardy.
Ferries north.
Additional public dock at Port Hardy:
Commercial but some transient moorage available.
Downtown Port Hardy location with access to shops and services.

Photo: Doug Pemberton

God's Pocket

God's Pocket

Harry Kerr & Molly Milroy
P.O. Box 471, Port Hardy,
BC. V0N 2P0
Phone: (604) 949-9221
Chart 3546, 3548 VHF 73
(Located at Hurst Island)

Marina:

Moorage: Limited, sheltered docks. Washrooms, laundry. Some accommodation on availability.

Services:

Cabins, excellent meals, good island walking. Scuba diving, fishing excursions and charters. Some provisions, gifts, arts and crafts. Coffee shop, lunches, pies.

Entertainment:

Walking trails on island. Hiking.

Bull Harbour

Hope Island
Fisheries & Oceans dock
Main Marina Chart 3549
Float length 35 m
No shore access

Quarterdeck Marine

Andy, Vern, Val
Box 910, 6555,Hardy Bay Road,
Port Hardy, BC. V0N 2P0
Phone: (604) 949-6551 Fax 949-7777
Chart 3548 VHF 73

Marina:

Moorage and RV parking.
Fuel, showers, laundry. Travel lift, charts, electronics, ice, licences, hardware, tackle.

Services:

Flights, bus service, ferry nearby.

Index

Active Pass 103
Alert Bay 235
Alert Bay Boat Harbour 235
Alert Bay public dock 236
Angler's Anchorage Marina. 56
April Point Fishing Lodge 192
Barbary Coast Yacht Basin 130
Bathgate General Store & Marina 169
Beachcomber Marina 183
Beach Gardens Resort 172
Beaumont Marine Park 74
Bedwell Harbour Resort 94
Belcarra Park Public Dock 133
Big Bay 216
Big Bay Marine Resort 216
Bird's Eye Cove 67
Blackfin Pub & Marina 184
Blakely Marina 36
Blind Channel Resort 220
Blubber Bay public dock 174
Brechen Point Marina 124
Brentwood Bay public dock 55
Brentwood Inn Resort 54
Bridgepoint Marina 128
Brown's Bay Marina 198
Browning Harbour public dock 97
Brown's Marina 244
Buccaneer Marina 154
Bull Harbour public dock 249
Cabbage Island marine park 74
Campbell River public dock 195
Canoe Cove Marina 52
Cape Mudge public dock 195
Captain's Cove Marina 127
Caulfeild public dock 142
Chemainus public dock 68
Chemainus 70
Coal Harbour Marina 130
Coho Marina 160
Comox Municipal Marina 187
Comox public dock 185
Comox, Royston public dock 185
Copeland Islands marine park 261
Cordero Lodge 219
Cortes Bay public dock 210/211
Courtenay Slough public dock 187
Cowichan Bay public dock 63
Crescent Beach public dock 127
Crofton public dock 68
Crofton 70
D'Arcy Island marine park 74
Deas Marina 127
Deep Bay public dock 182
Deep Cove public dock 133
Deer Harbor Resort & Marina 32
Degnen Bay public dock 115
Delta River Inn Hotel Marina 128
Denman Island public dock 182
Des Reid Marina 186
Desolation Sound 200
Desolation Sound marine parks 201
Desolation Sound, North of 222
Dinghy Dock Pub 122
Discovery Harbour Marina 197
Discovery Marina Sportfish Centre 194
Duncan Cove Marina 166
Echo Bay Resort 238
Echo Bay public dock 239
Egmont public dock 169
Evans Bay public dock 201
False Bay public dock 175
Fanny Bay public dock 182
Fernwood public dock 88
Fisherman Bay 39
Fisherman's Resort & Marina 162
Ford Cove public dock 182
French Creek public dock 182
Friday Harbor, Port of 24
Fulford Harbour public dock 81
Fulford Marina 80
Gabriola Island 114
Galiano Island 111
Gambier Harbour public dock 145
Ganges 84
Ganges Marina 85
Ganges public docks 88
Garden Bay Hotel & Marina 161
Garden Bay marine park 157
Genoa Bay Marina 64
Gibsons public docks 144/145
Gibsons Marina 146
God's Pocket 249
Goldstream Boathouse 57
Gorge Harbour Marina & Resort . 202/209

Greenway Sound Marine Resort 242
Gulf Islands 77
Gulf Islands Marine Parks 74
Halfmoon Bay public dock 153
Halkett Bay public dock 143/145
Harbour Ferries 130
Harbour's End Marine 87
Headwater Marine 167
Heather Civic Marina 132
Heriot Bay public dock 204/9
Heriot Bay Inn 204
Heriot Bay Public Marina 204
Hope Bay public dock 99
Hopkins Landing public dock 144
Horseshoe Bay public dock 139
Horton Bay public dock 101
Hospital Bay public dock 162
Howe Sound, Upper 148
Howe Sound Marinas 136
Howe Sound public docks 144
Indian Arm 133
Inn of the Sea Resort 73
Islander Lopez Marina Resort 41
Islands Marine Center 38
Irvine's Landing Marina & Pub 165
Keats Island public dock 144
Kelsey Bay public docks 225
Ladysmith 70
Ladysmith public dock 71
Lagoon Cove Marina 228
Lasqueti Island Hotel & Resort 175
Lions Bay Marina 142
Lowe's Resorts 167
Lund public dock 176/177
Lund Marine and Diesel 176
Lynnwoood Marina 131
Madeira Marina 166
Madeira Park public dock 166
Malcolm Island Inn 234
Manana Lodge & Marina 72
Manson's Landing 203/209
Mansons Landing marine park 201
Mayne Island 100
Maple Bay public dock 66
Maple Bay Resorts 66
Mill Bay Marina 58
Mill Bay public dock 58
Miner's Bay public dock 102
Minstrel Island public dock 226
Minstrel Island Resort 226
Montague Harbour 112
Montague marine park 74/111
Mosquito Creek 13
Mount Gardner public dock 145
Musgrave Landing public dock 88
Nanaimo 119
Nanaimo Boat Basin (& public) 121
Nanaimo Harbour City Marina 123
Nanaimo Shipyard 124
New Brighton public dock 145
Newcastle Island Marine Park 75/122
North Galiano public dock 111
Oak Bay Marina 46
Octopus Islands marine park 201
Okeover Inlet public dock 177
Orcas Landing 33
Otter Bay Marina 98
Owen Bay public dock 201
Pacific Playgrounds Resort 188
Page's Marina 116
Pelican Bay Marina 132
Pender Harbour 158
Pender Islands 91
Piers Island public dock 53
Pirate's Cove marine park 75
Plumper Cove public dock 143
Point Roberts Marina 42
Porpoise Bay public dock 152
Port Browning Marina Resort 96
Port Graves public dock 145
Port Hardy public docks 248
Port McNeill Boat Harbour 236
Port Neville public dock 225
Port Sidney Marina 48
Port Washington public dock 99
Porteau public dock 143
Powell River public docks 174
Princess Margaret marine park 75
Quathiaski Cove public dock 197
Ragged Islands Marine 178
Rebecca Spit marine park 201
Reed Point Marina 133
Refuge Cove 208/212
Retreat Cove public dock 111
Roche Harbor 22
Rosario Resort Marina 30

Rosario Resort Marina 30
Roscoe Bay marine park 201
Royal Reach Marina & Motel 171
Saanichton public dock 46
Salmon Point Resort 191
Salt Spring Marina 86
Saltery bay public dock 171
San Juan Islands 19
San Juan Islands Marine Parks 28
Salt Spring Island 79
Salt Spring Marina 86
Saturna Island 100
Saturna Point Landing 100
Schooner Cove Resort 180
Sechelt public dock 153
Secret Cove public dock 153
Secret Cove Marina 152
Sewell's Marina 139
Seycove Marina 133
Shawl Bay, Brown's Marina 244
Shoal Bay public dock 218
Shoal Bay Lodge 218
Shelter Island Marina 128
Sidney Spit marine park 75
Silva Bay Boatel 115
Silva Bay Marina 117
Skyline Marina 129
Smuggler Cove marine park 157
Snug Cove 141
Snug Cove public dock 145
Snug Harbor 26
Sointula public dock 234
Something Fishy 241
Sportfish Centre, Discovery 194
Squamish public dock 144
Squamish 146/149
Squirell Cove 211
Squirrel Cove Bakery 211
Squitty Bay marine park 157
Squitty Bay public dock 175
Steveston public docks 127
Stone's Marina and RV Park 125
Stubbs Island Charters 230
Sullivan Bay Marine Resort 246
Sunset Marina 142
Sunshine Coast 151
Sunshine Coast marine parks 246
Teakerne Arm marine park 201
Telegraph Cove Marina 230
Telegraph Harbour Marina 106
Thetis Island 104
Thetis Island Marina 109
Thunderbird Marina 131
Thurston Bay marine park 201
Tsehum Harbour public dock 51
Twin Islands public dock 133
U'mista Cultural Centre 235
Union Steamship Marina 140
Vancouver area 126
Vancouver Marina 128
Vancouver Island Central 179
Vancouver Island North 216
Vancouver Island South 43
Vancouver Marina 129
Van Isle Marina 50
Victoria 45
Wallace Island marine park 75
Walsh Cove marine park 201
West Sound Marina 34
Westin Bayshore Marina 130
Westview public dock 174
Whaletown 203/209
Windsong Sea Village 241
Winter Cove marine park 10

"Well, Honey, where should we go next season?"
"Mm?"
"Where should we go next year? Alaska? Princess Louisa?"
"I don't know–I kind of like it right here..."

Docks and Destinations

Some comments from marina owners and cruising yachtsmen

Thank you for the excellent write up on the marina and for delivering Docks & Destinations. You have obviously worked exceedingly hard at gathering together all of the information on all of the marinas and various facilities up and down the coast. It is an excellent publication and I'm sure it will become standard equipment on most boats cruising our coast.

–Mark Dickinson, Van Isle Marina, Sidney.

The books are great. We should have ordered more (for the first delivery).

–Lynda Brown, Ganges Marina, Salt Spring Island.

You dropped off six copies of Docks & Destinations today and four of them sold right away. Stay in touch as things change from year to year. Lots of luck.

–Pat Lovell, Refuge Cove General Store, Desolation Sound.

The diagram (of our marina docks) is excellent. Note some changes (for the next printing). Thank you.

–Bob Nissen, Pacific Playgrounds Resort, Vancouver Island.

Picked up a copy late last (1994) season. It gave us just the guidance we needed for some outstanding last minute cruising and we look forward to checking out some of the places in it next season.

–Ron Yates, RYM Propeller, Richmond, BC.

Thank you for publishing this guide. It's excellent. Just what cruising boat owners need.

–Peter Lazenby, yachtsman and former owner Telegraph Harbour Marina.

This guide is updated when reprinted. Major updates and changes will be made periodically when new editions are published. Please write to me if you have any information or suggestions for inclusion in future editions. Your comments will be welcome.

–Peter Vassilopoulos.

Docks & Destinations, Box 1312 Delta, BC. V4M 3Y8
or P.O. Box 984, Point Roberts, WA. 98281-0984

Suggested guides to the scuba diving opportunities in Washington and British Columbia:

99 DIVES.
101 DIVES. By Betty Pratt Johnson
These two guides describe dive sites throughout the waters of the Pacific Northwest and are divided into areas covering the San Juan Islands to the Gulf Islands and Vancouver Island in one volume, and the mainland of Washington and British Columbia in the other.

Also read **DIVER Magazine** which contains colourful regular features on diving in British Columbia and other popular destinations in North America and the tropics. It also features equipment reports, diving medicine, historic and wreck diving, technical diving, environmental issues, photographic and marine life articles.
–Available from dive stores or magazine stands.
–Subscriptions available from Seagraphic Publications Ltd., P.O. Box 1312 Delta, BC. V4M 3Y8.
Phone (604) 273-4333. Fax (604) 273-0813

The author's Monaro 27, used also for work with his Canadian national scuba diving publication, DIVER Magazine.

Notes: